IN THE FOOTSTEPS OF XUANZANG:
TAN YUN-SHAN AND INDIA

IN THE FOOTSTEPS OF XUANZANG: TAN YUN-SHAN AND INDIA

Edited	*by*	TAN CHUNG
Foreword	*by*	KAPILA VATSYAYAN
Preface	*by*	JI XIANLIN

Co-Publisher

GYAN

GYAN PUBLISHING HOUSE

INDIRA GANDHI NATIONAL CENTRE FOR THE ARTS

A Publication of Indira Gandhi National Centre
for the Arts, Janpath, New Delhi-110001, India

Editor : Prof. Tan Chung, Professor-Consultant,
Indira Gandhi National Centre for the Arts.

Assistant Editor : Dr. Sabaree Mitra.

In the Footsteps of Xuanzang: Tan Yun-shan and India

ISBN: 81-212-0630-8

Published in 1999 by
Gyan Publishing House,
5, Ansari Road, Darya Ganj
New Delhi-110002

Laser Typesetting at: Kamal Printing System, Delhi-110092
Printed at: Mehra Offset Press, Delhi.

DEDICATED TO

GURUDEVA RABINDRANATH TAGORE,
PANDITJI JAWAHARLAL NEHRU,
TAI CHI-TAO,
CAI YUANPEI,

and all Pioneers in founding the Sino-Indian Cultural Society and opening a new leaf in India-China cultural interface and synergy in modern times.

CONTENTS

सत्यमेव जयते

राष्ट्रपति
भारत गणतंत्र
PRESIDENT
REPUBLIC OF INDIA

MESSAGE

It is with great happiness that I associate myself with this literary project commemorating the late Professor Tan Yun-shan on the occasion of his centenary

Tan Yun-shan personified the deep and abiding ties of the civilizations of India and China. These ties go back to the great Chinese pilgrim, Xuanzang. That early visitor not only spent 15 years in India during the seventh century learning Sanskrit, Buddhism and Indian culture but also played a key role in establishing Buddhism and its cultural heritage on a firm footing in China.

It was this firm-rootedness of our relationship that inspired our first Prime Minister, Jawaharlal Nehru, to write to Professor Tan Yun-shan some sixty years ago

> "China and India have stood for certain ideals in human life for ages past. These ideals must be adapted to the changing circumstances of the world today. But they must remain to guide us in the future as they have done in the past.

Contd.

राष्ट्रपति
भारत गणतंत्र
PRESIDENT
REPUBLIC OF INDIA

I trust that it may be given to our two countries to cooperate together in the cause of world peace and freedom and that neither of us, in good fortune or ill fortune, will lose our souls in the pursuit of some temporary advantage."

Rabindranath Tagore, who visited China in 1924, was keen to revive the historical bonds between India and China. He offered Santiniketan as a centre for the activities of a Sino-Indian cultural society, to ensure a continual interflow of cultures between the two great civilisations. In order to translate this objective into reality Tagore invited Tan Yun-shan to come to Santiniketan, making him a "Professor" not only to teach the Chinese language but also to develop Chinese studies at Visva-Bharati.

As founder-director of Cheena - Bhavana, Tan Yun-shan was responsible for creating what could be termed as a centre of excellence in Chinese studies. He arranged to bring over 150,000 volumes of Chinese books and personally supervised every aspect of building up the institution.

Contd

सत्यमेव जयते

राष्ट्रपति

भारत गणतंत्र

PRESIDENT

REPUBLIC OF INDIA

The thirty years of his life and career that Tan Yun-shan dedicated entirely to Santiniketan and Cheena-Bhavana until his retirement in 1976, also saw him helping many universities and institutions in different parts of India to develop courses of Chinese studies and language.

It is worth noting that the Sino-Indian Cultural society centred at Cheena-Bhavana counted among its ordinary members, Dr. Rajendra Prasad, Dr S Radhakrishnan and Dr Zakir Husain all of whom later became Presidents of independent India. Pandit Jawaharlal Nehru was its honorary president from the early 1940s, long before he became the first Prime Minister of free India. Tan Yun-shan also had a part in arranging Jawaharlal Nehru's visit to China in 1938 and the visit of Premier Zhou EnLai to Santiniketan in 1957. That year marked the twentieth anniversary of Cheena-Bhavana and in a message to commemorate that event, Nehru wrote:

"Twenty years ago, the Visva-Bharati Cheena-Bhavana was started. It was intended to promote contacts between India and China and to encourage the study of the Chinese language in India. Since then, many changes have taken place both in China and India.

Contd...

सत्यमेव जयते

राष्ट्रपति
भारत गणतंत्र
PRESIDENT
REPUBLIC OF INDIA

But, whatever changes have occurred, the friendship of these two great countries has continued and will, no doubt, continue. The roots of that friendship go back thousands of years, and it has withstood many storms and stresses during the past because of those deep roots.

Cheena-Bhavana at Visva-Bharati has quietly and unobtrusively continued its work to increase mutual understanding. It is now entering a third decade. I wish it success in its work.

Learning, the great Tamil savant Tiruvalluvar has aphorized, is a shoreless sea and the learner's days are few. Professor Tan Yun-shan packed into his years in India a great energy both to teach and to learn. He also passed on this spirit to his daughter Tan Wan who learnt Bengali whilst at Santiniketan, standing first in class in Bengali in the M.A. examination. "This is a remarkable feat", wrote Nehru to Professor Tan Yun-shan, "more especially as the standard of Bengali at Santiniketan is a high one." It is equally remarkable that his son, Professor Tan Chung, has carried on the noble tradition of his great father for several decades now.

Contd

सत्यमेव जयते

राष्ट्रपति
भारत गणतंत्र
PRESIDENT
REPUBLIC OF INDIA

A lover of both China and India he has contributed to the development of Chinese Studies in Indian Universities and worked for friendship and understanding between these two great countries of Asia.

I am glad to learn that a commemorative volume to mark the centenary year of the birth of late Professor Tan Yun-shan is being published in English and Chinese by Indira Gandhi National Centre for Arts and the Chinese University of Hongkong respectively. I should like to take this opportunity to felicitate Professor Tan Chung on this occasion. The Tans are a unique family representing continuity, commitment and the highest scholarship and I would like to pay my tribute to them as cultural ambassadors in the tradition of Xuanzang. By honouring the memory of Tan Yun-shan, a great scholar, teacher and builder of bridges between the civilisations of India and China, the publication will inspire more scholars in the two countries to strengthen existing contacts and enhance the understanding between the two countries.

(K.R. NARAYANAN)

New Delhi
April 22, 1998

भारत के उप-राष्ट्रपति के सचिव
नई दिल्ली

SECRETARY
TO THE VICE-PRESIDENT OF INDIA
NEW DELHI

November 7,1997

MESSAGE

Vice-President of India is glad to know that a commemoratory volume of Tan Yun-Shan is being brought out in English and Chinese.

Vice-President sends his good wishes for the success of the publication.

(A.N. TIWARI)

ACKNOWLEDGEMENTS

I am greatly indebted to a number of scholars and friends who have made valuable contributions to this commemorative volume. Dr. Kapila Vatsyayan, Academic Director of the Indira Gandhi National Centre for the Arts (IGNCA), has so graciously included the publication of this volume in the annual action plan to enable this literary project to exist. I have enjoyed for more than a decade sharing her affection for a junior friend and colleague, sharing her dedications to the Indian and world cultural heritage, to what Gurudeva Rabindranath Tagore and other Indian Savants had stood for. It was this sharing that has enabled this volume to be produced to commemorate the birth centenary of my father, Prof. Tan Yun-shan.

Many friends have written for the commemorative volume, some in Chinese, some in English. These contributions have enabled us to bring out two different versions of this literary commemoration of Tan Yun-shan's centenary -- its Chinese version by the Chinese University of Hong Kong, and this volume by IGNCA. Our earlier intention of translating every article so that they all appear in both the volumes cannot be materialized because of want of human and temporal resources. While thanking all the contributors for their English and Chinese writings, this thanksgiving is also a sincere apology for what is being left out, depriving our readers opportunities to have a fuller view of all the intellectual properties lying in our files, all in various ways providing an insight into the life of Tan Yun-shan and Sino-Indian interface and synergy.

Prof. Bhudeb Chaudhuri was particularly kind for taking troubles in the cold winter to get an article written, typed by a helper, and checked personally while he had cold. Prof. Kalyan Kumar Sarkar was very prompt in sending his short and sweet article across the Pacific Ocean. Prof. B.K. Roy Burman and Dr. (Mrs.) Bina Roy Burman were very obliging too. Ambassadors K.P.S. Menon and C.V. Ranganathan were equally kind, prompt, and obliging as all the above scholars. Prof. Karuna Kusalasaya sacrificed his time of rest in retirement, and sent his piece from Bangkok. So did Lama Chimpa from Kalimpong. So did my old colleague and friend Dr. Haraprasad Ray from Calcutta. To Prof. Prasenjit Duara and Prof. Manoranjan Mohanty I am equally indebted. In fact, not only they never say ``no" to my request, but always give the "yes" in deed more than in word. Mr. Sampson Shen was generous and kind to let a part of his half-a-century-old Ph.D. thesis to be reproduced. Prof. W. Pachow who knows my father more than I know in many ways, is like an elder brother in our interactions. He, like many others among those I have mentioned above, has sent me not just the kind words, but a sea of sentiments for the departed soul, I am forever grateful to all of them.

So many friends from China have obliged me by sending their pieces quite early, and these pieces have enriched the Chinese version of the commemoration which has now been brought out in Hong Kong. I wish to thank all of them here. Thank you, Prof. Ji Xianlin, Prof. Huang Xinchuan, Prof. Jin Dinghan, Prof. Wang Hongwei, Prof. Wu Baihui, Prof. Geng Yinzeng, Prof. Lin Chengjie, Prof. Wang Bangwei, and Prof. Zhang Minqiu (all from Beijing), and Prof. Li Chih-fu (from Taipei).

I want to add my special thanks for Prof. Ji Xianlin, doyen of all contemporary Indologists and India experts in China, and Life Professor of Beijing University. His generous words are enshrined in his "Preface" which we have used for both the Chinese and English versions, which will forever be remembered by the descendants of Tan Yun-shan. Apart from this, I am profoundly indebted to him for all the kindness he has showered on me in the last two decades. I feel sorry for my inability to translate Prof. Jan Yun-hua's very learned article on Chinese Buddhism (which is abridged in the Chinese volume due to space) which would have been a special jewel in this volume. He and Prof. W. Pachow are the proudest products of my father and Visva-Bharati Cheena-Bhavana. In fact, Tan Yun-shan had such enormous affection and regards for them that made his children envy.

To the President of India, Honourable Mr. K.R. Narayanan, I shall not be able to express adequately my indebtedness and gratitude. Being a great President of a great country, his judicious safeguarding of the democratic values and political justice has become a household word. Yet from that lofty height and heavy responsibility in leading the Parliamentary democracy of India to a healthy development, the President still so graciously spare time and energy to make the birth centenary for Tan Yun-shan — just an ordinary associate and follower of Gurudeva Tagore — an event of significance in the annals of Sino-Indian intercourse. My gratitude is also due to the Vice-President of India, Honourable Mr. Krishan Kant whose message for the commemorative volume had arrived long before the contributions did.

When I express my gratitude for all the above mentioned dignitaries and scholars I do it on behalf of not only IGNCA, but also the departed soul and all his descendants. My brother, Tan Lee, has taken a special interest in helping the centenary activities. Instead of thanking him (which is not a tradition in both India and China), I put this on record. Mention should also be made about my late lamented sister, Tan Wen, of whose name President Narayanan has made special mention in his "Message" courtesy of late Prime Minister Jawaharlal Nehru. She put her emotions and memories together in a beautiful article in Bengali when she was suffering great pains of the body. Tan Lee has rendered it into readable English.

The Gyan Publishers are very cooperative in putting extra resources and energy to make this volume ready for Rashtrapati Narayanan to release at Santiniketan on November 7, 1998. I express my sincere thanks to them on behalf of IGNCA, and on behalf of the Tan family.

Seeing that I was in straits, fighting with datelines, my former students but now teachers of universities, Mr. Yukteshwar Kumar and Dr. Sabaree Mitra have come to my rescue by sharing my work of proof-reading. Helping me proof-reading is also Mr. Bijoy Das. Shalini kumar has been of help on the computer, and Geeta Manchanda for miscellaneous services. To them I express my thanks. I should also thank Prof. M.C. Joshi, Member Secretary and Pandit Satkari Mukhopadhyay, Co-ordinator of Kala Kosa of IGNCA for helping provide the fund for the book.

October 15, 1998

TC

FOREWORD

"My heart sings at the wonder of my place
in this world of light and life;
at the feel in my pulse of the rhythm
of creation
cadenced by the swing of the endless time.

I feel the tenderness of the grass in my
forest walk,
the wayside flowers startle me:
that the gifts of the infinite are strewn
in the dust
wakens my song in wonder."

(Quoted from Sisirkumar Ghose ed. *Tagore for You*, Calcutta: Visva-Bharati, 1984, p. 145.)

These words of Gurudeva Rabindranath Tagore's poem "Wonder" forever reverberate in our hearts. No matter how "the infinite are strewn in the dust" we, as the gardeners of the cultural treasures of "this world of light and life" always feel that we are treading on "the tenderness of the grass" when we take our daily "forest walk" in the city of Delhi which may soon become yet another real concrete jungle.

Tagore wrote to Mahatma Gandhi on Februray 19, 1940 that Visva-Bharati was both national and international: "national in its immediate aspect", and "international in its spirit". He wanted Gandhiji to note that he had offered at Santiniketan "India's hospitality of culture to the rest of the world".The same thing, probably, could be said about the Indira Gandhi National Centre for the Arts (IGNCA). Although sometimes we share the poet's feeling of the Infinite being "strewn in the dust", our hearts still sing at the wonder of our little places, in our humble voices.

The international aspect of Gurudeva and Santiniketan had attracted a unique family of Prof. Tan Yun-shan to settle down there for more than half a century, from the 1930s to the 1980s. Conversely, Tan Yun-shan and his family had enriched the international aspect of Santiniketan. In the same manner IGNCA has Prof. Tan Chung — a member of our family — and Tan Chung is no other person than Prof. Tan Yun-shan's eldest son. Both father and son of the Tan family have had only one agenda in their life, i.e. promoting friendship and understanding between India and China — the two nations and states having the largest populations and longest continuous civilizational experiences.

We bring out this commemorative volume for Tan Yun-shan's birth centenary in consonance with the Tagorean spirit, with what we are doing in awakening universal consciousness for the cultural heritage of both India and the world. Tan Yun-shan, as described by the former Prime Minister of India, Mrs. Indira Gandhi, had "identified himself with Santiniketan and contributed immensely to a better understanding between the civilisations of India and China". He was initially invited by Tagore (in 1927) to Visva-Bharati to help Gurudeva to revive "Great Pilgrimage" of ancient Indians going to China, and Chinese coming to India weave into a golden tapestry of a Sino-Indian Cultural interface and synergy. Tan made a great contribution in the establishment of the Sino-Indian Cultural Society (established in Nanjing, China, in 1933, and in India, 1934) and the Cheena-Bhavana (in 1937). In doing so, Tan Yun-shan himself has become a part of the modern phase of this "Great Pilgrimage". We commemorate his centenary in the hope that this "Great Pilgrimage" between India and China will develop further from strength to strength.

It is gratifying that Tan Yun-shan's centenary is being celebrated in Beijing on October 27, and at Santiniketan on November 7, this year. We are most grateful that the President of India, Honourable Mr. K. R. Narayanan, has not only written a long and warm "Message" for this volume, but is also going to release this book at Santiniketan, when he inaugurates the Tan Yun-shan centenary celebration. The President has taken a lead in reiterating the messages of India's savants, particularly, Gurudeva Tagore, Mahatma Gandhi, Panditji Nehru, etc. that India regards it vitally important to cultivate cordial understanding and co-operative relationship with her close neighbour China.

I am grateful to Chinese and Indian scholars, as well as scholars from other countries in making their contributions to this volume, and wish to thank them on behalf of IGNCA. I hope this volume will further widen and deepen understanding between India and China.

October 15, 1998 **Kapila Vatsyayan**

PREFACE (translation)

Both China and India are ancient civilizations of the world, both have been friendly neighbours for thousands of years uninterrupted. This is an unparalleled development in world history. The people of our two countries have made great contributions for the welfare of the humankind. Our brilliant inventions and creations have all along been the beacon lighting up the historical developments of the world. Today, the amity between the two most populous countries of ours is closely interrelated with world peace and the furture of humanity.

In a history extending several millennia we see a large number of eminent priests and political emissaries from our two countries going across deserts and oceans, risking their own lives, taking their own inventions and creations, both spiritual and material, to each other's country — giving a fillip to social developments enhancing people's welfare. Beneficiaries our peoples still are to these historical contacts.

Yijing (635-713), the eminent Tang pilgrim wrote at the very inception of his *Biographies of Eminent Monks of the Great Tang Dynasty Going on Dharma-Seeking Pilgrimages to the Western Regions (Da-Tang Xiyu qiufa gaoseng zhuan)* thus:

"It is observed that since ancient times there has been no death of people who would be willing to sacrifice their lives for the sake of Dharma, Master Faxian was the first to carve out a path in remote wilderness. Master Xuanzang futher trode it into a thoroughfare. Such pilgrims either blazed a lonely trail through alien lands of the Western Regions, or singularly disappeared in the ocean expanse of the South Sea. All of them looked forward to the holy shrines, and went on pilgrimage exhausting themselves physically with a strong wish to return so that they could redeem the four gratitudes (gratitude to parents, to all human beings, to the ruler of the country, and to the Grand Jewel of Buddhism) and leave behind a good name. However, perilous was the exalted journey separating the Treasure-land (of Lord Buddha) with an endless distance. What with scores of booming seedlings hardly one ultimately bore fruit. It was due to the daunting deserts with long rivers reflecting formidable sunlight, while dreadful waves in the ocean lining up giant columns covering the sky. When a pilgrim printed his lone steps beyond the iron gate of China, he threw himself into thousands of pinnacles. When he embarked on a voyage, his life was dispatched to the strange islands and shores. For days he had to make do without food to eat and water to drink. His spirit was consumed by anxiety, while his rightful countenance becoming a wreckage. Among several scores of pilgrims hardly a few could survive. Even after reaching the Western Country (India), one could not find a Chinese temple, seeking shelter became a great worry, landing oneself in a position of homelessness like a floating leaf, seldom having a fixed place for stay. Without a settled life how could Dharma prosper? Alas! The pilgrims are indeed praiseworthy, and their fame should be passed down to posterity. Here I have gathered some rough details to serve as their biographies."

The above passage vividly depicts the perilous journeys undertaken by eminent monks like Faxian (337?-422?), Xuanzang (600-664), Yijing etc. for India in the past in quest of *Dharma* across land and sea. Such undertakings would not be possible without an undaunting spirit and life-risking adventurism. Such people were lauded by Lu Xun as the "backbones of China" — how befitting this Laudation! Equally noble were also the eminent Indian monks who arrived in China. The personalities painted bv the brush of Yijing were the builders of the golden bridge of Sino-Indian friendship. Whenever we think of them even after the lapse of a millennium, we are filled with adoration and wonderment for them.

In modem times there has been a complete revolution of communication and transportation facilities. Nevertheless, the great significance of Sino-Indian friendship has not only been unaltered, but is even enhancing with each passing day. Notwithstanding the availability of aeroplanes and oceanliners which land you at the destination in a matter of twelve (even less) hours, interflow between our two countries has not entirely passed through highways — but so often through single log bridges. True that a much larger number of personalities are shuttling between the two countries with much enlarged activities which, in turn, have widened visions and complicated purposiveness. But, we see very few builders of the golden bridge of Sino-Indian friendship. Such a builder must be endowed with enormous courage and profound wisdom, with an insight much above their companions and a vision far beyond that of the ordinary people. In other words, such builders are not among the ranks of Tom, Dick, or Harry. They can be likened to what the Chinese proverb describes as "phoenix's feather and unicorn's horn" *(fengmao lingjiao).*

Do we have such people in China, or in the world? Yes, he is Prof. Tan Yun-shan. Prof. Tan Yun-shan has trodden on the footsteps of Faxian, Xuanzang, Yijing and other eminent monks and noble masters in extending and promoting the traditional friendship between the two great nations of China and India, throwing in the energy of his entire life into this noble pursuit. Though, indeed, he did not go through the ordeal of desert-crossing and ocean-faring as experienced by those ancients who had mortgaged their lives for their pilgrimage, his, after all, was also not a comfortable journey along a smooth highway. He made acquaintances with great personalities in India, like Mahatma Gandhi and Gurudeva Tagore, great statesman Nehru and his daughter Indira Gandhi etc. In China, he also had associations with some leaders of the Kuomintang. After the founding of the People's Republic he again, made friends with a few famous leaders of New China. He re-constructed a golden bridge of friendship — a bridge more brilliant and magnificent, more meaningful, more valuable than the one of the past, and perfectly meeting the conditions and needs of modern times — among these great personalities, and between China and India. Yijing observed that "with booming seedlings hardly one ultimately bore fruit", but Prof. Tan Yun-shan has yielded abundant fruits, far beyond what the ancients could achieve — thus all the more conforming to Yijing's laudatory. I am sure the peoples of our countries would forever remember Tan Yun-shan.

Prof. Tan Yun-shan was also an example of a patriotic overseas Chinese. He visited China in the 1950s, published an anthology entitled "Visit the Motherland — written with copious affection for the motherland that moves anyone who reads it. His son, Prof. Tan Chung, has stepped into his shoes to dedicate himself to an endeavour that promotes Sino-Indian amity, and is known in both the countries. Anyone who is a true internationalist must first be a true patriot. These two do not contradict, only complement each other.

The volume edited by Tan Chung in commemorating his father is nothing short of a shower for the drought, which gives me great pleasure to pen this "preface".

Ji Xianlin

(Translated by Huang I-shu)

INTRODUCTION

Gurudeva Rabindranath Tagore has become a "multi-national" in the sense that he has authored the National Anthem of two separate sovereign countries — India and Bangladesh, and is regarded as the common cultural savant of both the nations. When friends in Beijing started preparing for the Memorial Function-Cum-Seminar for Tan Yun-shan's birth centenary (scheduled for October 27, 1998), they accepted my request not to designate him as an "Overseas Chinese". Yes, Tan Yun-shan was a Chinese diaspora, but he is also owned by India and has become a "multi-national" — like his 'Gurudeva' Rabindranath. It is quite interesting to note that after accepting Tagore's invitation in 1927, and arriving at Santiniketan in 1928, Tan Yun-shan started following the footsteps of Gurudeva, and has gone so far with Tagore to become a common asset of two sovereign countries. This phenomenon has also registered the borderlessness between India and China in his being (during his life time), and in his symbol (after his demise).

On the surface, my taking initiative and also the troubled pleasure (or pleasant-trouble) in Tan Yun-shan's centenary celebrations seems in accordance with the filial piety of a Confucian Chinese tradition. But, the enthusiastic support from my Indian friends, particularly Rashtrapati (President of India) Honourable Mr. K. R. Narayanan's warm blessings for and gracious participation in this celebration has taken it beyond the narrow boundary of nation-state, let alone nationalism. Like Gurudeva, Tan Yun-shan was no nationalist from a narrow perspective. His loyalty always belonged to two nations — India and China. China was his first motherland, India was his second; China was his cradle, India was his cremation ground. He lived for 85 years of which nearly half a century was spent in India. Among his seven children, India and China have claimed an equal share of their birth places: (3 born in China, 3 born in India, one born in Malaya), and only the first two enjoy Chinese as their mother-tongue — the rest five have been essentially Bengali and English speakers. When we asked our late-lamented sister, Tan Wen, to write about father more than a year ago, she felt it better that the memoir should be couched in Bengali — which was practically her first language and strongest forte, although she had emigrated to the USA for nearly ten years because of her marriage with a US citizen of Bengali descent. All this speaks how national boundaries have become blur in the Tan family.

Why I should dwell on this point is to drive home another point that India and China should become one entity in the schema of TanYun-shan's spirituality which is basically not different from the Tagorean spirituality. The only unmatching element of the former to the latter is that while Tan Yun-shan's spiritual universe was largely that of two countries (India and China), and two civilizations (Indian and Chinese), Tagore's was of far greater dimension encompassing the East and the West — the entire humanity. Yet, this Tagorean schema of the "universal man" was not alien to Tan Yun-shan's intellectual and spiritual networking. For Tan had written the Chinese term "Datong" into the aims and objectives of the Sino-Indian Cultural Society, and christened the school he and his wife, Chen Naiwei, had jointly founded at Changsha in 1948 with it. This "Datong" is the abbreviation of "Shijie Datong" which means "one world" — the world of the Tagorean "Universal Man".

All this has helped me to exercise the element of narrow family piety and even narrow national jingoism fro the Tan Yun-shan centenary project. I think, humans are such cultural animals that they love symbolism, that they have a human touch in any spiritual wave or movement. The name "Tan Yun-shan" has already become a symbol, just as "Tagore" "Visva-Bharati", "Santiniketan" have become powerful symbols. The "Tan Yun-shan" symbol, of course, is a mini-symbol in comparison with the other three. It is a symbol that has linked up with Cheena-Bhavana which is but a portion of Santiniketan, and an integral part of Visva-Bharati's institutional structure. It is befitting that the birth centenary is celebrated at Santiniketan on November 7, 1998, and is inaugurated by the President of India in front of the erstwhile residence of the Nobel laureate Rabindranath Tagore. (When I pen this sentence, there comes the exciting news that Prof. Amartya Sen whose birthplace is Santiniketan has been awarded this year's Nobel Prize in Economics. Santiniketan, thus, has the unique honour of producing two Nobel laureates, and, surely ranks highest in the world now in terms of the per-acre share of Nobel Prize.)

Yet, in a sense, the "Tan Yun-shan" symbol has also gone beyond the boundaries of Santiniketan if the Beijing Centenary Celebration on October 27, 1998 is any indication. In this book, we have used another symbol — that of "Xuanzang" (spelled variously as "Hsuan-tsang", "Yuanchwang", "Hien-tsang" etc). This symbol, though quite endeared to Indian culture, Indian history and the Indian people, is essentially a Chinese symbol. It is the symbol known as "Xitian qujing", i,e. "The quest for truth (Buddhadharma) from the Western Heaven". This has been a symbolism that has had a powerful appeal among the Chinese intellectuals. Its spell has overpowered thousands or even millions of Chinese intellectuals, including Tan Yun-shan. There are three elements in this symbolism. First, to China India is the fountainhead of spiritualism. Buddhism is the essence of this spiritualism, no doubt, but out of a thousand Chinese who used to be under the spell of the Indian spiritualism only one had donned the Buddhist robe. Spiritual Buddhism, as Tagore, Nehru and many Indian savants had conceived, was acceptable to all Indians (even all foreigners) irrespective of their religion — if we care to separate spiritual Buddhism from monastic Buddhism. That the national flag of the Republic of India bears the *dharmacakra* is a ramification that in modern India spiritual Buddhism still survives.

Second, the symbolism of "Xuanzang's quest for dharma from India" (*Xitian qujing*, as I have just now alluded to) is an urge by a materialistic civilization to gain spiritual input into it. I have written elsewhere that China had two greatest poets Li Bai and Bai Juyi of Tang Dynasty styling themselves as "upasakas". Li Bai (701-762), whose poetic gems smell the aroma of Chinese whiskey, had left behind a poem "who am I?" which reads:

"Blue-Lotus Upasaka is my self-styled title,

An angel from Hevean I'm banished to this world,

My fame has been buried beneath the liquor of the pubs

And I have measured thirty springs with my wine cups.

Who am I ? Why on earth should anyone thus inquire?

I am Golden-Millet Maiterya's next life."

(See Tan Chung, *Classical Chinese Poetry* in the *Classics of the East* series, Calcutta: The M.P. Birla Foundation, P. 143, with translation modified.)

This "Golden-Millet Maiterya" was the powerful Indian legend, Vimalakirti whose Chinese name reads "wei-mo-jie" (the transliteration of the Sanskrit). Another famous Chinese poet, Wang Wei (701?-761) had a second name in "Wang Mojie", i.e. he tried to demonstrate in both his names that he was "Wang Vimalakirti" — "Wang" being his surname. Here we see Li Bai and Wang Wei vying with each other to claim themselves as the reincarnation of Vimalakirti who was the Indian symbol for a man higly enlightened (even more enlightened than the Bodisattvas) but remained married in the mundane world. I dare say that all the Chinese intellectuals who had self-styled themselves "Jushi" had cast themselves in this Vimalakirti mould. Tan Yun-shan never self-styled himself "Jushi", but was glad to be addressed as one, particularly by the devout Buddhists. Thus, we see a Chinese cultural drive from Xuanzang to Tan Yun-shan to synthesize spiritualism with materialism. We have included in this volume Gurudeva's inaugural address of Cheena-Bhavana in which he praised highly the Chinese culture's perfecting the material life without lapsing into materialistic obsession. That means the above mentioned Chinese cultural drive had yielded a positive result, and Tagore was a witness of it.

There is yet a third element in the Xuanzang Symbol, i.e. dedication and self-sacrifice. My Indian friends who have resurrected their memories of Tan Yun-shan have emphasized on this point.

All in all, the symbolism that has embodied the life and career of Tan Yun-shan is a three-in-one entity: (1)

Sino-Indian cultural affinity, (2) spiritual-material synthesis, and (3) dedication and self-sacrifice. It is such a symbolism that this volume intends to project — through Tan Yun-shanÕs centenary celebration. I must hasten to add that I have not consciously or unwittingly made any attempt to project Tan Yun-shan (who was my father) as a perfect saint. Because I know when we employ symbolism we only highlight the main strain. I may liken a human career to a river. In a river not every drop of water flows in the same direction, but the main direction of the flow is unmistaken. I want to make it crystal clear that there is no intention in this volume to eulogize Tan Yun-shan, but just to project him in a historical perspective, particularly in the spirit of promoting the "Xuanzang" or "Modern Xuanzang" symbolism.

This volume is quite hurriedly assembled trying to interweave various items and segments into an integral whole. The first part of it contains five articles under the caption of "Life of Tan Yun-shan". As they are written by five different authors, repetition and contradiction may be unavoidable. Tan Lee, who, in certain aspect, was the closest among all brothers and sisters to father, has taken pains to reconstruct the life sketch of Tan Yun-shan. In doing so, he has combined the information Tan Yun-shan himself had reluctantly revealved about himself under public pressure along with the little information that has trickled from China. There was no time to embark on a comprehensive research on Tan Yun-shan's life (which will be left to future scholars), but what Tan Lee has produced can become a base for further inquiries. Tan Chung's article tries to avoid repeating the "Life Sketch", yet providing an overview with a touch of historical discourse. I know that the readers will not trust my objectivity, but may gain a little insight from my narrative.

Mr. V. G. Nair was one time Tan Yun-shan's secretary. He was very nice to have brought out a book titled *Professor Tan Yun-shan and Cultural Relations between India and China: Commemoration Volume*, published in Madras by Indo-Asian Publication in 1958. This is the first commemorative volume of Tan Yun-shan. His article included in our volume is taken from that volume. (While I am forever grateful to Mr. Nair for having projected my father 40 years ago when my father was in the prime of his life and career, I never had any opportunity to meet him, nor know his whereabouts. Thus, I have taken the liberty of using his article without his consent.)

Prof. W. Pachow has specially written his piece for Tan Yun-shan. Though it is a mirror of how a favourite disciple remembers his most endeared guru, it covers almost all major dimensions of Tan Yun-shan's life and career. Prof. Huang Xinchuan, on the other hand, is looking at Tan Yun-shan from a distance (not like Pachow's close-quarter observations) with a macro perspective.

The second section: "Fond Memories" has gathered the remembrance of 18 persons, including 2 relatives, 3 children of Tan Yun-shan, 7 who had worked, studied, or lived as neighbours with Tan Yun-shan, 2 ex-Indian ambassadors to China (who knew Tan Yun-shan from the files), and 3 Chinese India experts to whose Indological careers Tan Yun-shan had provided the first lesson.

Ms. Chen Laisheng is my mother's younger sister who has been congratulated for her 90th birthday two years ago by the leaders and public of Hunan province. She is respected as a model teacher and social worker for the welfare of women. In 1929, immediately after my birth, she accompanied my mother to carry me to Santiniketan to meet father and to pay homage to Gurudeva. As she is too old and weak, I did not tax her too much, but what she has written which is included in this volume is itself a piece of document. Prof. Yang Yun-yuan (Y. Y. Yang) is my mother's first cousin. He, too, is over 80, and has lost quite a bit of his memory. But, his recollections are quite valuable, not in the know of any one of us in the family. As Tan Yun-shan's life and career involve many dimensions that, too, are geographically scattered, no single person can possess information to all these dimensions. But Prof. Bhudeb Chaudhuri, Prof. Kalyan Sarkar, Lama Chimpa, Prof. Karuna Kusalasaya, Prof. B. K. Roy Burman, and Mrs. Bina Roy Burman have given us titbits of insight into the personality and character of Tan Yun-shan. These are supplemented by the three pieces of recollections of brother Tan Lee, and Tan Arjun, as well as sister Tan Wen. In all these accounts, we see mother Chen Naimei's image as an avant-garde path-opener being transformed into a traditional "good wife and good mother" (*xianqi liangmu*) just because of her marriage to Tan Yun-shan. This reminds me that when I was studying in Hunan in the middle school, and when friends saw the handwritings of both father and mother, some of them remarked that my mother's hand was superior to father's.

Though this slightly hurt my imagination of father's "greatness", I was assured that mother, in her own right, was the material for a great career. But, she sacrificed her own to accomplish that of her husband, Tan Yun-shan.

In the next section, "India and China", we have 5 solicited articles specially for our volume in addition to the one written by Prof. Kalidas Nag for the 20th anniversary of Cheena-Bhavana in 1957 (which we have reproduced from Tan Yun-shan ed. *Twenty Years of Cheena-Bhavana, 1937-1957*, Santiniketan: Sino-Indian Cultural Society, 1957).

The name of Dr. Sampson Shen seems a little strange, but he is well known in India as Shen Chi (Shen Qi). After obtaining his Ph.D. from India, he joined the Nationalist Government of China and later distinguished himself as the Foreign Minister of the Taiwan regime. The article is an excerpt from his Ph.D. thesis entitled, "Tagore and Confucianism" with his consent.

Prof. Prasenjit Duara's is a modified version of a published article from his book, trying to examine nationalism and culturalism in depth from the developmental experience of India and China. It helps us to understand the cultural ecology in which the generations of Tagore, Tan Yun-shan and later intellectuals of India and China have grown up. Prof. Manoranjan Mohanty's focus is very similar but sharply focussed on the issue of colonialism and the Indian and Chinese discourse of it.

Prof. Lin Chengjie's article is a modified version of what he had written for the ICCR journal, *Indian Horizons*, in 1994. He has provided valuable information and insight about the echoes in China of what Tan Yun-shan and others had done in India or in between India and China. He is, I dare say, the most knowledgeable scholar about India-China friendship in modern times, particularly in the present century. It is his camera that has enabled us to see the role of Tan Yun-shan from a historical dimension. Dr. Haraprasad Ray's article, on the other hand, has focussed on a narrower area of the academic field.

In the next section we have included important writings not only by Tan Yun-shan himself, but also by Tagore and Nehru and others that can help understand the large dimensions participated in by Tan Yun-shan in the India-China relations. I also include an introduction to the Sino-Indian Cultural Society which, as President Narayanan has pointed out, enrolled the first three Presidents of India, Dr. Rajendra Prasad, Dr. S. Radhakrishnan, and Dr. Zakir Husain, as ordinary members long before their election as the Indian heads of state. President Narayanan's "Message" which enshrines the beginning pages of this volume helps us to realize Tan Yun-shan's role in bringing India and China together through his close contacts with leaders of the two countries.

We have photoproduced a few letters of the Indian leaders addressed to Tan Yun-shan, in addition to one addressed by Prime Minister, Mrs. Indira Gandhi, to me expressing condolence for Tan Yun-shan's demise. These letters are meant to strengthen the historicity of Tan Yun-shan's career and our commemoration of this career.

As I have alluded to earlier, this volume is not the fruition of research, but can serve as original and second hand source materials to future researchers to inquire into a chapter of India-China intercourse which has not been given adequate scholarly attention. I hope this publication will deepen mutal understanding between India and China, using the symbol of Tan Yun-shan as a "golden bridge" — as Prof. Ji Xianlin has so kindly described in his "Preface".

October 16, 1998

TC

A MOSAIC LIFE OF ORDINARY UNIQUENESS

1. Life Sketch of Tan Yun-shan
Tan Lee

2. Tan Yun-shan — A historical Role
Tan Chung

3. Tan Yun-shan: The Man and his mission
V.G. Nair

4. Tan Yun-shan and the Renewal of Sino-Indian Cultural Interaction
W. Pachow

5. A Cultural Envoy between China and India
Huang Xinchuan

1

LIFE SKETCH OF TAN YUN-SHAN

1898 Oct.10 — Born in Chaling County, Hunan Province, China, youngest child of a Confucianist scholar and teacher.

1902-1906 — Early education at home from father who ran an atalier in traditional Chinese style. Studied Szu Shu, the Four Books of Chinese Canons.

1906 — Father passed away suddenly.

1906-1910 — Sent to study in the county school Wen Chiang Shu Yuan under Master Chen Lan-Chi. Studied the first three books of Wu Ching or the Five Canons.

1910 — Mother passed away.

1910-1914 — Went to study in the district school Mi Chiang Shu Yuan under Master Lung Tzu-Yuan. Besides completing the last two books of Wu Ching, studied ancient and modern Chinese philosophy, history and literature, e.g. Lao-Tzu, Chuang-Tzu, Mo-Tzu, Kuan-Tzu, and Hsun-Tzu; the four Dynastic Histories Shik-Chi, Han-Shu, Hou-Han-Shu, and San-Kuo-Chi; and select ancient and modern books of poetry and novels such as Hsi-Yu-Chi, Shui-Hu-Chuan, San-Kuo-Yen-Yi, Ju-Lin-Wai-Shih, Hun-Lou-Meng, etc.

1915-1919 — Studied in Hunan Teachers' College, Changsha, graduating in 1919. First contact with western education imported mostly from France and United States.

1919-1921 — Post-graduate studies in Comparative Chinese and Western Education.

1922-1924 — Joined the Chuan-Shan Academy in the Provincial Capital of Changsha and carried out advanced studies and special research in Western Culture, Philosophy and Thoughts.

During this period, wrote a number of articles, stories and poems and published them in local newspapers and magazines. Organized the ``New Literature Society", edited a weekly named ``New Literature" as the Sunday Supplement to the daily newspaper "Hunan Jihpao".

At the same time, Tan was active in the progressive students movements and served as Head of the Provincial Students' Union and the College Students' Union, each for one year. Edited and compiled the Union mouthpieces and other publications. Joined Mao Zedong in two of his organizations: ``Hsin Min Hsuch Hui" or 'New Peoples Learning Society" and "Hsin Wen Hua Shu She" or 'New Culture Book Depot". Later, organized and headed a third society called "Chung Hsin Hsuch She" or "New Cultural Society".

Tan also had a baptism in Buddhist Studies under Rev. Tai Xu, the leading exponent of Buddhism in modern China.

Four main movements had engulfed China, two political and two cultural. First, the Kuomintang or Nationalist Party led by Dr. Sun Yat-Sen. Second, the Kungchangtary or Communist Party led by Mao Zedong. Third, Movement to South Sea Countries to spread Chinese education and culture. Fourth, Movement to Europe, particularly France, to learn modern European Culture. Not being politically inclined, Tan chose the last two.

1924 Went to Malaya with a plan to teach there for four years, go to India to seek Buddha-Dharma and Arya-Dharma for five years, then travel to Europe for three years, and finally return to China to continue work in the field of educational and cultural inter-change between China and India.

Taught in Vocational School of Industry & Commerce in Singapore. Also worked as part-time teacher of Chinese Philology in Singapore Chinese Girls' Normal School. Visiting teacher at Chinese School of Kuala Muar, Johore State and Chinese School of Kuala Trengganu, Trengganu State.

Pioneered Chinese literature in Malaya and championed modern ideas among overseas Chinese. Wrote articles and poems and published them in the three Chinese daily newspapers in Singapore, Lex Pao" or the "Journal of Singapore', "Kuo Min Jih Pao" or the "National Daily Newspaper" and "Shang Pao" or the "Commercial Daily". Edited a Sunday Supplement called "Hsin Kuang" or "New Light" to the "Journal of Singapore" in 1925. Later, edited a new supplement called "Sa Mo Tien" or "Oasis" to the "National Daily Newspaper".

1925 Spent four months in Johore State on an extraordinary and emergency assignment for the Government of Malaya.

1926 Met Miss Chen Nai-Wei, native of Hunan who had come to Malaya to teach, first at Kuala Lumpur, then at Matubahar, Johore as the Principal of Aiqun School.

1927 Met Rabindranath Tagore in Singapore for the first time in July. Tagore invited Tan to come to Santiniketan to teach. Tan and Chen got married in Singapore.

1928- 1930 Tan travelled to India for the first time. Joined Tagore's International University, Visva Bharati, Santiniketan as Professor of Chinese Studies. Classes in Chinese started in September with five students: Sri Prabhat Mukherjee Prof. F. Benot, Sri Sujit Mukherjee, Dr. Chowdhury, and Sri Pate. Free discussion sessions were held regularly between Tan and Pandit Vidhusekhar Sastri. At the same time Tan started to take lessons in Sanskrit from Pandit Kshiti Mohan Sen. He also helped linguist Mark Collins in his study of Lao Tzu.

During the next two years, Tan wrote a number of poems and articles on Indian culture, religion, philosophy, customs and manners.These were published in various journals in China. Of particular note was the article 'In-Du Quo-Chi Ta-Hsueh"or ``The International University of India'', which appeared in "Tung-Fang Tsa-Chih" or "The Eastern Magazine" in Shanghai. The other was an article on the Indian National Movement led by Mahatma Gandhi. Tan's poems were published in a booklet entitled "On the Indian Ocean" by the Youth Book Shop in Guandong.

Eldest son Tan Chung was born on April 18,1929 in Matubahar, Johore State. Mother and son visited Santiniketan in 1929 for a few months.

Tan had numerous meetings with Tagore to discuss ways and means of raising funds to build a permanent Hall for Chinese Studies. Re wrote letters to friends and wellwishers in China and South-East Asia soliciting help. The response was mixed. Promises from a major donor in Singapore failed to materialize.

1930 Took leave of Tagore and Visva-Bharati to go back to Singapore on a fund-raising mission. Stayed in Singapore for only two months.

Went to Rangoon, Burma to assume the editorship of the local Chinese language newspaper as an interim vocation. There he continued to promote the vision of the Chinese Hall in Santiniketan.

Left the editor's job and joined Mr. Xie Guoliang, Special Chinese Envoy on his mission to Tibet. Xie died on the way.

1931 Tan continued to Tibet and was guest of the 13th Dalai Lama at the Potala Palace. Tan delivered the government document to the Dalai Lama. Dalai Lama in turn asked Tan to carry a message from him to Mahatma Gandhi.

Mar. 7 Reached Kalimpong on his overland trip on horseback from Lhasa to India.

Mar. 23 Returned to Santiniketan but left soon after on a tour of India. Visited all the major Buddhist Centres of pilgrimage.

Apr. 27 Met Mahatma Gandhi at his Sabarmati Ashram, and delivered Dalai Lama's message. Gandhi and Tan had prolonged discussions about relationship between India and China and India's freedom movement. Gandhi encouraged Tan to adopt vegetarianism.

May 15 Left Calcutta for Singapore. Met up with wife and son to take them back to China. His plan was to stay in China for a few years to promote his vision of Sino-Indian cultural exchanges and to raise funds to build the China Hall in Santiniketan.

1931 Sep. Returned to China with family. Started to teach at the Lida Academy, Shanghai. Commuted between Shanghai & Nanjing (interim Capital of China) to canvass for establishing a Sino-Indian Cultural Society as a vehicle to realize Tagore's dream. Was successful in obtaining solid support from Tsai Yuan-Pei, President of Academia Sinica, as well as Tai Chi-Tao, President, Examination Yuan (China's Public Service Commission), and others.

1932 Second son Tan Chen was born in Changsha on August 10, 1932.

1933 The China Chapter of the Sino-Indian Cultural Society formally established in Nanjing, with Tsai Yuan-Pei as its first President and Tan Yun-Shan as the first Secretary. On February 18 Tan wrote to Tagore advising him of the progress much to the delight of the Poet.

1934 Returned to Santiniketan in February to organize the India Chapter of the Sino-Indian Cultural Society. The Society was established in September with Tagore as its first President and Rathindranath as the General Secretary.

In October, Tan returned to China to raise funds for construction of the China Hall and to secure books most essential for research activities of the institute. The response was overwhelming. With strong support from Tsai Yuan-Pei, Tai Chi-Tao and Rev. Tai Xu, adequate funds were raised for the building and furnitures. The Sino-Indian Cultural Society purchased over 100,000 fascicles of Chinese books on Buddhism, Classics, History, Philosophy, Literature and Arts. More books were donated by friends and publishers.

1934 Third son Tan Lee was born in Shanghai on November 30,1934.

1936 Returned to Santiniketan with Rs. 50,000 and 100,000 books. Tagore was thrilled and allocated a prime piece of land at the heart of the campus for the Institute of Chinese Studies or ``Cheena Bhavana". Construction started immediately under Tan's personal supervision. Suren Kar, the noted resident architect provided aesthetic touch to the functional plan chalked out by Tan. Biren Sen was the building contractor.

Eldest daughter Tan Wen was born in Changsha on July 4,1936.

1937 Cheena Bhavana was completed in record time. Nandalal Bose assisted by Binode Behari Mukherjee and other staff and students of Kala Bhavana adorned the Hall with beautiful frescoes and relief work. Chinese calligraphy written by Lin Sen, the President of China, was placed centre-front on the building with similar calligraphy by Tai Chi-Tao at centre-rear. Tan meticulously planted many native species of trees around the building to provide shade to what was then a barren piece of property.

Mahatma Gandhi was invited by Tagore to inaugurate the building, but could not come due to prior commitment to go to Belgaum. Jawaharlal Nehru, then President, Indian National Congress agreed to preside over the function but was prevented from attending due to sudden illness. Finally, it was left to Indira Gandhi to do the honours. On April 14, Cheena Bhavana was formally opened. Gandhi in his message to Tagore said: "May the Chinese Hall be a symbol of living contact between China and India".

1937 Tan was appointed the Director of Cheena Bhayana, the first institution of its kind in India, but because of the financial straits of Visva Bharati (then a private university), refused to take a salary. Instead the Chinese Government provided him an honorarium.

Tan continued his effort in fund raising. Seth Jugal Kishore Birla sent a donation of Rs. 5,000 to start some of the research projects with future donations to come.

Tan maintained a dialogue with Indian leaders on issues of Indian independence and the sufferings of Chinese people at the hands of Japanese invaders. Attended International Parliament of Religions in Calcutta as China's representative.

Delivered a series of 5 lectures at Andhra University, later published as a book entitled "Modern Chinese History".

Nov. 23 Nehru wrote to Tan informing him that the Congress had started campaign to boycott Japanese goods.

1938 Returned to China to report to his Chinese supporters progress in the establishment of Cheena Bhavana. The news was welcome in government circles as well as among the intelligentsia. Tan saught further help from the Chinese Government in the form of research scholarships.

Apr.10 Nehru wrote to Tan prior to his departure asking him to convey India's support to the Chinese people in their struggle against the Japanese.

Apr.12 Tagore wrote to Chiang Kai-Shek in support of China's resistance to Japanese aggression. utter delivered in person by Tan to Chiang.

1938 Apr. 23 Netaji Subhas Bose wrote to Tan asking him to convey the support of the Indian Congress to China's resistance against Japan.

Jul. 9 Tan met top leaders of China including Chiang Kai-Shek at Wuchang and discussed how China and India could support each other in their respective struggles.

Jul. 14 Chiang wrote to Tagore from Hangzhou thanking him for his moral support to the Chinese people.

1939 Tan returned to Santiniketan accompanied by wife and third son Tan Lee and eldest daughter Tan Wen, leaving the eldest son Tan Chung and second son Tan Chen in Changsha, Hunan.

Pandit Vidhusekhara Bhattacharya had looked after academic and research work at Cheena Bhavana during the absence of Tan in China. With his return, a major effort was made to recruit teaching and research staff. Those who responded included Dr. Vasudev Gokhale from Poona, Sujit Mukherjee, W. Pachow from China, Rev. Sumangala from Ceylon, Shih Shu-Lu from China, Wangdi from Tibet, Pandit Aiyaswami Sastri from Madras, and Chow Ta-Fu from China.

Xu Beihong (Ju Peon), the leading artist of modern China came at Tan's invitation and spent a year as Visiting Professor of Chinese Fine Arts.

At the initiative of Tan, the Sino-Indian Cultural Society organized a visit by Nehru to China. On August 18, Tan sent a telegram to Chiang to inform him of Nehru's arrival on August 20. Nehru spent August 20 to September 6 in China gathering support for India's independence from British rule.

1939 A close bond of friendship and mutual respect for each other's mission was thus forged between Nehru and Tan. This bond was to continue for the rest of their lives.

The first Chinese Buddhist Mission to India led by Rev. Tai Xu visited Santiniketan and spent a week as guests in Cheena Bhavana. Tan accompanied Tai Xu to Ceylon.

1940 Tan was instrumental in organizing a visit by Dr.Tai Chi-Tao to India and Santiniketan. Tai, a profound scholar in Buddhism, had been a staunch supporter of Tan's efforts. He was also a great admirer of Tagore and Gandhi. Tai donated Rs.10,000 of which Rs. 6,000 was to be used to build a quarter for the Tan family, Rs. 3,000 for a memorial to Maharshi Devendranath, and Rs.1,000 was to go to the Visva Bharati Relief Fund. As Tan had already built a modest home with his own money, the Rs. 6,000 was used to build quarters for other staff.

Second daughter Tan Yuan was born at Santiniketan on August 5, 1940. Tagore named her Chameli, the first child to bear an Indian name.

1941 Tan requested Government of China for more funds to expand Cheena Bhavana so that the valuable collection of books can be properly cared for. The Government of China responded by donating Rs. 13,000.

Wu Hsiao-Ling joined Cheena Bhavana as research scholar and lecturer. He spent four years and returned to China as a Professor in the Academia Sinica. His wife Shi Suzhen mastered the Bengali language and subsequently joined as Professor in the Institute of Foreign Literature, at Chinese Academy of Social Sciences, Beijing.

1941 Chin Ke-Mu spent several semesters in the Cheena Bhavana between 1941 and 1945 and returned to Beijing University as a Professor of Sanskrit.

From Thailand came Karuna Kusalasaya who spent two years as a research scholar and Assistant to the Director. He returned to Thailand to become Professor of Sanskrit at the Buddhist Academy in Bangkok as well as an Advisor to the Indian Embassy. Rev. Pannasiri came from Ceylon and spent five years in research work.

Tagore taken seriously ill in Calcutta. Tan spent several days by his bedside praying, but his Gurudeva could not be revived. Later, Tan was to lament that with the passing of Tagore, he lost the one person who could truly understand the scope and significance of Cheena Bhavana.

1942 But the task entrusted on Tan had to go on. He devoted all his energies to fulfill the dream that he was privileged to share with his beloved Gurudeva.

Feb. In the midst of the raging war in China, Generalisimo Chiang Kai-Shek and Madam Chiang decided to pay a strategic visit to India. Because of their awareness, they made a special trip to Santiniketan to see Cheena Bhavana. They were pleased with the progress of the institution that had already received financial support from China and announced a further donation of Rs. 50,000.

Tan helped in organizing a series of meetings between Chiang and Nehru which were of importance to China's destiny during the war with Japan.

Jul.8 Nehru conveyed Chiang's anxiety to Mahatma Gandhi and persuaded the latter to reply to Chiang with an assurance that: "whatever action I may recommend will he governed by the consideration that it should not injure China .... and .... must lead to the strengthening of India's and China's defence".

Rev. Fa Fang, a prominent disciple of Rev. Tai Xu joined Cheena Bhavana as a Research Fellow in Indian Buddhism. After three years he went to Ceylon to study the Southern School and returned to Santiniketan and taught for two years before going back to China. Wu Bei-Hui, another protege of Tai Xu joined Cheena Bhavana. He studied and did research in Sanskrit and Hindi for ten years prior to returning to Beijing University as a Professor of Sanskrit.

During this time, Tan became concerned about the education of the children of overseas Chinese. Tan was drawn to the large Chinese population in Calcutta and helped them with fundraising for the Chinese Medium School. He was also instrumental in establishing a Chinese School in the hill station of Darjeeling.

At the same time, Tan's deep-rooted interest in Buddhism drew him to places like Bodh Gaya and Sarnath.He became intimately involved in fundraising and construction of the Chinese Buddhist Temple and Lodge in Bodh Gaya. In the City of Calcutta he became a frequent participant in the activities of the Maha-Bodhi Society where his dear friend Rev. Jinaratna ran its affairs.

1942 Fourth son Tan Ajit was born on April 3,1942 in Santiniketan.

The research staff was strengthened with the addition of Santi Bhikshu Sastri and Krishna Kinkar Sinha.

1943 Through Tan's efforts, the Government of China sent ten students to study their chosen subjects in various universities in India. Three of them, Shen Chi, Ou- Yang Chung-Yang and Wei Kwei-Sun came to Santiniketan. After some months they transferred to Benares Hindu University, University of Allahabad and the Aligarh University repectively to obtain their doctorate degrees. Wei Kwel-Sun subsequently joined Cheena Bhavana and retired as Professor.

A Chinese Cultural and Educational Mission visited Cheena Bhavana and donated some funds for its library.

The fifth son and youngest child Tan Arjun was horn in Santiniketan on August 6, 1943.

Satiranjan Sen joined as a Research Scholar and became a Junior Research Fellow under the Chinese Government Cultural Fellowship. Was sent by the Indian Government to Beijing University for further Chinese studies. Founded Cheen Bharat Sanskriti in Calcutta. Amitendranath Tagore, likewise, was selected for a Chinese Government Cultural Fellowship and spent three years in Beijing University. On his return he became Lecturer in Modern Chinese Language and Literature. Later he became Professor of Chinese Studies in Oakland University, USA.

1943 Birendra Chandra Banerjee was hired by Tan as Office Assistant and later as Secretary to the Director. Subsequently, he went to USA for further studies and returned to take a librarian position in Visva Bharati.

1944 Further donations were collected by Tan for the expansion of the Cheena Bhavana Library. A second storey was added to the two single-storey wings of the main building to properly house the valuable collection of books which have now grown in numbers.

New staff who joined included: Yang Yun-Yuan, Research Fellow and Lecturer in Chinese Language and Literature who later became Professor of Chinese at the School of Foreign Languages, Govt. of India and still later Professor of Chinese, Berkeley; Mrs. Yang Lo-Heng, Research Scholar & Assistant Librarian; Chang Jen-Hsieh, Research Fellow & Professor of Chinese Archaeology; and Hsu Hu, Research Fellow in Indian Philology & Professor of Chinese Literature.

1945 Following the War, Tan Yun-Shan was awarded the ``Victory Medal" by the Government of China in recognition of his valuable services to the nation.

The Government of China continued its strong financial support by starting a Chinese Cultural Fellowship for three years, worth Rs. 25,000 each year.

Cheena Bhavana was strengthened by the addition of several senior staff. Dr. Probodh C. Bagchi joined as Senior Research Fellow and Director of Research under the Chinese Government Cultural Fellowship. He was later seconded to Beijing University as Visiting

Professor of Indology. On his return he becaine the Principal of Vidya Bhavana and subsequently the Vice Chancellor of Visva Bharati; Dr. P. V. Bapat joined as Senior Research Fellow and Professor.

Haridas Mitra was hired as Research Fellow; Prahlad Pradhan as Research Fellow; V. G. Nair as Research Fellow & Assistant Secretary to the Sino-Indian Cultural Society; and S. K. George as Research Fellow & Joint Editor of the Sino-Indian Journal.

1946 The Ministry of Education, China, gave a special grant of Rs. 12,000 each year for three years for scholarships. Another Rs. 12,000 per year for three years was received through the Sino-Indian Cultural Society of China.

1947 India became independent with Nehru as its first Prime Minister. Tan attended First Inter-Asian Relations Conference, New Delhi as a Delegate of China.

It was time for another visit to China. This time Tan was accompanied by his wife and the three youngest children. The family went back to Changsha where Mrs.Tan Chen Nai-Wei built the Datong School and ran it as Principal for two years.

Sisir Kumar Ghosh joined the Cheena Bhavana as Research Fellow & Joint Editor of the Sino-Indian Journal. Ghosh later became the Head of the English Department, Visva Bharati.

1948 Tan returned to Santiniketan with an additional title of China's ``Cultural Representative". By a letter dated August 26, Prime Minister Nehru congratulated Tan: ``I hope that with your assistance and advice we shall develop further cultural contacts with China".

1949 Under the leadership of Mao Zedong, a new People's Republic was established in China. Not knowing what the future cultural relationship would he between India and China, Tan decided to bring his family back to Santiniketan in May. There was a temporary hiatus in cultural exchanges between the two countries, but not for long. At the same time, Tan's honorarium from China stopped.

1950 Tan was invited by the Government of India to the Republic Day Celebrations in New Delhi as a representative of the Chinese people where he was received by President Rajendra Prasad.

Tan wrote to old acquaintance Mao Zedong with three policy suggestions for the New Government: 1) Not to lean on one side; 2) Strengthen Sino- Indian friendship; 3) Find peaceful solution to the Taiwan issue.

A Special Donation of Rs. 500,000 was received from The Sino-indian Cultural Society of China for a new Central Library for Visva Bharati.

1951 Visva Bharati became a Central Government University. With this came structural and organizational changes to many of the institutes including Cheena Bhavana. Some of the primary goals of this unique institute charted by Tagore himself got lost in the euphoria of run of the mill university expansion. This, no doubt, caused great disappointment in Tan. His strong discipline in the tenets of Buddhism, Confucianism & Taoism permitted Tan to endure this in silence.

On top of this Tan had no income and refused to take a salary from Visva Bharati. It was at the insistence of his dear friend of long standing Anil Kumar Chanda that he finally agreed to receive a salary from the university.

Around this time, Tan's spirituality and interest in religious matters made him explore the fertile fields scattered throughout India. Gandhi had already made a deep impression in his mind. Although, not quite able to convert to total vegetarianism, Tan nevertheless curtailed his meat intake, relying more on eggs for protein. He also started to observe Wednesday as a day of silence following Gandhi's lead.

Tan became interested in the work and writings of other spiritual leaders like Sri Aurobindo,

Acharya Kripalani, Vinoba Bhave, and Sivananda. He maintained regular correspondence with them and visited the Aurobindo Asram in Pondichery on a number of occasions. At the same time Tan kept touch with several academics who were keenly interested in his efforts. Some of the leading thinkers with whom Tan maintained regular dialogue included Dr. Kalidas Nag, Dr. Suniti Kumar Chatterjee, Dr. Amarnath Jha, Prof. Humayun Kabir, Dr. Kamta Prasad Jain, Prof. Nikshoy Chandra Chatterjee, Prof. Sisir Kumar Mitra, Swami Satyananda, and Sri Krishna Kripalani.

1952-1955 Teaching of the Chinese Language to Indian students and Indian Languages to Chinese scholars continued at an accelerated pace due to the emerging geopolitics in Asia. Unfortunately, the earlier emphasis on research and retranslation of Buddhist texts were relegated to a lesser position. This turn of events disturbed Tan a great deal.

However, Cheena Bhavana continued to attract new scholars. Some of the more recent arrivals included: Narayan Sen who taught for a few years; Jan Yun-Hua (1953), Research Fellow under Government of India Five Year Plan, who after completing his Ph.D. taught for a number of years before joining McMaster University, Hamilton, Canada as Professor of Chinese; Mrs. Jan who worked in the Cheena Bhavana Library; Sm. Ambulu Sastri (1953), Research Scholar who visited China as a member of Indian Professors and Students Delegation in 1955; Viswadev Mukherjee (1953), Research Scholar; Krishnanath Chatterjee (1953), Research Scholar.

Dr. Carrington Goodrich, Dean Lung Professor of Chinese, Columbia University spent two years as Visiting Professor of Sinology (1953-54).

Tan Chung, eldest son who grew up in China through the turmoils of the War expressed his desire to come to India to complete his studies. Tan obtained permission from appropriate Chinese and Indian authorities and Tan Chung and his wife Huang I-Shu were able to come to Santiniketan in 1955. After completing his Ph.D. Tan Chung taught at the NDA, Khadakvasla, then joined Delhi University as Professor of Chinese and subsequently became Head of the Department of Chinese and Japanese Studies in the Jawaharlal Nehru University, New Delhi. His wife Huang I-Shu also taught Chinese in Delhi University for several years.

1956 Zhou En-lai, Premier of China wrote to Tan extending his Government's invitation to visit his homeland. In September, Tan made his first trip to China since the change. On this trip he was accompanied by eldest daughter Wen who had completed a B.A.(Hons) in Bengali, securing the top position in the class. In Beijing, Chairman Mao welcomed his friend in presence of other Chinese leaders, former teachers and fellow students who were familiar with Tan's work in promoting Sino-Indian relations. Thus, the channels of communication with the Government of China were established much to Tan's delight. Of the leaders who showed particular interest in Tan's work, mention must he made of Premier Zhou, Minister Li Weihan, Minister Yang (Education) and Guo Mojo.

1957 On return to India,Tan reported on his China visit to Nehru and suggested that the Government of India invite Premier Zhou to visit India. This was duly arranged and in January, 1957 Premier Zhou became the first leader from Peoples Republic of China to visit India. Zhou came to Santiniketan to receive an honorary degree. He visited Cheena Bhavana & donated Rs. 60,000 for a Memorial to Tagore.

Daughter Wen was pursuing a Masters Degree in Bengali. Zhou offered her a job to teach Bengali in Beijing. However, circumstances did not permit Wen to accept this generous offer.

K. Venkataramanan, Prof. of Philosophy, transferred from Vidya Bhanana to Cheena Bhavana.

1958 Feb. 20 Tan invited to New Delhi where he was received by President Rajendra Prasad.

1959 Sep. Again invited by Government of China to visit. Received by President Prasad before leaving for China. In China Tan again met major leaders in Government including Mao Zhedong, Liu Saochi, and Zhou Enlai. Tan had many discussion with Premier Zhou focussing mainly on

Sino-Indian cultural relations but also on the border dispute.

1960 On his return to India, Tan was received by Prime Minister Nehru in New Delhi. They discussed Sino-Indian relations and the tensions at the border in the presence Anil Kumar Chanda, Deputy Minister of External Affairs. Tan reported on his discussions with the Chinese leaders.

1962 Border skirmish flares up between India and China. Tan was devastated. He felt his life long dream and efforts were about to crash. Question was raised at the Parliament of India regarding the activities of Tan, a Chinese national. Nehru made a strong defence of his old friend of thirty plus years.

Dec. At the Visva Bharati Convocation Nehru spoke passionately about the border war. Spotting his friend Tan in the audience, Nehru hastened to add that despite the border conflict which has to be resolved between the two Governments, the people of China would always be India's friends. Tan openly wept.

1963-1970 In spite of the mental anguish weighing heavily, Tan continued his teaching and research work. Years of disciplined life kept him in good health. He was given several extensions in service. Meanwhile daughter Wen completed her Ph.D. in Bengali in 1964, the first Chinese ever to achieve this distinction. One of Tan's cherished dreams was realized.

1971 Retired from Visva Bharati Cheena Bhavana. Donated the house he built with his own money to the University however, the University was happy to let Tan live in it as long as he wished. Tan's mind, however, was drawn to a new challenge, an even bigger dream.

1972-1978 On one of his ocean voyages, Tan had this other vision. He started preparing for the establishment of the World Buddhist Academy to be located in Bodh Gaya. Through his connections with Chief Minister Sinha of Bihar, Tan was able to acquire the necessary amount of land next to the Chinese Temple that he had helped build many years ago. This time, however, he decided to build the institution entirely from private donations.

Despite his advanced age, he was once again on the road, travelling to Hong Kong and Singapore to raise funds for the Buddhist Academy. And funds did pour in from many sources such that construction of the Academy could start. It would be a 4 storeyed building with a total floor area even larger than Cheena Bhavana.To most people much younger than him, the very scale of the building would be a formidable task, but not to Tan. He was always used to thinking big and no undertaking was insurmountable as long as the cause was justified. Tan took on the life of an ascetic living in a small room at the Chinese Temple. He was finally able to fulfill his earlier vow to Gandhiji of becoming a true vegetarian. A villager brought him a Spartan ration of some vegetables and pancakes. Tan plugged along and the Academy took shape.

In the meanwhile, the second son Tan Chen, who had remained in China also wished to come to India. Arrangements were made and he and his family came to Santiniketan in 1976. Tan Chen taught Chinese in Cheena Bhavana from 1979 to 1987 before emigrating to USA.

1978 The University of Nalanda conferred an Honorary Doctorate on Tan.

1979 Visva Bharati conferred the honorary degree of "Deshikottama" on Tan.

1980 His wife and companion of 54 years passed away. This was the ultimate shock of his life. But his second mission had to continue. Despite pleadings from his children he could not be pursuaded to come away from Bodh Gaya.

1982 The Academy building by now had its roof on. But for the flooring, it was essentially complete. A large statue of Lord Buddha carved in stone donated by a devotee in Singapore, had been flown in and installed. On a visit from Canada by his third son, Tan talked to him about how to get the work of the Buddhist Academy started. Tan by now was weak in health from years of neglect and deprivation, but his spirit was strong as ever. Tan took his son to each room of the

Academy and explained how he planned to use the space. He appeared almost etherial, being totally immune to suffering and pain. He was bent on finishing his mission. Perhaps he realized time was running out. But the good Lord had other plans.

On to the small village of Bodh Gaya descended the Dalai Lama and his entourage. Thousands of Tibetans from all over India flocked to Bodh Gaya to get his "darshan". They had no place to stay. Tan opened the gates of his Academy gladly to give them shelter and they remained there long after the Dalai Lama had left. That his Buddhist Academy could give shelter and warmth to devotees of the Lord must have given Tan a final satisfaction.

1983 At the ripe age of 85 Tan breathed his last in Bodh Gaya, the seat of Buddhism which drew him to India in the first place, his pilgrimage of life completed.

Prime Minister Indira Gandhi in her message of condolence said:

"Gurudeva and my father had affection and regards for him. He identified himself with Santiniketan and contributed immensely to a better understanding between the civilizations of India and China".

2

TAN YUN-SHAN — A HISTORICAL ROLE

1. The spirit of Hunan ox

According to the *Gazeteer of Chaling County,* Tan Yun-shan was born at the Shen hour (1500-1700 hours) on the 5th of the 9th moon of the Wuxu year of Emperor Guangxu's Era of the Manchu Dynasty, i.e. 1898. Tan Yun-shan was a man who was keen to embrace modern trends. He recorded the birth of all his children according to the solar calendar. This created problems for his second son, Tan Zheng, when he applied for passport to come to India in the 1970s. The Hunan passport office refused to believe that his date of birth was recorded in the solar calendar, as he was born in 1932. It promptly converted his solar birthday into another solar birthday. Few modern Chinese could imagine that Tan Yun-shan did this in the early decades of the century to his own birthday. One year, this 5th of the 9th moon coincided with the 10th of October which was the national day of the Republic of China. This gave him an occasion to switch calendar. Henceforth, everyone easily remembered that he was born on the "Double 10th Festival", forgetting the original date recorded in the lunar calendar.

His cradle was the Xiadong Village of Chaling County in Hunan Province — a place on earth which even today lies sleeping in the natural economy. Both his grand father, Tan Wenhan, and his father, Tan Hongmou, were village intellectuals with a smattering of scholarship but no outstanding distinction. His father, Tan Hongmou, earned an honorific imperial title of the lowest 9th rank which, of course, was something to boast of in the village surroundings of the 19th century. Economically, the family might be rated as "rich peasants" if only to apply the criteria of the Land Reform Movement of the early 1950s. Judging from the standards today, the word "rich" would be a total misnomer.

His grand father, Tan Wenhan, survived both son and daughter-in-law who passed away just a few years after they got their third son, Tan Yun-shan. This was the 4th child in the family after quite a gap between his birth and that of his two elder brothers and one elder sister. In my boyhood, I saw my elder paternal aunt, but never my uncles who were probably too old to journey from Chaling to Changsha (a matter of several hundred kilometres) to be our guests. But, their sons did come, and they were at least twenty years my senior. It was obvious that they inherited the poverty and rustic manners of their parents.

Tan Yun-shan was first given the name "Qixiu" while his elder brothers begot "Qiding" and "Qicai" respectively. (The sister probably had no name to herself as per China's male chauvinist tradition). The common syllable "qi" in all the three names represents the generation. Traditionally, a Chinese family adopted a passage of the classics the word-order of which became the order of the genealogical growth — a word in the passage is used as the marker of a specific generation according to the order of words which enshrines the generation sequence. While "qi" was the marker of my father's generation, mine is marked by another character "ke". But, father never passed the genealogical passage down to me, hence I could not use the marker of my son's generation. My son who never had any chance to work in a Chinese language environment, hence does not actually need a Chinese name. But, father named him "Fatian" which is the Chinese translation of "Brahma".

Coming back to the birth names of my uncles and my father, the eldest son was christened "ding" which means "population", the second son's "cai" meaning "wealth", while my father's "xiu" denotes "talent". Here is a reflection of the typical traditional rural aspirations of China. When the first son arrived, the parents were assured that the genealogical tree would grow. But, my grand father (and also the great-grand-father) wished that the growth should he exuberant which was depicted in Chinese as "Rending xingwang", i.e. "a thriving population". While my first uncle was named "population", the arrival of the second uncle evoked an additional hope for richness. While my second uncle's name was "wealth", my father's arrival after a considerable gap of the three births (of two sons and a daughter) made the patriarch of the family invoke the icon "talent" *(xiu)*, betraying his further ambition of getting a member to distinguish in the Imperial Examinations. ("Xiu" stood for "Xiucai" which was the name of the title conferred on a scholar who passed the first stage of the three-tier Exams.) Father was, indeed, a material for such a distinction. But, by the time he was old enough for the Exams it had already been abolished for quite a number of years (in 1905).

According to Chinese tradition, every man must have two names, one used officially and publicly, and the other to be addressed only by family members and intimate friends. When we were young, we saw mother marking all the houshold furniture by four characters of "tan qi xiu tang", meaning "the household of Tan Qixiu". We thought "Qixiu" must have been father's second name. Actually, it was his first, while his second name was "Lianke" which we never saw him using anywhere. But, "lianke" denotes "to qualify the Imperial Exams" which all the more reflects the family expectations of his academic excellence. As my father had ultimately distinguished himself in the academic world, that too in a foreign country, his christeners' wishes were over-fulfilled. But they (my grand father and great-grand-father) never lived long enough to know this.

I checked up the students' rosters of the First Normal School of Hunan (with the kind help of Mr. Zhao Lei who used to work for the China Association for International Friendly Contacts), and found the two names of father being "Yunshan" and "Shaoshu", none of which seems to originate within the family. Father entered the First Normal School at Changsha after completing his studies in the First Senior Primary School of Chaling. He was listed as "Tan Yun-shan" in the roster while his other name "Shaoshu" was noted in parentheses. Who gave him these names cannot he historically ascertained now.

But we know another development of father's early life. Ironically, after christening him "Qixiu" (talent of the Qi generation) and "Lianke" (qualifying the Imperial Exams), my great-grand-father (my grand father passed away early) was too poor to send the talented orphan boy to school. There was a relative named Huang Wuren living in a neighbouring village of Huangtang who was well to do. Huang (who probably had no son) virtually adopted Tan Yun-shan as his own son, and sent him to the local First Primary School of Chaling. Tan not only studied well, but eventually qualified the entrance exams of the Hunan First Normal School at the capital city, Changsha, which was not only the highest educational institution of the province at that time, but was extremely difficult to get in. It was likely that Huang Wuren had named him "Shaoshu" while sending him to school, and Tan himself adopted the name "Yun-shan" after entering the First Normal School.

Sources from his village trace the name "Yun-shan" (denoting "cloud mountain") to a famous hill in Chaling named "Yunyang" Hill. But, "yunshan" was a favourite imagery of classical poetry, having employed by famous Tang poets like Li Bai and Wang Wei, and many others. Wang Wei composed a poem in Hunan while he was only 19, depicting a legendary ideal society which is known as "shiwai taoyuan" or "the peach-blossom land beyond our world". In the poem, Wang Wei wrote: "Shizhong yaowang kong yunshan" describing the utopian "peach-blossom land" as an "illusory cloud mountain" when looked from our human world. In these lines, the ancient Tang poet showed that he had already adopted the Buddhist philosophy of Sunyata. As Tan Yun-shan had surely read Wang Wei before entering the First Normal School, and as he was also inclined to the Buddhist way of life, it was possible that he discarded all his given names, and used "Yun-shan" (the cloud mountain) to mark his entrance into a new world of hope and challenge.

During and before Confucius' times the pale of Chinese culture concentrated along the middle and lower streams of the Yellow River. Hunan, a region which lay south of Yangtse, was conceived as a part of "Nanman" (southern barbarians). I have, a little earlier, alluded to Taoyuan, a part of northern Hunan, being conceived as a happy and peaceful land beyond the hustles and struggles of China. This myth was created by a scholar from neighbouring Jiangxi, named Tao Qian (or Tao Yuanming) (365 427). Tao's famous essay "Taohuayuan ji" (An Account of the Origin of the Peach Blossoms) presented this part of Hunan as the habitat of ancient Chinese refugees who knew nothing about the Han Dynasty. This was probably an indication that Hunan was hardly integrated into the mainstream of China by the powerful Han Empire (206 BC - 220 AD). During the post-Han period, there was a large exodus of Chinese northeners into the areas south of Yangtse, and Hunan began to have Buddhist temples built at its scenic spots which, in turn, attracted famous writers of the Tang

Dynasty (618-907) as tourists. But, it was only in the last couple of centuries that Hunan distinguished itself as a cradle of talented people both on the civilian and military fronts.

Situated at the centre of the country, and the midway station along the Yangtse river with a railway passing through it from Beijing to Guangzhou (Canton), Hunan was not cut off although deep in the interior. In the 20th century, its capital city, Changsha, was humming with new trends, new ideas, and new-wave activities. For instance, my mother, Chen Naiwei (1905-1980), was born in a village in the Dongshan hills north of the old small city of Changsha (but now very much a part of the enlarged Changsha city). Her grand father, Chen Xiaolou, was one of old China's millions of ambitious rural intellectuals who was unlucky in qualifying the Imperial Examinations. But, he decided to play an active role in his rural surrounding, teaching youngsters and also treating the sick with his self-made medical expertise. Unlike others in his profession, he travelled to the houses of his patients without being carried by the palanquin, without accepting fees and gifts. When Dr. Sun Yat-sen rose in rebellion against the Manchu Dynasty in the southern neighbouring province of Guangdong, the senior Chen emulated Sun's example to cut his own pigtail (which was the symbol of enslavement forcibly imposed upon all Chinese nationalities by the ruling Manchu race). Under his influence, his eldest son, Chen Zihou, resigned from his government job in the High Court of Hunan and joined the communist movement, and died a martyr in 1927. Chen Naiwei was the eldest daughter of Chen Xiaolou's fourth son. She and her younger sister were among the first Chinese women to enlist themselves in public schools. When she started teaching during her teenage in the Taokan School in Xiangxiang county not far away from the birthplace of Mao Zedong, the village urchins used to regard her as a rare animal — an unmarried young woman running away from home, teaching other's children in a strange place, unheard of in the thousand-year-old tradition of China!

In comparison, father's own village was not so advanced. But, the moment he landed in Changsha (to study in the First Normal School) he became thrilled by the new things he saw. Incidentally, this was also the school where Mao Zedong and a host of other revolutionary leaders had had their education. Father was all admiration for Mao. He joined the Xinmin (New people's) Society, a revolutionary organization founded by Mao, and often followed Mao to his swimming exercise in the rivers. One episode he told his children was Mao's not fighting shy of changing his underwear after swimming in front of a group of young men and women. This was abominable enough (according to Hunan's conservative decorum) to earn him the nickname of "Madman" (fengzi) even by his close friends and admirers.

As if following Mao's footsteps, Tan Yun-shan went for further studies in the Chuanshan Academy in Changsha which was founded by Hunan's first great scholar, Wang Fuzhi (better known as Wang Chuanshan) (1619-1692). Tan also was the President of the Hunan Students' Union, and his close associates, Xia Xi and Guo Liang both became activists of the communist organizations in Hunan, and died young. Tan bid his farewell to his Maoist friends in 1924 when he went to Malaya to join one of the two movements beckoning the intellectuals of Hunan. The first movement was, again, launched by Mao and his associates, to mobilize young students to go to France to work and study which was a boon for China's having sent workers (not soldiers) to join the anti-German front during the World War 1. Out of this movement arose famous leaders of the Communist Party of China (CPC), like Zhou Enlai, Zhu De, Deng Xiaoping etc. The second movement was to help educating the children of China's diaspora in Southeast Asia who had been sold to the British and other European colonisers as indentured slave- labourers (nicknamed "Pigs"), but turned to be nouveaux riches after gaining freedom from their colonial masters. Tan's initial plans were to join both these movements. He made his first step to Singapore, waiting for an opportunity to travel further to Europe. Spiritually, he did not actually break away from the movement led by his cynosure — Mao Zedong — in his formative years. ne entirely different road he ultimately took was because of new developments in Singapore.

As he never gave up his Hunan accent, Tan had also remained a Hunanese till the end of his life in many ways. The Hunanese have been known in modem times among fellow Chinese as people extremely hard working, honest, loyal, stubborn, courageous, with a fighting spirit against injustice. A befitting nickname for them is "Hunan niu" (Hunan Ox). Tan Yun-shan had all these traits. The "Hunan idiosyncrasy" was also decided by its geographical location. Their's not being a frontline province, the Hunanese seldom stood out as a pioneer, blazing a new trail in any movement. Yet, Hunan's being a province which was well connected with the frontline regions, these Hunanese showed great sensitivity to new movements, and always ready to join them. I term this as a "rear- wave tendency" which could give a strong backup force to the pioneers. Tan Yun-shan had such an idiosyncracy as well.

I must mention another special feature of Hunan, i.e. a strong impact of Buddhism both in the great and little traditions. There was a famous saying which might or might not originate from Hunan, but well known to the Hunanese. The saying goes:

Shishang haoyan Fo shuojin, tianxia mingshan seng zhan duo.

"All good words have turned out to be the Buddha's sayings,
Most of the famed mountains are in the monks' possessions".

Tan Yun-shan had developed a positive response to such a pro-Buddhist culture of Hunan, and learnt to recite many Buddhist scriptures which came easily to him just like the Bhagwat Gita to an Indian intellectual who has a traditional inclination. This cultural inculcation from his home province played no small part in his choice of settling down in India — which was quite unthinkable not only to his contemporaries, but even to so many Chinese today. Every time when Tan was in China, whether in the 1920s, 1930s, 1940s or 1950s, he was invariably greeted by an unbelieving inquisitive: "You live in India?!" And after his demise, this greeting has now passed on to me. "There is a famous Chinese saying: "As water flows downwards, man climbs upwards." Going abroad is called "dujin" — to gild — but only to the affluent countries and the Western Hemisphere. In modern times and among the modern Chinese, going to India is almost unheard of, and incomprehensible. Gone is the ancients' enthusiasm in modern China in the pilgrimage to the "Country of Buddha". To Tan Yun-shan who had grown up as one of the millions of modern Chinese eager to embrace the Brave New World across the Pacific and Atlantic, his choice for settling down in life was still a pilgrimage unaffected by the earth-shaking changes of the 20th century — while nothing short of abnormality and imbecility according to many a materialistic modern Chinese.

2. A Passage to India

I have already written elsewhere about the invisible linkage between Gurudeva Rabindranath Tagore and two modern Chinese personalities. One of them was Guo Moruo who was, as it were, China's Tagore or Gorky, and the other was Tan Yun-shan. One commonality between the two was when Guo was studying in Japan and Tan working in Singapore, both were fond of going to the sea side. Facing the sea's endless expanse, both Guo and Tan developed a feeling of frustration and uncertainty about their own future, while their own country was in shambles. Both, it so happened, could. not suppress an idea of either committing suicide, or renouncing the world as a Buddhist monk. That both of them were rescued from mishap was partly because of Tagore. Readers who want to know how Tagore had saved the life of Guo Moruo and given China her own Tagore may read my article, "Tagore's Inspiration in China's New Poetry" in Tan Chung (ed.), *Across the Himalayan Gap: An Indian Quest for Understanding China*, New Delhi: Indira Gandhi National Centre for the Arts, 1998.

That Tagore was the turning point of Tan Yun-shan's life and career I shall now spell out. Tan was a bunch of contradictions when he sauntered on the sea shore. Various voices from the sea waves were calling him — an ambitious young Chinese in quest of future career. He had left behind his school-mates and close companions who had dedicated their lives to the creation of a new nation. He would not shed tears for the *ancien regime*, but he had grown up from a great tradition which became endeared to him, while what shape the new order of China might take he could not see clearly.

Hunan, as has been alluded to above, had deeply ingrained in the young mind of Tan Yun-shan not only a strong dosage of Chinese cultural tradition, but also a strong fancy for India — through Buddhism. Besides a strong desire among the Buddhist-inclined Chinese intellectuals to pay homage to the "Country of the Buddha" (Foguo), there was even a wider tradition (call it superstition if you like) to wish the deceased to ascend to the "Western Heaven" (xitian) —which was a synonym of "Foguo", i.e. India. (The catch phrase is "Rong gui Xitian", i.e. "May the departed soul return gloriously to the Western Heaven" and it has been a standard condolence message for more than a thousand years which survives even today among the Chinese both in the mainland and overseas.) Of course, as I have alluded to earlier, it is also true that the progression of the 20th century in time and space means that all roads of China are leading to the Western Hemisphere. Tan may be regarded as one of the last Mohegans (sic.) who had preserved in him the potential to tread the faded footsteps of Xuanzang and other ancient Chinese pilgrims.

That India had lost her age-old charm among the modernites in China was also due to her being enslaved by British colonialism. Those Indians who appeared in China from the 1840s onwards begot India an image of "a country that has died" (wangguo). They came to China to serve their colonial masters as soldiers, police, watchmen, cooks, and domestic servants without dignity, giving a strong exogenous shock to patriotic Chinese that never should they follow the negative example of the Indians — existing only as "wangguonu" (slaves of a country that has died). Yet, there came the surprising news that one among such Indians "Taige'er" (Chinese transliteration of Tagore) won Nobel Prize in 1913, and that this "Tage'er" was busy travelling in the western countries lecturing to the royal families and ruling elite of the Western powers whose representatives were treating the Chinese in China as dirt — not allowing "Chinese and dogs" into their public parks. Tagore had set fire to the brambly fields of Europhiles in China. When he embarked on a lecture tour there in 1924, educated Chinese youths greeted him as if a god had resurrected. Meanwhile, some leftists were deeply worried that Tagore would prevent the Chinese youths from responding positively to the call of revolution, hence they made a point to disturb Tagore's lectures. (See Sisir Kumar Das, "The Controversial Guest: Tagore's 1924 Visit" in Tan Chung (ed.) op cit.)

Tan Yun-shan belonged to those who regarded Tagore as a god-figure. But, when Tagore sailed to China, he was onboard of a ship sailing away from China. He lamented the loss of the opportunity to see the "saint-poet" ("shizhe", as Chinese called him). But, what had been slipped away turned to be a godsend — Tagore came to Singapore to lecture in 1927. Tan availed of the first opportunity to meet Gurudeva and was given a warm audience by Gurudeva. It so happened that the latter had already been trying to get a suitable Chinese scholar to start Chinese studies in Visva-Bharati.

Just at that time Tan Yun-shan fell in love with a fellow Hunanese with whom he got married. Mother was an ardent admirer for father's writings (for, in addition to teaching in a school in Singapore, father was helping the couple of Chinese language newspapers there to start literary supplements, and also used the papers to publish his prose and verse). Mother was the Principal of a new girls' school named Aiqun (loving the humanity) at Matubahar in Johore (still there even today) north of Singapore. She encouraged father to go alone to India after hearing his exciting account of meeting Gurudeva. Her sister was also staying with her, which made father feel safe in leaving behind the newly married and pregnant wife (with me on my way) to the care of a loving sister and a school of helpers. Her handsome salary from the Principal's post made mother a reliable backup to father's new adventure.

Far from being an established university, Tagore's Visva-Bharati was only an ashram in disguise in those years. Not only were the students sending in their contributions (however meagre they might be), but even the teachers volunteered their services without salaries. They were provided with a subsistent living in addition to a free supply of stamps for letters to be sent out of the Santiniketan post office. Tan Yun-shan, however, was given a special treatment by Gurudeva, being allotted a room in the most luxurious facilities of the then "Tata Building" (now "Ratankutir") with free lodging and boarding. He was given a choice to opt for Western food which he declined. Why? His explanation was: "I would not have the heart to eat Western food even if I wanted particularly after seeing the frugal life of the professors." One of such professors was Vidhushekara Shastri, the pillar of Visva-Bharati, veteran Sanskrit scholar who was the "in-charge" of research. Tan had these descriptions about the pandit:

> "What I admire him most was his frugal and disciplined life as well as his hardworking spirit. Like Gandhiji, he covered himself with only two pieces of coarse cloth. He ate two vegetarian meals a day all cooked by himself."
>
> (All the above and the ensuing quotations are from his book in Chinese, entitled "Yindu Zhouyouji", !.c. An Account of My Travels around India, Nanjing, 1933.)

No sooner had Tan Yun-shan made the option for Indian food from the Tata Building which was served in his room than he began to regret. For neither did it appeal to his gourmet humour, nor was its hygienic standard approvable. But, Tan's "Spirit of Hunan Ox" now rose to the occasion. He not only got used to it, but also composed a poem for self-amusement:

"As if the broom on the floor sweeping
That's the bearer gets your plate clear;
Rice served amidst plenty of sands

Falling as the bell's "ding dong ding".
Potatoes with ingredients boiled
And tree leaves make a depressing hue,
There is curry always with bean soup
Thus everyday your food stares at you.
Meal time is ritual, you remember past sages
(Yan Yuan's frugality echoes Confucius' praises.)
After food you never forget the innumerable poor.
When you are fed what happiness you want more?
Aren't you one who is really privileged,
Hardship isn't the adjective for how you live."

Gurudeva appointed Tan Yun-shan as a Professor of Chinese Studies when the latter was merely thirty. He had the most learned scholars at Santiniketan enlisted as his students in the Chinese language class. Everyone on the campus of Visva-Bharati respected and showered affection on him. However, such a lifestyle was not what Tan had been looking forward to. His plans were first to learn, not to teach. He wanted to learn Sanskrit and Indian cultural traditions. He wanted to travel and see India. Though he was prepared to spend five years for a settled life, but two of the five at Mahatma's Sevagram at Sabarmati, and the rest three at Gurudeva's Visva-Bharati. It looked like that such a plan of pilgrimage would come to naught.

Another distraction was domestic problems. After all, he had just got married, and a baby son was born in his absence. His wife, sister-in-law, and baby visited him at Santiniketan once in 1929 which was only a very brief reunion. It was an express telegram from Malaya which made him decide to leave India after a three year sojourn at Santiniketan. He returned to his wife and son, but left them immediately to work in Rangoon as the chief editor of a Chinese language newspaper. Then, there was a mission for him to accompany an aged and sick Hunanese to go to Lhasa to deliver government documents to the Dalai Lama. He brought the mission to a successful conclusion although the elderly emissary passed away on the Himalayan tracks. After that, he paid homage to Gandhi's Satyagraha Ashram, met the Mahatma to fulfil his dream, and also to convey the Dalai Lama's blessings as he had promised in Lhasa. After all this, he left India and took his family back to China.

This first phase of Tan Yun-shan's three-year sojourn in India had virtually transformed his vision, and his ambition. He was fascinated by the Indian civilization about which he had had only bookish knowledge before, but had now gained an insight into it. He was fascinated by the Gurudeva, by the Mahatma, by what little he had Learnt about the Indian cultural tradition, particularly its spiritual culture and its holistic perspective. He began to write about India — with curiosity and affection. His writings earned many readers' sympathy for India, and earned himself a reputation of an "Indian expert' — an entity which was virtually non-existent in contemporary China. His *Yindu Zhouyouji* (cited a moment ago) and a later book *Yindu congtan* (A Discourse on India) had been, for many decades, the best introduction and reference on India for the beginning scholars. In 1957, when Premier Zhou Enlai visited the Cheena-Bhavana Library, and saw on exhibition a copy of *Yindu congtan*, he opened its leaves and exclaimed, "Why, I have not seen this book!" Tan Yun-shan readily allowed him to take the book away for reading. But, this was the only copy he had left. Later, he often regretted that he had allowed the book to be taken away, or he had not made attempts to retrieve it. Since then, the family library has lost this book for ever.

Tan Yun-shan's three year sojourn at Santiniketan was also a very special experience which one could not easily find anywhere. Though a quiet campus of simple living, it was the habitat of a world famous poet — a cynosure to writers and intellectuals all over the world. The tiny post office at Santiniketan was one of the busiest in the world, with letters of admiration and inquiry arriving like snowflakes. Visitors tracked their ways to the tiny village of Santiniketan which had had no motorable road until the middle of the 1950s. It was here that Tan Yun-shan could get the acquaintance of all kinds of people from all over India, and even from the remote corners of the world. Inside Tan Yun-shan's young mind. Tagore had implanted his huge magnet. Though physically he was compelled to be away, his heart had stuck in Santiniketan. He had decided to come back, come what may. Of course, the seniors of Santiniketan had already been endeared to him, and he to them — a spiritual bond had been lined up. That was why after returning to China he was so eager in writing about India, about Tagore, about Santiniketan, about the Mahatma, as if this was his own country. The fish that was reared up in Hunan Province in China had now been turned into an amphibian — at home both in the Chinese and Indian cultural milieu.

Another discovery of Tan Yun-shan was the virtually non-existence of understanding about China on the part of Indian intellectuals. Though he was not the most educated and most knowledgeable representative of China, he was treated as one. People, including very learned scholars at Santiniketan, and sometimes from other places, came to him to ask very elementary questions about China, about China's sages and philosophical thought. In such interactions, Tan Yun-shan discovered a great deal of commonalities and similarities between both India and China. In Santiniketan, he lived in a life of human and spiritual concord between the two great civilizations. Echoes from both the civilizations became his daily intake of spiritual food. His being treated as a "Professor" in status and an expert of China in reality made him feel the need of studying more of his own cultural traditions. Moreover, he also could deepen his understanding about his own cultural heritage when he was forced to explain it to others. So often, when you are inside the cultural milieu you take everything for granted, never really giving deep thought to them. But, now, in a foreign country, when you look at your own traditions you look at them from a distance. You are putting yourself in the position of a bystander which helps you to inject an element of objectivity in your analysis. All this was very rich living experience and exciting mental exercise for Tan Yun-shan. His stay at Santiniketan was three years of an immersion course in cultural interface and synergy. All this has predetermined that he would be back, and would settle down in India in life.

3. Visva-Bharati Cheena-Bhavana

When Tan left Santiniketan in a hurry after receiving an express telegram from his wife in Malaya, he could not bid goodbye to Pandit Vidhushekara Shastri (who was like a Registrar, particularly when Gurudeva was away staying at Calcutta). He only left a note behind. This attracted a desperate and near-angry reply from the senior who wrote: "Your absence will very keenly be felt by us and specially by those who have been directly connected with you ... I do not know what will now happen to our Chinese Studies in the institution. Only the other day it was arranged that a student would come to us from Nepal to learn Chinese." But he added with affection: "When are you coming back? We shall always be looking for your return." Incidentally, a few months later (after Tan had completed the mission to deliver the Chinese government's documents to the Dalai Lama at Lhasa), Tan did return to Santiniketan and stayed for eight days. Prof. Kshiti Mohan Sen was so excited that he took the trouble to go to Calcutta to escort Tan back. After affectionately embracing him, Prof. Sen asked with anxiety: "What would become our plans, and how to put them into practice?"

The "plans" had been cooked up in the previous three years between Tan Yun-shan, Vidhushekara Shastri and Kshiti Mohan Sen on how to translate into reality the Gurudeva's dream of creating a strong centre for Chinese studies at Visva-Bharati. Gurudeva himself had tried to persuade his Chinese hosts and whomsoever he had met in China in 1924 but to no avail. After Tan had landed at Santiniketan, he also tried to contact people in Singapore and China. He had written to millionaire Hu Wenhu of the "Tiger Balm" fame asking for a couple of ten thousand dollars to build an institution of Chinese studies at Santiniketan, and did obtain a prompt reply that "it's not a big sum, there wouldn't be any problem". Yet, this promise never turned into cash. Tan also wrote to Cai Yuanpei (who was then the President of Beijing University) and a few other influential intellectuals without even getting any reply.

Returning to Kshiti Mohan Sen's question about the "plans", Tan, with his typical innocent optimism and the Hunan Ox spirit, hastened to offer a reply: "Our plans would be transformed into reality only after I return to China." There was laughter before Tan's words had died down. Clearly, no one took what he had promised seriously. The only exception was Tan himself.

To look back, Gurudeva Rabindranath Tagore's idealism about reenacting the pilgrimage of ancient times between India and China would have remained only in the conceptual stage if no powerful human and material push arrived in practical life. Under the circumstances of Tagore's time such a push could not have come from India which was still a British colony ruled by predatory colonial masters. As the famous Chinese abortive reformer, Kang Youwei, had insightfully realized in Darjeeling and other places in India, the country was simply the paradise for the Britons and hell for the Indians. (See Prof. Lin Chengjie's article in this volume.) Even rich Indians were in a pitiable situation of sharing some leftovers of the British spoils. No Indians, individually or collectively would be able to render much help to Tagore to realize even a fraction of his dream of an India-

China fraternity. The other and only possibility of the push would have to come from China.

Tagore had realized this and had tried to create a congenial atmosphere for such a human and material push to emerge. In this respect he did have considerable success. The Chinese intellectual atmosphere after Tagore's 1924 visit was favourable to the launching of a programme to strengthen cultural interactions between China and India. What Tagore had failed in the same trip was in finding a concrete person — a Chinese comrade of his idealism — to convert the favourable atmosphere into material input. In Singapore, when he met Tan Yun-shan — a young immature idolatrous idealist — Tagore might have cherished some illusion, but there was nothing from Tan that could assure Gurudeva that the Chinese comrade he had been looking for had arrived.

Nor was Tan Yun-shan himself sufficiently sure when he made the promise in his parting words to Prof. Kshiti Mohan Sen. That he had finally made it was because of two factors: his unearthing the potential among the Chinese ruling elite to render spiritual and material support to Tagore's agenda, and his own spirit of Hunan Ox. This can be illustrated by a letter addressed to Tagore from Cai Yuanpei, the first Executive President of the Sino-Indian Cultural Society:

"Academia Sinica
Brenan Yuyuen Road,
Shanghai China

February 5th, 1936

Sir Rabindranath Tagore,
Uttarayan,
Santiniketan,
Bengal, India.

Dear Sir Rabindranath,

Owing to my prolonged absence from Shanghai on account of health, I did not see Prof. Tan Yun-shan until the beginning of the present year when he transmitted to me your charming letter of the 28th September. At one time India exerted an overwhelming influence upon the culture of China. Although intellectual contact between the two countries has become less intimate during the past few centuries, nothing is more welcome to us who value our cultural heritage than to resume that contact in order to learn from your country the ways and means of adapting an ancient culture to the conditions of the modern world.

All of us are grateful to you for your great kindness in allowing the Sino-Indian Cultural Society to use your university at Santiniketan as its headquarters. I will do my little part in cooperating with Prof. Tan Yun-shan in his courageous effort to work for the endowment of a Chinese Hall, although the present financial conditions in China are bad enough to discourage a less brave man than Prof. Tan..."

(This letter seems to have disappeared from all the archives in India and China except a hand- copied version preserved by Wei Fengjiang, the first Chinese student sent by the Sino-Indian Cultural Society to Visva-Bharati. See his *Wode laoshi Taige'er* (My Guru Tagore), Gulyang: Guizhou People's Publishing House, 1986, pp. 127-8.)

In this letter, Cai Yuanpei has objectively testfied to the fact that there was a favourable atmosphere in China to help Tagore revive the ancient intimate cultural interactions between India and China on the one hand, and the bad financial situation of the country to be materially of help on the other. But, he also saw a ray of hope in the unusual courage and perseverance on the part of Tan Yun-shan. Indeed, Tagore's comrade had arrived after Tan Yun-shan had made the courageous promise to Prof. Sen at Santiniketan in 1931.

As the chronological sequence of Tan Yun-shan's near-heroic efforts in first getting the Sino-Indian Cultural Society founded, and then mobilizing the requisite funds and books for the establishment of Cheena-Bhavan (the "China Hall") has been given by Tan Lee in the preceding "Life sketch of Tan Yun-shan", I shall only make a few observations to help put the important episode in proper historical perspective.

I should view Tagore, Nehru, Tan Yun-shan, Cai Yuanpei, Tai Chi-tao and many other intellectuals of India and China as representing a historical force generated by the close proximity of two great civilizations of the world — the force of befriending each other and even closing ranks with each other to face the daunting tasks of repulsing the oppression of the Western Hemisphere as well as finding their rightful places in the modern world. Such a historical force was led by Gurudeva with a strong support from Nehru and other enlightened Indian public leaders. But, its field army was first recruited and commissioned in China around the standard of Sino-Indian Cultural Society whose avowed aims are:

Pursuing Sino-Indian Studies,
Linking up the cultures of China and India,
Forging Sino-Indian fraternity,
Uniting the nations of China and India,
Creating peace in humanity,
Making the world a utopia of *Datong* (Ramarajya).

These words are my translations of their Chinese equivalents which were obviously penned by Tan Yun-shan. This was Tan's composition giving full play of what he had understood from the inspirations of Gurudeva.

I wish to dwell a little on this lest the noble ideals of the pioneers of Santiniketan becomes a total loss. Ours is a mundane materialist world in which consumerism has taken command in all spiritual and intellectual arenas. People praised Tan Yun-shan because he had helped Tagore erect an impressive monument at Santiniketan. But, if Cheena-Bhavana is to last as a shining monument the spirit behind its creation should never die — or more accurately, be given a burial as developments seem to point to that direction.

I have earlier highlighted Tan Yun-shan's spirit of Hunan Ox to attribute it as a vital factor to his success in creating the Sino-Indian Cultural Society and Cheena- Bhavana. However, the Tan Yun-shan as the creator and founder-director of Cheena-Bhavana would never have arrived without Gurudeva's idealism which is clearly spelled out in his two famous letters to the "Chinese friends". In his letter addressed to "My friends in China" dated April 23, 1934, Gurudeva wrote:

> "The truth that we received when your pilgrimage came to us in India and ours to you, — that is not lost even now.
>
> What a great pilgrimage was that! What a great time in history! It is our duty today to revive the heroic spirit of that pilgrimage, following the ancient path which is not merely a geographical one but the great historical that was built across the difficult barriers of race differences and difference of language and tradition, reaching the spiritual home where man is in bonds of love and co-operation."
> (See Tan Yun-shan ed., *Twenty Years of the Visva-Bharati Cheena-Bhavana 1937—1957*, Santiniketan: Sino-Indian Cultural Society of India, p. 37.)

In another letter addressed by Gurudeva to the "Chinese friends" who were members of the Sino-Indian Cultural Society dated April 18, 1934, he wrote:

> "There was a time when India and China stood very near, when they joined their hands and their hearts in one common homage to the spirit of Love and Renunciation. Today when the world is being divided into hostile camps, each ready to strangle the other, let us recall that spirit, which still lives among us and permeates our being, and prove in our relations that the forces of love and understanding are greater than those of hatred and aggrandisement."
> (Ibid. *D.* 36.)

Clearly, Tagore's aim of establishing a Cheena-Bhavana in Visva-Bharati was to revive the ancients' spirit of "Love and Renunciation" exemplified by the pilgrims — Indians to China and Chinese to India. The word "Renunciation" has a reference to Buddhism, but Tagore had no intention, and Tan Yun-shan did not mechanically understand it to mean turning Cheena-Bhavana into a monastery. Gurudeva mentioned it along with the predatory world-order of modern times which had not only hopelessly divided our earth into "hostile camps", but such mutually hostile components of the modern world were doing their best "to strangle" each other. Tagore, of course, would not like India and China to fall into such a jungle, instead would let his Visva-Bharati become an exemplary place for international amity and cooperation in general, and Cheena-Bhavana to dedicate to the amity and cooperation of India and China in particular. Tagore had mentioned in his 1924 talks in China that his Visva-Bharati was meant to be "a meeting place for individuals, east or west, who believe in the unity of mankind and are prepared to suffer for their faith". Such a conviction he had repeated in his address at the inaugural function of Cheena-Bhavana on April 14, 1937.

Why "suffer for the faith"? The answer is found in his above mentioned inaugural address in which Tagore said:

> "It is indeed true that we are weak and disorganised, at the mercy of every barbaric force, but that is not because of our love of peace but because we no longer pay the price of our faith by dying for it." (*Ibid*, p. 44.)

It is in this spirit that we should understand Tagore's emphasis on "renunciation", i.e. renouncing the human cowardice before the barbaric forces, and renouncing the obsession for material values.

All this is not to blind us from Tagore's positivism and healthy and optimistic expectations for the establishment of Cheena-Bhavana. Let us review what he had said when he inaugurated Cheena-Bhavana:

> "Let us therefore abide by our obligation, to maintain and nourish the distinctive merit of our respective cultures and not he misled into believing that what is ancient is necessarily outworn and what is modern is indispensable ... can anything be more worthy of being cherished than the beautiful spirit of the Chinese culture that has made the people love material things without the strain of greed, that has made them love the things of this earth, clothe them with tender grace without turning them materialistic? They have instinctively grasped the secret of the rhythm of things, -- not the secret of power that is in science, but the secret of expression. This is a great gift, for God alone knows this secret. I envy them this gift and wish our people could share it with them."
> (*Ibid.*)

While Tan Yun-shan had helped Tagore to build up a Cheena-Bhavana at Santiniketan, Tagore, in turn, empowered Tan Yun-shan to run this newly created institution with a free hand, not as an ordinary organization paying attention to quotidian affairs only, but as a monument of noble idealism. Tagore had particularly given Tan Yun-shan a difficult task of implanting into the campus of Santiniketan the "Chinese secret" of caring for material pursuits without becoming materialistic — the ramifications of this secret was even difficult to find in China in the days of Tagore and Tan Yun-shan, let alone today.

Other authors of this volume have detailed what Tan Yun-shan had built up at Santiniketan in terms of material achievement. I think we ought to scrutinize Tan's achievement by the criterion of Tagore's noble idealism especially his wishing to transplant the spiritual excellence of Chinese civilization onto the soil of Santiniketan. An immediate satisfactory answer to this exercise may not be expected from this essay. But, I have two points to offer. One, I think Tan Yun-shan had understood Gurudeva's message, and had tried to make Cheena-Bhavana a living temple of Chinese civilization howsoever imperfect it might be. For some time, Santiniketan did have a mini-China Town because of Cheena-Bhavana (and a part of it was made up by the family members of Tan Yun-shan). This mini-China Town offered a favourable comparison to its big sister — the China Town in Calcutta just a hundred miles away. At its best times, Cheena-Bhavana did live up to the expectations of Gurudeva although he was no more there to see the fruition of his own idealism. Another point I would wish to make is that Cheena-Bhavana did make Tagore's Visva-Bharati a place true to its name — as an international commonwealth. Conversely, had Cheena-Bhavana not existed, Santiniketan would have been very difficult to justify its claim as an international university. Uptil several years ago, "Cheena-Bhavana" had remained as the only "foreign" member of Tagore's international community. Even today, the second "foreign" member, the Nihon Bhavana, is only the symbol of a building without much cultural contents and academic activities. These two points, I think, make us cherish the memory and contribution of Tan Yun-shan when we commemorate his birth centenary.

Many eminent Chinese monks a millennium ago visited India and went back to build spiritual temples in their country according to the idealism of the Indian saints — the Buddha and the Bodhisattvas symbolizing them. Tan Yun-shan had traced their footsteps to India. Instead of going back to build a temple of spiritualism in his own country, he build it in the "Land of the Buddha". In the past, an Indian monk saw a hill in Hangzhou and claimed that it had flown there from Magadha. Tagore saw the hill (which was named the "Hill of Heavenly India") and was told the story. He hailed it as an example of unity of hearts between the peoples of the two countries. In building up a Cheena- Bhavana at Santiniketan, Tagore had virtually got a Chinese hill flown to India. In the past, people did take pride of Cheena-Bhavana; scholars would go back to China or move to other countries claiming their pilgrimage to Cheena-Bhavana, to Visva-Bharati. Today, not only has Cheena-Bhavana ceased to enjoy such a reputation, but even its name has been erased from the administrative infrastructure of Visva-Bharati — only a Department of Chinese Language and Culture exists. The climb down from the holy hill of Cheena-Bhavana to today's diminished Department of Chinese Language was partly because of the departure of its dynamic founder-director, but more due to the loss of Gurudeva's spiritual idealism. This saddens people more than the loss of reputation. There is a Chinese saying: "Ai mo dayu xinsi." — Nothing is sadder than the death of the heart. I wish we pay attention to the problem of how to revive Cheena-Bbavana when we commemorate the birth centenary of Tan Yun-shan, and how to revive the idealism of Gurudeva that had conceived Cheena-Bhavana, and that had been transformed into practice by Tan Yun-shan.

Another point I must highlight is that from its inception upto 1949 the expenses for running Cheena-Bhavana were not from the treasury of Visva-Bharati, but was remitted from China to Visva-Bharati for the management of Cheena-Bhavana. In other words, Visva-Bharati was only at the receivng end, but how money had come was entirely Tan Yun-shan's personal effort with the blessings of the Government of China. There was a delicate relationship between the Visva-Bharati authorities and the Director of Cheena-Bhavana, and between Visva-Bharati and the Government of China. Much of the success of Cheena-Bhavana during this period was due to its generous Chinese donors (including the government) in contrast to the financial difficulties of the university particularly after the passing away of Gurudeva. In 1951,Visva-Bharati became a national university, while the Chinese government had ceased to finance Cheena-Bhavana since 1950. Yet, the semi-autonomous status of Cheena-Bhavana was still maintained so long as Tan Yun-shan was its director (till 1967).

Because of this semi-autonomous status of Cheena-Bhavana, it could function as an open house. Scholars were welcome to visit and stay in Cheena-Bhavana from a few days to a few years, and were provided. Tan Yun-shan obtained donations from China and built many living quarters behind Cheena-Bhavana for the visiting scholars from China. Students could live in single rooms inside the Cheena-Bhavana building as well. In this way, Cheena-Bhavana gathered a good concentration of Chinese — scholars and students. They, in turn, attracted a lot of Indian intellectuals (scholars and students) to benefit from the rich resources of Chinese studies housed in Cheena-Bhavana. Today, such a character of Cheena-Bhavana is totally lost and impermissible. In fact, how a modern Indian university can observe discipline and simultaneous enjoy a degree of permissiveness (not in sexual sense) of an autonomous institution is a problem that has belied solutions. Under a rigid regulation it may he impossible to revive the past glory of Cheena-Bhavana.

The Cheena-Bhavana that was created and moulded by Tan Yun-shan was, in fact, a multi-national institution with an element of cultural infiltration into India from China. But, this was in partial fulfilment of Gurudeva's dreams. In ancient times, there was never an immigration office anywhere, and no visa was required for entering into any country. It was as the Chinese saying describes: "There is you in me and I in you." (Nizhong you wo, wozhong you ni.) This, I think, is the true spirit of the global village, and was strongly advocated by Gurudeva. Cultural infiltration is the requisite for building the ideal society of *Datong* (Ramarajya) as advocated by the Sino-Indian Cultural Society. This would inevitably clash with the policy that jealously guards the educational and cultural sovereignty against the infiltration of foreign influences (including the influence of the Almighty Dollar). One could debate on this issue (whether it is wise to maintain a dog-in-the-manger attitude) when we consider the revival of Cheena-Bhavana.

4. Needle for Cultural Tapestry

As cited above, Tagore's idealism of reenacting the ancient Sino-Indian pilgrimage had a much greater dimension than building a monument at Santiniketan. He wanted to bring the two ancient civilizations together. In his inaugural address, he made it even more clear about the direction which the activities of Cheena-Bhavana should head to:

> "The Hall [Cheena-Bhavana] which is to be opened today will serve both as the nucleus and as a symbol of that larger understanding [between India and China] that is to grow with time. Here students and scholars will come from China and live as part of ourselves, sharing our life and letting us share

theirs, and by offering their labours in a common cause, help in slowly re-building that great course of fruitful contact between our peoples, that has been interrupted for ten centuries."
(*ibid*, p. 42.)

The moment when Tan Yun-shan completed the work for Tagore to inaugurate the historic Cheena-Bhavana, he himself, became a part of the historical task set forth by Tagore, i.e. to embark on the "great course of fruitful contact" between India and China. Looking from inside the complex of Cheena-Bhavana, Tan Yun-shan, from 1937 onwards, was the head of a new family within the joint family of Visva-Bharati. If weighing with the tasks propounded by Gurudeva there would be no great responsibility falling on Tan Yun-shan's shoulders, but as the head of such a unique institution, he was already transformed into a tiny needle, and his role was weaving a tapestry of Sino-Indian cultural contact. The two dimensions of this "great course" were: (a)events developing within and around Cheena-Bhavana, and (b)those beyond Cheena-Bhavana and Visva-Bharati — but we see the thread of the Tan Yun-shan needle. Both these dimensions have been detailed in other articles of this volume. I shall just summarize the broad significance of the events and activities.

Cheena-Bhavana may be likened to a hen which performed two duties: laying eggs, and hatching eggs into chicks. When it celebrated its 20th anniversary in 1957, Cheena-Bhavana could parade a list of 44 Indian and Chinese scholars (including Tan Yun-shan himself) who had been associated with it. Barring a few exceptions, all of the scholars have not only distinguished themselves in the academic fields, but a distinctive contour of the "great" course of Sino-Indian cultural interactions has been drawn through the efforts of these scholars. All their writings, whether written at Santiniketan or elsewhere, have enriched the field of "Sino-Indian Studies", a term originally conceived by Gurudeva, but more vigorously introduced to the academic public by Tan Yun-shan — all studies about the great civilizations of India and China with a Sino-Indian perspective belong to the arena of Sino-Indian Studies.

While with no intention to discriminate, I wish to highlight the achievements of a few of the ex-Cheena-Bhavana scholars alluded to above. Cheena-Bhavana was fortunate to have the association of Dr. P.C. Bagchi who himself represented a movement of marrying Indology with Sinology. Had he not died on duty as the Vice-Chancellor of Visva-Bharati in the beginning of 1956 — living only 57 years — he would have made much greater and more significant contributions to the development of Sino-Indian Studies. His joining the Cheena-Bhavana for two years (1945-47) signified the confluence of two streams — that of Begchi and Tan Yun-shan.

Similarly, Cheena-Bhavana was enriched almost from its inception by the contributions of Dr. P.V. Bapat, Dr. Vasudey Gokhale, Prof. Prahlad Pradhan and the famous American scholar Dr. Carrington Goodrich (in 1953-54). These and some others were the creators, not products of Cheena-Bhavana. Among other names that Cheena- Bhavana has proudly associated is the great Chinese painter Xu Beihong (Ju Peon) who was also a founding member of the Sino-Indian Cultural Society. Xu's brief association with Cheena-Bhavana (1939-40) resulted in the entrance of Indian flora and fauna, landscape, and Santiniketan personalities (including Tagore) into his artistic creation. Xu Beihong's immortal paintings, thus, also immortalized Tagore, Santiniketan, and India. But for the needle of Tan Yun-shan such a fraternization would not have taken place.

Ambassador C.V. Ranganathan related to an interesting evening in Beijing when Prime Minister Rajiv Gandhi's special envoy, Mr. P.N. Haksar, and a Chinese scholar, Prof. Wu Xiaolin vied with each other in reciting verses from Kalidasa's *Meghdoot.* (See Tan Chung ed., Across the *Himalayan* Gap, p.443.) How Gurudeva would have smiled if he had come to know this small realization of his "Great Course". Prof. Wu learnt to read Sanskrit in Cheena-Bhavana (in 1941-45). He led a group of Santiniketan-returned scholars to build up Indian studies in China for which he was awarded *Desikottama* by Visva-Bharati (which was, incidentally, presented by Ambassador Ranganathan in the Indian Embassy in Beijing.)

I must particularly mention two more cases which belong to the "products" category. Dr. W. Pachow had had a long association with Prof. Tan Yun-shan and Cheena-Bhavana whether he was in or outside India. Buddha had only five disciples when he first turned the *Dharmacakra* (the wheel of truth). When Tagore started his ashram at Santiniketan, he also had only five students. Tan Yun-shan started Cheena- Bhavana also with this lucky number, while a young intellectual who had just taken off the robe of a Buddhist monk was one of the five. His name was Pachow. Now, he is retired in USA after distinguishing himself as one of the leading Buddhist scholars in modem times. Another young man, Jan Yun-hua, arrived from Hong Kong at Santiniketan in the early 1950s. When Prof. Tan Yun-shan first initiated him into Buddhist studies, he found it a totally unknown field. Now, he is one of the world's greatest authorities in religious studies, particularly Buddhism. People have been proudly talking about the rich collection in the Cheena-Bhavana Library of Chinese classics and other books of the civilization that had invented paper and printing, that had produced more books than the rest of the world before the middle of the 18th century. No one had more efficiently used this Cheena-Bhavana Library than Jan Yun-hua when he was also the custodian of it in the 1950s and 1960s. I saw with my own eyes how even university professors of eminent standing went to Prof. Jan to ask for information, and how the latter just offered it from his finger tips. In Prof. Jan Yun-hua we see the true value of Cheena-Bhavana if people want to encash it. Both Prof. Pachow and Prof. Jan have given me encouragement in organizing the centenary activities of Prof. Tan who had always treated the two as his most favourite disciples.

I have already touched upon both the functions of the Cheena-Bhavana *hen*. It is not only modern India's first institution of Chinese Studies and Sino-Indian Studies, but has had no predecessor in the long history of Sino-Indian cultural intercourse. Partly because of the fame and importance of Tagore and Santiniketan, and partly due to the proactive spirit of Tan Yun-shan in disseminating Chinese studies to other parts of India, Cheena-Bhavana has assumed the role of a lead-point in expanding the study of China and teaching of Chinese language all over India. After independence, particularly during the 1950s and 1960s, whenever there was the starting of an academic project and a course on China or teaching Chinese language anywhere in India, the advice of Tan Yun-shan would be sought. He had associated himself in various manners in helping selecting teaching staff, drawing up curricula etc. In some cases, when the requisite certificates were wanting for academic appointments, a testimonial in Tan's signature could enable the Vice-Chancellor or Director of an institution to exercise his emergency power to make a recruitment. In such cases, the needle that was Prof. Tan was transformed into a stamp.

Tracing the cultural needle of Tan Yun-shan to activities that moved far away from Visva-Bharati Cheena-Bhavana, the China visit by Pandit Jawaharlal Nehru and Dr. S. Radhakrishnan during the war time have often been cited as eminent examples. In this volume, Prof. Lin Chengjie, famous authority on Sino-Indian friendship and comradeship in modern times, has cited a telegram which was sent from Santiniketan by Prof. Tan informing the Chinese leaders in Chongqing about the exact date of Nehru's arrival in China. In the same telegram, Tan wrote that he had already welcomed Nehru to China on their behalf, which is rather interesting, reflecting the important role of an intermediary.

I myself never have had such a privilege in becoming a bridge between political leaders of India and China, but have, nevertheless experienced the performance of an intermediary, and the amount of anxiety involved in such activities. But, to an intermediary, every successful interaction or intercourse between India and China becomes far greater satisfaction than any personal achievement. In this way, I am able to appreciate what father had been doing almost all his life and career. A self-centred person might remember the famous line of the Tang poetry: "Wei taren zuo jia yichang" (stitching wedding dress for other girls). But, Tan Yun-shan took up such a role with wholehearted enthusiasm. History though written by millions of unsung heroes would never recognize them. Tan Yun-shan did not mind to be one of such unsung heroes. As Prof. Huang Xinchuan has observed, perhaps such a mood was inseparable from his embodiment of the Mahayana tradition of the altruist Bodhisattva.

I have already alluded to the want of basic understanding of China among Indian intellectuals when Tan Yun-shan first arrived at Santiniketan in the end of 1920s. Today, of course, things have been vastly improved. Cheena-Bhavana has, indeed, played the role of disseminating information and knowledge, building bridges between the two great civilizations. In playing his role as a needle, Tan Yun-shan had had the disadvantage (which was also an advantage) of not being educated from a western university. Disadvantage it was because a section of Indian intellectuals would always like things presented in an impressive western package, whether or not the content was good or genuine. Neither did they show much appreciation for Tan Yun-shan's scholarship, nor was Tan mindful of that. He, in fact, took great pride in presenting things with his Sino- Indian perspective which was immensely appreciated by Gurudeva and the old generation Ashramites of Santiniketan. Of course, owing to heavy administrative duty, Tan did neglect in writing what he had conceived as the cultural affinity between India and China. Much of this insight he had carried away to his Heavenly abode without benefitting the posterity. Even what he had penned and published might not have been agreed universally because of his strong accent on the positive side — the brotherly feelings between the Indian and Chinese peoples.

Today, we see the Indian intellectual world sharply divided on the perception of China which reminds us the ancient debate between Mencius and his contemporary, Xunzi (also spelled as Hsun-tsu). While Xunzi thought human nature was evil (something like the Christian belief of man being born in sin), Mencius strongly refuted it and forcefully expounded Confucius' basic idea that "Men are by nature inclined towards each other, but social practices created a distance between them". (Xing xiangjin ye, xi xiang yuan ye.) It is also like the Rama and Ravana dichotomy in the Indian religious preachings. (In north India Ravana is a devil, but in south India and Sri Lanka he is a hero.) At the root of such controversy we see Sino-Indian understanding much influenced by the views, perspectives, information, disinformation, distortion etc. that have infiltrated through the westem-culture-dominated mass media. But, all those who have cared to study China based on truth and true information are@by and large agreeable with the Tan Yun-shan school that the two great civilizations are not poles apart, but are closest cultural cousins.

We are fortunate to have a few contributions from eminent Chinese scholars who are in the forefront of Indian studies in present China. They all testify to the influence from Tan Yun-shan's writings in their formative years, and the inspiration from him to promote Sino-Indian understanding. Prof. Lin Chengjie and Prof. Huang Xinchuan, with their vast knowledge of Chinese source materials, have revealed things about Tan's impact which 1 have not heard of (perhaps Tan Yun-shan himself had not too). One instance was an exchange of correspondence between Gandhiji and H.H. Kung (Kong Xiangxi or Kung Hsiang-Hsi), Vice-Premier of the National Government of China, both of whom had used Tan Yun-shan as their messenger. In 1939, when Tan returned to India from China (via Chongqing or Chungking), H.H. Kung asked him to carry a letter to the Mahatma wishing to strengthen friendship between the two peoples. In 1940, when Tan again visited Chongqing, he carried with him a reply from Gandhiji which said that Kung's desire for strengthening India-China friendship had evoked a strong response from his heart." (See Lin Chengjie's article in this volume.) 1 have searched the Collected Works of Mahatma Gandhi, but have missed this letter which, as Prof. Lin informs us, was carried by Xinhua Ribao (Xinhua Daily which was the mouth organ of the CPC) on February 13, 1940 and created a strong impact among the people of China.

Although being alluded to in this volume by others too, I should not omit mentioning the most important errand in Tan Yun-shan's life as a messenger of important messages. This was his carrying a letter from Tagore to the head of state of China, Chiang Kai-shek written on April 12, 1938 in support of China's fighting against the Japanese aggression. The letter was delivered personally by Tan when he was given an audience by Chiang at Wuchang on July 9 of the same year. Chiang's reply to Tagore was dated Hangzhou July 14. In this letter, Chiang addressed Tagore as "Gurudeva" which was quite unusual. One can see the needle of Tan Yun-shan working, trying to make friendly contacts between the great personalities of the two countries more affectionate, and striking a greater echo. One cannot but point out that the Nationalist Government of China showed great sensitivity in cultivating friendship with public leaders of India, like Tagore, Gandhi, Nehru, and many others. This paid rich dividend, particularly in winning the sympathy of the Indian public for China's Anti-Japanese War. Here, once again, we see the needle of Tan Yun-shan moving. On February 18, 1933, when Tan informed Tagore about the establishment of the Sino-Indian Cultural Society, he also told Gurudeva that he had had an audience with Chiang Kai-shek who was supportive of the idea. Later events showed that Chiang was generous in sanctioning funds and even donating from his own pocket for the creation and maintenance of Cheena-Bhavana. It is immaterial how much credit should be given to Tan's efforts in enlisting Chiang Kai-shek's government as a strong supporter to Tagore's endeavours in Santiniketan. That the needle of Tan Yun-shan could reach the high circles of the two countries is all what the chroniclers should take cognizance of. It was Tan's and many others' needles which have created a tapestry of Sino-Indian cultural interface and synergy.

5. Anti-Japanese War

Just after Santiniketan had given birth to the new institution of Cheena-Bhavana, Japan donned the mantle of an anti-China imperialist power and launched a full scale war against China. "There is not a single peaceful desk in the entire North China" was the description of the Chinese response to the new situation at that time. Tan Yun-shan's new desk in Cheena-Bhavana was equally disturbed even before he had time to settle down in his work.

I was in Changsha at that time just an 8 year old boy. Father had sent money and mother had got a two-storeyed red brick house built up outside the Northern Gate of the city. Tne house was surrounded by green vegetable fields. After starting the war on China, Japanese planes raided the interior of the vast country hitting civilian targets with the aim of demolishing China's anti-Japanese fighting morale. Our house became an eminent target of this senseless Japanese bombing. I still remember vividly that one day when my mother took four children and a maid hiding in the anti-air-raid shelter, leading the kids to chant the name of Avalokitesvara to pacify the nervousness that had seized all of us, there was such a tremendous explosion nearby what I thought was the announcement of the doomsday. After the alarm was lifted, we rushed outside to see what had happened. Our house which had been locked had its doors broken open. All the windowpanes were smashed. It was as if the God of Death had inspected the house. The Japanese pilot missed the aim of our house by about ten yards, killing a peasant working in the field. Mother was panicky and immediately sent a telegram to Santiniketan. In this way, Tan Yun-shan and the newly established Cheena-Bhavana were cast under the shadow of the Japanese aggression against China.

Though India was not directly involved in the Sino-Japanese War, then, and the colonial masters — the British — were dubious in their attitude, the people of India, led by Tagore and others, were loud in voicing condemnation against the Japanese aggressor. Tan Yun-shan had contributed to this sympathy wave in India and also benefited from it. He sent reports and articles to China, conveying to the Chinese government and people about India's support which was no small encouragement as I have already alluded to. Meanwhile, Tan was instrumental to the obtaining of information and reports about the heroic struggle on the part of the Chinese soldiers and civilians in resisting the formidable Japanese invasion. Furthermore, Tan himself joined a public campaign in India with speech and writing in support of the Chinese war effort and denouncing the Japanese aggression.

On October 13, 1940, Tan Yun-shan published an article in the *Hindusthan Standard,* Calcutta entitled "China and the European War". In this article, he wrote "in spite of all diversities, this small world of ours forms an integral whole". Then, "China needed and still needs much help, and she has got and is getting it from countries all over the world, excepting one — her own enemy. But China did not and does not depend on any country besides herself." He continued, "The arrogant and rabid Japanese militarists thought that they could conquer China in three months. The outside world also was of the same wrong opinion." After reminding the readers that China had already successfully resisted the Japanese aggressors for more than three years, Tan reiterated, "Under whatever circumstances and in whatever difficulties, China will not cease to fight, until she will achieve her ultimate victory. She will never stop to resist unless the Japanese themselves withdraw or are wiped out from China."

On June 13, 1943, Tan Yun-shan delivered the Presidential Address in the United Nations' Day Public Meeting organized by the Provincial National War Front of Bengal in which he made four points. First, the Anti-Japanese War was a world war, "very really our war, and we all must fight in it to the best of our ability". Second, the war was fought "between democracy and tyranny, between justice and injustice, between decency and indecency and between humanity and brutality". Third, "We must have complete faith and full confidence in the United Nations' victory." Fourth, "we must not only win the war but also win the peace", "we must not only win the war for the present time but win the war for ever".

In another speech delivered on July 7th, 1943 at the meeting held at Santiniketan celebrating "China Day" and commemorating the 6th anniversary of China's Anti- Japanese War, Tan Yun-shan pointed out that the Japanese militarists were the most guilty among the three criminal states of the Axis. He listed 1 1 events of the crimes committed by the Axis in 11 years between 1931 and 1941 out of which 6 were committed by Japan. Responding to Real Admiral Yarnell's statement in the USA that "there is a possibility that the Chinese Nationalist Government may collapse unless effective aid is forthcoming soon", Tan wrote, "we want aid to come through our merit in the war, not through any kind of pity on the part of our allies. We want our allies to help us to defeat our common enemy but not for any charitable purpose. We can claim every aid and help from our Allies because we are also helping and aiding our Allies in the war."

These examples show that the Professor of Chinese Studies had transformed himself into a diplomat, even a spokesman of the Chinese Government which was very unusual of Tan Yun-shan's character. China was at the juncture of a life-and-death struggle, and almost all Chinese intellectuals got agitated and threw themselves into the national crisis. Tan Yun-shan did not lag behind such a national mood.

A significant thing Tan Yun-shan did was his issuing "An Appeal to Conscience" on September 24, 1942 which was carried by all the Indian newspapers, and was published as a special article in the *Modern Review*, Calcutta, and the *Blitz*, Bombay. The full text of the "Appeal" is included in this volume for the reference of our readers. It is a daring statement first appealing to the "Indian brethren" to join the international fight against the Axis, particularly Japan. He appealed: "My dear and respected Indian brethren, cease your present mass movement against the British Government, join the United Nations, and fight the aggressive Axis, especially the Japanese invaders!" Then, he appealed to the British Authorities to immediately declare India as an independent nation, and, then, handing over power to the Indian leaders. "if" Tan stated, "you declare India independent and free just now, you will not only gain the heart of the 400 million Indian people, but also obtain the praise, enthusiasm, appreciation and admiration of the United Nations." In the end, he appealed: "I most earnestly and humbly appeal and pray to you, far-sighted British statesmen, for everybody's sake and for many reasons, to declare India independent and free, and to form an Indian National Government, enabling the Indian people to join the war totally and wholeheartedly to finish the Axis as soon as possible."

I wonder what Gurudeva would say, if he had read Tan Yun-shan's appeal. But, Gurudeva had already condemned the Japanese aggression on China most strongly, expressed sympathy for the Chinese government and people, and demonstrated his confidence about China's final victory. This he did in various letters and statements, particularly his correspondence with the Japanese poet Noguchi (see "Poet to Poet" in this volume). The Japanese had tried their best to win support from Tagore (at least securing his neutrality in the Sino-Japanese War), knowing that Tagore not only had a great influence over Indian intellectuals and the common people, but also had enjoyed tremendous prestige among the international community. Japanese agents tried to present Tagore with valuable antics in order to "bribe" Gurudeva. However, Gurudeva was very firm in his attitude. Tan Yun-shan's vantage point vis-a-vis the Japanese in influencing Tagore, and Cheena-Bhavana's being a part of Visva-Bharati were not insignificant factors in defeating the Japanese efforts in winning Tagore over.

There is yet another episode worth mentioning. Chiang Kai-shek, being the Commander-in-Chief of the Chinese Theatre of the Allied Forces in World War II, wanted to secure the Indian rear to backup the war efforts. But, the deteriorating political situation in India worried him extremely. Thus, he and Madam Chiang Kai-shek visited India in 1942 to persuade the leaders of the Indian independence movement to see that the Indian situation would not become out of control. Initially, the Chiangs had planned to go to Sevegram to meet Mahatma Gandhi, but the programme was cancelled (causing Gandhiji's displeasure). Chiang Kai-shek had no special interest in visiting educational institutions, while Tagore had already passed away. Yet, he made it a point to visit Santiniketan, and spent a couple of hours in Cheena-Bhavana. This might be interpreted as the Chinese government's recognition of the importance of Cheena-Bhavana and Prof. Tan Yun-shan, but there was a secret agenda, i.e. to meet Jawaharlal Nehru. It was all arranged, and Nehru was there at the gate of Cheena-Bhavana to welcome the Chinese head of state and the first lady whom he had already met in Chongqing. Nehru and the Chiangs carried on talks from Santiniketan to Calcutta inside the special train for the Chinese head of state, accompanied by Tan Yun-shan who acted both as a liaison and also an interpreter, sometimes. The visit was fruitful because of Gandhi's special letter to Chiang later in June that year pledging that (a) "I would personally agree that the Allied Powers might, under treaty with us, keep their armed forces in India and use the country as a base for operations against the threatened Japanese attack", and (b)"whatever action I may recommend [for the Quit India Movement] will be governed by the consideration that it should not injure China, or encourage Japanese aggression in India or China". (See *Collected Works of Mahatma Gandhi*, Vol. 76, pp. 223-26.)

Such a pledge not only stands in the history of India-China relations as an exemplary instance of friendship and self-sacrifice, but is also very rare among friendly nations of the world. Nehru had played a vital role in the whole episode, and Tan Yun- shan's contribution also cannot be denied. Perhaps, this was one of the main considerations for the National Government of China to award the "Victory Medal" to him after the victory of the War in 1945.

Tan Yun-shan's role as a weaving needle of friendly bonds between India and China continued. Dr. Basu, who was one of the five doctors sent by the Indian Congress and Nehru to the Chinese anti-Japanese war front (along with Dr. Atal, Dr. Cholkar, Dr. Kotnis, and Dr. Mukherji) once said in a public talk in Delhi that when they reached Wuhan in central China they were looked after and helped by Tan Yun-shan who was also there. Tan told his children that the first thing he did for the Indian doctors was to give each of them a Chinese name. Name-giving is an art, particularly christening foreigners in Chinese. Tan used the transliteration method but also inserted the letter "hua" (meaning "China") in all the names. While other doctors left China one after another, Dr. Kotnis alone breathed his last in China's war front. Chinese leaders, from Mao Zedong onwards sent affectionate condolence messages, and there is now a Kotnis Memorial at Shijiazhuang in Hebei Province. Kotnis has become a household name in China. But, the Chinese know him not as "Kotnis", but "Ketihua" — the Chinese name created by Tan Yun-shan.

6. Reunion with Past

Tan Yun-shan's life and career in India had witnessed earth-shaking changes in both the countries. First, India obtained her independence, and many of his old acquaintances became the leading figures of the Government of India. Jawaharlal Nehru whose friendship with Tan could he traced back to early 1930s was free India's first Prime Minister and Foreign Minister. Moreover, Nehru took away from Santiniketan, Mr. Anil Kumar Chanda, Gurudeva's secretary, and the closest friend of Tan at Santiniketan, and made him Deputy Minister of Foreign Affairs. Another interesting and significant happening was that all the first three Presidents of Republic of India, Dr. Rajendra Prasad, Dr. S. Radhkrishnan, and Dr.Zakir Husain had all joined the Sino-Indian Cultural Society as ordinary members before the Independence.

Things were developing from the Indian side in a manner that Tan Yun-shan was destined to play a greater role now that so many of his old friends had moved into the Indian government edifice. The Nationalist Government of China had realized this development. In 1947, when it appointed its first Chinese Ambassador to independent India (in the person of Luo Jialun or spelled as Lo Chia-lun), it also designated Tan Yun- shan as "Wenhua daibiao" i.e. the 'Cultural Representative" of China. Tan told his family that some Nationalist leaders felt a little apologetic that he was not chosen as China's Ambassador to India. Here also there was some delicate relationship between Tan Yun- shan and the Chinese Government which father had confided to me. The Presidentship of the Chinese chapter of Sino-Indian Cultural Society, after the passing away of Cai Yuanpei, passed on to Zhu Jiahua (or Chu Chia-hua) who was the Chief Secretary of the Kuomintang (KMT). I remember when I was taken to the receptions for father in Hunan during his brief visits, many among the hosts were Kuomintang Party workers, perhaps because of the influence of Zhu Jiahua. As Tan worked so closely with the KMT leaders, there invariably emerged the desire to absorb him into the Party which Tan had repeatedly declined with polite firmness. Tan, in his early years had followed Mao Zedong and other progressive youths who had all distinguished in the CPC either as martyrs or as surviving heroes and leaders. That probably inhibited him a bit from joining the KMT. But, he was basically a man not cut out for politics, and he would like to keep himself aloof from the political struggles in China. When friends in Chongqing asked him whether he was unhappy to have missed the ambassadorship, he laughed and replied that never had he expected or aspired for that appointment.

Indian leaders welcomed Tan's new designation with warm feelings. Rajaji (C. Rajagopalachari), the first Indian Governor General of independent India, said in his message of July 7, 1948 that "It gives me great pleasure to note the renewal of your office of culture in India as representative of China." Nehru wrote on August 26, 1948: "I am glad to learn that the Education Ministry of China have appointed you to act as China's Cultural Representative in India. I hope that with your assistance and advice we shall develop further cultural contacts with China."

But, there was no change in the function of Tan Yun-shan after donning the new hat. He continued to be a teacher, and an academician, the Director of Cheena-Bhavana in Visva-Bharati. He had always been (even when he was not officially designated) and continued to be more than a head of a department of an Indian university, and his activities continued to exceed the boundaries of the university and the country (which had started from day one when he had just been a man without government designations). Again, he continued to be a bridge between the two cultures, and a needle trying to weave cultural bonds between India and China. As usual, the funds for running Cheena-Bhavana continued to come from the Chinese government and public till the overthrow of it on the mainland. Of course. now that he was a government "representative" fund raising would become easier than before.

Then, came the earth-shaking changes in China — the fall of the KMT regime, and the establishment of the People's Republic of China. A close friend and powerful patron of Tan Yun-shan, i.e. Tai Chi-tao (thinktank of Chiang Kai-shek), did not follow the KMT withdrawal to Taiwan. Instead, he committed suicide at Guangzhou, the last KMT bastion on the mainland, in 1949. This gave Tan Yun-shan the greatest shock in life.

The revolutionary change of China could be clearly visualised in India, while Nehru had already seen the writings on the wall even a couple of years before. Giving the special nature of Cheena-Bhavana and its close financial dependence on the KMT government, Tan Yun-shan's position became somewhat precarious, and he was prepared to withdraw himself from the scene. Nehru stabilized his unstable mind and asked him to continue to function as a bridge between the two cultures. However, whether he and Cheena-Bhavana could continue to play its erstwhile intermediary role in between the two governments would have to depend on the negotiations between India and the new Chinese regime in Beijing. Such a negotiation, unfortunately, never took place. But, Tan Yun-shan stayed on pursuing his work in promoting cultural relations between China and India irrespective of the changing political scene.

While the mental stabilization had to take a course, it had been very well known that Tan Yun-shan had shared the education of the same school with the top Chinese communist leader, Mao Zedong — at the First Normal School of Hunan. People began to gossip, speculate, and some of it did feed back to Tan Yun-shan. Never an insensitive conservative or an ivory-towerish pedant, Tan was seized by turbulent surging emotions which resembled what he had experienced when he stood at the beach of Singapore almost three decades ago. The year 1950 was a difficult year for Cheena-Bhavana as its financial resources were cut off, and he had to go to Calcutta and Darjeeling to seek donations from the Chinese community to meet the maintenance expenses of the institution.

He composed a few poems in this year from which his unstable mind can be detected. One poem reads (in English translation):

"Confucius codified historical vicissitudes
With a spell of mighty canonical speech.
Buddhadharma dwarfed lords and empires
An eternal course to practise and preach.
With an un-erasable heart I tread sages' steps
For centuries and millennia never laid to rest.
Missions fulfilled, I am happy and my mind runs out,
Why on earth should I worry my whereabouts."

Another poem reflects a totally different mood, its translation reads:

"Lofty is the Heng Mountain shrine
With exuberant scenaries around,
Hunan abounds in rivers and ponds
Heroes innumerable beyond count.
I long for the romantic memories
Where are they now? I wonder.
Beyond the sea at the corner of yonder
Land the old country is beckoning to me".

In the first poem the idea of "whereabouts" (meaning where to go) was definitely haunting him, although he wanted to take refuge in the nobleness of missions that made him emulate the past sages like Confucius and the Buddha. But the second poem took his mind to his native province Hunan which was famous for the holy shrine at the top of the Heng Mountain. He was chasing the romantic memories out of which had emerged the innumerable heroes, some dead, some were now presiding over the state affairs of China.

Another thing Tan Yun-shan did in the same year was to address a letter to Chairman Mao Zedong with the aim of reviving the erstwhile acquaintance. Lest it would be taken as one of the thousands of self-seekers to touch the feet of the new masters, his was an entirely different letter with three serious suggestions:

(1) Stop leaning on one side (referring to Mao's famous essay of 1949 in which Mao had advocated

leaning on the Soviet Union),

(2) Pursuing Sino-Indian friendship,

(3) Peaceful solution of the Nationalist-Communist dispute.

He waited and waited, for many years there was no reply. Later, when Mao received Tan in Beijing in 1956, Mao said two things. First, when he read the letter he could not connect the name of Tan Yun-shan with one of the old boys in his memory, but after some time he remembered. Second, about the three suggestions he decided only to accept the second. Then, he began to lecture Tan about the world equations, and how the new Republic could not afford to be without international support, and how the Soviet Union was truly reliable'. Tan was only too happy to meet the cynosure of his young days and to revive the lost association. He was not in a mood to defend his suggestions, nor to argue with this much greater Hunan Ox famous for his enormous self-confidence and obstinacy. Later, Tan was invited to Beijing for the second time in 1959. In that year schemism had started to develop within the Communist Bloc, and Mao had stopped reiterating his favourite "leaning on one side". Unfortunately, Tan's itinerary had listed no meeting with Mao while he was dying to hear what Mao would have to say about his original suggestion of not leaning on one side.

Perhaps, Tan's letter which had suggested the strengthening of Sino-Indian friendship was treading on the territory of Premier Zhou Enlai who had been given a free hand in handling China's foreign affairs, while, on the other, Zhou was also on the look out for people outside the government who could help in strengthening China's diplomatic efforts in winning international friends. The two directions must have converged. However, the Chinese government was extraordinarily cautious in enlarging the sphere of its "united front", hence the long wait. Finally it was Zhou Enlai who signed the invitation to Tan to visit China. By that time, Tan Yun-shan had already stabilized his unstable mood, and started a new phase of his old role as the Director of Cheena-Bhavana on the payroll of Visva-Bharati which was now funded by the University Grands Commission. As Nehru was the Chancellor of the University, and during his annual visit to Santiniketan to preside over the Convocation he always made it a point to visit Cheena-Bhavana and talk to Tan Yun-shan for some time, the University authorities continued to allow Tan to operate beyond the boundaries of the campus, even to freely correspond with the Chinese government as he had been doing in the good old days.

Tan's two visits enjoying the hospitality of the People's Republic of China (by now the meagre salary of a university professor prohibited him from going to China at will as he had been doing before 1950) in 1956 and 1959 resulted in totally different impressions and moods — the first visit was extremely enjoyable while the second not so much. In his first (1956) visit because Chairman Mao's willingness to renew the past friendship, Tan had virtually met all the top leaders. Also the economy of the country was not as bad as in 1959, and the political stability of the new Republic in a much stronger position than in the later year. Another factor that contributed to the diminishing excitement of the 1959 visit was the mishap in the western sector of the India-China border resulting in the killing of Indian patrolling police, and the ensuing tension between the two governments. However, Tan had strengthened the friendship with Zhou Enlai whom he met for the first time in 1956. Zhou not only had a charming personality, but with enormous capacity in seeking and accepting suggestions from all quarters. He asked Tan for advice to improve relations with India in a long session in his office in 1956. Tan suggested the commemoration of Tagore's birth anniversary, and Zhou's visiting Santiniketan to see Cheena-Bhavana and receiving the Desikottama from Visva-Bharati in addition to minor things such as the famous silk factory at Hangzhou making special weaving portraits of Tagore, Gandhi and Nehru. All the suggestions were accepted and implemented. Zhou Enlai visited Santiniketan in January 1957, merely two months after Tan had returned from China. Visva-Bharati Cheena-Bhavana, thus, has the rare distinction of being visited by two heads of state from China (Chiang Kai-shek in 1942, and Zhou Enlai in 1957) — an honour probably no other university of the world has enjoyed.

During Tan's 1959 visit, the border incident took place, and Zhou Enlai proposed that the security forces of both sides withdrew 20 kilometres from the disputed border. Just after this proposal was sent to the press, Tan was invited to Zhou's office and the two had a long session of talks. Zhou wanted Tan to tell Nehru and his other Indian friends that he wanted the border to be tranquil, and the two countries to maintain friendship while seeking a resolution of the border dispute. Marshal Chen Yi was the Foreign Minister at that time. He also invited Tan to his office and talked about Sino-Indian relations. In his typical unsophisticated manner and with a forceful Sichuan accent, the Marshal suddenly said: "You know I am a soldier. If there is fighting I would like to join. But we don't want to fight with India." After his return to India, Tan tried to convey to his friends in the Indian government his conversations with the Chinese leaders, except, of course, what the Marshal had said about "fighting".

The Sino-Indian border conflict of 1962 had wounded many lives and many hearts of those who had been advocating amity and friendship between the two countries. Those who cherished Sino-Indian friendship more than others also suffered heavier pain. But, Tan worked as usual. Earlier, when Zhou Enlai visited Cheena-Bhavana (in early 1957), his portrait and that of Prime Minister Nehru made by the Hangzhou Silk Factory in fine weaving were hanging on the wall of the Cheena-Bhavana library to welcome the rare Chinese guest. They were still hanging there after the 1962 War. Cheena-Bhavana was such a place during the time of Tan Yun-shan that it was daily visited by scores, sometimes hundreds, of tourists. Reports began to get into Tan Yun-shan's ears about some visitors' objecting to the hanging of Zhou's portrait. Tan ignored them initially. Later, when anti-China atmosphere was on the rise, he thought it wise to remove Zhou's portrait. But, he did not want to do injustice to Zhou, so he asked both Nehru's and Zhou Enlai's portraits to be removed simultaneously.

Nehru, on the other hand, did not want Tan's usual work to be affected by the governmental enmity. The most moving scene took place at Santiniketan when Nehru was there to preside over the convocation hardly a month after the war was over. Naturally, Nehru felt very angry and humiliated by the War, and people expected that he would talk about the War and severely criticize the Chinese government during his speech. But, swing Tan Yun-shan sitting in the crowd, his heart melted. His speech was mild and friendly, as he said the following:

> "...while performing the duty of protecting the country, we should keep in mind the principles which form the basis of Indian culture.
>
> In the Visva-Bharati, for instance, you have got the various departments. You have got the Cheena-Bhavan, under a distinguished Chinese scholar [Tan Yun-shan]. That is a good thing to remind you always that you are not at war with China's culture or the greatness of China in the past or in the present. You have no bitter feelings against the Chinese people as such. You are against a certain deed which the Chinese Government has done which is very wrong ... if you think that China as a country or the hundreds of millions of her people are your enemies, let me tell you they are not...
>
> ....
>
> That is why I am glad that you have got here a symbol of international co- operation, of co-operation between India and China in the Cheena-Bhavan. While we fight the aggressor, we do not fight culture and we do not fight the people who are friendly to us..."
>
> (Jawaharlal Nehru Speeches, 1957-1963, vol. 4, New Delhi: Publications Division, Government of India, 2nd ed., 1983, p. 27, 28.)

The speech moved Tan Yun-shan who could not hold back his tears. And the moving scene was reported by all the Indian newspapers the next day. Perhaps, this episode would be remembered for a long time to come.

Five years after that Tan Yun-shan retired from Cheena-Bhavana. More earth- shaking changes took place in China, while Tan Yun-shan felt very confused. But, as usual he hoped for the return of friendship between the two countries, much as he hoped China to maintain stability and good progress towards prosperity. He spent a lot time in reading newspapers, and whatever was about China he would cut it out. When we cleaned his drawing room after his demise, there was a huge pile of such cutting which we could not dispose of but to burn them. I stood beside the fire for hours thinking that I was burning father's longing for his motherland that he had never visited after 1959.

7. The Modern Xuanzang

Calling Tan the "Modern Xuanzang" is a spontaneous phenomenon in both India and China. My friend, Zhao Lei, told me the excitement expressed by the people he had interviewed in Hunan while talking about Tan Yun-shan. They called Tan the "modern Xuanzang of Hunan". The comparison between Tan Yun-shan and Xuanzang is both valid and inappropriate. Xuanzang declined the offer of a top imperial post made by the all powerful Chinese Emperor Taizong of the Tang Dynasty so that he could remain in the holy order to concentrate powerful Chinese Emperor Taizong of the Tang Dynasty so that he could remain in the holy order to concentrate on translation of Buddhist scriptures and dissemination of the Buddhadharma. In this way, Tan Yun-shan belonged to an entirely different world than that of Xuanzang. However, the two had some commonality in their dedication to the promotion of Sino-Indian amity and understanding, in taking both the countries as their homeland, in their concentration and confidence in the noble cause of working towards a better future for humanity. Another similarity between the two was their acquaintance and personal friendship with the leaders of both the countries. On the whole, what Tan Yun-shan had done in his entire life and career was to revive the "great pilgrimage" described by Gurudeva, in which Xuanzang was the most brilliant symbol. Tan's journey on earth was the continuation of the same journey of Xuanzang. Tan was treading on the footsteps of Xuanzang.

Tan Yun-shan was a man of very regular and simple living habits. His Public activities, particularly moving with great personalities of both countries, had invariably involved him in many drinking and feasting sessions. But, he did not drink (only wet his lips symbolically when the occasion demanded). Whatever delicacies on earth were a total waste on him. He never discussed cuisine just as he never bought a novel. Everyday, he got up before daybreak, and climbed on the roof of Cheena-Bhavana to start his daily "lesson" (gongke as he called it). This was a course of physical-cum-mental exercise combining Indian and Chinese philosophies. During the exercise, he merged himself with the universe. Alas, much as he was eager to pass this exercise down the family line he did not succeed. I, being his eldest son, having maximum contacts with him than all other brothers and sisters after I came to India, was the culprit. I was young and believed nothing in body and mind cultivation. More than once did he express his regret that I had declined the cultural gift passed down by the two great civilizations.

Santiniketan knows nothing about the word of "pollution". When he stood on the roof of Cheena-Bhavana, it was that hour of the day when the sky revealed the most genteel, kind, harmonious, and affectionate face of Mother Earth. The air was at its purest best, and there was no hustle and bustle on the ground. He stood there to greet the rising sun with gentle movements of torso and limbs according to a course which he had invented himself. The exercise was, in fact, to integrate his somatic existence with the rhythm of Nature. It was a kind of Kungfu (martial art) cultivating not the physical power, but the mental steadiness, stability and strength. It took the best part of an hour for him to finish. When he walked down from the roof top, his face was radiant, and his movement resembling that of a walking Bodhisattva. But, his "lesson" was finished only by half. You would see him entering his study, and, then, hear a bell ringing gently. He had, by that time, lit a bunch of incense, and begun to pay homage to his "gods" who included the Buddha, Confucius, Ramakrishna, and Sri Aurobindo. He would gently chant a Buddhist sutra (in Chinese) or say his prayers silently. He prayed for the safety of all family members, friends and colleagues, for smooth conduct of work in Cheena- Bhavana, for success of children's examinations and careers, but never for himself. Money never entered his mind during his communion with his "gods".

By nature he was wedded to ahimsa and santi. "Auntie Zhang", a lady who was with him in Singapore (who later treated me like her own son while I was in Changsha), told me that in the early years of Singapore, everyone was harassed by bedbugs. Tan Yun-shan would diligently get up at midnight, hunt for the bugs, catch them, but not hurt them. He threw them out of the window. Auntie Zhang used to tell him: "In this way, you only send them to bite others!" But, he would not change his temperament of non-killing — not even a bug. This obsession of his with ahimsa sometimes created problems for family members, particularly mother. In Chinese cuisine, chicken soup was believed to be the safest and not-too-expensive tonic for health, and mother made it a point to serve this to father regularly. But, killing the chicken was an idea repulsive to father. So, mother had to ask the maid to do it in the faraway corner of the garden.

If there is one element in which the Indian and Chinese civilizations hold contradictory positions, it is "simple living and high thinking" in India, and almost the exact opposite among many Chinese people. Tan Yun-shan, as alluded to earlier, was at once struck by the examples of "simple living and high thinking" among the learned pandits, the moment he arrived at Santiniketan. Later, he became an ardent admirer of Gandhiji — another ramification of "simple living and high thinking". Tan who had promised to be a vegetarian in the face of Gandhiji, tried to emulate the Mahatma by maintaining frugality in life. in addition to observing a day of silence on every Wednesday (the Sunday of Santiniketan). This sometimes caused inconvenience to the family, particularly when visitors from Calcutta made it a point to call on the Tans on Wednesdays. So often, like what Gandhiji did, he would carry on conversation with a pen. But, there were also occasions that he had to break his silence if the visitor turned to be important, or a VIP, or had come from afar. Short of the Gandhian spirit of "walking alone", Tan Yun-shan tried his best to walk on the borderline between the spiritual and the quotidian worlds.

Included in this volume is Prof. Yang Yun-yuan's (Y.Y. Yang) article remembering Tan Yun-shan, the elder fellow-Hunanese who had married his first cousin. Prof. Yang dug out from the old files many Chinese poems presented by Tan Yun-shan to him. One of them reads (in translation):

"Exciting meetings atop holy mountains,
Long ago event now I reckon.
How many times have I stood on high
All surrounding scenes before the prying eyes?
Let our Saha-lokadhatu metamorphosize
Into the Pure-Land Paradise,
Where the West Wind succumbs
The East Wind is blowing strong."

In this poem, Tan remembered his going to the Heng Mountain to pay homage to the Buddhist shrines in the company of Yang Yun-yuan in early 1930s. Then, his thought travelled to the present and future. While he revealed that his world-view was basically that of a Buddhist, he also paraphrased Mao Zedong's famous words: "the East Wind prevails over the West Wind" (Mao launched this "East wind" wave in China after the successful Soviet launching of the sputnik in the latter half of 1950s). Here, the eclectic mind of Tan Yun-shan comes to light, trying to synthesize the spiritual with the mundane. Just like Gurudeva, Tan also believed strongly in cultural synthesis and synergy. By quoting Mao, he had no intention to involve himself in the Cold War stuggle between the Communist Bloc and the Western Capitalist Bloc. He was simply using a modern metaphor to advocate the revival of the Eastern spiritual values.

There was yet another poem of Tan Yun-shan cited by Prof. Yang which, too, can help us understand the inner ambitions of the former. The translation of the poem reads (as quoted from Yang's article in this volume):

"Riding on the white horse I head
Towards the path trodden by old sages,
Something I hold close to my chest:
My great ambition yet to manifest.
Gone are the Tripitakas into antiquity,
Supplementaries are needed for posterity.
Who is ready to undertake the task
To make moderns better than men of the past?"

In this poem Tan Yun-shan revealed himself the ambition to surpass Xuanzang and other historical pilgrims and translation masters. The "great historical pilgrimage" described by Gurudeva has bequeathed to us the Tripitaka literature which is a vast literary treasure embracing all historical writings of past Buddhist masters, most of which are Sanskrit- Chinese translations. Tan Yun-shan's ambition was to compile the modern Tripitakas, i.e. to reconstruct a Buddhistic culture that could be relevant to the modern social conditions. If any individual or a group of individuals could achieve this, as Tan thought, they would certainly surpass the achievements of the past pilgrims. Of course, he himself would not have been excluded from the task. However, the poem also shows that such an ambition still remained only in the conceptual stage.

With such a mind, and his never-say-die spirit, Tan Yun-shan embarked, after retirement from Cheena-Bhavana (in 1967), upon another ambitious plan of building up a "World Buddhist Academy" at Bodhgaya. Starting from early 1970s, he got busy by going to Hong Kong and Singapore to collect donations, and to, begin construction at the site of the Chinese Temple just a few hundred yards from the Mahabodhi Temple of Bodhgaya. After the building was almost complete, the money was exhausted, and Tan was too old to get further work going. Virtually, the project was stopped, but he still insisted on staying in the temple. Every summer vacation when my sister, Tan Wen, my wife and I went to Bodhgaya to take him to Santinketan, he had already been reduced to a skeleton. After reaching Santiniketan he was sleeping day and night as if making up all the lost hours of rest during the previous months. Then, with rest and nutritious food his usual healthy and active self returned. But, not many days later the three of us had to go back to Delhi to teach, while he was frimly determined to return to the Bodhgaya temple. Next year, the same thing repeated. In the third year I decided to stop this vicious circle. There was a Seminar in the Department of Buddhist Studies coming up in the Autumn, and he agreed to be taken to Delhi to attend the Seminar. It all went on very well for a few months. But, after the Seminar was over nothing could make him stay away from Bodhgaya. He had no health problems, and with good rest and good food would have enjoyed many more years of life. The life of the temple was too hard for an octogenarian (He had corssed to the wrong side of 80 by the end of 1978). It was sheer want of food and care that had hastened the arrival of the end. I felt terribly sorry about it for not giving every care to him judging from the standard of filial piety in the Chinese tradition. However, as Prime Minister Mrs. Indira Gandhi rightly said: "It is a befitting close to his life of devotion that he should die at Bodhgaya." It was the attraction of the Buddha that had defeated all the affection and attentions of his children. But, he did not suffer before his heart beat stopped. When we rushed to his death bed with great lamentation and inner disturbance, he was sleeping there so tranquil and unperturbed as if still doing his daily exercise. He was really in the state of Nirvana.

The life of Tan Yun-shan tells us that the life-span of an ambitious person falls too short to realize what one wants to do in life. Yet, if without ambition life is not even worth living. Those who equate life only with enjoying comfort and luxuries is no different from the white tiger in the zoo. That majestic show piece is but a pitiable beast who knows nothing about the meaning of living. Achievement can be great or small, but one must leave some mark behind when one bids farewell to mankind so that people will continue to remember you. Today, we commemorate the birth centenary of Tan Yun-shan only because he had left behind some mark, and there is something to write about him, to appreciate what he had done.

Tan Yun-shan could not be compared with Gurudeva Rabindranath Tagore. But, it was Tagore that had attracted him to India, to commit three generations of his family to embrace India. When my younger brothers and sisters. Tan Lee, Tan Wen, Tan Chameli (now Chameli Ramachandran), Tan Aujit, and Tan Arjun meet or speak over the phone, they always speak in Bengali because that was how they had started talking to each other since birth. My parents had tried to arrange Tan Lee and Chameli to marry a certain girl and boy from the Chinese families of Calcutta, but failed. Tan Lee, Tan Wen, and Chameli all married Indians — their own choice. India and China are married to each other within the family of Tan Yun-shan. They are also married in the mind and heart of Tan himself, his wife, and everyone of his children. The great union of India and China that was the dream of Gurudeva is realized in a capsule form in the Tan family. This can be regarded as the best dedication of Tan Yun-shan to Gurudeva.

However, when we look again at the aims of the Sino-Indian Cultural Society, we feel that very little has been achieved, and a lot much remains to be done. This is not meant to be any criticism of Tan Yun-shan or Gurudeva, or his followers at Santiniketan. In the long course of the river in which time flows, Gurudeva, Visva-Bharati. Cheena- Bhavana, Tan Yun-shan, and all those who had gathered around them were just the first swell of waves. They just made a beginning to work for the "Pursuance of Sino-Indian Studies", the "Linking up of the cultures of China and India", the "Forging of Sino-Indian fraternity", the "Unity between the nations of China and India", the "Creation of peace in humanity", and the "Preparation for a utopia of *Datong* (Ramarajya) in the world". Not much has been achieved in our continuous endeavour after the pioneers have passed away. Let us hope that the examples of Gurudeva, Tan Yun-shan, and many other examples before us can stimulate generation after generation of Indian and Chinese intellectuals to work ceaslessly towards the realization of the idealism which the name of Gurudeva, the name of Tan Yun-shan have symbolized. Let us hope, more Gurudevas, more Tan Yun-shans, more Cheena-Bhavanas and the Chinese counterparts of Cheena- Bhavana would emerge in the coming century and millennium. Let us hope that when people are called upon once again hopefully in the not-too-distant future to commemorate Gurudeva, Tan Yun-shan and others, there will be something to console the departed souls: "May you rest in peace. For, your dreams have now become a part of our living."

3

PROFESSOR TAN YUN-SHAN

The Man and His Mission

I

Among the few notable names associated with the movement of reviving Sino-Indian cultural relations in India during this century that of Professor Tan Yun-shan, founder Principal of Visva-Bharati Cheena-Bhavana, in Santiniketan occupies an honoured place unparalleled in the history of resurgent Asia. Thirty long years of ceaseless service in the cause of strengthening Sino-Indian relations, the major portion of it spent in the sweet company of India's beloved Poet Rabindranath Tagore, is the proud record of this Chinese savant who personifies all that is highest and noble in Sino-Indian culture. As the pioneer of the movement of Sino-Indian cultural Ambassador of modern China to the Indian people who has opened a new chapter of progress and reform in all affairs that affected the welfare of India and China. To the task of restoring the broken cultural ties, of bringing together all that is best and noblest in Indian and Chinese races and of blending each other's culture and force of his brilliant intellect and personality ever since he landed in India in 1928.

A native of Hunan Province, Tan Yun-shan came to Santiniketan at the instance of Gurudeva Rabindranath Tagore with the mission of creating better understanding between India and China. And in collaboration with the Poet he organised the Chinese Department, Cheena-Bhavana, in the Visva-Bharati University and initiated the Sino-Indian Cultural Society in India and China. In this endeavour he succeeded in enlisting the active support of such leaders like Mahatma Gandhi, Pandit Jawaharlal Nehru and other well-known personalities of India. As a close associate and trusted colleague of Poet Tagore, his work in India brought him into intimate contact with the leaders and people of all nationalities and religions. He was especially fortunate in winning the esteem of Gandhiji with whom he was in constant contact for several years. Gandhiji had promised him on several occasions that he would visit China the moment India attained independence. And while Tan Yun-shan was in his motherland a few months before Gandhiji's martyrdom, he had made all arrangements with the Chinese Government and leaders to invite Gandhiji to China. But shortly after came the tragic news of the Mahatma's passing away. In Gandhiji's moral weapon of `soul force' Tan Yun-shan saw the most powerful implement ever invented by the wisdom of modern man for rooting out all evils and alleviate human sufferings. He is also one of the trusted friends of Jawaharlal Nehru, whose inborn passion for all that is best in Chinese culture and civilization has become almost proverbial in India. It is no wonder that our Prime Minister has become capativated with the magnetic personality of Tan Yun-shan, because he could be rightly chosen as the Mahatma of China.

Tan Yun-shan is of varied temperments; silence being his golden rule in every day life mingled with occasional flashes of polished talks on culture and wisdom. He is spiritually a Buddhist, intellectually a Confucian, a Humanitarian in social out look and Gandhian in daily life. A college mate and personal friend of Mao Tse-Tung, the supreme leader of New China, he is held in high esteem by all parties and people of China. A firm believer in the "one word" ideal of Confucius, China's ancient sage, it is his conviction that this life preserving ideal could be realized only through the adaptation and practise of Gandhiji in the socio-economic and political affairs of mankind. It is his wish that every one should learn and understand more about the fundamentals of the Confusian precept, "All within the four seas are brethren" which according to him is intrinsically based on the doctrine of Ahimsa expounded by the Buddha, Mahavira and Christ in the ancient times and propagated by Gandhiji in modern times with such far reaching and glorious achievement for the peace and progress of India and the world.

Professor Tan Yun-shan can rightly claim as the foremost Chinese savant of all the past ages who has lived in India for over thirty years in pursuit of Indian culture and wisdom, not only for his own enlightenment but also for the benefit of the entire mankind. By his long stay in India, he has eclipsed the record of Huien-Tsang, the celebrated Chinese Buddhist monk of the 6th Century A. D. who lived in India for about fourteen years studying Buddhism at the Nalanda University in Bihar and visiting educational centres and holy spots hallowed with the memory of the Buddha.

May the mission of Professor Tan Yun-Shan, the Sage of Santiniketan meet with everlasting success in sustaining human brotherhood and world peace is my ardent prayer to the Omnipotent Power that moulds the destinies of mankind.

II

In the galaxy of eminent Chinese savants whom the Han race has produced during its long history of Sino-Indian relations commencing from the first century A. D. onwards, Tan Yun-shan, collaborator with Gurudev Tagore in inaugurating the Sino-Indian Cultural Society of India, and Founder-Principal of Cheena-Bhavana, the Department of Sino-Indian cultural studies in Visva-Bharati, occupies the is (sic.) not only an erudite scholar and Buddhist philosopher widely known in this country, but he is also the twentieth century, is standard-bearer of Fa-Hien, Hsuan-Tsang and I-Tsing, the three celebrated Chinese Buddhist monks, who were the pioneers in the field of Sino-Indian cultural co-operation, and who first blazed the trail into India across the Himalayas to realise this objective followed by the exchange of pilgrims and scholars between the two greatest countries of Asia. Tan Yun-Shan can be rightly called the HsuanTsang of Modern China, for it is he who is responsible for reviving the broken cultural bonds of India and China after an interregnum of nearly one thousand years. Unlike Hsuan-Tsang, who came to India to learn and carry her wealth of learning and philosophy for utilising them to the benefit of his countrymen, Tan Yun-Shan not only drank deep into the fountain of Indian culture but lidi a true Confucian, imbued with the thoughts of benevolence and charity, he made India his second home, and settled down at Santiniketan for teaching Indians the glories of Chinese culture and civilisation. An ardent Buddhist scholar of rare merit, deeply religious, unassuming and silent, he represents all that is best in Chinese civilisation. The Poet's bosom friend, collaborator, disciple and co-worker, Tan Yun-Shan is not a visionary, but a man of action. He is undoubtedly the most fascinating personality today in Visva-Bharati. He is still in the vigour of youth and has many years of active service before him.

It was by accident that Tan Yun-shan came to India. Gurudev Tagore discovered him in Malaya in 1927, just three years after his historic cultural mission to China. Inspired with Gurudev's message of achieving world peace through international co-operation Tan Yun-Shan came to Santiniketan in 1928 and took up cultural studies among such intellectuals and stalwarts as Abanindranath Tagore, Vidushekhara Sastri, Kshitimohan Sen, C. F. Andrews and Nandalal Bose. After a few years, the idea struck Gurudev and Tan Yun-shan to organise a permanent institute in Visva-Bharati which should serve as a nucleus for the interchange of students and professors between India and China. With this object, Tan Yun-shan visited China in 1931, to acquaint his countrymen with the ideals of the Visva-Bharati and appealed to them to support the movement of Sino-Indian cultural co-operation. The response to the call was good; and the Sino-Indian cultural Society was initiated by him in Nanking in 1933. He returned to India the next year and in collaboration with Gurudev Tagore, the Sino-Indian Cultural Society was organised in 1934. The Cheena-Bhavana, with its imposing building and huge library, which is considered to be the biggest in the whole of Asia, outside China, came into existence at Santiniketan in 1937.

The Chinese Library in Cheena-Bhavana owes its existence to professor Tan's herculean efforts. It consists of 100,000 volumes including the Sung Edition (10th Century A. D.) and the reproduction of the Ch'ing or the so-called Dragon Edition (1936) of the Buddhist Tripitaka along with many separate volumes of important Buddist works and a large number of selected Chinese works representing the Chinese classics, history, philosophy and literature. Ten sets of the Shanghai edition of the Chinese Buddhist Tripitaka were presented to the library by the Chinese people of which Professor Tan has presented nine sets to the universities in India.

This edition of the Tripitaka contains 1916 different books consisting of 8,416 Fascicles of which most were translated from Sanskrit and the originals are now lost in India. It took about twelve hundred years to translate them into Chinese. The translators numbered more than two hundred, all of them were great scholars, both Indian and Chinese. The translation work was executed under the patronage of Chinese Emperors who lavished millions of money for this noble cause. These books are bound into 414 combined volumes and packed with Camphor boards into 40 bundles. The present collection of Chinese books in the Cheena-Bhavana deserves to be described as magnificient and unique. Due to the destruction of universities, libraries and publication depots during the war some of these books have kept in twenty double-faced glass cases in the first storey of the main hall in the Cheena-Bhavana.

Tan Yun-Shan, who is mainly responsible for this great achievement within a short span of time, was born in the province of Hunan in a distinguished family of scholars. Before coming to India, he devoted himself to several years of vigilant study on Chinese classical literature and philosophy. If he had settled in China, there is no doubt that he would have proved a valuable asset to the ranks of public men of that country; but China's loss has been the gain of India. Though he is confined to Bengal, he is not parochial. He has presided over several cultural and educational conferences in various parts of India.

Tan Yun-shan is essentially a man of peace. He is not an orator, but he is gifted with the power of expressing his views in a simple and straight forward way which always capture the imagination of this audiences. He is not a prolific writer, but he likes writting the press whenever time permits him to do so. He has contributed a good number of articles to Indian journals and peridicals, some of which have been published in book forms. Of his publications in English and Chinese, noteworthy are his speeches on the political, historical, social and religious evolution of China delivered by him at the Andhera University, which are published by Kitabistan under the title of "Modern China". Among his several Chinese works, the most significant are his "Gandhiji's Hind Swaraj", "Saint-Philosopher Gandhi" and "Poet-Saint Tagore", all of which had a popular reception in China.

He is simple in habits. He never smokes and eats only meagre food. Always an early-riser, he could be seen in his study amidst his voluminous books. Sometimes, a distinguished scholar, or cultural leader from the remotest part of India or from some foreign country, steps in for a discussion on Confucian Classics, Lao-Tse's philosophy, or on the intricacies of Chinese metaphysics. He satisfies his hearers with his sober arguments. Polite in conversation, he makes an unforgettable impression in the minds of those with whome he comes into daily contact .

He is well-versed in Yoga philosophy and practises the Asanas daily in the early dawn. He observes Wednesday as his day of silence.

The life work of this "Chinese Mahatma" , as some of his numerous disciples and admirers lovingly address him, is centred round Sino-Indian cultural co-operation. In the realisation of this great ideal, he foresees a Greater India and Greater China, rejuvenated and united in common bonds of fellowship and love, the forces of which, he believes, will undoubtly contribute to a larger extent towards the making of a new world of peace and security.

In the course of a message, Mahatmaji once described the Chinese hall in Visva-Bharati as the symbolises Mahatmaji's ideal of that 'living contact' in the human form which is so rare a phenomenon to witness either in China, India or in any part of Asia.

A great legacy has been left to the world by Gurudev Tagore in flesh and bones in Tan Yun-shan, the Chinese Sage of Santiniketan.

III

A trusted friend, collaborator, disciple and co-worker of Poet Rabindranath Tagore is Prof. Tan Yun-shan, the Chinese Savant of Santiniketan, popularly known as the Hsuan-tsang of modern India, Tan Yun-shan's life mission is to futher the cause of Sino-Indian cultural understanding, Ahimsa and world peace.

Tan Yun-shan came to Santiniketan in 1928 and took up Indological studies under the guidance of Gurudev Tagore. His colleagues and co-workers were C. F. Andrews, Rabindranath Tagore, Tucci, Kshitimohan Sen, Indira Rani and Nandalal Bose. Inspired by the Gurudev, Tan Yun-shan founded the Sino-Indian Cultural Society of India and the Cheena-Bhavana, the department of Sino-Indian Cultural Studies in the Visva-Bharati University. As the Principal of the Cheena-Bhavana he has trained many Indian and Chinese scholars who are now holding high positions in the educational and cultural life of India and China.

"What is the most unforgettable episode in your life"? I asked the Professor. After some thoughts, he said smiling "It was my first meeting with Mahatma Gandhi. I went to Bardoli in April1931 to see the Mahatma . "Deliverance of China and the world is through Ahimsa — pure and unadulterated" was Gandhiji's message to me. "I was also Gandhiji's Ambassador of peace and goodwill to Tibet. During my visit to Lhasa in 1930, the 13th Dalai Lama gave me a message to Gandhiji. The Mahatma later replied to it in Gujarati" said the professor.

Tan Yun-shan is essentially a man of peace. "Culture sees no colour, race or political denomination. It is universal" — emphasised the Professor. The present century's standard bearer of Fa-hien, and Hsuang-tsang, the Chinese Buddhist monks who came to India centuries ago in pursuit of learning and inaugurated the era of Sino-Indian cultural understanding, Tan Yun-Shan is responsible for reviving the broken Sino-Indian cultural bonds after an interregnum of more than one thousand years.

A calligraphist, poet, essayist, author and writer, Tan Yun-Shan is also a linguist. He is a devoted Mahayana Buddhist and a Confucin scholar of distinction. He is well versed in the Jaina and Yoga philosophies. He practises the Asanas daily and observes Wednesday as his day of silence. To his large circle of students, friends and admirers, he is known as the Chinese Mahatma of India.

Tan Yun-Shan has visited China serveral times on his mission of peace. About last year, he was specially invited by Premier Chou En-Lai to visit New China, In recognition of his services to the cause of Sino-Indian cultural understanding, the People's Republic of China nominated him as a Member of the People's Political Conference. It is the highest honour to be conferred on an overseas Chinese national who has distinguished himself in developing international understanding and world peace.

Professor Tan Yun-Shan symbolises the Confucian concept of the universal Man. He is a citizen of the world and not of a particular country. He has crossed the barriers of religion and nationality. He is a humanitarian, an internationalist, a Man of Peace and an ardent devotee in the Temple of Universal Spirit.

The following message to the people of India given to me in response to my request on the completion of his thirty years in this country contains the Gospel of Tan Yun-Shan, the Universal Man:

"Among all the races of the present world, the Chinese and Indian amount to about nine hundred millons, and their cultures have also spread over half of mankind; so it is the duty of these two races to create a universal civilization for the present world.

The total amount of the people of India, one fifth of the world population and those of china, one fourth, is nearly equal to a half of all mankind in the world. Such a big number of honest souls, the well combined and struggling for the common fecility of human life, must have a herculian force and be able to produce a marvellous effect. The time has now arrived for the Indian to join hands with the Chinese for producing that long expected marvellous effect which will save civilization from total annihilation".

May All Living Beings Be Happy.

Diwali Day, **V.G. NAIR**

November, 10, 1958

(Reprint from V.G. Nair: *Professor Tan Yun-shan and Cultural Relations between India and China, Madras, 1958.)*

4

TAN YUN-SHAN AND THE RENEWAL OF SINO-INDIAN CULTURAL INTERACTION

The early cultural contact between India and China could be traced back to about 2,000 years ago. The Buddhist missionaries from India and the pilgrims from China braved the hazardous journey of the Gobi deserts and the snowy peaks of the Himalayas. They did not seek fame, riches or conquest but endeavoured to promote the Buddhist message of peace and compassion, and to collect sacred scriptures for translation. As a sequel it is recorded in the Taisho edition of the Chinese Tripitaka (1929) that there are 3283 titles of sutras, sastras, vinayas, commentaries, compositions and other items bound in 85 volumes. The size of this collection is ten times thicker than that of the Encyclopedia Britannica. Undoubtedly this is a monumental achievement of cultural cooperation between the two countries. Among the Chinese participants the names of Fa-hsien (399-416 A.D.), Hsuan-tsang (630-642 A.D.), and Yi-tsing (671-695 A.D.) are well-known, and their counterpart from India such as Parmartha (546-567 A.D.), Kumarajiva (401-413 A.D.) and Amoghavajra (723-756 A.D.) were outstanding. The contents of these translations cover not only Buddhist philosophy and literature, but also Indian philosophy, religion, literature and art including the concepts of karma and rebirth. Thus, Indian influence penetrated deeply into the daily life of the Chinese people, and in due time there emerged many new sects known as the T'ien-T'ai, Ch'an (Zen), Hua-yen and Pure Land in Buddhism, and the school of Mind along with the school of Li (reason) in new Confucianism. They came into existence from the 6th to the 11th century. Initially China was the beneficiary. However, owing to this development Indian Buddhism has been enriched and transformed to a great height. For instance, the essence of Ch'an (Zen) is fundamentally different from that of Indian dhyana, and the Platform Sutra of Hui-neng, a Ch'an classic has received the same veneration as that of the Saddhammapundarika Sutra or the Bhagavad Gita. These are the successful stories of international cultural cooperation, and we are proud to declare that it is a glorious chapter in human history. Unfortunately the law of mutation (anicca) remains constantly in motion, and nothing in the world is free from its subjugation including the fortune of nations. Over the centuries both India and China were subjected to tremendous vicissitudes on account of foreign invasions or internal strife. In the case of India, she suffered a spell of misfortune from the Muslim (1526-1858) and the British domination (1858-1948) which lasted for 422 years. A nation that loves freedom and spiritual emancipation it was natural that Indian patriots sacrificed everything in order to regain their independence. Due to this and other factors the opportunity of dispatching Buddhist missions abroad was not available for many centuries. In the case of China she suffered from a similar fate, namely, the Yuan dynasty replaced the Sung rulers in 1206 until 1368, and the Ch'ing dynasty (1644-1909) dethroned the Ming dynasty (1368-1638) in 1644; Thereby the Manchu rulers took control of the Chinese empire until 1909. Under these circumstances from the 15th century on down nothing was heard of the cultural interchange between the two countries. Indeed, for the sake of freedom everything else has to be kept on the back burner.

1. Poet Tagore's visit to China and the Sino-Indian Cultural Society

In the 20th century there are many conveniences of communication, the general public are able to travel freely to distant destinations. One feels as if all of a sudden the earth has shrank and the metropolises in the world have become one's nextdoor neighbours. This is a blessing of the modern age.

Rabindranath Tagore, the famous Indian poet, winner of the prestigeous Nobel prize for literature in 1913 was invited to visit China on a lecture tour by the intelligentsia and universities of Beijing. When he arrived at the Ch'ien-men station in the Spring of 1924 he was accorded an extraordinary welcome by a large number of people outbursting of enthusiasm which was beyond all precedent, Prof. Lianger Ch'i-Ch'ao, a prominent scholar, in his welcome speech addressed him as the Indian sage and poet-philosopher, and expressed the sentiment that China had looked upon India as an elder brother, in that she had learnt from India various branches of arts and sciences. In addition, he pointed out that there were 187 Chinese pilgrims, who had visited India, in order to return the courtesy calls of 37 Indian missionaries in the past. He urged that the friendly cooperation which had existed previously between India and China should be renewed, and the poet's visit should mark the beginning of a new era.

While in China Gurudeva Tagore visited many cities such as Beijing, Shanghai, Nanjing, Hangzhou including a visit to Pu Yi, the ex-emperor in the Forbidden Palace. Wherever he went he was showered with love and admiration. At the Chinese scholars' dinner party in Beijing Mr. Lin made this remark:

"We cannot tell him how moved and touched by his presence. His appearance, his eyes, his deportment, his beard, his clothes—everything about him is poetic. He is in-fact poetry itself."

As a token of affection he was given a Chinese name "Chu Chen-tan" engraved on a seal stone. "Chen-tan' is a translation of "Rabindra" = Sun and thunder and also a poetical name for China. "Chu" is the Chinese term for India derived from Sindu or Hindu. Thus it signifies the unity of India and China in the great personality of the Poet. He was much delighted to be honoured in this fashion.

During his lecture tour in China Poet Tagore many a time focused his attention on the cultural renewal between the two countries. The following quotation may illlustrate his genuine concern on this subject:

"My friends, this is my mission. I have come to ask you to reopen the channel of communication which I hope is still there; for though overgrown with weeds of oblivion, its lines can still be traced. I shall consider myself fortunate if, the through this visit, China comes nearer to India and India to China, — for no political or commercial purpose, but for disinterested human love and for nothing else."

— Address to Students at Hangchow

At a farewell party the Poet was assured by Dr. Hu Shih that his mission to China was a great success, and many skeptis had been converted to support the renewal of cultural ties between the two great peoples. He stated that his visit was a successful beginning which would grow and show results far beyond everyone's expectation in ages to come. This prophecy came to pass, and it came much sooner than expected. Within a decade of this visit, the Poet actually realized his great dream of Sino-Indian cultural coopration before his own eyes.

2. Professor Tan Yun-Shan and the renewal of Sino-Indian cultural activities

If Gurudeva Tagore was a finger post, then, Prof. Tan Yun-Shan was a construction worker, who laid down the building blocks piece by piece, and built a bridge leading to the forgotten path of cultural fellowship between India and China, although that channel of communication had been covered with wild weeds of oblivion for centuries. We may say that Gurudeva Tagore was the teacher and guide, and Prof. Tan was his chief disciple. Together they formed an ideal team in erecting an edifice of cultural exchange in the name of Visva-Bharati Cheena-Bhavana.

Professor Tan Yun-Shan was born in Ch'a-lin, Hunan province, China in 1898. In 1927 he had the opportunity of meeting Gurudeva Tagore in Singapore. On that occasion the Poet informed him in detail of the objective of the Visva-Bharati University, viz., it is a center of learning which promotes the best in world culture, upholds the ideal of universal brotherhood and welcomes everyone to participate in this endeavour. Besides, it does not discriminate in terms of race, nationality, colour, religion, caste and other prejudices. He also revealed a plan which was formulated in 1924, in that it would initiate an exchange of professors to teach Sanskrit and Chinese at Beijing and Santiniketan respectively. However, it did not materialize.

In 1928 Prof. Tan visited India for the first time. In the beginning he had the intention of going there as a pilgrim to pay homage to the sacred sites associated with the life of the Buddha, such as Bodh Gaya and the Deer Park (Sarnath) near Benares, and to study Indian philosophy and religion at Santiniketan. On hearing of the Poet's grand scheme of cultural revival and at the request of Prof. Vidhusekhara Bhattacharya, Director of Post-graduate Studies, he gladly agreed to start a Chinese class at Santiniketan with five students. Among them three were college teachers and two researchers, and among the teachers Prof. Prabhat Mukherjee, a wellknown Bengalee writer and librarian of the Visva-Bharati University was one of his pupils. This was the official introduction of Chinese studies, although earlier Mr. Lin Wo-chiang has taught Chinese for a short time.

In 1931 Prof. Tan returned to China taking with him Gurudeva Tagore's blessing and inspiration in regard to the cultural renewal. For the sake of the noble cause he visited many eminent personalities, intellectuals, scholars and educators and urged them to support the Sino-Indian Cultural Society by becoming active members. As the response was overwhelming and beyond his expectation, the said society was successfully inaugurated in Nanjing in 1933. Soon after that he returned to India in 1934 to report to the Poet the successful story. In the same year under the guidance of Gurudeva Tagore the Indian branch of the society was established with greater speed and success. The Poet was very pleased to assume the presidency of the society and Prof. Tan became its Secretary-General. The ideal and objective of the society are as follows:

1. To study the advanced learning of India and China.
2. To facilitate the understanding of Sino-Indian culture.
3. To enhance the friendly fellowship between India and China.
4. To unite the two nations of India and China.
5. To create a lasting peace among mankind.
6. To promote a World Commonwealth.

It appears that the first four in the list concentrate on the improvement of relations between the two peoples through the study of their cultures and languages, and the last two are aimed at achieving a lasting peace and creating a World Commonwealth. If there is peace, then there will be happiness among mankind.

According to the schedule the next important step was to acquire books and to collect funds in order to build an edifice for housing the China Institute, the Library and other facilities. For this Prof. Tan returned to China in 1934 for the third time. He stayed there for over a year and was able to collect sufficient funds to start the required construction work, although the total receipts were below the original expectation. On the other hand, the collection of Chinese publications including the Buddhist scriptures amounted to a total of 500,000 faciculi. It was an unexpected success. Thus the Cheena-Bhavana library is the only facility that has the richest collection of Chinese books in India.

These are Some of the Initial Activities

The Visva-Bharati Cheena-Bhavana (The China Institute-Chung-kuo Shuehyuan) along with several structures was undertaken by the local contractors. In the course of time all were completed. The official inauguration of the Cheena-Bhavana took place on April 10, 1937 which coincided with the Bengalee new year's day. Gurudeva Tagore presided over the function with great joy, because his vision of a cultural renewal between the two nations had been translated into reality, and the Cheena-Bhavana is a living symbol of this reality. Earlier Pandit Jawaharlal Nehru, president of the Indian National Congress had consented to preside over the celebrations; owing to a sudden indisposition he was unable to travel, and had to deputize his daughter Srimati Indira Nehru to represent him instead. She read her father's inspiring message which states:

"It is a very rare opportunity in my life to participate in such a grand ceremony. Therefore, with infinite delight I made a promise to come and take part; I firmly believe that I must come and join in the celebrations. Because the greatness of this ceremony does not confine itself to the ever lasting memories of these two countries in the past, but also points to the great expectation of their friendship in the future. Thus, it will forge a new link which will enable our two countries, India and China to come closer to each other in due time."

Besides, Mahatma Gandhi also sent a message to bless this historical event. His cable says:

"I hope this Cheena-Bhavana is a symbol of renewed relations between India and China."

The newly established China Institute known as the Visva-Bharati Cheena-Bhavana at Santiniketan, India is an imposing concrete building consisting of a ground floor and an upper story. It houses an auditorium, a library, offices, class rooms, a reading room, research rooms and living units for students and staff. Owing to its symbolic significance linking the two great nations, it has been a show piece for visitors to Santiniketan.

In regard to the excellent collection of Chinese books its library has four different editions of the Buddhist Tripitaka such as the Chi-sha edition of the Sung (960-1278), the Dragon edition of the Ch'ing (1644-1909), the Shanghai edition or P'in-Chia edition and the Taisho edition (1929) along with many valuable publications concerning Chinese philosophy, history, classics, literature and other classifications amounting to over 150,000 volumes. No other educational institution in India can claim to own such a rich collection of Chinese texts.

As Cheena-Bhavana is a special research department of the Visva-Bharati University, its primary objective is to enable Chinese scholars to study Indian philosophy, religion, history, literature and languages, and to render assistance to Indian scholars to carry out research on Chinese philosophy, literature and other subjects including the study of Chinese language. As a necessary tool Chinese scholars are encouraged to learn Sanskrit or Pali and modern languages like Hindi or Bengalee. Most of the students from China have followed this guideline and it is to their advantage.

It may be noted that the study of Buddhism occupies a prominent place in the research programme of this institute, in that the translation of Buddhist texts from Sanskrit or Pali to Chinese and vice-versa is encouraged. As a sequel many scholars from India, China, Ceylon or other countries devoted themselves to this area in the early years. For instance, Aiyaswami Sastri translated the Ch'eng-shih lu=The Satyasiddhi Sastra of Hari Varman from Chinese to Sanskrit as the original Sanskrit text was lost; Sujit Kumar Mukherjee translated the Vajrasuci Sastra into English from Chinese; V.V. Gokhale edited a Sanskrit manuscript of the Abhidrama-kosa-karika in the Roman script; P.V. Bapat who did not go to China, but joined the team of researchers of the Cheena-Bhavana to continue his comparative studies. Later, Prof. Bagchi was appointed Vice-Chancellor of the Visva-Bharati University and Prof. Bapat became the director of Buddhist Studies at the Delhi University.

Among the Indian scholars, who went to China to study Chinese, were Amitendra Nath Tagore, a great grandson of Poet Tagore's younger brother, K.Venkata Ramanan from Southern India and Paranjpe from Western India. Having completed their studies in Beijing, Amit Tagore in due time was appointed to teach Chinese at the Oakland University, Michigan, U.S.A. Ramanan continued his study on the Madhyamaka Sastra philosophy at Santiniketan and Paranjpe served as a diplomat of the Indian embassy in Beijing. These were the scholars, who went to China, through the official channel. An exception, however, was the visit of Mr. K.K. Sinha. In 1943 the Kun-ming Oriental Languages School, Yun-nan, China requested Prof. Tan to an Indian scholar to teach Hindi there. Mr. Sinha, who had been a student of the Cheena-Bhavana, was selected to take up that appointment. He stayed in China for a period of three years (1943-1945). Here we see an opening to new opportunities, viz., Hindi, the national language of modern India was introduced to China for the first time. It signifies that progress has been made in accordance with the changing times.

Among the recepients, who had been selected to go to India for advanced studies, were Shen Chi, Wang Han-chung and Wei Kuei-sun. In a few years time they received the Ph.D. degree from their respective Indian universities. Later, the first two in the list returned to China and served in various official positions while Dr. Wei Kuei-sun preferred to remain in India and continued his studies in the Cheena-Bhavana.

Apart from the official exchange of scholars, from the inception of the Cheena-Bhavana in 1937 until the late 1960s there were about 40 known researchers or students from India, China, Japan and Ceylon who had, at different times, studied in the Cheena-Bhavana. Consequently most of them returned to China to engage in academic pursuits, and three of them were invited to the West to teach Asian studies in American and Canadian universities. We regret that space does not permit us to go into details.

5. A gift of the Chinese Buddhist Tripitaka

There is a saying in Buddhism that the best gift is the gift of Dharma. The introduction of Buddhism to China was a gift of Dharma. It preaches the message of peace, compassion, love and emancipation which is similar to the teachings of Laotzu and Confucius. Through the uninterrupted effort of both Indian and Chinese scholars a monumental achievement was created in the form of a collection of Chinese translations of Sanskrit or Pali texts known as the Buddhist Tripitaka. In terms of time it took more than 15 centuries, in terms of human labour, many thousands of people was engaged in this project as volunteers, and in terms of value, it is absolutely priceless. It has been regarded as the national treasure by many Asian countries, and if we appreciate the moral and ethical teachings of ancient Asian sages, we ought to pay profound respects to the said Tripitaka. Under these considerations it is appropriate for China to offer India a gift of the Chinese Tripitaka as a token of gratitude. Besides, the original Sanskrit texts which had been lost in India a long time ago, were carefully preserved in these translations. If China was not in a position to offer India anything in return, the gift of this Tripitaka should receive a warm 'welcome home' from the people in India.

On the basis of the above Prof. Tan Yun-shan urged the highest authorities in China and the ministry of education for their sponsorship of donating ten sets of the Shanghai edition of the Tripitaka known as the P'in-chia edition to ten cultural and religious organizations in India. It consists of 1916 titles amounting to 8416 fasciculi, bound in 414 volumes. For the sake of easy handling every 10.35 volumes are kept in a champhor-board binder. The whole set has a total of 40 bundles.

The following is a list of beneficiaries in India:

1. The University of Calcutta, Calcutta, Bengal.
2. The University of Patna, Bihar.
3. The Hindu University, Benares, The United Province.
4. The University of Andra, Andra.
5. The Bhandharkar Oriental Research Institute, Poona, Bombay Province.
6. The Venkateswara Oriental Institure, Tirubhati, South India.
7. The International Indian Cultural Institute, Lahor (Now in Pakistan).
8. The Maha-Bodhi Society, Sarnath, Benares, The United Province.
9. The Buddhist Association of Bengal, Calcutta, Bengal.
10. The Visva-Bharati Cheena-Bhavana, Santiniketan, Bengal.

From the point of geographical distribution there are three sets in Eastern India (Nos.1,9,10), two in Southern India (Nos. 4,6), three in Central India (Nos. 2,3,8), one in Western India (No. 5) and one in Northern India (No. 7). The reason for selecting them was that there were scholars in some of these centers of learning, who had shown a keen interest in Sinological studies. The names of Prof. P.C. Bagchi and Prof. V.V. Gokhale were well-known in this regard. To have a set of the Tripitaka it would facilitate their research on Buddhism and strengthen the Sino-Indian cultural activities.

6. An Appeal for India's Independence

On many occasions Prof. Tan declared publicly that the Sino-Indian Cultural Society would remain strictly non-political. This guideline had been faithfully observed. However, during the Second World War he wrote an article entitled, "An appeal to conscience" fervently appealing to the concerned parties. It was still under the control of the British, inspite of the fact that her southeastern corner had been raided by the Japanese. The enemy stationed an imposing army near the border, waiting for the right moment to advance into Indian territory. In the meantime some political parties planned to utilize this opportunity to regain independence and expel the British Raj from India. It was reported that in order to achieve that goal they would even cooperate with the Japanese invaders. On the other hand, Mahatma Gandhi and the Indian

National Congress Party would tread the path of non-violence to achieve the same objective. It was critical moment for India, the Alliance and mankind. Can one imagine what would happen if the Axis had won and Japan had become the master of the whole of Asia? It would mean a victory for aggression and defeat for justice and righteousness. Fortunately the outcome was in favour of the democratic forces.

Out of genuine love and concern for the Indian people, he passionately implored the British government, Indian leaders and the leftist parties to cease immediately all violent actions such as bombing, arson, robbery, assassination and other acts of sabotage. He argued that violence would benefit neither India nor the British, but the Japanese invader. He compared the aggressor to that of a fisherman, who captured both the victims, a kingfisher and an oyster, when they were in a heated dispute. He warned the parties that such a fate might be waiting for them, if they did not change their course of action. On the other hand, if they could cooperate with the Alliance, India would certainly regain her independence when the Axis were defeated. The second world war came to an end in 1945, and the dream of Hitler, Mussolini and the war criminals of Japan was shuttered to pieces, Indeed, this was a great victory of the good over the evil. In 1947 the British left India returning the empire to its rightful owners. India has been an independent nation ever since. We pay our tributes to Prof. Tan for his endeavour in this regard.

As for his appeal to the British, he beseeched the British authorities to declare immediately India an independent sovereign state, so that a nation of over 400 million people would gladly join hands with them to fight against the Axis aggressors; It would also tear asunder the mask of Japanese propaganda, "As the British will not give you freedom, we shall come to liberate you." Further, he argued that such a move was not only the wish of the United Nations, but also of the British people, and that being a nation of advanced culture, India would treat the English people with courtesy and kindness. If such a step could take place, it would definitely help the Alliance achieve a great victory, and a new link of friendship between India and the British would be forged. At the end of the war, Indian was liberated from the British rule of over 150 years in 1947. There were many Complicated factors involved in this subject, we hope, however, that Prof. Tan's "appeal to conscience" might have exerted some influence on either parties.

7. A Proposal for World Peace

The history books inform us that among men and nations war occurs constantly, and its consequence is the terrible sufferings of the unfortunate victims. They suffer from the loss of lives, of property, of happiness and of being separated from their loved ones. In examining the cause of war and its prevention, Prof. Tan concured with the Buddhist assessment that the three poisons, namely: Greed, Hatred and Ignorance are the root cause of all evil deeds including war. Being inherent in human nature, everyone seems to have desires for fame, riches, power, influence and sensual pleasures. When these wish are not fulfilled anger and hatred will arise within, and in turn there will be war, murder, arson, violence, death and destruction. These are daily occurrences before our own eyes. All these activities may be ascribed to ignorance (Avidya) or stupidity. The individuals, who tread a path of evil, may be regarded as insane, such as Adolf Hitler and his associates. At the end of the second world war they were duly punished for their crime against humanity.

As a supplement to the three poisons Prof. Tan added the following six evil views which should be discarded:

1. The evil view of individual and racial superiority.
2. The evil view of private and national self-interest.
3. The wanton ambition for social and political power.
4. The wanton ambition for personal and state vainglory.
5. The stupid fears and suspicions of others.
6. The stupid jealousy and envy towards others.

On the basis of the above, events concerning the strong oppress the weak, and the majority humiliate the minority have been reported daily, and the practice of discrimination regarding race, colour, nationality, religion, sex and so forth is still being observed in many communities. This would bring them misfortunes and strife. In view of the nuclear weapons race and its fatal consequences, Prof. Tan proposed the following 12 principles as a remedy and a prescription for world peace:

8. His friendship with Poet Rabindranath Tagore

The awakening of Sino-Indian cultural renaissance in the 20th century is mainly due to the vision and effort of two great souls: Gurudeva Tagore and Prof. Tan Yun-shan. Poet Tagore was the finger post and Prof. Tan a bridge builder. Through their cooperation they translated a dream into reality, and brought the peoples of India and China closer to each other. In this chapter we shall learn of the relationship between these two personalities. The following may serve as an illustration:

When Poet Tagore visited China in 1924 Prof. Tan was teaching in the Southseas. Therefore, they could not meet at that time, but three years later. However, before the said date he had read many of his works in English and Chinese translations as well as his lectures delivered in China. Through these writings he felt as if he had known the Gurudeva for ages, except for a personal interview. Thus, a seed of friendship was sown, eventually it will grow, bloom and yield beautiful fruition in time to come.

In 1927 they met for the first time in Singapore. Prof. Tan enthusiastically supported Gurudeva Tagore's mission of renewing the cultural ties of these two nations, and declared his unconditional devotion to serve him and the good cause. According to him that the Poet's deep concern over, and understanding of China surpassed that of everyone including the Chinese themselves. He cited Gurudeva's advice to the Chinese people that the Russian type of communism should not be blindly imitated, as no benefit would be derived from it. He believed that the Poet loved China as much as his love for India, if not more. Moreover, as the Buddha was born in India, he regarded Gurudeva Tagore to be the most outstanding representative of the Buddha's kingdom. For these reasons he joined the Visva-Bharati University at Santiniketan in 1928 at the invitation of the Poet. He worked there wholeheartedly until his retirement in 1971. While at Santiniketan Prof. Tan had the opportunity of seeing the Poet almost daily. He was a trusted friend, collaborator, disciple and co-worker of Gurudeva Tagore. However, he never attempted to beg favours of him, nor put questions to him like other visitors, but paid sincere respects to the Gurudeva. In turn, the Poet receprocated with warm affection and trust, and he would occasionally initiate an interesting topic for conversation. We shall cite a few in the following page:

One day the Poet showed Prof. Tan a book entitled, “My country and my people" by Lin Yu-tang, and enquired whether Prof. Tan would like to make a comment. “This is a very fine and interesting book, but you may not like it" the poet added. In response, Prof. Tan said, “I also like it. But it does not interpret the whole and the real aspect of my country and my people." The poet rejoined: “That is why I say you may not like it. Perhaps I should say you may not appreciate it." This exchange suggests how profound and penetrating was the Poet's understanding of China and the Chinese people. As a token of gratitude Prof. Tan wrote in “My dedication to Gurudeva Tagore" showing an outburst of appreciation : “O beloved and revered Gurudeva, you indeed grasped the soul of my people, and embraced the heart of my country." It was written on August 7,1942 in memory of Gurudeva Tagore's first death anniversary.

At a later date touching on the topic of the Poet's passing away, Prof. Tan told a friend : ``Alas, only he understood me in India. Now Gurudeva is no more and I am like Krishna's abandoned flute." With tears flowing from his eyes. We are moved by his heartfelt sorrow and love for Gurudeva Tagore.

On another occasion, the discussion was centered on whether people from different cultures would consider ‘beauty’ differently. Prof. Tan quoted a saying from Mencius : “All men's eyes agree in recognizing the same beauty. “To this the Poet did not concur and said, “No, it is not always so.” Then, he related a story, saying, “The young poet Susima (Tse-mo hsu) who came here, you know, who was quite a handsome person. I asked our girls if they appreciated his beauty. All of them said ‘No.’ At this juncutre Prof. Tan advised him that the girls might not be trusted if they were shy. Therefore, they did not frankly admit having appreciated the young Chinese poet's beauty. This explaination caused an outburst of laughter among all those who were present, including Gurudeva himself.

On August 6, 1942, one day before the passing away of the great poet, Prof. Tan went in a hurry to

Calcutta to see him at his residence. He was in a critical condition and there was hardly any hope of recovery. Prof. Tan sat by his sickbed silently; He prayed and recited Buddhist sutras for several hours. He hoped that the blessing of the Triple Gem would prolong his life. As the physicians could not render any appreciable improvement, Gurudeva Tagore passed away on August 7, 1942. The sad news spread rapidly to every corner of the country and the world. At that time all florist stores sold out their stock of wreaths and flowers, and one could not purchase any garland at any price. As a token of love and veneration he took off from his own hand a string of amber beads and placed it in the hand of Gurudeva Tagore. This may symbolize the intimate friendship between the two great nations, and the final offfering from his devoted Chinese disciple.

9. His Friendship with Mahatma Gandhi

In modern India there were two great leaders : Rabindranath Tagore and Mahatma Gandhi. The former was bright star in the spheres of culture, literature, peotry, art, music and social reform, and the later a national hero and a firm believer in Non-violence (Ahimsa) with which he achieved independence for India without shedding a drop of blood. He was lovingly addressed as `the father of Indian freedom'. In reality he was a saint, a holy man and an extrarordinary politician. They had their own spheres of influence. Such being the case there were many people from far and near eager to seek his darsana. When Prof. Tan visited India for the first time he intended to pay his respects to both of them along with a pilgrimage to the sacred sites of Buddhism. His appointment with the Mahatma had many changes of time and venue. It was from Delhi to Sabarmati, and from there to Bardoli. The changes were necessary because Gandhiji had several urgent calls requiring his presence at those locations. Anyway, they finally met at Bardoli in April, 1931.

We must, however, report an important event which altered Prof. Tan's travel plans. In the Winter of 1930 he was suddenly requested to visit the 13th Dalai Lama in Lhasa on certain official business. While staying in the Residential Palace (Noblingone) of the `Living Buddha,' the late Dalai Lama and his high officials were very keen to learn of the various activities of Indian political leaders, especially of Gandhiji's way of living and his satyagraha movement. On his return to India, His Holiness entrusted him with a personal message to be delivered to the Mahatma. As this was an important mission he requested Gandhiji to grant him a darsana, and that was readily given.

On the day of their first interview Prof. Tan solemnly handed over the letter to Gandhiji from the Dalai Lama. It was discovered, to the surprise of everyone, that the letter was written in Tibetan. As no one was able to translate it into English Gandhiji could not know what was the message. In a flash the Mahatma said that he would send an acknowledgement to his Holiness in Gujarati (the mother tongue of Gandhiji) so that the Dalai Lama would similarily be unable to know what was the response. As one was a `Living Buddha', and the other a `Great Soul' (Mahatma), perhaps they could communicate with telepathy, and would dispense with the conventional practice. However, Gandhiji's letter was sent to Lhasa, Tibet, through the postal service in May, 1931.

During the interview Prof. Tan informed the Mahatma how the Chinese people had expressed their deep veneration for him and Poet Tagore, how they prayed for his success in regaining India's independence, how they aspired to renew the historical ties between the two countries, India and China and how they hoped to invite him to visit China. In response to the last point, he said that he could not and would not leave India until she was free. He also stated that he had great admiration for China and the artistic living of the Chinese people. Then, he referred to Chinese food. He was under the impression that all Chinese people were found of meat-diet. To this Prof. Tan corrected him and said that was not the case. According to him cows used for agriculture were not slaughtered, and the country folks used to eat meat only on rare occasions such as the new year or wedding celebrations; The folks used living in big cities would have frequent access to a meat-diet. On the whole more vegetables were consumed than meat. At this point Gandhiji enquired of him whether he was a vegetarian, if not, whether he could become one? In response, Prof. Tan said that he would endeavour to become a vegetarian on account of the Mahatma's personal advice, and he would dedicate his conversion to vegetarianism to the happy occasion of meeting with the Mahatma. On hearing this Gandhiji was highly pleased.

Before his departure from Bardoli he quested the Mahatma to send a message to the students in China.

He wrote with his own hand the following message in English :

"Dear friend,

You must come again whenever you like. My message to the Chinese students is: — Know that the deliverence to Chinese is through Ahimsa-pure and unadultrated.

Yours Sincerely,

M.K. Gandhi

As at Sabarmati, 4-5-31.

Since this visit they had remained in touch. At a later date when the Mahatma was on a hunger strike in Western India, Prof. Tan travelled there to visit him in prison. It would be a happy occasion for both of them to meet once again.

10. The Sino-Indian Good-will Missions

The inauguration of the Visva-Bharati Cheena-Bhavana took place in 1937. From 1937 to 1962, a period of 25 years we witnessed an increase in the frequency of good-will missions from China to India and vice-versa, some of which were very extraordinary ones. The most outstanding event was the visit of Generalissimo and Madame Chiang Kai-shek in 1941. They saw the Cheena-Bhavana and made a brief stay in the Utarayana, the Poet's residence at Santiniketan. This occurred in the midst of the second world war, and China was a member of the Alliance. Next was the good-will mission of Chou En-lai, premier of the Peoples Republic of China, who visited Santiniketan in 1957. To honour him the Visva-Bharati University conferred on him an honourary doctorate. Later he donated many valuable books to the Cheena-Bhavana library. Prior to this there was the good-will mission of Venerable T'ai-hsu during the Sino-Japanese war and the mission of Tai Chi-tao, president of the Examination Yuan of the Nationalist government in 1940. As a pilgrim he visited various Buddhist sacred sites such as Bodhgaya, the Deer Park and so forth. He wrote an essay in Chinese tracing the historical relations between India and China and praying for its renewal. This document being engraved on a plaque was installed on a wall of the Cheena-Bhavana hall. During his visit to Santiniketan he made a donation towards the construction of a sacred shrine where Mr. Devendranath Tagore (father of Poet Rabindranath Tagore), a spiritual leader of the soici-religious reform movement, had set foot on the soil of Santiniketan for the first time. From this humble beginning it has become the beautiful Visva-Bharati University as we see it today.

Moreover, there were private and semi-official missions to India in the 1940s and 1950s. One mission was led by Ting Hsi-ling and Hsieh Ping-hsin ( ) both were well-known writers, and the lecture tour of Prof. Chang Chun-mai who visited many cultural centers in India. It is obvious that Prof. Tan played a very significant role in some of these missions. For instance, he accompanied Mr. Tai Chi-tao to visit the Buddhist sacred spots and acted as a personal guide. The increased traffic of good-will missions between the two countries is an indication of their good friendly relations.

In the 1950s several good-will missions went to China from India, such as visit of Prof. S. Radhakrishnan, an internationally renowned philosopher, and later he became the President of the Indian Union : The visit of Mrs. Vijayalakshmi Pandit (sister of Jawaharlal Nehru), Indian ambassador to the United Nations, and the good-will mission of Pandit Sundarlal of Allahabad, India. When he returned to Allahabad, through the suggestion of the present author, he donated all the gifts he had received in China to the University of Allahabad Department of History museum for permanent exhibition. In addition there was an Indian Medical Mission of five physicians who went to China for relieving the sufferings of war victims. Among them one died in China. A book entitled, ``One did not come back" was published to record the services of this mission. This must have occurred during the Sino-Japanese war years (1936-1945?).

Besides, there were individuals who had visited China or India in a private capacity. Unfortunately their activities or dates of their visits were shrouded in the mist of oblivion.

One may be surprised to learn that the leaders of the official Chinese good-will missions such as Ch'iang Kai-shek and Chou En-lai were paramount personalities of the Nationalist and Communist parties respectively. It appears that Prof. Tan was equally comfortable in the company of Ch'iang or Chou, and he was a good friend of both. This is because he was neutral, impartial and detached from any political party affiliation. Similarly the nature and purpose of the Sino-Indian Cultural Society and the Cheena-Bhavana have been non-political. This is proved by the fact that some housing units of the Cheena-Bhavana are named after Ch'iang Kai-shek : and Tai Chi-tao, and many valuable books donated by Chou En-lai have been preserved in its library. It should be borne in mind that Cheena-Bhavana means ``An Institute for Chinese Learning". Therefore, let us keep it in the way, and every Chinese should make a point of respecting its independent status.

11. Professor Tan's way of life

Being thoroughly imbued with the teachings of great religions of India and China, Prof. Tan's way of life reflected the essence of Confucian humanism and Buddhist universal compassion. He was an embodiment of sincerity, simplicity, modesty, humility, enthusiasm, determination and of being eveready to render a helping hand to the needy. In the area of religious observance, he used to recite Buddhist sutras, to worship the Buddha, to meditate and to practise Yogic exercises in addition to his official duties of teaching and administration. In the area of self-cultivation, the practice of T'al-chi chuan or Pa-tuan chin and a morning walk was his daily routine. He observed silence on Wednesdays, and would answer questions in writing if such an occasion should arise. On Sunday evenings an informal gathering for the imates of the Cheena-Bhavana was held. The participants observed silence for a few minutes. Then, he would recite the objective of the Sino-Indian Cultural Society and prayed for world peace. At the end of the session he would answer questions concerning current affairs or events related to the Visva-Bharati University. To participate in this event was optional. In a way, this might have been influenced by the evening service of Mahatma Gandhi.

During his lifetime many people showed him great esteem regarding him as an ambassador of Sino-Indian cultural revival, a scholar, a writer, a poet and even a Chinese Mahatma. As a tribute to Prof. Tan, Mr. A.K. Chanda, a former secretary of Gurudeva Tagore, had sent this message : ".... a perfect gentleman, a man of extreme charm and piety, and in fact a God's own man." This shows how he was respected by others.

Being a good father, he educated and brought up seven of his children, five sons and two daughters with great love and care. All are college graduates, two engineers, one specialist in Bengalee language, one artist, and three teachers in higher education. As a way of strengthening the Sino-Indian friendship one son and two daughters are married to Indian families. It is reported that these children have settled down in India, Canada and the United States.

Around 1971 Prof. Tan retired from the Visva-Bharati Cheena-Bhavana and moved to Bodhgaya, where the Buddha had attained to his enlightenment, for the purpose of establishing a world institute for Buddhist studies. It was an uphill task for him to collect funds for this project. For a period of twelve years he could complete only one-half of the construction due to the lack of funds and other difficulties. In early 1983 he passed away peacefully in Bodhgaya at the age of 85.

A sad note may be added here. When Prof. Tan was very ill and alone, and owing to his extreme compassionate nautre, he had entered his signature on a sheet of blank paper which was given to a tibetan person as requested. After his death, making use of that piece of blank paper signed by him, the said forged a false claim stating thet Prof. Tan Yun-shan had gifted all the buildings and other assets to him. Such being the case, nothing could be done to recover the loss. It is an irony of fate that due to this treacherous fraud, the splendour of Prof. Tan Yun.shan's immeasurable compassion and achievement will shine more brightly for ever.

12. Conclusion

The foregoing chapters may serve as a survey of Prof. Tan Yun-shan's achievement is strengthening the link of friendship and cultural interchange between India and China in the 20th century. Now, both Gurudeva Tagore and Prof. Tan are no longer with us there might be a bumpy journey ahead in Sino-India relations. We are of the opinion that it is the moral responsibility of our two countries to maintain the existing friendly ties through academic and cultural activities. It would be tragic, if this cordial cooperation should silently fade away due to negligence.

A few decades ago the present writer was privileged to pay homage to Gurudeva Tagore, and to sit at the feet of the revered Prof. Tan Yun-shan. In the capacity of a former student and Colleagues, I would like to share with my friends my personal impression concerning his good qualities. As the founder-principal of the Cheena-Bhavana and Secretary-General of the Sino-Indian Cultural Society he had multiple responsibilities. For a period of 45 years, he toiled indefatigably and sacrified the prime of his life in order to accomplish his mission. Further, in the capacity of an unofficial cultural ambassador, his modest residence at Santiniketan was used to entertain many distinguished visitors by his personal meagre resources. Inspite of all the difficulties he was generous and compassionate going out of his way to help anyone in need. He sympathized deeply with those who were in sorrow, and rejoiced the success of others. He treated his colleagues and pupils as his equals. He was always their sincere friend and guide. Such were some of Prof. Tan Yun-shan's great qualities. We always cherist the memorable days spent in his company.

On the occassion of Prof. Tan Yun-shan's centenary commemoration, I solemnly express my deep gratitude and appreciation, and salute him with a verse which was composed by Si Ma-chien the great Chinese historian of the Han dynasty, who had dedicated it to Master Confucius. It runs as follows:

"High is the mountain,

I gaze in wonder.

Though I can't be there,

My mind goes younder."

W. Pachow

Professor Emeritus

University of Iowa, USA

October 10,1998.

BIBLIOGRAPHY

Paul Demieville, (ed) Hobogirin Fascicule Annexe, Tokyo: Maison Fransco-Japonaise, 1941.

Rabindranath Tagore, Talks in China, Calcutta: Arunoday Art press, (Ca., 1942).

P.C. Bagchi, India and China: A thousand years of cultural relations, New York: The Philosophical Library, 1951.

V.G. Nair, (ed) Professor Tan Yun-shan and cultural relations between India and China commemoration Volume, Santiniketan: An Indo-Asian Publication, 1958.

Tan Yun-shan, The Visva-Bharati Cheena-Bhavana, Santiniketan: The Visva-Bharati Press, 1944.

My dedication to Gurudeva Tagore, Santiniketan: The Visva-Bharati Press, 1942.

Chinese studies in India, Santiniketan: The Visva-Bharati Press, 1942.

My devotion to Rabindranath Tagore, Santiniketan: The Visva-Bharati Press, 1942.

``My first visit to Gandhiji" in the [Sino-Indian Journal] Vol. I, Part II, and in Nair's (ed) Commemoration Volume, pp. 19-30.

Ways to Peace, Sanitiniketan: The Visva-Bharati Press, 1950.

An Appeal to conscience, Santiniketan: The Visva-Bharati Press, 1942.

W. Pachow, The collected works of W. Pachow (Pa Chow Wen-Tsun — in Chinese), Taipei: New Wen-feng Press, 1985.

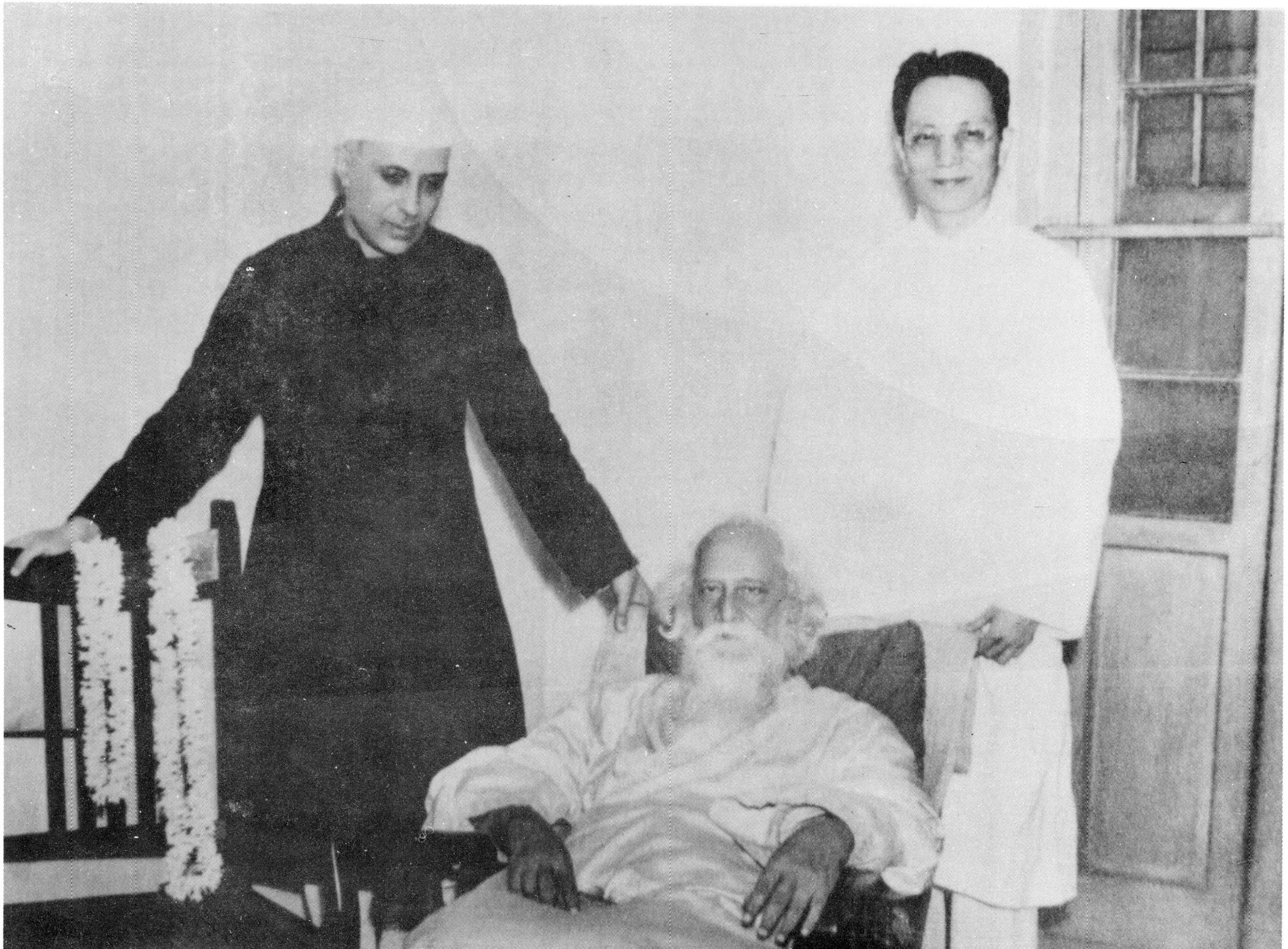

Tagore (centre), Nehru (left), and Tan Yun-shan (right).

Tagore and Tan Yun-shan.

Nehru presiding over the General Body Meeting of the Sino-Indian Cultural Society, December, 1945.

President Dr. Rajendra Prasad and Prof. Tan Yun-shan in the Rashtrapati Bhavan, January, 1950.

Premier Zhou Enlai and Prof. Tan Yun-shan in the Premier's residence, Beijing; October, 1956.

Prime Minister Lal Bahadur Shastri visiting Cheena-Bhavana.

Premier Zhou Enlai visits Cheena-Bhavana, January, 1957.

Prof. Tan Yun-shan and family members; Santiniketan.

Prime Minister Indira Gandhi and Prof. Tan Yun-shan, 1971.

Prof. Tan Yun-shan receiving the Deshikottama Award, December, 1979.

5

TAN YUN-SHAN: A CULTURAL ENVOY BETWEEN CHINA AND INDIA

India is the close neighbour of China. Two thousand years ago the peoples of China and India have started friendly contacts and cultural interactions, resulting in a profound fraternity. Such interactions commenced in the beginning of the Qin Dynasty, which gradually increased during the former and later Han, and reached the climax during Sui and Tang. During Song and Yuan they became further deepened. After entering the modern era there has been a new development, with new input. The Sino-Indian cultural interaction was unique in the history of world cultural interaction. All the great inventions and creations, both spiritual and material, of the Indian people were introduced into our country with blossom and fruition. Hence, the great thinker and writer of China, Lu Xun, observed: "Since ancient times India has communicated with us, made great presentation to us, whether it is philosophical thought, or religious belief, or morality, or art and literature, even brother and relatives would not be so generous".

When we look back at the history of Sino-Indian interactions we cannot but remember the large number of Buddhist monks, scholars, emissaries, scientists, technical experts and merchants etc. who had carved their ways out of the brambles with an undaunting spirit, braving heat and cold, embarking on long journeys, submerged by diligent work, creating remarkable careers which inspire both eulogy and tears. Some of them recorded their names in history, but many more have vanished into oblivion. According to historical records, from the end of Han Dynasty till the end of Song Dynasty, i. e. in the space of 1,000 years from the second to the 12th century A.D. there had been more than 150 scholars who had been frontline participators in the gigantic undertaking of translating the *Tripitakas* [from Sanskrit or Pali into Chinese]. Among them those whose details are confirmed by historical books included 70 monk-scholars from India. During the period from 10th to 13th century, there were 160-170 translation masters in Tibet among whom 70-80 were from Kashmir and eastern India.

The most famous Indian monks who came to China from India were Kang Senghui, Buddhabhadra, Dharmaraksa, Bodhiruci, Paramartha, Kumarajiva, *Subhadrasangha,* Amoghavajra, Vajrabodhi, Dharmadeva, Devabhaya, Dhanabhadra etc. Those who went from our country to India were Faxian, Xuanzang, Wang Xuance, Yijing etc. These personalities who had made outstanding contributions to Sino-Indian cultural interaction and friendship have evoked an enduring longing with affection among us. In 1994, we organised an international seminar commemorating the 1,650th birth anniversary of Kumarajiva at the Kizil Grottes in Xinjiang. In 1997-98 India has had commemorative activities for Dr. P. C. Bagchi, famous Indian Sinologist and former Vice-Chancellor of Visva-Bharati. In 1998, we shall be celebrating the birth centenary of the outstanding cultural envoy, famous Buddhist scholar, Prof. Tan Yun-shan.

After India and China falling into colonies and semi-colonies, although the Sino-Indian relationship were hampered by the colonial authorities, friendly intercourses between the people of the two countries have never stopped. The people of China and India particularly forget a common front-fighting against the imperialist aggression. Leaders of the Indian National Congress led by Gandhi, Nehru, Subhas, Bose, and patriotic poet Tagore had all along cherished deep sympathy and the maximum support for the struggles of China for anti-imperialist national and democratic revolution. In the beginning of this century Gandhi had expressed sympathy and support to the revolution led by Dr. Sun Yat-sen. During the Anti-Japanese War, he sent a telegram of congratulations to the Director of Cheena-Bhavana, Tan Yun-shan, expressing good wishes and warm regards for China. The poet sage of India. Tagore, had a very profound affection for China. He admired the outstanding ancient Chinese culture, and repeatedly condemned the Japanese aggression. When China was in a precarious juncture, Tagore asked Tan Yun-shan to carry two letters back to China: one to the highest authority, Chiang Kai-shek, another to the Chinese people. When he was the President of the Indian National Congress in 1937-38, Nehru launched the "China Day" movement, advocated a universal boycott of Japanese goods, mobilizing donations to rush medicines and even sent a medical mission to China — all concrete actions in support of China's Anti-Japanese War. And about all this the first person to be informed by Nehru was Tan Yun-shan. In August 1938, Nehru visited Chongqing, and the trip was arranged by Tan Yun-shan and the Sino-Indian Cultural Society. During this visit, Nehru presented "A Note on the Development of Contacts between China and India" (dated August 29, 1939) to the Chinese leaders in which he made seven proposals:

1. To organize an efficient and regular service of information between China and India,
2. To exchange visits between the special experts of the two countries,
3. To establish contacts between the universities of the two countries,
4. To have direct contacts by post between the movements of the two countries,
5. To have Chinese representatives to attend the annual session of the Indian National Congress,
6. To develop a common Sino-Indian policy vis-a-vis great changes in Europe and the world,
7. To establish direct contact between specialized organizations of India (like the All India Village Association at Wardha, the All India Spinners' Association at Ahmedabad) and China.

The highest Chinese authorities formulated an "outline of Sino-Indian Cooperation" based on Nehru's suggestions, and promptly implemented it. All this not only boosted up the morale of the Chinese people, but also pushed the sympathy of the Indian people for China's anti-war cause to its high tide.

After that, the Sino-Indian Cultural Society under the leadership of Tan Yun-shan was instrumental to Tai Chi-tao's visit to India which further strengthened the relations between the two countries. After the Pacific War broke out, and the opening of the East Theatre by The Allied Forces, Chiang Kai-shek was appointed as the Commander-in-Chief of the China Theatre. In order to break the British-Indian stalemate, mobilize the gigantic economic and military power of India as input into the Anti-Fascist War, and strengthen Sino-Indian cooperation, Chiang Kai-shek personally visited India. In this visit, Tan Yun-shan arranged Chiang to visit Visva-Bharati Cheena-Bhavana and Calcutta, carrying out talks with Nehru. The above mentioned activities during the war time revealed that Prof. Tan was an ardent patriot. For the sake of Anti-Japanese War he tirelessly shuttled between the leading personalities of China and India, mobilized the support from all walks of life of India for China's Anti-Japanese War efforts, made a unique contribution to the liberation of the Indian nation and Chinese people to the final victory of the Anti-Japanese War.

Prof. Tan Yun-shan was a renowned Buddhologist, Indologist, educationist and social activist known in both India and China. In his early life, he was a student of China's revolutionary senior Xu Teli, Zhang Zhizhao and Buddhist reformer Reverend Taixu (Tai Hsu) and others, receiving their revolutionary ideas. He participated in the Xinmin (New People's) Association, New Cultural Books Society and the progressive activities led by comrade Mao Zedong and others. Later, he started newspapers among the overseas Chinese in Singapore, Burma and other places, advocating new culture and new thought. He created the literary supplement "Xingguang" (star light) in *Le Bao* (Singapore Newspaper) and wrote in its first editorial that "we want to light up the dark lonely night with our tiny star light."

In 1927, he met Tagore in Singapore. On the poet's invitation he went to Visva-Bharati to teach (in 1928), and settled down in India since then. While teaching in India, he wrote a large number of articles reporting and commenting on the modern development of India for the newspapers and journals of China. During India's second Non-Cooperation movement, he wrote several pieces for *Dongfang Zazhi* (Oriental Miscellany) like "The Indian National Congress of 1929 and the initial step of the Indian National Movement", "The progress of India's independence movement", "My visit with Gandhi". These articles enabled the Chinese intellectuals to have a comprehensive understanding of the development of India's national movement. His forceful comments registered a mental shock in the minds of his compatriots in the motherland. He specially commended Gandhi's doctrine of non-cooperation which made an impact among China's followers of Gandhism. In 1931, he wrote in *Yindu Zhouyou ji* (An account of my tour round India) the information he had gathered about the Indian society, folklore, relation, monuments, Indian-British relationship and his observations. The book created certain impact in China. Yu Youren, who penned the calligraphy for the book, called him "An intermediary of the Chinese and Indian nations, of Chinese and Indian cultures." In 1935, he published another book *Yindu Congtan* (General talks on India). This book made a completed and in-depth record about the colonial era of India. During the Anti-Japanese War he brought out *Zhongguo Yindu yu Dazhan Lunji* (China, India and the War) and other books. They helped us to understand the positions and contributions of China and India, and gave us a comprehensive and real understanding of the complicated in international relations.

With a noble resolution of promoting Sino-Indian cultural interaction Prof. Tan Yun-shan went to Visva-Bharati. First, he initiated in 1931 and established in 1933 the Sino-Indian Cultural Society in China. Strengthening Sino-Indian friendly relations were originally the ambition and idealism of Tagore and Gandhi. In 1924 when Tagore visited Beijing, he proposed to him that "a 'Sino-Indian Cultural Society' could be organized to facilitate mutual exchange of information". Tagore immediately agreed and said that it was his idea before coming to China. He wished a spiritual reunion between the personalities of the two countries to give play to the oriental culture. This thinking of Tagore fitted the Sino-Indian fraternity cherished by Tan Yun-shan. In his *Yindu zhouyouji*, Tan wrote, "... specially the Sino-Indian relations is the most important of the most important. Apart from our relationship in the past, if we just consider the current situation, it is my firm conviction that if there is no real unity between the Chinese and Indian nations and without their joint endeavour they would achieve nothing be it the strive for world peace or that for world revolution, be it the cause of human civilization or that of the human fraternity."Again, "If we want to save China, and save India, without the real unity of the two nations and their joint endeavour nothing can be achieved."

Tan yun-shan busied himself in mobilizing and organizing support in 1931 and 1933, shuttling between Nanjing and Shanghai. He obtained support from a large number of famous personalities in both politics and academics, like Cai Yuanpei (Ts'ai Yuan-p'ei), Dai Jitao (Tai Chi-t'ao), Liang Shuming, Rev.Taixu, Xu Beihong (Ju Peon) etc. The Sino-Indian Cultural Society was formally inaugurated in Nanjing on May 3rd, 1933. Cai Yuanpei was elected its Executive President and Dai Jitao its Supervisory President, while Tan Yun-shan, its Secretary. The constitution of the Society issued at that time announced the tasks of the Society as "pursuing Sino-Indian Studies, channelizing Chinese and Indian cultures, cultivating Sino-Indian fraternity, uniting the people of India and China so that world peace will be prevailing and an ideal world of Grand Equality and Fraternity will emerge." The Indian chapter of the Sino-Indian Cultural Society was established the next year after Tan Yun-shan returned to Santiniketan. Tagore assumed Presidentship of the Society. Later after the Poet passed away, Nehru agreed to become its Honorary President. The establishment of the Sino-Indian Cultural society saw it doing a great deal of work in strengthening the contacts between the scholars of the two countries, organizing mutual visits between famous personalities of the two countries, organizing mutual visits between famous personal ities of the two countries, exchanging studentsbetween the two countries, presenting books to each other country's institutions, mobilizing donation and relief for natural calamities etc. Prof. Tan always played central role and shouldered the major responsibilities. The Sino-Indian Cultural Society laid a good foundation idea-wise and organizationally for the future development of Sino-Indian friendship.

The greatest achievement of the Sino-Indian Cultural Society was to help the Visva-Bharati (International University) of India establish the Cheena - Bhavana (Chinese Institution). During the preparatory stage of the Sino-Indian Cultural Society Tagore had started talking to Tan Yun-shan about the establishment of such an institution. In 1934, Prof. Tan came to China for help in raising funds for its establishment. He carried from China Rupees fifty thousand and 110, 000 volumes of books to India. Among the books he took to India some were very rare and valuable, e. g. the Ming Dynasty edition of Daozang (the scripture of Taoism). In 1937, Gandhi could not attend the inauguration function of Cheena - Bhavana, but sent message to Tan Yun-shan and Tagore.

In his inaugural address, Tagore said:

Tan Yun-shan did commendable work in promoting the studies of Chinese and Indian Buddhism, as well as rearing up talents in Buddhist studies. He carried on his research in Sino-Indian Buddhist studies and his educational work while he was in Cheena - Bhavana, and has left behind 38 English writings and 10 odd Chinese writings, some of which are related to Sino-Indian Buddhist studies. He had considerable achievement in Buddhist studies. In 1979, in order to recognize his achievements, Visva-Bharati conferred on him the highest honour — Deshikottama. His keen interest in Buddhist studies led him to start building the world Buddhist Academy at Bodhgaya when he was an octogenarian. In 1980, when I first visited Visva-Bharati I was fortunate to see him. He talked to me about the prospect of the World Buddhist Academy and various difficulties in establishing it. According to his plans, he wanted to build this Academy into the centre of Buddhist studies in the world. It would include the "southern Buddhism", i. e. the Chinese-text and Tibetan-text Buddhism, linking up the "Southern" and "Northern" Buddhism with the world Buddhist studies. For the sake of establishing this World Buddhist Academy he set aside considerations of old age and fatigue to go to Hong Kong and Singapore to collect donations. He also exhausted his own savings. His expectations were also rested on Chinese Buddhist organizations and devotees. When this writer visited Bodhgaya, I saw with my own eyes a huge building coming up from the ground, and a feeling of unbounded admiration for him sprang from my heart. His spirit of service is the very ramification of the ultraic doctrine of Mahayana Buddhism.

Prof. Tan had all along been concerned with the activities of Chinese Buddhists. At Sarnath there had been a Chinese Buddhist temple which was built on by a Chinese mission on the imperial order of the Tang ruler, but had vanished for many centuries. The Buddhist masters Reverend Daojie (Tao-chieh) and his disciple Deyu (Teh-yu) of the Fayuan Monastery had made a resolution to revive it. They faced innumerable difficulties. Later, with the help of Prof. Tan Yun-shan and Indian overseas Chinese Qiu Qingchang and Liang Xiegui, building was completed, and was inaugurated in 1939. Today, this solemn edifice of the Chinese temple eminently stands put among temples of all other countries, symbolizing the long history of Chinese Buddhism. In 1940, Prof. Tan was instrumental to the visit to India of a Chinese Buddhist delegation led by Rev. Taixu who was the leader of the modern movement of reform of Chinese Buddhism. This further promoted the intimate contact between the Buddhist followers of both the countries.

Viewing from all the above events we see that Prof. Tan Yun-shan was the foundation-layer for Sino-Indian friendship in modern times, and was an important emissary of Sino-Indian cultural intercourse. He was the architect and builder of the edifice of Sino-Indian friendship in modern times. With his persevering efforts and self-sacrifice, he had promoted the understanding and friendship between the intellectual and cultural circles of the two countries. Special mention should be made about his all-out efforts in awakening the sympathy and support among all walks of life in India for China when she was at the most critical juncture fighting the life-and-death battle against the Japanese aggression. Of course, in his entire life he had encountered innumerable difficulties and obstacles which can be understood. 1998 will be his birth centenary. We shall for ever remember his feat, and march forward treading on the footsteps of Xuanzang and Tan Yun-shan with courage and confidence.

FOND MEMORIES

6

REMEMBERING MY SISTER AND BROTHER-IN-LAW TAN YUN-SHAN

My nephew, Tan Chung, wrote from India asking me to write for the commemorative volume of his father. I am on the wrong side of 90, and troubled by bad health. There is an overall deterioration in energy and strength, in eye-sight and audition. Fortunately, my mind is alert. It is good to remember the birth centenary of Tan Yun-shan, and we must warmly celebrate, complimenting his life and career.

Tan Yun-shan was an orphan, he began studing under the tuition of village teachers. When he grew older he eagerly looked for opportunities to develop his intellectunal facilities. Success never denied one who was so determined. He got admission in the First Normal School. In that school, he worked very hard in studies. He had immense thinking power, had a knack in writing both prose and verse, was one of the best in his class.

He had great ambitions since young. After completing his studies he sailed abroad and reached Singapore. Through the introduction of a fellow-Hunanese who worked in the Zhongnan School he started teaching in the Mapo Middle School. After 2-3 years, he married my sister, Chen Naiwei who also hailed from Hunan, and had arrived in Singapore to teach. After their marriage, a boy arrived, and was christened ``Fruit of Love''. I was in Singapore, too, staying with my sister and the baby.

After marrying my sister, he was addressed by me as ``Brother Yun''. He put his heart in teaching, was fond of reading, diligent in practising the Mandarin accent, in learning English, started creative writing, published his poems and essays. In 1927, the famous Indian poet, Rabindranath Tagore, visited Singapore and invited Tan to go to India. At that time my sister and I had just jioned the Aiqun Girls' School at Madubahar in Johore. But we supported his plans to go to India.

After going to India, Tan Yun-shan helped Tagore to establish the Sino-India Cultural Society and Cheena-Bhavana in Visva-Bharati, and started dedicating to the cultural interaction between China and India. His contribution has become an immortal chapter of Sino-Indian friendship.

China's victory over Japan in the War brought Brother Yun and my sister back to the country. When he saw the poor children nearby the residence at Changsha, he didn't want the sad condition to last. He consulted my sister and me, and decided to establish the Datong School. At the inception there was the regular course and service course for kids. The women's department was added later. The regular course charged tuition fees according to government regulations. The service courses for kids and women were free. In this way the Datong School has made a contribution to the education of the motherland.

Both Brother Yun and my sister compiete their lives in the country of the Buddha. I always longed for them. Now that the motherland is propering, also there is increasing improvement in Sino-Indian relation. These are happy developments which can make them smile in Heaven.

7

MY ACQUAINTANCE WITH PROFESSOR TAN YUN-SHAN

I was born in the same province, Hunan, as Tan Yun-shan was. But, his birth place was Chaling, a county at the eastern edge of the province while my County ,Xiangyin, was in the middle section. Our home village, though a part of the Xiangyin County, was only some 30 miles away from Changsha, the capital city of Hunan Province. (Today, it is a part of the now much enlarged Changsha City). Tan Yun-shan who was senior to me by sixteen years was married to my first cousin sister, Chen Nai-wei. Sister Chen was a very brave woman. She belonged to almost the first generation of the Chinese women who broke the age-old tradition of keeping unmarried girls away from career-seeking ventures. She started studying at a very young age in a modern-type of school in Changsha as a hosteller. After graduation from the school but still in her teenage, she went to teach the primary school kids in Xiangxing more than a hundred miles away from home. Then, she went out of the country to teach the children of the overseas Chinese in the "South Ocean"(Nanyang) which was what Singapore, Malaya, Indonesia and other parts of the mainland and islands of southeast Asia were called by the Chinese at the time. In 1931, she returned to her home village with her bridegroom — Prof. Tan Yun-shan (already so designated by the famous Indian poet and Nobel laureate, Rabindranath Tagore, after the young Tan had had a stint at Tagore's university called Visva-Bharati). It was first visit to our native place.

That time, I was still in my teenage — a country lad who had seen very little of the outside world, nor met any outsider from afar. I developed a great fascination towards my new relative from Chaling. My father was a Confucian scholar and middle school teacher. He, too, was quite cut off from the modern world. But my father had a hobby — playing Chinese chess. Prof. Tan was also good at it. Thus before they could get along in common conversation they had quite an encounter at a Chinese chess table. (This turned out to be the first and also the last time I saw Prof. Tan playing Chiness chess.) Then, my father and the guest who was not much younger than him became endeared to each other. He took Tan around in the countryside, showed him the hilly charm, lectured to him about the traditional Chinese geomancy. For, to my father's generation, the landscape inherited by men had a decisive influence on their fortunes. As a lad, I was keenly watching the reactions from Prof. Tan who listened attentively to my father without any comment.

My maternal grandfather, i.e. Tan's father-in law's father, and his two sons lived in the Eastern Hills while my parents lived in the plain by the side of many rice fields.It was comparatively quiet and cooler in summer on the small hill top, and I took great delight to go there. Much of my childhood I spent in my maternal uncle's house. The arrival of Prof. and Mrs. Tan with their first and second sons to spend some time was an exciting event among all of us. The lifestyle of a traditional Chinese scholar he carried with him, Prof. Tan set up his own study room in the cottage. When he inaugurated the study, he wrote a poetic couplet on two sheets with his beautiful calligraphy and displayed them. Hunan was a province quite strong in classical Chinese culture, and kids of my generation had a good exposure to good and simple poetic compliments. I could comprehend the couplet that he had pasted on both sides of the entrance to his study and immediately liked it. Since this never entered into the curricula of my long academic career, I never had the compulsion to memorize it. Yet, even after nearly 70 years, after a lot of memory has escaped my head, I can still vividly recall what he had composed. The couplet reads:

Dongshan Zhanji er san yue

Shushi changliu qianwan chun

(Left)

Just a brief sojourn

Of two three moons

At these East Hills.

(Right)

Forever to endure,

A thousand springs or more,

My study will grow.

Though already an accomplished "Mandarin", Tan did not give up his innate peasant nature. Every day he carried home from a well outside the house, with a pole on his shoulders, buckets of water for the large family. This he did to share the burden of household chore, and also to faithfully carry out the duty of a devout Buddhist according to the age-old Chinese Chan (Zen) Buddhist tradition (enjoying daily life by fetching water and cutting firewood).

One day, suddenly, he decided to proceed on pilgrimage to the Southern Holy Mountain (one of the five holy mountain shrines of China), Heng Shan, which is situated within Hunan, south of Changsha. I was glad that he took me in the trip. During the pilgrimage he observed that according to the Chinese saying, "Wuyue guilai bu kan shan". (After ascending on the five holy mountains one finds no interest in looking at any other hill.) But, he had already climbed the Himalayas, the loftiest mountains in the world. And this never diminished his interest in ascending mountains and hills again and again. In fact, he made another trip to Heng Shan soon after. I notice that pilgrimage to the Buddhist shrines to him was perhaps not as important as availing of the opportunity to distribute alms to the poor all along the way.

All this I still recall with vivid pictures in my mind. After my first round of acquaintance with Prof. Tan in my grandfather's house, he left for India and returned to his endeavour in developing Sino-Indian studies and the promotion of cultural relations between India and China. I remained in my home province to pursue my future career. Though I continued to obtain tidings of Prof. Tan and his family through the source of my maternal relatives, I missed him for quite a long duration.

Like my cousin sister Chen, I, too went to Changsha as a hosteller, first of the Changjun School, then of the First Normal School where Prof. Tan and many famous modern leaders of China, like Mao Zedong, had studied. I then, got admission in the Central Political University in Nanjing which was essentially the cradle for government officers. No sooner had I joined this prestigeous institution than did Japan invade China in the fall of 1937, and the Sino-Japanese War broke out. Then the university moved to Chongqing, the war capital. After graduation from the university, I got a teaching assignment in Guiyang which was situated in southwest China. There I started correspondence with Prof. Tan in India. In August, 1945 the Japanese surrendered and World War II came to an end. Prof. Tan was awarded the victory medal by the National Government of China for his contribution in mobilizing international support to China's war efforts. He went from India to Chongqing to receive the medal.

I was thrilled to know the news, and took a trip from Guiyang to Chongqing to meet him. Apart from sharing his pride and joy, I was keen to meet him for some personal reasons. When I told him that I would like to pursue research in India he showed great delight. He went out of his way to help me to obtain permission from Chinese authorities, and also a scholarship from the Ministry of Education (which was meagre in sum though). Of course, the invitation to me to go to India came from himself as the Director of Cheena - Bhavana of Visva-Bharati.

I should like to record an important thing which happened to Prof. Tan towards the end of 1945 in Chongqing which, probably has escaped notice by the chroniclers. He took initiative to convene a conference on the development of Sino-Indian cultural relations which was attended. by Dr.Tai Chi-tao, one of the top leaders of the Kuomintang government, who addressed the conference, and dwelt on Sino-Indian cultural affinity. Dr. Tai was not only a devout Buddhist but also lent a powerful support to Prof. Tan to help Rabindranath Tagore establish a permanent institution on Sino-Indian studies in his university. He had travelled to India a few years earlier and had pleasant meeting with Mahatma Gandhi and Jawaharlal Nehru.

While in Chongqing, Tan gave me opportunities to share some of his itinerary. One evening he took me to see Rev. Taixu (or Tai Hsu), an eminent Buddhist sage of modern China who had also led a Chinese Buddhist delegation to India. One thing I vividly remember was to watch how Prof. Tan knelt down before the patriarch to pay his respect. Tan was a man always humble, never rest on his own laurels. It also reflected his unbounded devotion to the high ideas and ideals of Lord Buddha of which the Reverend was a symbol.

With the invitation from Prof.Tan on behalf of a renowned Indian university, the Visva-Bharati (a Sanskrit name meaning "International University"), and with the blessings of my eminent relative who was quite influential in the national government, I did not have much difficulty in getting the green signal from the Chinese Ministry of Education. I left Chongqing by a military plane available at the time, flying over the Himalayas, and landed at Calcutta. Then, I took a train to Santiniketan (a very poetic Sanskrit name meaning "the abode of peace") which was a tiny village of serene atmosphere true to its name, with many eminent scholars pursuing high academic activities quietly. I was happy for many reasons. First, I had my reunion with not only Prof. Tan, but also my first cousin, Mrs. Tan who now had many more children. I admired the manner in which she had set up a happy home far away from her homeland. The idea that I was in what the Chinese literature used to describe as "Foguo" (the Buddha's country) and "Tianzhu" (Heavely India) made me very excited. India was a country that I had been longing to see, a country with powerful spiritual values and sophisticated philosophies. I was even more excited when I discovered the presence of many famous and learned scholars of Indology and Buddhism around the quarter I lived, and so easily accessible.

I arrived in India to become a visiting scholar of Visva-Bharati Cheena Bhavana, an insititution that was created jointly by the founder of the university, Chancellor Tagore and Prof. Tan in 1937. I joined it in early 1946, five years after the great poet had passed away. As soon as I joined the Cheena Bhavana, I became a part of the international fraternity in which Chinese scholars met Indian scholars and assisted each other like brothers. The mutual feeling of brotherhood was spontaneous, this was not to be compared with the slogan, "Hindi Chini Bhai Bhai" (Indians and Chinese are brothers), coined by an Indian poet and much trumpeted by the Chinese government in the 1950s.

I can never forget my associations with some Indian pundits at Santiniketan, many of whom were outstanding scholars trained both in India and abroad. Dr. P. C. Bagchi was then giving a series of lectures on the cultural relations between India and China.I was happy to attend his lectures. He was later to be visiting professor of Indian Studies at Beijing University, China. His most important publication was *India and China: A Thousand Years of Sino-Indian Cultural Contacts.*

Another professor of Sanskrit was Dr. P. V. Bapat who, like Bagchi, also had a good command of Chinese language. He was always intimate and humorous especially towards Chinese scholars. To Chinese beginners Sanskrit is a very hard language to learn. But Bapat had enormous patience with us. Later, during the year of Buddha Jayanti (celebrating the 2,500th Anniversary of Lord Buddha) in 1956, Prime Minister Nehru appointed him as the founder-head of the Department of Buddhist Studies in Delhi University. I was, then, working in Delhi and had more interactions with him. My wife was asked by Prof. Bapat to teach Chinese language to the students of the Department. Dr. Bapat's personal friends with Prof. Tan had, thus, extended to me and my wife who were related to the Tans.

Among the Chinese scholars there were two professors from China. One was Xu Hu (or Hsu Hu), who had studied in Germany. He was well versed in Chinese classics and preferred to write Chinese in its old literary style. He had also learned much Sanskrit. Another Professor from China, Chang Renxia (or Jen-hsia) specialized in archaeology and ancient Chinese art. Prof. Xu was very close to me. In a way I respected him even as my teacher. After leaving Cheena Bhavana later, I met Prof. Chang in New Delhi once, but never Prof. Xu. He went to the ashram of Sri Aurobindo at Pondicherry and translated a large number of the modern Indian sage's writing into Chinese. In late 1970s he returned to China and joined the Chinese Academy of Social Sciences as an India-expert. With regret I came to know that both of them had passed away.

Two disciples of Reverend Taixu also joined Cheena Bhavana, both having returned, to the mundane world form priesthood. One of them, Pachow, has become the renowned authority on Chinese Buddhism (now settled down in USA), after a fruitful teaching career in the universities of Allahabad, Candi (in Sri Lanka), and Iowa. He was a favourite disciple of Prof. Tan, and had been very attached to the Tan family ever since. Another ex-Taixu disciple, Xulu, taught Chinese in Cheena Bhavana for many decades, leading a simple and singular life, and passed away in Uttar Pradesh.

We also had a lady scholar from China living in Cheena Bhavana who was a painter. Her name, then, was You Yun-shan, sharing personal name with Prof. Tan. She is a leading Buddhist priest and educationist in Taiwan now — the renowned Rev. Hsiao-yun (Xiaoyun). Not far away from Taipei, Rev. Hsiao-yun has carved out a hill into a campus resembling Santiniketan. She named her higher educational institiution "Hua-fan", meaning 'China-India'. We see the spirit of Sino-Indian fraternity of Gurudeva Tagore first extended to Prof. Tan, and then to Rev. Hsiao-yun.

Prof. Tan lived wholesomely in his idealism of universalism,and his path was shone upon by the noble ideas of both China and India. This was enshrined in the "Sino-India Motto" composed by him. The Motto has 32 Chinese characters, beginning with "li de li yan". All Chinese scholars of Confucian tradition in the past had a task set for themselves to achieve three things: "li de" (to attain a moral character), "li gong" (to achieve a meritorious feat), and "liYan" (to perfect a speech which can propagate truth and noble ideas). Prof. Tan dropped the second as if to say: "I must cultivate my character and perfect my speech to set an example for posterity".

Then, the next four characters to follow in the Motto are "Jiu ren Jiu shi" — to save other and save the mankind. Here, he expounded the noble spirit of a Bodhisattva, viz. sacrificing oneself to rescue all beings of the universe from misery. This Bodhisattva spirit was brought alive by Mahatma Gandhi who said: "Who would go to the Hell if I don't take the lead." Mahatama Gandhi was the human being Prof. Tan admired the most — even surpassing his admiration for Gurudeva Tagore.

The next eight characters of Prof. Tan's Sino-Indian Motto are:

"Zhi gang zhi da" — To be extremely strong and grand;

"You shou you wei" — To contribute but adhere to Principle.

The second part of the Motto is in keeping with the Confucian norm that there are things which a gentleman will do, and things which a gentleman will not do. Judging from this light, the concept of "Zhida" (extremely grand) should be understood as "Zhi gong da yi" i.e., extremely selfless and grand righteousness.

The last half of Tan's Motto is more transparently a Buddhist spirit:

"Nan xing neng xing"— To be able to do what is difficult to do;

"Nan ren reng ren" — To be able to tolerate what is difficult to tolerate;

"Sui yuan bu bian" — Adaptable to circumstances yet remaining unchangeable;

"Bu bian sui yuan" — Remaining unchangeable while adapting to circumstances.

In later Prof. Tan self-styled himself as "Renxian" which is the Chinese rendering of the Sanskrit term "Ksantirishi"— the saint who suffers insult patiently. Prof. Tan was the last human being on earth on whom anyone might like to hurl insult, perhaps. His self-styled title of "Renxian" was just in keeping with his Sino-Indian Motto to set an example of noble and magnanimous behaviour.

Knowing that I, too, had a smattering of classical Chinese poetry which I had inherited from my family background, Prof. Tan, time and again, presented me with verses which he had made it a point to pen with his calligraphy. I particularly remember the four pieces he sent to me in September, 1958, in reply to my offer of poetry to him, after he had made a brief visit to New Delhi and been entertained by my wife and me in my house. Let me quote what he has composed:

Verse One

I visited the ancestral house
Eight and twenty years from now.
You were just a bud, and
I, not much older a man.
Memories of the Eastern Hills
As if gathered only yesterday,
A happy though that thrills
Of new achievements already made.

Verse Two

I have from the inception
Adopted the world as home.
What a rare fortune to share here
My years with the near and dear!
I owe you and family many thanks
For delicious eats and *amrita* drinds,
And momentarily excited and happy
To become guest while in a great country.

Verse Three

Riding on the white horse I head
Towards the path trodden by old sages.
My great ambition yet to manifest.
Gone are the *Tripitakas* into antiquity,
Supplementaries necessary for posterity.
Who's ready to execute such task
To see moderns exceed men of the past?

Verse Four

Exciting moments atop holy mountains,
Long ago event now I reckon.
How many times have I stood on High
All surrounding scenes before the prying eyes?
Ler our *Ssha-lokadhatu* metamorphosize
Into the Pure-land *sukavati* paradise.
where the Western Wind may succumb
There the Eastern Wind blows strong.

When I go through these verses once again, memories of half a century emerges beginning from the beginning of the 1930s when I first met him in the Eastern Hills, when I accompanied him to the holy mountain of HengShen. That time, I was just a "bus", beginning to see the contours of the brave new world. The prying eyes of this marvellous young man had already visualized the Pureland *sukavati*. That was the kind of man Prof. Tan was. He was the rider of the "white horse" — a metaphor that can trace its genesis to the stories about Buddha's life with a white horse carrying Prince Siddhartha into the womb of Mayadevi, and once again carrying him out of the palace in quest of enlightenment. It was by no accident that the two first eminent Indian monks arrived in the Han imperial capital, Luoyang, by white horse during the reign of Han Emperor Ming in the first century. By identifying himself with this white horse image, Tan Yun-shan had unmistakably placed himself among the ranks of idealists. It was his quest for *sukavati* that had build up his life and career in India where he also breathed his last — a great fortune and honour cherished by many among his and my generations. Unfortunately, his ambition about adding supplementaries to make the Tripitaka relevant to the modern age has remained unfulfilled.

A man of modest experior cherishing great ambitions, Prof. Tan Yun-shan was not only a close relative of mine, but quite an inspiration to me. It was he who was instrumental to my departure from my motherland — China. While my steed, once set in motion, seemed never tired of galloping — from China to India, from India to Mexico, and then to USA — his white horse never carried him beyond the 'guest country'. According to Chinese tradition, he must have been some one who had reincarnated in China, and has reincarnations alternately in India and China eternally. He is truly the symbol of Sino-Indian amity and fraternity.

8

TAN YUN-SHAN: PERSONIFICATION OF RABINDRANATH'S VISVAKARMA

A hundred years have rolled on since the advent of Professor Tan Yun-shan (1898-1983); and admiring hearts, near and dear ones, are aspiring to cherish him afresh, in devout remembrance.

Rabindranath Tagore once felt not withstanding the intrinsic vigour of genius all around, commemorable are only those, who offer a whole life for consummation of a definite cause — a specific value. Rabindranath's, again, was a pivotal role in nurturing the unpreconceived blooming of Professor Tan Yun-shan, thoroughly consecrated to the enthralling cause of Sino-Indian cultural concord. The monumental edifice of the Cheena-Bhavana, at the heart of natural serenity of the Santiniketan Ashrama, still bears the eloquent exterior testimony to the innate vitality of that total dedication, all born in a meditative mind.

Professor Tan, in fact, flourished in a turmoiled juncture of modern China's history. Age-old lofty traditional values of all-found spiritual — certainly not all etherial — sustenance waned in utter material depredation; and western colonialists, with subverting designs, wrought havoc unabatedly. Rabindranath, even when comparatively young in age, scorned that perfidious onslaught in a remarkable paper: Cheen Maraner B yabasay' — Trade of Death in China.

During the maturing days of Tan Yun-shan and his contemporaries, a vibrant resurgence rebounded in the ancient land, with a newer conviction of emancipation. This time, exclusively mundane in nature. As a result at a particular level of youthful exuberance, a rebellious negation of the contemplative past, together with a vigorous craving for unmitigated techno-scientific progress, as of the modern age, gave vent to a confrontational atmosphere. Yet, the inlaid quest, even then, was for an assimilative consonance between the traditional fibre of the people and the newly usurping urge for unstinted corporeal advancement. Rabindranath himself, also got entangled, unknowingly, into that agitative jolt, during a visit to China, in 1924.

Tan Yun-shan, as of himself, was a visionary and an activist at the same time. He came in close contact with the Xinmin Association led by Mao Zedong and his comrades, cherishing a western intellectual proximity, particularly, then, with France. Equally, he was drawn to the world of eastern wisdom, that Rabindranath had been striving to renovate in the modern context, with its enduring lusture.

In 1924, Tan could not meet Rabindranath in the mainland. Yet, reverently, he noted the messages of the poet. In fact, at a stage, he of his own, thought of a voyage to India, before venturing for one to France. In the mean time, in 1927, he came in contact with Rabindranath, for the first time, at Singapore, where he happened to be a teacher then. The poet, quite impressed, invited him to Santiniketan, the seat of the newly sprouting university of his dream, where the world would meet in one nest. Tan responded in 1928; and the poet immediately offered him the Professorship of Sino-Indian Studies at his university. Gradually, the visionary-cum- activist in Tan got so usurped in the mission, that all other programmes, envisaged earlier, got abandoned, even unperceived. In fact, Tan got usurped by Rabindranath, and his vision.

That vision of the poet, of the universal mind commingling in the precincts of his budding institute, acquired its first dominant pragmatic exposition in the pursuit of Sino-Indian Studies, and Tan Yun-shan happened to be the lone architect.

Rabindranath was of the firm conviction that true knowledge emanates from within the life-spirit of the people; knowledge, that breathes the vibrant exposition of a people's collective wisdom, and not all a conglomeration of variously assorted informations. Knowledge in that perspective, is capable of stimulating a supraphysical — an innate cohesion between man and man, all the world over. Hence the poet contemplated that Visva-Bharati, the just originating university of his conception, would devote entirely to the study of that aspect of knowledge spiring out of the meditative acumen of the east. There, this nest of universal concord, would invite scholars from all parts of the world, irrespective of east or west, in a collaborative venture of a fresh appraisal and expansion of the wisdom.

In pursuit of the novel idea, Rabindranath comprehended study of Sino-Indian cultural relations as one of the focal themes. The message of universal compassion and love, as propagated by Buddha, was of supreme attraction to Rabindranath. That, again, had an all-found impact on the Southeast Asia of yore, as also on China, Tibet and others. In this context, cultural interaction between India and China had been most abiding through ages. Illustrious deliberations on Buddha's humanistic reflections had been translated, with indepth commentaries, from the languages of India into Chinese; and that instilled in the land, a special humane glow. There had been direct exchange of scholars as well. Yet, with the lapse of time, Buddha's message gradually got over-shadowed in its land of origin, and many an invaluable text vanished in the process. A vast treasure of enduring reflections indeed ! A lot of those, again, were retained, in translations, amongst others, in China. After centuries of oblivious secretion, a new urge for resuscitation emerged in the modern context; a new scope for Sino-Indian interaction at academic level; a melodious venture of reconstructing the lost original texts from translations, through a process of Interlocution. To that, Rabindranath added the new dimension of cultural amity and transfusion. This was the idea of replenishing a total image of the wisdom of the east as a bond of universal understanding, and amalgamation.

In fact, investigation into the new arena of oriental knowledge, commenced in the west also, almost around the same time. Rabindranath invited Professor Sylvain levy, the much adored sino-Indo-Tibetologist as the first Visiting Professor of his university. And thence commenced, in right earnest, a well orchestrated study in the verity of Sino-Indian cultural identity, in modern perspective. At the end of his short tenure, Professor Levi left behind a warm inquisitiveness for the quest, and Rabindranath was all the more eager to perpetuate the legacy. Yet, inconceivable resource crunch seriously impeded on the way. Only a course of Chinese language study could be organised for an intervenning short period, while the poet was eagerly looking for a permanent centre of Sino-Indian cultural study. In Tan Yun-shan he visualized the potential and vigour of fulfilment of his dearly cherished programme.

That the poet was not mistaken in his selection seldom was he so, if ever, is embalmed, even today, through the multifarious impressions of thoroughly dedicated flamboyant services of Tan Yun-shan. Cheena Bhavana, the celebrated centre of Sino-Indian cultural and academic collaboration at Visva-Bharati, was ushered in through unilateral contributions of most eminent Chinese personalities and scholars. And all that could be organized through unstinted, singular efforts of Professor Tan. As the solid structure of the Bhavana, so also commenced intimate inter-courses between Indian and Chinese scholars, and that continued with unabated enthusiasm. To start with, some one and a half lakh erudite volumes of Chinese books were procured from the mainland, and much had been added to the stock with progress of time. And today, that treasure of rare books, manuscripts and others is simply matchless in the academic domain of the discipline. And all these could be attained through the tireless endeavour of Professor Tan Yun-shan. Himself an unsparing ardent scholar, he organised a reverberating hub of radiant vibration between souls of India and China. And the process transcended the academic limits to encompass dignitaries like Chiang Kai-shek at one end and Jawaharlal Nehru at the other, Rabindranath being always at the centre.

All these, and many others, are records of history today; history, not only of Visva-Bharati, Santiniketan, but also of the Sino-Indian cultural relations prevailing through decades. And, so far, I have ventured to scrible a very inadequate outline of that.

But, my ovation, at the moment, seeks a much more intimate perspective; personal, indeed. I have the privilege of witnessing Professor Tan from close quarters, and yet, outside the orb of his inexorable, glorious, activities. He retired from Visva-Bharati services in 1967; and I joined the university just the following year, with a residential accommodation adjacent to that of the Professor, the only barrier being a thin flowery hedge, as usual of Santiniketan. Yet, the constructions were such that though the inner meadow of his quarters could be seen from mine, there was hardly any avenue for contacting that Way. A tiny lane had to be crossed, to be able to reach to his doorway. Inspite of a piquent desire to meet my venerable neighbour, from the very first day, I dared not quite for some time, lest my intrusion disturbed his normal routine.

At last, on a Wednesday morning, the weekly holiday of Visva-Bharati, I knowcked at his door. An attendant appeared and guided me to a big room, wide open on east and south, a sort of a one-in-all sitting-cum-bed-room, as well as a study-room. The Professor, a slim elegant figure, with his bright eyes and calm face, all dazzling in seducing smile, clasped both my hands with an inexplicable warmth of intimacy; and I got entranced immediately. We talked quite for some time; mine were short queries, his responses also were thoroughly prescise, yet complete. Soft and sweet spoken, he tried, always, to evade points leading to his remarkable success in career. He escorted me, finally, up to the gate, and I left charmed by the rare grace of his personality.

Within a few minutes of my returning home, came an attendant with a basketful of fresh vegetable grown in the kitchen garden of Madam Tan. We all were surprised, but learnt, instantly, that was an indispensable trait of Chinese hospitality; to entreat the guest with some endearing present. Madam Tan's was an equally fascinating, graceful role in the neighbourhood. She was 'a mother figure', all the houses around pertained to her household. And, we, the new comers, got automatically enrolled to that long list, since that day.

Gradually, I had occasions to come closer to Professor Tan, a self-absorbed, calm personality, and myself a thorough introvert. His residence, constructed out of the fund he collected for Cheena-Bhavana, was actually an annexe to the main building, just on the other side of the narrow lane. And he left that to be acquired by Visva-Bharati, after his demise. Quite a time, I could be with him, when the Cheena- Bhavana used to be humining in the midst of its daily routine work. I tried, often, to draw the Professor to a comparative deliberation on the plan and programme of the Bhavana, as envisaged by him, originally, and the contemporary exposition of the same. Every time, he skipped with soft, kindling smile, obviously to avoid any possible reference to self-appreciation. Instead, he often used to divert to topics relating his daily routine of the time; and they were no less attractive to me.

An early riser, he left his bed quite before dawn, undertook some open air exercises on the roof of his house or of the Cheena-Bhavana. I surmised those might have been of the traditional nature. Then, after bath, he offered solemn prayer, as I could gather from the evasive expressions, so wont with him. Finally, he prepared for the day's work. That, of course, was, mainly a deep, absorbed study. Once, he led me to an otherwise closed room in his quarters, which was adorned with piles of neatly arranged books, all over the spacious floor. Study, I felt, could be a meditative exercise in the environ. There was another room in the main building of the Bhavana, even more spacious, which served as the seat of the Professor's studies in seclusion. There, also, was an image of Buddha, I could trace, amongst heaps of books.

Professor Tan never could project himself in eloquent conspicuity, and preferred, ever, to keep mute in a self-receding abstraction. That's how I was led to draw my own inferences of what I saw and heard during those precious contacts.

And there, revealed to me a unique personality; a speechless, innate devotee of Buddha. Buddha, to Rabindranath, was the ideal man of his contemplation. And, there, not really abnegation of the world, but an ineffable compassion for mankind as a whole, was the true tenet. Time and again, my short-spanned contacts with Professor Tan Yun-shan, dragged me to the sprinkling reflections of the poet. What Buddha wanted to be renounced, I felt, was not the unfathomable world, but the very intricate self the avid self-interest of the individual man.

World, as it is, transpires, definitely, in man's perception. When man is dipped deep into self-indulgence, he cannot look beyond which is the immanent source of compassion. I wondered how ardently the Professor strove to build the edifice, not only of the solid construction of brick and mortar, but even more, one of illuminous love and compassion, through a deep bond of cultural knot. Yet, how unbelievably, he could withdraw himself, completely, from the apex of his lifelong glorious service. The whole Bhavana buzzed in exalting activities, and Tan Yun- shan, by no means, was to be duped, even for a moment, to peep into those enthralling scenes, cherished, so dearly, for a full life time. That, by no means, was any aversion, but a total self-withdrawal abnegation of self-interest and self-exertion, with a view to self-assumption to plunge into the core of universal compassion.

Even today, when I remember Professor Tan-Yun-shan, Rabindranath's vision of Man ushers within me; and I deem myself fortunate that I was given to witness a lively meaning of that inexplicable idea :-

"It is only when his [man'sl] efforts take him beyond all personal interests and the inertia of customary habit that he becomes 'Visvakarma', a world-worker. (It is only when his love transcends his self-seeking that man becomes 'mahatma' — great soul — through his relationship with all creatures."

Solemnly, I do salute that "Man", that "Visvakarma" — that "Mahatma", when I pay my humble homage remembering Professor Tan Yun-shan on the gracious occasion of his first birth centenary.

9

MY TRIBUTE TO TAN YUN-SHAN

The hall mark of history of Sino-Indian relations is cultural intercourse and affinity. The two great peoples, wedded to civilized living in the ways of peace, naturally find in the exchange of culture the truest expression of their being. Not for them the covetous eyes of rapacious plunder nor territorial aggrandizement.

Jawaharlal Nehru, the great statesman of Modern India, had this description for Sino-Indian intercourse in his broadcast from London on January 12, 1951 : "When we hark back to that long past [of Sino-Indian friendship] something of the wisdom of that past also helps us to understand each other." On another occasion, Nehru talked about the "thousands of golden links" that had bound the two peoples in the past.

Some of the actors of this moving history are well known, such as the legendary Chinese pilgrims Faxian and Xuanzang: some, such as Bodhidharma, deserve to be better-known; but one name stands out in contemporary history, and will become still better known as India and China settle down after their present years of social and economic transformation, that of Professor Tan Yun-shan, the revered Director of Cheena-Bhavana at Santiniketan for more than thirty eventful years, from 1937 till 1967.

Professor Tan was not only the Director of the Cheena-Bhavana: he was its inspiration and founder; it would not be too much to say that but for him it would not have come into being. Tan had been "discovered" by Tagore in Singapore in 1927. He was then only 29 years old, but Tagore saw in him the dedication, the empathy he was looking for; and at the young age of 30 Tan came to Visva-Bharati without his bride of two years to take over as Professor in charge of Chinese studies. Young in years he might have been, but he had already been teaching and writing in Malaya for more than four years. It was in Malaya that he had met his bride to be, Chen Naiwei, who had also come out from Hunan, Tan's own province, to serve as a teacher and principal of a school in Malaya. Except for brief interludes, Tan was to remain at Santiniketan for the next forty-four years.

During his absence from Santiniketan Tan was increasingly occupied with affairs of state, but running through all his activity one senses the *leit-motif* of Sino-Indian friendship. In 1931 he accompanied a special Chinese government mission to Tibet when he delivered letters from that government to the 13th Dalai Lama. The Dalai Lama asked him to convey his blessings to Mahatma Gandhi. This Tan did in person when he met Gandhiji in Sabarmati in April the same year. Tan and the Mahatma talked about India and China; and the subject of India-China relations was also the subject he was to discuss subsequently with other leaders of India, such as Jawaharlal Nehru, Subhas Chandra Bose, Dr. Rajendra Prasad, Dr. S. Radhakrishnan and of course, Rabindranath Tagore.

For some time, Tan shuttled between Shanghai and Nanjing (the Chinese capital), putting into service all his persuasive power, calling on his compatriots to reenact the historic pilgrimage that saw eminent Chinese monk-scholars in their quest for Buddha Dharma from the "Western Heaven" i.e. India. 1933 saw the light of realization of one of Tagore's dreams when Tan was able to report that, after two years of shuttling back and forth between Shanghai and the capital Nanjing, he was in a position to establish formally the Sino-Indian Cultural Society in Nanjing. This had won the powerful support of Tsai Yuan-Pei, President of the Academia Sinica, and Tai Chi-tao, President of the Examination Yuan, equivalent to India's UPSC. In fact, Tsai Yuan-pei was the first President of the Society with Tan as its Secretary.

But Tan did not rest on his laurels. After a brief visit to Santiniketan in 1934, he returned to China and for the next two years gathered support there for the Cheena-Bhavana to be established in Santiniketan. His efforts were marked with success for he returned to Santiniketan in 1936 with Rs. 50,000, a not inconsiderable sum those days, and one hundred thousand books for Cheena-Bhavana. Tagore was thrilled, allotted the best plot of land for Cheena-Bhavana and requested Tan to have it built. This Tan did, personally supervising every detail, from the blueprint to the laying of bricks and the planting of trees. This hallowed testimony to Sino-Indian friendship, one of the most impressive buildings in Santiniketan, was completed with frescoes painted by Nandalal Bose and inscribed with Chinese calligraphy by the President of China, Lin Sen, to which was added, a few years later, the fine specimen of Chinese writing of Tai Chi-tao. The Bhavana was inaugurated by Tagore. Nehru could not attend on account of illness, but Gandhiji sent a message: "May the Chinese Hall be a symbol of living contact between China and India." This it truely became, with Tan, its first Director, continuing to collect support and funds from China for salaries and scholarships.

With the naked Japanese aggression unleashed upon China, Tan's role in public affairs became ever more exigent. Towards the end of 1937 Nehru wrote to him that the Congress would boycott Japanese goods in India; in 1938, just before Tan left on a visit to China, Nehru wrote him again, asking him to convey India's support to the Chinese people during the anti-Japanese war. This was followed by a letter from Tagore to Chiang Kai-shek, to be delivered in person by Tan, assuring Chiang of India's support to China in resisting Japanese aggression, and a letter from Subhas Chandra Bose, asking Tan to convey Congress' support to China in the war. Tagore's letter was delivered directly by Tan to Chiang; and within a week a letter of thanks from Chiang was despatched to Tagore.

On his return to India in 1939, Tan busied himself in promoting visits between the two countries. With the help of the Sino-Indian Cultural Society, Nehru's visit to China was organised between the 20th August and the 6th September. On the eve of Nehru's departure Tan had sent a telegram to Chiang informing him of the exact date of Nehru's arrival. In 1940 and 1941 Tan was instrumental in arranging visits to India of a Chinese Buddhist delegation led by the Rev. Tai Hsu and the visit of Dr. Tai Chi-tao. In 1942 came the visit to India of Generalissimo Chiang Kai-shek and Madam Chiang. They visited Santiniketan and made a donation to Cheena Bhavana; and, although India was not yet free of British rule, Tan was able to arrange a series of meetings between Chiang and Nehru. This could not but have a profound influence on the thinking of both men, on the one about India's independence and on the other about China and the war. Lest Chiang harboured any fears that India's struggle for independence would impede the war effort, Nehru got Gandhiji to send Chiang the assurance that "whatever action I may recommend will be governed by the consideration that it should not injure China ..... and ..... must lead to the strengthening of India's and China's defence."

For his tireless efforts, Tan was awarded the Victory Medal in 1945 by the Chinese government. The same year he went back to China with his wife to found the Datong school at Changsha, but he was back again in Santiniketan in 1948 in continuous pursuance of the added responsibility which had come along with the eminently appropriate title of China's "Cultural Representative", already bestowed on him at the time when China appointed its first ambassador to independent India. Why not "Cultural ambassador," one wonders. Perhaps protocol came in the way but, protocol or no protocol, Nehru, now Prime Minister, wrote to Tan, "I hope that with your assistance and advice we shall develop further cultural contacts with China."

But it was more than cultural affairs that Tan found himself drawn into. Years earlier, in the days of his youth in the early 1920s in Changsha, he had joined the progressive students' movement when he was pursuing his studies both at the first Normal School and at the Chuanshan Academy. The movement had been led by Mao Zedong, several years his senior at both the Normal School and Chuanshan. Now, almost three decades later, Tan wrote to his former acquaintance Mao, advising, firstly, that China should not lean to one side or the other; secondly, that Sino-Indian friendship be strengthened; and, thirdly, that the Taiwan issue be settled peacefully. As, unfortunately, the border situation between India and China took a turn for the worse, one notices a flurry of activity on Tan's part. In September 1956 he was invited to visit China where he met in Beijing Mao and other Chinese leaders, former teachers and fellow-students. In January 1957 he was instrumental in getting Premier Zhou Enlai to visit Santiniketan where Zhou received an honorary degree. Zhou also visited Cheenas Bhavana and decided on a donation of funds and books. Early in 1958 Tan was received by President Dr. Rajendra Prasad in Delhi and again in September, 1959, just before Tan left for China at the invitation of the Chinese government. In his 1959 visit, he had several rounds of discussion with Premier Zhou and followed these up with discussions with Prime Minister Nehru on his return to India in 1960. But political events moved to their tragic denouement and when, at the Santiniketan Convocation in December 1962, Nehru spoke about the border-war but, seeing Tan, added immediately that the people of China would always be India's friends, Tan was overcome by emotion and could not withhold his tears.

In 1967 Tan retired from Visva-Bharati but continued to live at Santiniketan. In the twelve yeras left to him he still busied himself with matters close to his heart, for we find him engaged in preparations for the establishment of the World Buddhist Academy at Bodhgaya and he visited Hong Kong and Singapore to collect donations for this purpose. His work at Visva-Bharati, already acclaimed by those who knew, found formal recognition in the award to him in 1979 of Visva-Bharati's highest academic award Deshikottama. Perhaps it was political vicissitudes that had delayed an honour which, one feels, should have been his much earlier, but at least one must be glad that his wife lived to see it, before her death in 1980.

Professor Tan Yuan-shan passed away at Bodhgaya in 1983. Fate, one thinks, showed a nice sense of understanding in choosing Bodhgaya as the final resting-place of one who had studied Buddhism under Rev. Tai-hsu, the leading Chinese exponent of Buddhism in his time, and who had spent so much of his life in sylvan Santiniketan. As a matter of fact, when Tan first saw the sacred seat where Gautama Buddha had attained Bodhi under the Bodhi-Tree behind the imposing Mahabodhi Temple at Bodhgaya in 1931, he could not suppress his excitement, and violated the decorum by sitting on it with closed eyes, praying for a long while. Inspite his frail health in his last years, of nothing could separate him from Bodhgaya, and his eldest son, Prof. Tan Chung, had a tough time to take him away to Santiniketan and Delhi to replenish his much exhausted body. On his death Prime Minister Indira Gandhi said in her condolence message, "Gurudeva and my father had affection and regards for him. He identified himself with Santiniketan and contributed immensely to a better understanding between the civilisations of India and China." This was the least that could be said of one who devoted his life to understanding between the two countries. Both countries must regard it as most fortunate that they have in his son, Dr. Tan Chung, now Professor-Consultant at the Indira Gandhi National Centre for the Arts in New Delhi after his retirement from Jawaharlal Nehru University as Professor of Chinese, one who carries on that proud legacy.

10

FOLLOW THE FOOTSTEPS OF SAVANTS: PROMOTE DEEPER UNDERSTANDING AND GREATER PARTNERSHIP BETWEEN INDIA AND CHINA

The year 1998 has ushered in many birth centenaries. Four are related to the development of relations between India and China. Born a hundred years ago in China were Zhou Enlai and Tan Yun-shan; and in India were P.C. Bagchi and K.P.S. Menon. Tan Yun-shan and P.C. Bagchi were the pioneers in Sino-Indians studies advocated by India's first Nobel laureate, Rabindranath Tagore. K.P.S. Menon was the first Indian Ambassador to China. I have the honour of succeeding that post vacated by him and a dozen of his successors. I and many others who held that office had shared his enthusiasm and enjoyment in building up bridges between the two great civilizations of the world. Zhou Enlai, of course, belonged to another category. I was still a student when he started visiting India renewing friendly contacts with Indians who had not long ago attained independence of their motherland. I am glad to know from my good friend, Prof. Tan Chung, that his father, Prof. Tan Yun-shan, was consulted by Zhou Enlai on how to improve relations with India. It was Tan Yun-shan's suggestion that has brought the Chinese Premier to Santiniketan in 1957 to receive an honorary degree from Tagore's university, Visva-Bharati. It is both rare that Visva-Bharati confers an honour on a foreign politician, and a Chinese leader of Zhon Enlai's stature arriving in India to receive an academic degree from an Indian University.

Many Indians know the illustrious family of Tan Yun-shan which has made India its second home. My connection with this family is cemented by a personal friendship between me and the Tan couple, Tan Chung and Ishu, with whom I started my acquaintance in early 1960s after I had just returned to New Delhi from my diplomatic assignment in Beijing. Both of them were the pioneers in setting up a Department of Chinese Studies in Delhi University. Tan Chung and his colleague used to hold a regular small group discussion on China's current developments, and I used to attend whenever I could take time off from the South Block (where the Foreign Office is). In one session, I was struck by Tan Chung's candid talk describing Jawaharlal Nehru as a Sinophile. It was then that he revealed the intimate relationship between Nehru and his father Tan Yun-shan.

A vivid case demonstrating Nehru's regard for Tan Yun-shan was in difficult times when he addressed the Visva-Bharati convocation at Santiniketan on December 24, 1962. The bitter memory of the Sino-Indian boundary war was just fresh, and Nehru was very hurt and wanted to vent his strong sentiments against the Chinese government. But, he spotted Prof. Tan Yun-shan in the audience with white Indian dress sitting on the ground like a Buddha. His heart melted. Before he started criticizing China, he began by these words :

In the Visva-Bharati ..... you have got various departments. You have got the Cheena-Bhavan under a distinguished Chinese scholar [Tan Yun-shan]. That is a good thing to remind you always that you are not at war with China's culture or the greatness of China in the past or present. (See *Jawaharlal Nehru's Speches*, vol. 4, p. 27.)

After hearing this, warm tears gushed out from Prof. Tan's solemn face, and he immediately caught the limelight of the media. The episode was reported by all major newspapers the next day. I think it remarkable that when bilateral relations between India and China fell to the nadir such an exhibition of soft and kind affection between the two great civilizations occurred. This all the more places Tan Yun-shan at the centre of cultural relationship between India and China.

In history we have many such touching stories between Indians and their Chinese brethren. We have the story of the Chinese emperor of Houqin named Yao Xing (reigning from 394 to 415) who admired Kumarajiva's genius so much that he even resorted to blasphemy to get the Indian saint to leave a number of progeny behind in China after he attained his *nirvana.* When the great Chinese pilgrim, Xuanzang, made it known to his colleagues at the Nalanda Buddhist University his intentions to return to China, the Indian monk-scholars did not want to miss him and tried their level best to persuade him to stay. Then, Xuanzang asked and extracted an answer from those who deeply loved him that even the sun had to travel to bring light to all the dark corners of the world, and he begged support from those much endeared fellow-Buddhists for his returning to his country to spread Buddha's enlightenment to the vast areas of darkness and ignorance.

But, Tan Yun-shan, the modern Xuanzang, had far exceeded Xuanzang's 15 year pilgrimage to India. Tan was teaching in Singapore for a number of years and Tagore was visiting Singapore. Tan was invited to Santiniketan in 1927 by Tagore when the two met there. He promptly arrived at Santiniketan the next year.

From 1928 to 1983 (when he breathed his last at Bodhgaya), he had virtually stayed in Santiniketan (and also Bodhgaya) all his life with occasional sojourns to China, that, too, to get support for his work and career in India. When he first arrived, he came alone leaving a newly married bride behind in Malaya. Although Tan was immediately appointed as a "Professor" by Tagore, he drew no pay from Visva-Bharati which was practically an ashram, and an extended family gathering of dedicated scholars around the "Gurudeva" (Tagore) to build up an international commonwealth which is suggested by the name "Visva-Bharati". Tan Yun-shan (then only 30) partook in this spiritual atmosphere of service, sacrifice and dedication while his new wife slogged in Malaya to send him financial support. Then, there was the well-known story of Tan's shuttling between Santiniketan and Nanjing-Shanghai to get Tagore's dream realized. It was by Tan Yun-shan's sheer personal persuasion that he got Tagore's long cherished Sino-Indian Cultural Society formed with eminent scholarly support from China, and subsequently got a handsome donation from Chinese leaders and government to have the Cheena-Bhavana built at Santiniketan and sustained for 12 years without asking for a penny from Tagore and Visva-Bharati. Prime Minister Nehru knew all the, details from the beginning. That was why he spoke with so much emotion about Cheena-Bhavana and Tan Yun-shan (without naming him) at the convocation when he was at the height of his anger and anguish about what had happened between India and China.

So, Tan Yun-shan's modern pilgrimage to India is very different from Xuanzang's in the 7th century. While Xuanzang spent all his post-pilgrimage life spreading Buddha's messages among the Chinese, and building up a sound intellectual and emotional friendship between the two civilizations on the soil of China, Tan Yun-shan's pilgrimage to India has extended to the life and careers of his children in spreading information and insight about China among Indians, and sound intellectual and emotional friendship between the two civilizations on the soil of India. In my limited contacts with Indian educational institutions from the Ministry of External Affairs, I could feel the impact of Tan Yun-shan and also his extended pilgrimage carried on by his eldest son, Tan-Chung from strength to strength. It is, like Nehru said in 1962, the spiritual bonds that Tan Yun-shan and his family struck with Tagore and the disciples and followers of Tagore at Santiniketan for many decades that has reminded India that we are never at war with China's culture or the greatness of China in the past or present, or even future.

Immediately after Independence, Nehru and other Indian leaders sent a message to the entire world that India wanted to be friends with all, and enemy to none. I joined my IFS colleagues from 1959 onwards to spread this message wherever I was posted. I have learnt from experience that it is easier to make enemies than making friends. There is so much ego, selfishness, suspicion, jealousy, and enmity among humans that only those who are honest, unselfish, dedicated, sincere, generous to others and treat others as their own near and dear can win trust and friendship. I have come across so many such people in my three-and-half decades of diplomatic career, and many of them are Chinese. There is a lot in common between the peoples of India and China. We have in our blood a thick cultural sediment which, sometimes, prevent us from knee-jerk reactions and a quick change of faces as if changing masks. Again, both the peoples have immense endurance and toleration, capable of absorbing shocks and sufferings. Even when I was in China during the days of tension and mutual distrust I discovered the innate affection and friendship on the part of Chinese people for India and the Indian people. My life-long experience of a diplomat also tells me that apart from a handful of us who are ambassadors accredited by the government, there are innumerable cultural ambassadors among the people who come to play the bridge-role on their own volition without accreditation and unmindful of reward. Such cultural ambassadors can easily put to shame some professional diplomats whose covetous self-serving is unproportionately greater than their devotion to duty — to the cause of building friendly bridges between nations. It is such an experience that has made me admire the cultural ambassadors.

Tan Yun-shan should be remembered as a cultural ambassador of the highest stature. Throughout his life he had spent time and energy to serve others. I am told that he had great talent in writing in both classical and modern Chinese, both poetry and prose. But, he sacrificed his own chances of becoming a great writer to facilitate others to achieve in knowledge and scholarship. Yet, the greatness of Tan Yun-shan did not lie in his self-sacrifice only. He had an unusual conviction in human kindness, in forging a synthesis between all the noble values of the civilizations of India and China. I was invited to Tan Chung's house many times, and saw hanging on the wall his father's fine calligraphy framed in a "Sino- Indian Motto" (Zhong-Yin zhenming). I tried to decipher those seal-script characters quoting Confucian teachings of "Li de li yan" (establishing one's virtue and also one's speech), and the Buddhist preaching of "Jiu ren jiu shi" (rescuing others and also the human kind). I, then, realized that what had attracted Tan Yun-shan to settle down in India, particularly at a place like Santiniketan where life was spartan, was not India's want of luxuries and material facilities, but her spiritual greatness and high thinking. It was not for nothing that on the Visva-Bharati campus Tan Yun-shan was revered as the "Chinese sage".

From what little I know about the nature and character of this "Chinese sage", I am greatly impressed that although he had attended innumerable Chinese banquets in the exalted company of VVIPs, Tan Yun-shan was basically a vegetarian, and his favourite things to eat throughout his life were sweet-potatoes and monkey -nuts. In Santiniketan, sitting on the floor without shoes was the daily practice. Many Indians much younger than Tan Yun-shan could not feel comfortable after a while, while Tan remained motionless for hours in the pose of (lion's sitting) like the Indian deities. I am also impressed by the fact that Tan Yun-shan had, in late life, styled himself as *"Ksantyrishi"* (renxian) which meant the saint who could tolerate all humiliations and outrages. This needs an enormous spiritual power which even escapes very great personalities whose public image is one thing and private life is another. No one, even his children, had seen Tan Yun-shan flared up. His children testify that on no occasion did their father lose his cool. I know from my own family tradition that to win universal admiration in India one needs not only to have a fine mind, but also an exemplary personal behaviour at any time and place. Tan Yun-shan belonged to this precious category, hence his "sage" image. Tan was, of course, not the only Chinese who had adopted India as his homeland. Many other Chinese have done so in Calcutta and other Indian cities. But as a Chinese who could be regarded as a sage in his adopted land — India — Tan Yun-shan has stood alone without match.

Culture is created by humans, and there can be a great culture only when there is a great people. Tan Yun-shan personifies the great people and great culture of China beyond doubt. But, he had enjoyed in his own personal cultivation the inspiration of many an Indian great man, like Gurudeva Tagore, Mahatma Gandhi, and Sri Aurobindo with all of whom Tan had maintained personal contacts. Thus, Tan Yun-shan was the embodiment of the virtues of both the Chinese and Indian cultures which, I think, is a rare feat, unachieveable by ordinary souls. Today, when we commemorate the birth centenary of Tan we must see that such a fine example gets multiplied in dozens, hundreds, and thousands. We must see that every Indian and every Chinese reflect the good points of their own cultural traditions first, and then absorb each other's admirable cultural traditions. This would require that the peoples of India and China enhance their mutual understanding, and promote their cultural synergy. Against the background of universal moral degeneration, if not decadence of our times, such a coming together by Indians and Chinese to uphold the highest spiritual standards and moral values is absolutely necessary. Only in this manner can the two nations enter the new century and new millennium as the frontline members of the world commity.

Prof. Tan Yun-shan has left us for 15 years now and during these 15 years much water has flowed down the Ganga and Yangtse. As the Chinese leaders are fond of saying, we are faced with great opportunities and great challenges. Opportunities are plentiful after the end of the Cold War and the universe is sailing into a new culture of dialogue, accommodation, engagement, cooperation, and genuine peaceful coexistence. Opportunities lie before the two nations as all countries, all nations, and all peoples are greeted by the incoming new revolution of humanity, i.e. the information technology and soft culture without universal discrimination and externally imposed handicaps. Challenges we face because both India and China are still in the developing stage, and it is a herculean task for the two billion people of India and China to catch up with the advanced science and technology which climb to higher classes and generations not in the courses of centuries or decades, but in every few years, even few months. Without catching up with the frontline achievements of humanity, India and China will not become the frontline countries for sure. Thus, we need to emulate the tenacity of Tan Yun- shan to create institutions and provide facilities for the talents. We need the example of Tan to shine upon the future Sino-Indian relations to build up a partnership of synergy. India and China should and could throw up more bridges like Tan Yun-shan, and cross the bridges to march together into the future.

11

MY TRIBUTE TO PROFESSOR TAN YUN-SHAN

Let me express my profound sense of appreciation to the distinguished sons and daughters of Professor Tan for organizing their father's birth centenary. Sincere congratulations for taking this commendable initiative.

Professor Tan has been and will be recognized as the living symbol of Sino-Indian friendship. Cheena-Bhavana remains and will constantly remind us for years to come the eternal ties that bind the two countries together, namely India and China. The Sino-Indian Cultural Society, now defunct, will continue to inspire the posterity with a great ideal of human endeavour to bring together two peoples with similar aspirations.

This birth centenary celebration of Professor Tan, in my humble opinion, is also an occasion for introspection. It gives us an opportunity to reflect and reassess the true value of our dreams we cherished for a long time and reaffirm our faith not only in the noble mission of fostering Sino-Indian amity for which Professor and Madam Tan strove and made great sacrifices, but also in some eternal verities of humanity which shaped those noble ideals like peace, harmony and compassion.

For me, Professor Tan was primarily a teacher in the noble sense of the term. No wonder, this great ideal of a true teacher closely resembled in both ancient India and China. Professor Tan's life demonstrates this noble ideal in action. Indeed, he practised what he taught. His compassion and affection for his students will never be forgotten and will remain an inspiration for those who follow his line.

I think Professor Tan imbibed some of the great ideals of both China and India in a very realistic and pragmatic way. In him I found a very refined blending of Confucian, Taoist and Budhist traditions. In our conversation it was hard to distinguish between various schools of thought, because in the ultimate analysis they tend to merge into the great ocean of humanity. The most remarkable feature of his personality was that he became spiritually an Indian without losing his Chinese identity. His personality was very classical in the real sense. At the same time he had an enormous strength of character to constantly welcome and practise in his own life the path of Mahatma Gandhi and the humanistic ideals of Poet Tagore. He never ceased to be active. A time came when he realized, in my opinion, that his active role of building in Santiniketan had been complete, he decided to move on to Bodh Gaya to initiate yet another noble dream of his life -- the World Buddhist Academy. I have noticed the foundations of both Cheena-Bhavana and World Buddhist Academy are really strong (both physically and spiritually). Obviously after the demise of Professor Tan, the functioning of the Academy suffered a lot, but that does not take away the value of that great ideal that worked behind its creation. The spirit of Professor Tan's relentless efforts to implement great ideas will never fade.

Today by paying tribute to the sacred memory of Professor Tan we are in fact honouring our own ideals and noble missions which always guide and provide light to the wayfarer in the midst of darkness.

12

REMEMBERING PROFESSOR TAN YUN-SHAN

I, as a raw young man, joined the Visva-Bharati Cheena-Bhavana in 1942. The Professor slowly and steadily moulded me through a new channel, taught me Chinese language, directed me in studying the Chinese Classics, sent me to China and got me appointed as the first Indian Professor on Hindi and Indian Culture in the Oriental Languages College at Kunming. Since then till today, my life's entire activities have been centralised and concentrated to materialise his cherished dreams, to promote the cause of Sino-Indian Cultural relations. He has the habit of penetrating so deeply in his students that every one of them will proudly confess, "His thoughts are our ideas, his programme is our programme and he is the only source of inspiration for us." He is second only to men like Jesus and Ramakrishna in his singular devotion and unlimited affection for his diciples. He often tells, "My students are my only hope and capital." Immortal are those words uttered by his noble lips in his characteristic low and ringing strong voice. "My boys, mark my words. From the cultural union of India and China will spring forth a spiritual awakening a spiritual light and this spiritual force alone can save the humanity from the impending annihilation and total destruction. Our ambassadors were men like Kumarajiva and Huen-Tsang, Lmmortal blossoms of the humanity in every sense. They are almost worshipped even today and what are the achievements of these present day political ambassadors! We will have to follow the footsteps of Kumarajiva to complete his unfinished work." He as a matter of principle, never gives much importance to men of knowledge. For him, men of devotion to the cause, the ideal and the programme are the real power. He used to say a critic co-worker is a dangerous hindrance in any work.

The Professor made Santiniketan his home. The Visva-Bharati Cheena-Bhavana at Santiniketan is his life's monumental work. For him, Gurudeva was not merely a master or a father but in true sense a God. The research department of the Visva-Bharati Cheena-Bhavana is one of the most outstanding centres of Oriental Learning of the entire Asia. Indian monks who went to China in ancient days took with them thousands of Sanskrit classics. They, there, studied the Chinese language and translated all those Sanskrit books into Chinese. Such Chinese books are now held like the Upanishads by the Chinese people. Now in India these Sanskrit texts are not available. The Professor brought all such Chinese books into the Visva-Bharati Cheena-Bhavana and it is his life's sacred dream to translate all such books into Sanskrit again. It will take hundreds of years to complete this great work for such is the vast volume of books he brought and collected in the Cheena-Bhavana Library at Santiniketan.

The Professor is now completing thirty years of his selfless service in India. It is the sacred duty of every one of us in India to pray for a long life for this great self-appointed Chinese Cultural Ambassador in India. His life will become one of the brilliant chapters of Sino-Indian Cultural History.

13

LONELY TRAVELLER

The measure of the vigour of a culture is the capacity to nourish individuals who can embrace the `beyond' without loosing their own; who can see in the mirror of "other" cultures the humanist essence of their own culture. Chinese culture has undoubtedly nourished many such individuals; but to us in India, it is the name of Prof. Tan Yun-shan which looms like a shining star. On the occasion of the opening ceremony of Cheena Bhavan (Chinese Hall), as part of Visva-Bharati University Santiniketan, Prof. Tan remined the audience of the Statement of Dr. Sun Yat-sen, the founder of modern China, to the effect that all the depressed nations in the East, specially India and China, must be naturally sympathetic towards one another and must cooperate in striving together for the common objective. Amplifying this statement Prof. Tan observed "By Cooperation and striving together, we do not mean any such alliance or league as those so-called modern powers and Eastern and Western imperialists have made to crush the weak and plunder them outright. We simply join in our mutual sympathy and love. We simply strive for our own equality and freedom. We will never stand against the good of any country and people."

Speaking about Prof. Tan Yun-shan himself, the Chinese scholar W. Pachow observed. "He always advocated the spiritual culture of China and India, and wished that the two peoples get a good example in their modern practice for other nations to emulate. In this way, confict and war could be eliminated, and world peace prevail. Human kind would enter the *datong utopia* in which the people could sleep at night with their doors open, and wealth would scatter on the roads without anyone claiming it as his/her private property, or the world would become a *Sukhavati* in which the people would live amidst charming music and fragrant flowers, without desire, greed, hatred and conflict. Prof. Tan was such a visionary whose vistas did not limit within the boundries of Sino-Indian Culture, but enhancing the prospects of the happiness of entire humanity."

I had the privilege of enjoying the affection of prof. Tan in the late 1970s, when I joined Visva-Bharati as Professor of Anthropology. It was four decades too late. In the 1930s, as a restless adolescent, I was extremely unhappy at the act of aggression Japan was perpetrating on China. My imagination, as that of many others of my generation, was fired when on the initiative of Jawaharlal Nehru a medical mission from India left for China. I wanted to reach China and give a good fight to the Japanese. But also I thought I must make some preparation before starting the one-man mission to China. I had heard about Prof. Tan and his Centre for Chinese Studies in Santiniketan, one of the items in my agenda was to meet him. But I did not do it. Perhaps prudence had the better of the enthusiasm. I ran away from my home and could manage to reach only upto Burma, where I was located by the Burmese police and sent back home.

When I joined Visva-Bharati, Prof. Tan was not permanently living there. He was spending some time at Bodhgaya where he wanted to build up a World-Buddhist Academy. During one of his prolonged visits to Santiniketan, my wife who was attached to Cheena Bhavan for her post-doctoral work on Tibet, came in contact with him. Some how she felt that he was a lonely traveller in a mindless crowd. On her invitation Prof. Tan and Mrs. Tan visited us at our house. During our discussion I told him about my adolescent chivalrous venture to assist China in her fight to maintain her freedom. Prof. Tan savvied an amused smile but quietly placed his hand on my shoulder. I knew he conveyed to me the muse of his soul. After that we met several times. From Bodhgaya he wrote to me to be a member of the Council of the World Buddhist Academy he was planning to set up. I felt greatly honoured and readily responded.

Though Prof. Tan weighed down by age, had formally relinquished the charge of Cheena Bhawan in 1967 to all of us he embodied the spirit of the institution. But he represented more. He was the symbol of the intellectual-spiritual universal brotherhood that Rabindranath Tagore, the activist poet ried to create at Santiniketan. There were many at Santiniketan who thought that Tagore's was a failed experiment. But Prof. Tan was an incorrigible optimist. His frail body carried an iron will. During his visits to Santiniketan, in his characteristic mild manner he always conveyed the massage: there may be temporary set-backs, but in the aeon of time there is nothing called defeat for any authentic endeavour in the journey towards a common human presence.

In our paying homage to the memory of Prof. Tan Yun-shan we actually renew our pledge to ourselves to be active partisans in the struggle for creating a universal one-ness of freedom and peace. If we are there, truly to ourselves, the `others' are truly with us; If `others' are there true to their-selves the truth of us, resides in them. Prof. Tan might or might not have spoken this in so many words; but his life, his living in manking, is an affirmation of this.

14

MY ETERNAL MEMORY OF PROF. TAN YUN-SHAN

I deem it a great honour to be invited to contribute an article in commemoration of the Birth Centenary of Prof. Tan Yun-Shan which falls on October 10, 1998.

My relationship with Prof. Tan covers a period of almost four decades and a half. At the time I was a student at the Maha Bodhi Sciety, Sarnath near Varanasi, India.

Prof. Tan, with the blessings of the then fore-front leaders of India such as Mahatma Gandhi, Rabinadranath Tagore and Jawaharlal Nehru, founded Cheena-Bhavana as a faculty in the Visva-Bharati University. Cheena-Bhavana, devoted to the promotion of Sino-Indian cultural friendship and understanding, was under the management and direction of Prof. Tan.

Sarnath, the place where the Buddha preached His first sermon, is one of the Holy Sites of the Buddhist World. Here stands the well-known Buddhist Temple, Mulagandhakuti Vihara, built several decades ago by the Venerable Anagarika Dhasmapala, Founder of the Maha Bodhi Society of Sri Lanka and India. Every year, in the month of November, Buddhists from far and near, gather at Sarnath to celebrate the inauguration of the temple.

So far as I can recollect, I had the good luck to meet Prof. Tan some time in 1938 at Sarnath. The prof. went there to participate in the temple celebration. I expressed my desire to him to join the Visva-Bharati University for advanced studies in Sanskrit and Indology. The good-hearted Prof. readily agreed to do what he could for me.

Early in 1939, I received a call from the Prof. to be admitted to Cheena-Bhavana, Visva-Bharati University.

Thus began my association with Prof. Tan whom the inmates of Visva-Bharati University used to call reverentially "The Chinese Sage of Santiniketan."

Under the guidance of Pandit Sujit Kumar Mukhopaddhya, staff-member of Cheena-Bhavana and a Bengali Brahmin well-versed in Sanskrit learning, I pursued my studies most profitably at Santiniketan till the Japanese War broke out on December 8, 1941. On January 25, 1942, Thailand, occupied by Japanese Forces, declared war on Great Britain.

On February 8, 1942, I was arrested and interned in Civilian Internment Camp at Purana Qilla, New Delhi, and later on at Deoli Camp, Rajasthan, till the Japanese War ended in 1945. The reason for my internment was because I was a national of Thailand which declared war on Great Britain; those days India was a part of the British Empire.

After the war I was repatriated to Thailand, my mother country. The Prof. in India and I in Thailand, however, kept on writing to each other.

In the middle of 1973 Prof. Tan visited Thailand and spent several days in Bangkok. I introduced him to several local Chinese Buddhist Organisations where the Prof. delivered learned lectures on Indian culture and learning.

I would be untrue to myself if I do not put on record here the fact that both during the time I was in Santiniketan and even while an internee during the war, I received so much kindness, both material and moral, from the "Chinese Sage of Santiniketan".

* The writer, now aged 78, was an alumnus of Cheena-Bhavana, Rabindranath Tagore's Visva-Bharati University at Santiniketan.

Yes, in my case, the proverb "Friends in need are friends indeed" proved fully valid !

In 1981 my wife and I went to India on a pilgrimage to various Buddhist holy places. We stopped at Bodhgaya where the Prof. was busy with the World Buddhist Academy of which he was the founder. To our own observation the Prof. was, no doubt, advanced in age but not quite infirm as yet. Little did we realise that would be our last chance to see the noble-hearted scholar in person.

To our endless grief and sorrow, one day we received a message from India that Professor Tan Yun-Shan, the Chinese savant who had devoted his life to the cause of Sino-Indian cultural friendship, breathed his last on ...February 12....., 1983.

``Rupam jirati maccanam

Namarupam na jirati."

``Human bodies perish

But not their names and lineages."

(A Pali buddhist Saying)

15

PROFESSOR TAN YUN-SHAN AS I KNEW HIM

Soon after joining the Visva-Bharati University in 1962 I had heard of Professor Tan Yun-shan who was the main figure of Chinese Studies at Visva-Bharati, then. Fortunately I was invited by him for a tea party. Finally, a smiling sober gentleman received me saying "Welcome Lama Chimpa!" on my bowing down to him, "I am Tan Yun-shan, living here, looking after this Cheena-Bhavana for a long time." Then he introduced me to Madam Tan who was as dignified as Professor Tan himself. Both of them talked nicely as if they were talking to a highly eminent person. Being much junior to them I felt ashamed and could not say much. Madam Tan told me about the difficulties to live in Santiniketan. She and Professor Tan reached Santiniketan by bullock cart from Bolepur and she used to go to Bolepur, a small township three miles away from Santiniketan just to buy some vegetables, on foot. "But now we are very happy, we can ride a rickshaw wherever we go, because of the newly constructed road by the West Bengal Government, one can even drive a car."

At that time there was not a single car to be seen in Santiniketan. While I was listening to the senior couple their younger children walked very well mannered and disciplined in their behaviour. Like their parents the children were so simple, having no sign of being the children of a great man. One girl about 18 years wearing a locally made cotton sari, barefooted, came to me, bowed down touching my feet. Madam Tan said: "This is my daughter Tan Wen, quite good in her studies." Later on I read in newspapers that she stood first in Bengali literature in the entire university. Yes, not only Tan Wen, but all of her sisters and brothers have distinguished themselves in their studies. On my departure Professor Tan said: As a new comer let me tell you that you must speak less and that will make your stay here in Santiniketan very happy."

The English Buddhists monk Sangharakshita remembered Professor Tan in his book "*In the Sign of the Golden Wheel*" (Windhorse Publications, Birminghan, 1996, p. 47):

> "Professor Tan Yun-shan wore the traditional black dress of the Chinese scholar. He had been at Cheena-Bhavana since its earliest days, having in fact been responsible for starting the school and being, even now, the moving spirit behind the place. He had started it with support of General Chiang Kai-shek and his Kuomintaug Government. With the defeat of Chiang and the Nationalist forces by the Communists in 1949, and the former's withdrawal to Taiwan, Professor Tan had lost that support, and the nature of Cheena-Bhavan's position in relation to the government of the People's Republic was unclear. Indeed, like that of many overseas Chinese, Professor Tan's own position was unclear, not to say ambiguous, it being rumoured that the new regime in Peking wanted to replace Chiang Kai-shek's protege with a nominee of their own. Naturally nothing of this was said in the course of our meeting. Professor Tan showed me the Bhavan's collection of Chinese books, the centrepiece of which, at least in my eyes, was the Taisho edition of the Chinese Tripitaka, the one hundred thick, closely printed red volumes of which were said to contain more than 1,600 separate Buddhist texts, both canonical and extra-canonical. The following day I had tea with him, and he showed me his house and garden, which he evidently had tried to make as much like the traditional Chinese scholar's house and garden as Indian conditions permitted. Professor Tan had, it seemed, put down roots in the land of his adoption."

Anyway, all the Santiniketan people know that Professor Tan Yun-shan was responsible for collecting the money for the construction of the huge building Cheena-Bhavana. Elderly people of Santiniketan say that they have seen Prof. Tan physically working with masons standing in the hot sun, saying." This building must stand for at least 500 years." So the noble man was right, even now one can see that not a small piece of plaster has dropped from this building, standing like a steel construction.

Cheena-Bhavana contains a huge library and many smaller libraries, class rooms, office and scholars' rooms, meeting halls, garden and every facilities of a good independent complex. Prof. Tan managed to fill the libraries with good books, tasteful furniture and maintained it as a sacred place of worship. One has to enter Cheena-Bhavana without shoes. A pleasant fragrance of incense and disciplined clean surroundings used to welcome the visitor.

Prof. Tan was a good friend of Jawaharlal Nehru. Perhaps through Nehru, he was invited to Beijing by Zhou Enlai who presented him a huge quantity of rare books which are preserved in Cheena-Bhavana.

After Madam Tan's expiry, Prof. Tan became so lonely with all of his children employed at some other places while he himself retired from the post of Visva-Bharati. But his evergreen spirit took him to Bodhgaya where he again started building a huge complex with physical help of some fellows who turned out to be very crafty and cheated him with much of his money and in other ways. He expired in Bodhgaya turning his face towards the sacred temple of the Buddha.

Kalimpong, April 1998.

16

THE GREAT SCHOLAR PROF. TAN YUN-SHAN

Prof. Tan Yun-shan can be described as the modern Xuanzang. As Xuanzang spent a considerable part of his life learning Indian religion, specially Buddhism and visited and stayed in Indian Buddhist universities, similarly Prof. Tan has done his best to promote Chinese studies in India and spread Indian thoughts in China through various means.

My first encounter with him took place when as a post-doctoral fellow I had joined Cheena-Bhavana of Visva-Bharati University at Santiniketan.

I was proceeding to attend a reception of the visiting Chinese delegaton. Though I had not been formally introduced earlier to Prof. Tan and Madam Tan, I recognised them very well. Prof. Tan was walking with the help of his walking stick towards the meeting place — the Uttarayan. I went to Prof. Tan and Madam Tan and said, 'Uncle, please wait."Soon a car of the West Bengal government was coming by the road, towards us. Without asking anything, I stopped the car and put Prof. Tan and Mrs. Tan inside the car and told the driver to take them to Uttarayan. The driver replied that he was from Calcutta and he did not have any idea regarding the place of the meeting. Prof. Tan who was sitting in the car held my hand and said, "Neice, you also come with us." Thus we went to the reception ground, and though he was ushered into the enclosure for the distinguished guests, he made me sit in between himself and Madam Tan. Thus our association started.

Rabindranath Tagore invited a good number of eminent scholars both Indian and foreign, to build up Visva-Bharati. Prof. Tan was one of them who had lifelong association with Visva-Bharati and who had dedicated his life, time and energy to build up the Cheena-Bhavana of Visva-Bharati.

Tagore first met Prof. Tan in Singapore in 1927. Prof. Tan was a brilliant and scholarly young teacher in Singapore at that time. Tagore was so impressed, that he invited Prof. Tan to come to Visva-Bharati and teach Chinese language. Of course, teaching of Chinese had started earlier there and Dr. Lin Wujiang taught Chinese, Silvain Levi and Tucci also had joined. But the Cheena-Bhavana was not born till then.

In 1928 Prof. Tan came to Santiniketan. In his own country he was a meritorious student of traditional Chinese literature and culture. He was born on 10th October in 1898. After the completion of traditional Chinese courses, he made a comparative study of methods in the sphere of traditional Chinese teaching, and western methods of teaching. Later he took up research in western culture, philosophy and thoughts which was completed in 1924.

As Prof. Tan was coming to India in the month of September, in 1928, his ship was caught in a storm. Then he wrote a poem on the Indian ocean and its fury. In another poem he expressed his respect and love for India. As he reached Santiniketan he expressed his joy in a third poem.

In Santiniketan Prof. Tan was called "Tan Saheb" by the Visva-Bharati community. He spent his life in constructive work, teaching, studying Indian culture and writing. The Cheena-Bhavana and the Sino-Indian Cultural Society became his centres of activities. When Tagore visited China in 1924, discussions had taken place there about exchange of scholars between India and China. For building a guest house for the visiting Chinese scholars, Yugal Kishore Birla was to donate Rupees twenty thousand to Visva-Bharati. But nothing happened. At his arrival, Prof. Tan was till enthusiastic about the programme. Prof.Tan went back to China in 1931 and he met important persons, who could help him for making this plan a success. Due to their help and co-operation at Nanking [Nanjing] the Sino-Indian Cultural Society was established in 1933. Thereafter in 1934 the Society was formed in India by Prof. Tan and Tagore became its president. Prof. Tan again went to China and started collecting funds for construction of buildings which were needed at Cheena-Bhavana for its library, guest house, hostels for teachers and researchers. He was successful in collecting funds and at the same time he collected a good number of books on traditional literature of China, Buddhism, philosophy and religion, literature and history. In 1936, the construction of Cheena-Bhavana was started and in 1937 it was completed. Apart from the hostels, a few quarters for the teachers were also built.

Prof. Tan was not only the founder-Director of the Cheena-Bhavana, he was also the Professor of Chinese Studies. He visited many institutions in India, where he delivered lectures on Chinese culture and philosophy. He placed emphasis on synthesis of Confucian ethics with the tenets of Buddhism. He highlighted the values of human kindness, righteousness, *Karuna* or compassion, Prajna or wisdom, and tolerance. He wished that the people of China and India would set a good example by showing these virtues even in the modern world, and should work jointly for world peace. He always spoke about these ideas.

With Prof. Tan heading Cheena-Bhavana, Santiniketan could attract many tens of scholars from China. Afterwards many of them returned to China to become the mainstay of Indian studies in China. Pachow and Jan Yun-hua distinguished themselves as authorities in Buddhism in North America. They all felt indebted to Prof. Tan. Several good will missions came from China to Visva-Bharati and Cheena-Bhavana. In 1940 the Buddhist mission came, and another good will mission came. In 1943, the cultural and educational mission from China visited the Cheena-Bhavana. Chiang Kai-shek visited it when he came to India in 1942. Later, Zhou Enlai also came and received Deshikottama from Visva-Bharati in 1957.

Prof. Tan did not stay uninterruptedly at Santiniketan. He had to visit China many times, for collecting funds, books, manuscripts etc. and arrange for guest-scholars. Even when Dr. Kotnis, and the Indian medical team had visited China during China's peril, Prof. Tan looked after this team there. He was like an ambassador. In India also he had to give lectures in different institutes or universities. He was busy in organisational work as well as teaching, writing, publishing etc. Through the Sino-Indian Cultural Society he published books and bulletins, where he mostly wrote about cultural traditions of China, unity of all nations, equality and friendship and about similar ideas.

He was a quite, dignified, dutibound, just and affectionate person. Cheena-Bhavana generally had paucity of funds. Prof. Tan led a very simple life, completely dedicated to the cause of spread of education and the ideals of Sino-Indian friendship and enhancement of positive thoughts among mankind.

Madam Tan was with him in his efforts. Prof. Tan brought up his children in that atmosphere in such a way that all of them are following the path shown by their great father.

Though Prof. Tan did not join any political activity in India, during the 1941 movement he apealed to the Indian political activists to avoid violence. At the same time he appealed to the British government that India must be given freedom. According to him there was no power which could refuse the right to India to regain her independence.

Times have changed. Visva-Bharati became a central university. Secondly, Sino-Indian relations suffered a lot due to harsh political situation. In 1959 Prof. Tan went to China, and he tried to ease the situation. But there was no improvement. Both Cheena-Bhavana and the Cultural Society had to suffer. As financial resources dried up, enthusiasm of some scholars also became reduced. It became difficult even to pay Prof. Tan's salary. Finally Visva-Bharati fixed an honorarium for him. But the institute became reduced to the status of a language teaching institute only. Gradually it lost its glory.

From 1971 Prof. Tan spent his time and energy to build the World Buddhist Academy at Bodhgaya. At first the temple was constructed and he had a plan to build it as an institute for study and research. Unfortunately he could not complete the work in his life time. He expired on 12th February in 1983.

I shall never forget that this eminent scholar and a great soul with a kind heart had to come to receive me at the Gaya railway station. But we could not find each other. When I wrote to him, he replied in such a way — I felt both sad and happy. I was very fortunate as I could maintain such a close contact with this great scholar who was like a saint. Madam Tan used to see me with a bunch of flowers or a few fruits.

It is not possible for anyone to forget him, who had been in close contact with him, such was his personality. His ex-students, and a few persons who had worked under him cherished him with great regard and reverence. It is not possible to describe adequately, his life and his work in these few words.

17

IN MEMORY OF FATHER

During a visit to America in 1985, while travelling on a California highway, an amazing scene unfolded in front of my eyes. Against a backdrop of deep blue sky, there appeared a swath of white cumulus clouds in the form of a mountain range. Our eldest brother who is the most knowledgeable in Sinology uttered: "look at the cloud-mountain". Father's name "Yun-shan" literally means "cloud-mountain". Prior to this spectacle, I had no notion of what "cloud-mountain" meant. This sudden revelation sent a pleasant spine-tingling sensation through my entire body.

My father was born nearly a hundred years ago in a village called Chaling in the Province of Hunan. He came of a literary and religious family. These two traits were inherited by father in good measure. Moreover, from an early age, father displayed such strong principles and a thirst of knowledge that the native soil could not contain him very long. After completing his education he left for Singapore in 1924. In his words, this period was spent in teaching, in writing poems and articles for various journals and newspapers, and in contemplation of his mission in life along the sea-shores in his spare moments. He was young and full of self-confidence.

During the four years in Singapore, the most memorable moment in Father's life was his first meeting with Gurudeva Rabindranath in 1927. On hearing about Rabindranath's tour of South-East Asia, father went to meet him. Coincidentally, Rabindranath was looking for a qualified Chinese teacher for his Visva-Bharati University. In the meanwhile, the thought of reviving the ancient cultural interchange between China and India was crystallizing in father's mind. Rabindranath's invitation to come to Santiniketan to teach was, therefore, a command, hard not to accept.

However, a personal matter unexpectedly and temporarily came in the way. This too I leamt from my father. Before leaving Singapore father went to bid goodbye to his close friends. One of them happened to be a young teacher in the Chinese Girls' School. She was also from Hunan Province. One of the pioneer Chinese teachers in Malaya, she was a great admirer of father's poetry. In fact, she had learnt by heart all the poems that father had published in the local journals. At the time of parting, her tear-filled eyes were evidence of a deep relationship that had already emerged between the two.

After father's departure for Santiniketan, mother remained in Malaya for sometime in her teaching profession. In those years, because of shortage of funds in Visva-Bharati, father did not take any salary. It was mother's income that supported the two establishments. In reply to mother's first letter from Singapore, father responded in poetry: "Your letter filled my two eyes with tears". After mother's death, I heard this poem in its entirety from father for the first time. The first child was born in Malaya in 1929. He was not only the eldest brother, but also the follower in the footsteps of father's life long mission.

In 1937, the China Hall or Cheena Bhavana was built and inaugurated as an important institution within Visva-Bharati. This auspicious occasion was graced by Rabindranath himself. Because of Jawaharlal Nehru's indisposition, his daughter Priyadarshini Indira conveyed Nehru's good wishes. Behind the success of this remarkable institution was the dream, planning and tireless efforts of one dedicated seeker. The rare and valuable collection of books and their careful upkeep was meticulously planned. The teaching curriculum and the research programs in the Cheena Bhavana are silent testimony to the strength of his vision.

China and India, two neighbouring civilizations. In their ancient history (from the fifth to the twelfth centuries), close ties between the two countries were established through the medium of Buddhism. China's way of life and philosophy was greatly influenced by Buddhist scriptures. Unfortunately, those ancient ties have been severed for many centuries. My father's mission for life was to bridge that chasm and to firmly re-establish the cultural ties. The vicissitudes of personal life, its joys and sorrows, its pleasures and pains, its glories and pitfalls became secondary to this dream. His arena of activity was spread between these two expansive nations. However, behind this life long undertaking lay the tough sacrifice of another person, that of our mother. She took on the responsibility and burden of running the household and raising a large family of five sons and two daughters, tirelessly and without complaint. On top of this, she took care of the hospitality of many friends and guests who frequently visited father in connection with his work. Mother's household itself changed venues several times. From Singapore to Santiniketan to Shanghai to Changsha and back to Santiniketan. She never had the pleasure of enjoying the company of all seven children in one location. The pain of separation from some of the children remained with her throughout, but she never let this pain get the better of her responsibilities. My mother started her career as a teacher. After a lapse of many years when she stood beside her husband and raised a family, mother went back, in late life, to her teaching profession. She built her own school in Changsha and named it Datong or "Great Confluence". This school will celebrate its Golden Jubilee next year.

After three sons, Tan Chung, Tan Chen and Tan Lee, I am the first daughter Tan Wen. Because of this, I received special affection from mother. However, in my childhood, father appeared remote. I did not get to see him in the first few years. This caused me to avoid him as a child. China was then engaged in war with Japan. There was bombing and destruction everywhere. Our city of Changsha did not escape from this rampage. I have heard from mother that during air raids she would gather me and my three brothers hurriedly to head for the bomb shelters. There, she had taught all the children to utter the words "Nomo Amitofu" or "Greetings to Amitava", and we would all chant them. Leaving the family in China under these conditions was a concern. On the urging of Rabindranath, father returned to China to bring mother and the two youngest children to Santiniketan, leaving the two eldest sons in China. This split in the family caused endless concern in mother and cast a shadow in our young lives.

My younger sister was born a year before Rabindranath's death. He named her "Chameli". He said the word had phonetic resemblance to Chinese. After that two younger brothers were born in Santiniketan. They also received Bengali names: Aujit and Arjun. The youngest was born when the dance-drama Chitrangada was being staged in Santiniketan. The song "Arjun Tumi Arjun" was reverberating in our minds. That's how the youngest brother acquired the name. Today, when I think of father, I remember his strong straight body, his bright dignified face. His bearing and personality set him apart from most men. Even in his dress he was distinct. He always wore clothes of his own particular design. He was remarkably self-disciplined. I have never seen him utter a harsh word even when someone offended him. He lived a life of strict regularity and control. In the morning he would get up long before sunrise and go to the roof of Cheena Bhavana to do his morning meditation and exercise. Following that he would come down to say his prayer to Buddha and start his day's work. The whole day would be spent in pre-planned activities. Everything was done like clockwork. Even while bathing, the number of pails of water used was predetermined.

Father tried to teach his children by example and expected them to follow his disciplined life. Thus he appeared rather strict to my young mind. That behind this formidable facade was a kind loving heart was revealed to me in later life, much later. Laxity and shoddiness in work was against his character. He expected the same high standard of behaviour and work ethic from his children.

Besides being blessed by Rabindranath, father received encouragement and co-operation from many leading personalities in India and China which helped him immensely in fulfilling his life's mission. The exception was Mahatma Gandhi which father acknowledged with due respect and humility. When father had approached Gandhiji for his support in re-establishing the ties between India and China, his response was straightforward and direct: "My first duty is to look after the welfare of my own country. Beyond that, where is the time for anything else?" These words rang true in father's ears.

The existence of Cheena Bhavana and father's life long efforts came to the attention of many intellectuals in China. The Chinese Government had given full financial support for the works carried out in Cheena Bhavana for many years. Although this support was halted in 1949 with the change in the political structure in China, the new Government respected the research and teaching at the institute. In 1956, the invitation to father to visit China came from the Premier himself. In his letter to father, Zhou Enlai said: "We are fully aware of the valuable work you have engaged in for such a long time. But you have not visited your homeland for many years. Come, take a look at what we have accomplished?" At the suggestion of the Chinese Consul-General in Calcutta, I accompanied father on his trip to China. During the trip, I became aware for the first time of the ease with which father's person could attract the attention and respect of the political leaders in China.

Two encounters deserve special mention here. First was the meeting with Chairman Mao Zedong. Father had written a letter to the Chairman criticizing his one-way leaning in foreign policy. Mao mentioned this letter and said that in the effort to help improve China's industrial wealth quickly, no super-power other than the Soviet Union is likely to come forward. And this was the reason for China's one-sided policy. He spoke those words with such passion that even my uninitiated mind could respond to them. In retrospect, father's far-sightedness in this matter becomes more apparent today.

The second was the meeting with Premier Zhou Enlai. The appointment was at midnight! We were given to understand that was the customary time for serious discussions. The Premier's graceful demeanour impressed me very much. When I garlanded him in traditional Indian style, he immediately said it was a photo-op not to be missed. A photographer was summoned right away and pictures were taken. I remember that my artist sister Chameli had sent a hand-made batik table cloth depicting Saraswati as a present. Zhou received it and looked at it carefully. He said regretfully that it was not customary for the new Government to exchange gifts. But later he sent autographed copies of four albums of paintings by famous Chinese artists. Father's visit with Zhou Enlai lasted for three hours during which he listened carefully about the Visva-Bharati University and the Cheena Bhavana. When my father invited him to visit Santiniketan, he sent for his itinerary to see if it was included. Subsequently, Santiniketan was added to the list. Following the long meeting we had a light supper of simple food. The entire ambiance was spartan, but the Premier's personality lent a special aura to the occasion.

In this context, let me touch upon an event that took place during Premier Zhou's visit to Santiniketan. The Premier's special train arrived at Bolpur station the evening prior to his tour of Santiniketan. Father went to Bolpur to meet the Premier. Of the many topics of discussion he carried with him was a special request. That request came from no other than Pratima Bouthan, Rabindranath's daughter-in-law through her confidant Kshitish Roy. Bouthan was aware that in the past the Chinese Government had helped Visva-Bharati with generous financial support. She was hoping that the present Government would likewise support the construction of a memorial to Rabindranath where his archival materials could be properly preserved. Initially, father was somewhat hesitant to broach the subject with Zhou. Father's connections with the previous Chinese Government was strong. But he was not sure of the support he would get from the present Government. However, his deep dedication and commitment to Rabindranath came on top. Next day it was announced that the Chinese Government had donated Rs. 60,000 towards the establishment of a memorial to Rabindranath Tagore.

It is appropriate here to correct a misinformation. There is a common belief that father was a class mate of Mao Zedong. This is incorrect. Although the two went to the same school, Mao was senior to father by a few years. When Mao was an established leader among the students, father was still an up-and-coming flag-bearing junior among the younger crowd. However, some close associates of Mao, one of them a Minister, remembered my father well. Moreover, during our visit father met an old teacher who had very fond memories of both Mao and my father.

In 1959, border dispute between China and India reared its ugly head. The hurt and disillusionment caused in father's soul can not be comprehended by ordinary mortals like us. The life long dedication of father to build up cordial relations between the two great countries appeared to be at the point of crumbling. There was only pain and suffering on his countenance. One person who could bring a sliver of joy in the face of my father was his longtime dear friend Anil Kumar Chanda. He tried his best to cheer up father by saying "even brothers some times fight". The tension was felt by other members of our family as well. The poet's words: "So much joy has turned to sorrow, so many friends will turn tomorrow" symbolized the pain in all of us.

One afternoon I went to visit my respected teacher at his home. He welcomed me and said in the presence of others: "She is not one of the bad guys". I came home with a heavy heart, having been branded by a racial identification that I was oblivious of. In his novel "Gora" Rabindranath has said no one is born with racial markings. I felt this was only an ideal. In reality, it was very difficult to reach that lofty height of colour-blindness that our father achieved.

After retiring from Visva-Bharati, father's work ethic once again made him restless. The result can be seen in the start of the gigantic World Buddhist Academy in Bodhgaya which was, once again, my father's brainchild. Unfortunately, before this project could be completed, father's life-flames were extinguished.

Father's last days were spent as a mendicant. In fact, his whole life was lived in sacrifice and not in luxury. Even in old age, when most mortals break down in health and require assistance, father had no such need. After our mother's death, the children tried hard to keep father in some semblance of comfort. But no amount of pleading would succeed in keeping him close to us. Again in the words of the poet: "You want to keep me in bonds of love, but do you have that capability?" He took shelter in a small room in a temple in Bodhgaya. A simple ration came from a poor family in the village. Father subsisted on it contentedly year after year. Even in his last days father was free of any ailment. His mind was strong as ever. But unfortunately, his weakened constitution ultimately succumbed to a bout of flue. In 1983, father breathed his last in his favourite place of pilgrimage, Bodhgaya. None of his children nor any friend was present at the time of his demise.

The funeral pyre was built on an open field next to his incomplete dream, the World Buddhist Academy. Our eldest brother lit the flame. The harsh environment became aglow with the ultimate sacrifice of father's life-long pursuits. The two Chief Bhikshus from Bodhgaya and father's long-term friend Reverand Jinaratna of the Mahabodhi Society stood in front of the pyre and chanted Buddhist scriptures in Pali. I felt that in the modern annals of exchange of knowledge and culture between India and China a major chapter had come to a close.

Translated from original
Bengali by Tan Lee
November 30, 1997.

18

TAN YUN-SHAN: THE ESSENTIAL MAN

INTRODUCTION

In writing an article to commemorate some one's Birth Centenary, it is easy for the author to fall into the trap of turning his article into an eulogy. This is particularly true when the writer is also a son of the person being remembered. This I want to avoid. Instead, my attempt will be to look at the persona of Tan Yun-shan dispassionately from a distance while at the same time maintaining a close perspective -- in the architect's parlance, a "worm's eye view'-- that only a son is privileged to obtain, and in so doing, get to the essence of the man. A truly formidable task!

For Tan Yun-shan was no ordinary mortal. In his chosen field he was a giant among men. Not perhaps to the many casual acquaintances who knew the mild-mannered Professor merely as the builder of Cheena Bhavana in Tagore's Visva-Bharati University in Santiniketan, or as the creator of the monumental but incomplete World Buddhist Academy in Bodh Gaya. But to, those who could grasp the significance of the vision of this cultural ambassador between China and India, and the zeal with which he carried out his calling, his stature approached that of a modern day Xuan Zang.

There are few in this world born with the knowledge of their life's mission. Fewer still who have actually carried out their mission to fruition. Tan Yun-shan belonged to this select group. Yet, all his achievements were realized without any fanfare and much less publicity. Because, essentially he was a modest person, with a sense of humility that only a firm belief in the tenets of Confucianism and Buddhism could bring. His modesty, however, was possible only due to a supreme confidence in the calling that he chose for his life. The feeble attempt to trace this Journey is the tribute the author would like to pay to the memory of Tan Yun-Shan.

FORMATIVE YEARS

Like many young intellectuals growing up in the early years of this century, Tan Yun-shan was struck by the inhumanity suffered by colonized nations at the hands of conquering nations. Although China was nominally independent, the fate of its people was no better than those in India. Tan would find around him many young revolutionaries who wanted to set things right. "The end justifies the means" was a common slogan and Tan would empathize with many of those who chanted that tune. However, he was strongly opposed to any kind of violence, even if it was to achieve the emancipation of the down trodden, the freeing of a nation from foreign subjugation. In this regard, his training in Buddhism led him towards the path of "ahimsa". This explains why, in spite of his early contact with Mao Zedong and his "comrade" in their student days, Tan remained somewhat aloof from the political currents that were sweeping through China.

Tan's early initiation to Buddhism naturally attracted him to India, the birth place of the Enlightened One. He drew upon the recorded history of cultural exchanges and amity between the two ancient nations of India and China and wondered how they could coexist without ever raising arms against each other. How could they flourish and build up their own respective civilizations without design on each other's territory? Why could not the modern Western countries learn the path of peace, non-violence and coexistence from these ancient Eastern nations?

Yet, through all these mental turmoils, Tan, like many of his Chinese contemporaries, could not ignore the strength of the modern West. He wanted to travel to France to learn about "liberte, egalite, fraternite". But the gravitational pull towards India was just as strong. A choice had to be made. Tan waited for some signal. That signal came to him in a roundabout way.

By this time Tan had read up on India, its history, culture, people, and above all its struggle to gain independence from the British. Two modern Indian giants caught his attention: Mahatma Gandhi and Gurudeva Rabindranath Tagore. While Gandhi's practice of non-violence appealed to his spirituality, Tagore's broader cultural outlook was more appealing to his intellect. Somehow Tan yearned to meet both of them to draw inspiration from them for the work that lay ahead. In 1924 Tan left for Singapore to take up a teaching assignment. About the same time Tagore and his entourage had set sails for China. They literally crossed paths on the high seas. Tan was disappointed in missing the opportunity to meet Tagore in China. However, he kept track of Tagore's itinerary and read all his speeches which appeared in the newspapers.

Tagore's lecture tour of China was not without controversy. It appears that the Chinese audience was split in two camps: the Traditionalists who praised his literary and cultural accomplishment, and the Modernists who thought his concepts belonged to the past. Tan was firmly entrenched in the first camp. In fact he was trying to determine how close Tagore's concept of internationalism came to his own inclination to rejuvenate Sino-Indian relations. The more he read about Tagore, the more attracted he became to Tagore's Visva Bharati. But would that school be the right arena for a vigorous effort to renew cultural exchanges between the two giant nations? Tan had to wait till 1927 for an answer. That year Tagore came to Singapore and Tan was able to meet him. The meeting was fortuitous in many respects. Tan expressed his desire to go to India to start his mission. Tagore was anxious to find a suitable Chinese scholar to come to Sāntiniketan to establish his fledgling Institute of Chinese Studies on a firmer footing. When Tagore asked Tan whether he was interested, it sounded like a command that Tan could not turn down.

LAYING THE FOUNDATION TO SINO-INDIAN CULTURAL EXCHANGE

Perhaps Tan's decision to come to India was taken in haste. He had no idea of the remoteness of Santiniketan, nor the financial strength and capabilities of Visva Bharati as an institution. But no matter. The concept sounded perfect and Tagore's words were more than convincing. It did not take long for the two to chalk out a course of action. Tan was to come to Santiniketan as soon as he could wrap up his work in Singapore in order to revive Chinese Studies in Visva Bharati. At the same time he would work towards the establishment of a Sino-Indian Cultural Society with branches in China and India.

That decided, Tan started preparing for his pilgrimage to India. And a pilgrimage it was. For, to Tan, visiting the birth country of Lord Buddha was a long cherished dream. But something stood in the way. Tan had met a bright young teacher from his native Province of Hunan who was among the pioneers who came to Malaya to teach the children of the overseas Chinese. The chemistry between the two was right but the goals in life were quite different. However, they got married about the time when India beckoned at Tan.

Whiile Tan had set his goals at a lofty altitude, his wife Chen Nai-Wei, though dedicated to her teaching career, was more down to earth and pragmatic. The former was determined to move ahead along his chosen path, but the latter was quite content in shelving her career to raise a family. In 1928 Tan sailed for India to put the plan he had carefully prepared with the advice of Tagore into action. But the finances at Visva Bharati did not permit the university to offer him a salary. Chen stayed back in Malaya and supported the two establishments with her teacher's salary. On the surface it would appear that Tan was somewhat harsh and premature in his actions and must have placed a heavy burden on the shoulder of his young wife. But later events were to prove that his timing was impeccable. Moreover, Chen was fully supportive of the noble mission embarked by her husband and never complained.

The vicissitudes of life were to keep the Tan family splintered on numerous occasions and for prolonged periods of time. But that was the price that had to be paid to carry out Tan's mission. The establishment of the Sino-Indian Cultural Society, first in Nanjing, China and then in Santiniketan, India took enormous effort and dedication. Although soft-spoken and reticent by nature, Tan was persuasive and convincing in face to face dialogue. His command of English was good but his erudition in his mother tongue was awesome. Having listened to him on a few occasions speaking to large gatherings in Chinese, in order to raise funds for some worthwhile cause, I remember the spell he could cast on his audience. However, he preferred to discuss things in smaller groups. That was where his charm and erudition was most apparent. I have an impression that he was very aware of his own distinctive personality and was not hesitant to use it in furthering his mission. Thus, convincing the Govermnent of China to give generous sums of money to build Cheena Bhavana in Santiniketan was not a problem. Tan used his ability to write articles in newspapers and journals in China and South-East Asia to advance Tagore's concept of an International University and his own notion of an Institute for advanced research on Sino-Indian cultural, linguistic, religious and philosophical exchanges within the umbrella of that University. That the magnificent building of Cheena Bhavana could be built in record time is a testimony of the success of his efforts in China.

One of the strengths that became apparent was Tan's ability to keep politics outside his cultural pursuits. He knew that politicians came and went. But his dream of Sino-Indian cultural revival must endure the vagaries of political change. Therefore, while he did not hesitate in cultivating his contacts in the Government, both in China and in India, he always took pains to reiterate that his efforts were apolitical. This proved far-sighted when the Kuomintang Government which had responded generously with financial support for Cheena Bhavana was replaced by the Peoples' Republic led by Mao Zedong. It did not take long for the new Government to recognize the valuable work done at the Cheena Bhavana.

I will not deal anymore with the Cheena Bhavana as an institution, nor its accomplishments. These are matters of record and I am sure other contributors to the Commemorative Volume will cover that ground. I just wish to touch one area where I have heard criticism about Tan's achievements. That area deals with his own research efforts. There have been comments that Tan did not publish enough. This is a valid comment, but here is my response.

Tan was a visionary, a builder and an organiser. Having watched him from close quarters, I and some who had ringside seats, have been impressed by the herculean efforts he put in travelling back and forth between China, India and South-East Asia, corresponding with endless people, lobbying governments and individuals in fund raising to build the infrastructure and the superstructure, acquiring a most valuable collection of books for the library, actual planning and supervision of construction of the many buildings which constitute the Cheena Bhavana, and preparing detailed research plans and programmes for the institution. Where on earth would he have any time or energy left to do research of his own? However, I know (because he told me himself on more than one occasion) that he would have preferred nothing better than to do research on many topics that he had identified for attention at a future date and perhaps write books on. But his first priority was to build up the institution itself so that others could start the monumental research programs he had already chalked out for them. He wielded a powerful pen, particularly in Chinese; and understanding of Mahayana Buddhism would have been the richer if only he was spared some time to use it more often. And obviously that was not to be. He encouraged his children to take up subjects dear to his heart. Perhaps he wished that through their research efforts he would derive some vicarious satisfaction that his responsibilities denied him. It must have pleased him immensely that his eldest son Tan Chung and his eldest daughter Tan Wen were able to Fulfill some of his unrealized desires.

PERSONAL TRAITS

Now I wish to devote some time to talk about the personal traits of Tan Yun-shan. This effort will be mostly anecdotal. The reason is obvious. To his children, Tan appeared larger than life. Citing anecdotes may help demystify some of that perception.

I shall start by saying that Tan Yun-shan lived the life he preached. He set high standards for himself and tried to live by those standards as best as he could. But he was also human. When he slipped in his day to day activities, which rarely happened, he was very sad and the pain would be clearly visible on his face.

Some of his students have said that Tan was the "Chinese Sage" in Santiniketan. This may be an apt description. But it was also a wrong one. His countenance and bearing could certainly be described as sage-like, but he had no illusions of ever becoming one. He wanted to be remembered as a devout Buddhist who had found his calling early. And no amount of adversity or pressure could dislodge him from his chosen path. His commitment was unshakeable. I have to state here that the atmosphere in Santiniketan in the early years was ideally suited to Tan's personality and temperament. And that is why when he arrived there for the first time in 1928, the harsh barren landscape, the peaceful environment, and the spartan existence instantly won his approval. What better place could he find for "simple living and high thinking"? Many who came to know Tan in later years were impressed by the courtesy and patience he showed to others. But those qualities were acquired through years of practice and self discipline. It is true that when it came to dealing with a native either of his motherland or of his country of adoption, Tan was particularly generous. However, he was not always that kind while dealing In fact, he had certain amount of contempt or disdain for the British. One incident clearly showed his bias. The summers in Santiniketan could be quite oppressive. In order to escape the heat he would take his family to Darjling for a couple of months. That was when the British Sahibs would also congregate there. The train to Darjling was full of them in those years. On one of these trips, although father had made reservations on the Darjling Mail for the family, on arrival in Calcutta, he found that those berths had been allocated to a British family. Tan was furious and immediately demanded to see the officer-in-charge of reservations who also happened to be British. He made such a fuss that the British officer had to reverse his decision and reallocate the berths so that we could travel in comfort. I have no doubt that he could take such a strong stand because of Gandhiji's influence and his own sympathy towards India's struggle to rid the country of the British yoke. That was a rare display of anger by Tan that I witnessed. The red face of the British officer who was at the receiving end of father's tongue-lashing is indelible in my mind.

DEALINGS WITH HIS CHILDREN

In dealing with his children, Tan was kind but firm. He rarely proselytized, preferring instead to teach by example. Although a practising Buddhist, he was tolerant of other religions, in particular Eastern. He never tried to Instil his religious beliefs in his children, and was not offended if they showed an interest in other faiths. On one occasion his eldest son, who was left to grow up in China during the Second World War, wrote a letter announcing that he had fallen in love with an American girl, the daughter of a missionary. Therefore, he was thinking of conversion to Christianity. Father showed me the letter, and rather than expressing any displeasure, merely chuckled and had a good laugh with my mother. He knew that his children would be able to make their own decisions regarding their religious inclinations as they grew up. On another occasion, when I was still quite young, I had committed an indiscretion that deserved a reprimand. Father took me to his study where he also said his daily prayers and asked me to promise in front of Lord Buddha that I would not commit the same indiscretion again. My flippant response was: "But I do not believe in Buddha". Father let me off without further admonition.

Father's treatment of his children was not always even-handed. This no doubt caused pain to some of his children and embarrassment to others. Father also believed in divine intervention in the birth of some of his children. He used to tell me how the young Dalai Lama was chosen when the old passed away, with his followers searching far and wide for the perfect reincarnate who displayed unmistakable divine signs. For some reasons he saw signs at the time of my birth, and I became the favourite child. This caused no end of embarrassment for me, particularly in front of my immediate younger sister Wen, for I had no such illusions of my own. But because my father mentioned this a number of times, Wen was somewhat mystified and looked upto me with a degree of deference that I did not deserve.

Father's beliefs in me as a special child received further encouragement on a trip to Bodh Gaya. The devout Buddhist that he was, father spent most of his time praying near the Great Pagoda. I was left to wander by myself away from the temple. While running around in the grass I stumbled over a piece of stone which, on closer examination, turned out to be a mini-pagoda. When I eventually had the opportunity to show the stone to my parents, my father was struck by awe. We brought the stone to Santiniketan and father installed it on a pedestal in his study. Thereafter, it became the symbol in front of which he said his daily prayers to Lord Buddha.

Mother, on the other hand, was much more evenhanded. To her, all children were equal, and she displayed no bias in favour of anyone. As a matter of fact, because father leaned in my favour, mother showed particular affection towards Wen, as if to balance things somewhat. In later life when Wen distinguished herself in the study of the Bengali language, father was ecstatic and showered her with all the parental pride and affection that he was able to display.

Our eldest brother Chung had a special place in our parents' minds. He displayed talents in many areas and eventually became a renowned historian and China scholar. However, in 1939, at the height of the war with Japan, our parents decided to bring the two younger children, myself and Wen to India, leaving the two older sons in China. The family was split. My mother was worried sick about the elder children and we could see the sadness in her face. Father, however, confranted the situation more philosophically, and did not display any external anxiety. Perhaps he was confident that Buddha would protect the sons from harm caused by the Japanese occupation of China. Years later, these two elder brothers were able to come to India and the family was reunited. It then became apparent to the younger children how fond our father was of his first son. The second son, however, did not receive the same amount of attention, which was most unfortunate. For, he was just as talented as the other children, particularly in the field of fine arts. Perhaps he did not have the opportunity to display his talents to his parents as did the other children. He suffered his pain with dignity and grace which endeared him to all his siblings.

There is no question that father wanted all his children to excel in their studies, and irrespective of his biases, whenever a child showed good result in school, he would unequivocally recognize the achievement. Sometimes I felt he drove his children rather hard. One episode comes to mind. A close friend of father who was a successful businessman in Hong Kong was childless despite his three marriages. In desperation, this friend wanted to adopt a child from our family. Our parents at that time had five children, three sons and two daughters. The eldest four were considered too old for adoption. The youngest one, a daughter, was a favourite child. Therefore. my father decided that the next child would go to his friend for adoption. The next was a son named Aujit and he was sent to this rich family in Hong Kong while still a baby. Father did not think much about it, but mother shed many a silent tear to let go of the newborn. This brother grew up in luxury and his adopted parents doted on him. Unfortunately, the mother passed away shortly thereafter and the father married a fourth time. This marriage produced some children and it was time for Aujit to return to his natural parents. When he came "home", Aujit was clearly unhappy. Coming from the luxuries of Hong Kong to the spartan life in Santiniketan required a good deal of adjustment. Consequently, the first few months were quite difficult for Aujit. His grades in the school suffered. Father was critical of his performance at school and compared his marks with those of his younger brother Arjun who was doing better. This made Aujit doubly sad. We felt father was unduly harsh towards him. To the credit of Aujit he recovered from this temporary setback and was soon performing at the top of his class. He proved to his parents that he was equal to the challenge thrown at him and father was quick to acknowledge it. Later on, Aujit became a skilled mechanical engineer and made his parents proud. Father particularly admired Aujit's skill with his hands. He became the inhouse repairman.

Father was a well organized, meticulous man. As his favourite child he tried to inculcate many of his talents and skills in me, which I learned by osmosis. He gave me the penchant for reading books and taught me how to take care of them. When I was still in elementary school, father was in the process of building up a magnificent personal library. Almost every mail brought in parcels containing books. I had the privilege of going to his library at will. There I would watch father open the parcels with infinite care. He would show me the new titles which ranged from history to religion to philosophy to architecture to gardening, and so on. One category of books that were conspicuous by their absence were novels. He did not seem to have any use for them.

It was in father's study that I came across H.G. Wells' "The Outline of History". I was fascinated by the title and borrowed it. After spending many months reading the book, it was time to return it to father's library. Unfortunately, by this time the book was somewhat frazzled with many of its pages dog-eared. When I took it back to father, he looked the book over and returned it to me saying: "You can keep it". I knew instantly what he meant. The book was too mutilated to go back on the shelf I was ashamed and learnt a valuable lesson. Next day father called me to his library. Some shiny new books had arrived on his desk. With infinite patience he showed me how to put a brown paper jacket on one of his new books so that it could withstand the rough handling that all books go through. It was then that I noticed that all his books on the shelves were carefully wrapped in brown paper jackets. This subtle training stood me in good stead in my later life.

Growing up through school was peaceful and easy in Santiniketan. We were insulated and, by and large protected from the influences of the outside. This created problems for me, because I had become interested in the bigger world at an early age. The call of the big blue yonder rang in my ears with increasing regularity. I was yearning to get out of the manger but knew that it was too early for a twelve year old to leave home. What made things worse was I had two sets of friends and they transmitted different and often conflicting signals to my adolescent mind. The first group consisted of children of parents who worked in Santiniketan. They were the local boys and girls, considered to be simple, naive, country bumpkins who rarely stepped outside of Santiniketan. These became my playmates during the prolonged summer recess when we would cruise the entire campus looking for fruit to pluck and other adventure. We knew every tree that grew around us. We played simple rustic games and sometimes indulged in activities that were considered taboo, such as smoking a few puffs of tobacco. I was happy with these friends until it was time for the school to reopen. Then I looked forward to my other group of friends, the sophisticates from the big city of Calcutta. These were students who lived in hostels and had a distinctly urban bearing. I felt drawn to them as they always seemed to bring news of some new innovation or fad that we village folks were too ignorant to know about. Some of them, the more outrageous ones, talked about the glamorous girls of the big city; this peaked my interest as I had just begun to notice the biological differences between boys and girls. My urban friends often invited me to-visit their homes in the big city and I was yearnng to their invitation. But my father would not allow that. It so happened that one of my classmates had to receive an extended course of treatment that was not available in Santiniketan. On one of these occasions, I told my friend that I would like to come with him for a visit of the big city. In the middle of the night I sneaked out of our home and met my friend and soon was on a train to Calcutta. When my parents found out about my absence my mother panicked. But father was nonchalent, saying: ``Oh well, he will be back when he has seen the excitement and runs out of cash." Sure enough, after a day, I returned home rather sheepishly, and all was forgiven. It showed me the inner fortitude that father had. He always appeared tranquil and calm even in the face of great adversity. I often wondered where he found all that strength?

My immediate younger sister Wen was a bright and precocious child. She was only three when mother took us to India. As the two older brothers were left in China, Wen grew up knowing me as her only elder brother. She used to follow me around and mimic whatever I did until she was old enough to have her own coterie of friends. Although she was two years younger than me, she was intellectually sharp enough to be only a year behind me in class. At that rate she would have completed her Matriculation Examination at age thirteen. Wen continued to do well in her class and was promoted to Junior high when she was only nine years old. At that point, father, in his wisdom, decided that Wen was too young to have advanced so far in school. He met the School Principal & and demanded that Wen be demoted to a lower grade. The Principal was flabberg asted. He told father that during his entire tenure all the requests he had received from Parents were to promote their children who had failed in their classes. This was the first request to dernote a child who had actually passed her examinations. However, father was quite persistent and his wishes were granted. Later in life, when I pondered over this incident, I was able to understand father's wisdom. Although Wen was scholastically able to finish the courses, she would have been at a physical and cultural disadvantage dealing with her classmates who were much older and more mature than her. Subsequent events proved that the decision was appropriate and Wen went on to top her classes through college and graduate school, eventually earning a Ph.D. in Bengali. Wen became the cynosure of father's eyes. What gave father the most satisfaction was that Wen mastered the mother tongue of Rabindranath and proved that cultural integration between China and India had been achieved in the Tan family.

Throughout our adolescent years in Santiniketan, we were exposed to streams of visitors to our home. Our parents would go out of their way to show their hospitality and make their stay as comfortable as possible. While they lived simple and frugal lives themselves, our parents were generous to a fault when it came to treating their guests. The phrase "Charity begins at home" was foreign to them. These were important lessons that all their children were able to pick up. The wise saying of Mother Teressa - "Give until it hurts"-- was practised in front of our eyes.

I started a stamp collection at a young age. It grew rapidly as father used to get mail ftom many countries. Besides, there were a number of foreign scholars in Visva-Bharati in those days and we could approach them for the stamps on their mail. Pretty soon I needed a larger stamp album to put them in. I asked father to buy me an album on his next trip to the big city. Father asked me to save my pocket money if I was so keen to get the album. I began to save the pennies and eventually accumulated enough and gave them to father. When he returned from his next visit to Calcutta, I was full of anticipation. But father did not mention anything about the album. Eventually, I gathered enough courage to ask him. He said his busy schedule did not allow him the time to shop for the album. I felt completely deflated and went to my room and refused to appear for dinner. Finally, father came to my room. He carried a package inside which was the much coveted album. I was thrilled. That taught me another lesson: in life we value rewards that we work hard for, even if the reward was as modest as a stamp album. I cherished that album for many, many years.

As I entered senior high, my interest in English literature grew exponentially, thanks to some

English teacher, I captured the "Aujit Chakravarty" Memorial Prize in English-an award of of thirty rupees. It was a handsome amount in those days with which I could buy a number of English books. Father was so pleased that he matched that amount and had my own mini-library. These are wonderful memories of father that I cherish to this day. Around the same time, father started to show me drafts of articles in English that he was writing for various journals, and I would proof-read them for him. He started to treat me as an adult and I felt proud of that honour. In 1947 when my parents went back to China with the three youngest children, Wen and I were left in Santiniketan to pursue our studies. I was barely thirteen then. But father thought I was old enough to look after my younger sister. We had a maternal uncle who taught in the Cheena-Bhavana. He was nominally named our guardian. Father opened a bank account which I would operate each month withdrawing just enough cash to pay for our expenses. Again a valuable lesson was learnt.

My younger sister Chameli was another favourite child of our father. She was a beautiful bonny baby that brought joy in the family, being the first child born in the country of our adoption. In those days child births took place at home but there was no midwife around. "Thandi", the wife of the venerable Pandit Kshiti Mohan Sen stepped forward. Having helped deliver many a child, she took charge of the situation, and everything went smoothly. The baby was christened by Gurudeva Rabindranath himself. He named her Chameli and said this name had close phonetic resemblance to Chinese. She was a happy child, had an excellent academic career and grew up to become an accomplished artist.

The youngest brother Arjun received the greatest display of affection by both father and mother. Having raised their other children with controlled discipline, it was time for them to let go and splurge a little. We all accepted this with grace and understanding. In fact, Sister Wen who named him, also doted on her kid brother. All this attention did nothing to spoil him, and Arjun grew up to be a kind hearted person and a brilliant physicist.

JOY AND SORROW

When Tan returned from China in 1949, the Kuomintang Government had been replaced by the Peoples' Republic. Financial support of Cheena Bhavana by the Chinese Government was suspended. It was time for Tan to launch another fund raising drive which took him to various places where his many friends and well wishers resided. One of these places was Kalimpong where he knew a wealthy Chinese businessman who had prospered through trade with Tibet. He was also a devout Buddhist and invited Tan to visit him. Father took me with him on that trip. After dinner, the two started to discuss Buddhism. The discourse went deep into the night. The rest of the people in the household retired to thier bedrooms. The next day I learnt from father that their discussion lasted all night. At the end of it the host was very pleased and wrote out a cheque for a handsome amount to promote the study of Buddhism. This was yet another example of the gift of persuation that Tan possessed which helped him advance his mission.

However, in spite of all the major accomplishments, it was not a life of unmitigated joy for Tan. Like the proverbial yin and yang, joy came with sorrow and Tan had his share of the latter. But in the end, Tan's eternal optimism always pulled him from darkness to light.

Tan used to lament to his children that there was only a handful of people who understood the real significance of what he was trying to accomplish. However, within that small group he could count stalwarts like Tagore, Nehru, Tai Xu, and Tai Chi-Tao. As these giants passed away, one by one, no other visionaries would step forward to fill the gap. One exception was his friend and life-long well-wisher Anil Kumar Chanda. He did all he could within his powers to lend support to Tan's projects, but he too passed away prematurely. Each passing away was filled with pain for Tan but he endured them all with the strength that his faith in the good Lord Buddha gave him.

1951 was a momentous and painful year for Tan. That year, Visva-Bharati was taken over and became a Federal Government University. The intentions were no doubt honourable, for Nehru had promised Gurudeva to take care of the university after his death. However, once the takeover was completed, Nehru left the administration of the university in lesser hands. These people did not have the benefit of sharing Gurudeva's vision and the character of Visva-Bharati changed dramatically. No longer did it retain its unique characteristics of an international centre of learning. It became a run-of-the-mill university. Tan was disillusioned by the turn of events. The institutions that Visva Bharati was known for, Patha-Bhavana, Kala-Bhavana, Sriniketan and Cheena Bhavana were all relegated to secondary positions. We wondered what Gurudeva would have thought about these transformations !

Visva-Bharati grew rapidly with funds pouring in from the Federal Government. Many new faculty members were hired from outside. Unfortunately, most were now drawn to Santiniketan because of the higher government salary scales and not because of their commitment to the ideals espoused by Tagore. Tan used to return from Faculty Meetings disgusted by the tone of discussions that were taking place. Most discussions were focussed around what salaries the staff would demand of the administration in the next round of negotiations. There was hardly any time or interest in discussing the promotion of academic and research excellence in the institution. The physical growth of the university was achieved at the cost of the quality of academic pursuits that Visva-Bharati was once known for. It was a sad period for Tan indeed!

The next period of sorrow came in the early sixties when the political relations between India and China became strained due to disputes along the border. It was a cartographical nightmare left by the British who were unable to complete field survey over some no man's lands that caused the initial disagreement. But no matter. It was enough excuse for the two countries to go to war for the first time in thousands of years of peaceful co-existence. Tan was absolutely devastated. It appeared to him that all his life-long efforts to build cultural ties and political understanding between the two countries were about to shatter. Only the encouragement of a few steadfast friends in India, including Nehru, was able to bring some peace to Tan's mind.

Tan's retirement from Visva-Bharati Cheena-Bhavana in 1967 almost came as a relief to him. By this time he had already lost his last staunch supporter Nehru and his last close friend Anil Chanda. His mind was now focussed on the next major challenge in Bodh Gaya which had beckoned him ever since he set foot on Indian soil.

Was this a unique life-career? I would say, definitely. Was it an ordinary life-career? Only the readers of this article can judge. On the occasion of the Birth Centenary of Tan Yun-shan, I present this humble account to help understand the life and works of this contemporary cultural ambassador between India and China.

January 1, 1998
Vancouver, Canada

19

FOND MEMORY FROM A SON

As I gather my thoughts to write this article for the Centennial volume on my father Prof. Tan Yun-shan, a vast amount of memories and impressions race through my mind. After much self-debate as to what to put in black and white, I decided to write about both of my parents, since my mother was an inalienable partner of my father in whatever endeavour he undertook. This article is about both of them from the frame of reference of their children, as we viewed them and perceived them while we grew up and matured under their care into adulthood.

I will begin with a small supernatural event which my father encountered over the South China Sea which is now being brought out for the first time. On one of his voyages between India and China, he went to the deck of the ship at sunrise and saw what he described as the "Heart of Lord Buddha" floating on the sea. He went to summon his family, but when they arrived at the deck, the "heart" had disappeared. It is this event which probably later dictated what he would undertake after he retired as the Director of Cheena-Bhavana.

He was going to take up the monumental task of single-handedly creating the "World Buddhist Academy" in Bodh-Gaya in his sixties from private donations alone and without government help. To any sane person, this was like trying to climb Mt. Everest alone without oxygen. But no matter. For, this was the call from a higher authority and must be carried out. From a physicist's perspective, this was like Einstein's quest for a Unified Field Theory, which he could never accomplish in his lifetime.

Father was a very quiet, soft-spoken and humble person, who never became angry at anyone and always avoided argument. But he was also a very sensitive individual who was easily wounded by unfair criticism of him. Instead of confronting his critics, he withdrew himself to his study in silence and often refrained from talking or taking food for the rest of the day. Usually, he would slowly return to normal the following day.

His association with Tagore, Gandhi and Nehru is well-known. But it was the Mahatma who had by far the deepest influence in his life, surpassing even that of Gurudeva. In his mind, Gandhiji was the closest human being to God: in fact he was God in a human body. When Gandhiji visited Santiniketan, father spent many hours with him seeking answers to intractable questions and general guidance in life. To him, Gandhiji seemed to have answers to all the questions he was seeking.

Santiniketan observed Wednesday as the weekly day of rest as that was the day the Mahatma first set foot on Ashram soil. Following Gandhi, father observed a day of silence on Wednesdays. Later on, as life became more complicated, and pressure of work became more intense, he was forced to curtail his silence. First he ended his silence after lunch on Wednesdays, and later after breakfast.

Following Gandhi again, he wanted to be a complete vegetarian, but here he had difficulties. He was the head of a large family with several growing children, and he understood the importance of a balanced nutrition. I used to sit closest to him around the dining table and I vividly remember that every time he was served meat by a family member, he would let out a gentle groan as if to ask for forgiveness. One item he relished was eggs, for Gandhiji had given him full permission to treat eggs as vegetarian food.

Father lived a saintly life in a family setting. He woke up every morning and witnessed sunrise as he did yoga commencing with "Surya Namaskar". He would then pick a basketful of flowers and laid them on his prayer table in his study at Cheena Bhavana. He would light up incense and pray to Lord Buddha. He would repeat his prayers at the prayer table in the family residence. His family often joined him in his prayers but were also frequently absent. I often felt that the second prayer was on behalf of the family. He would repeat his prayers after practising yoga in the evening.

Father was an avid reader who compiled his own library in his study at Cheena Bhavana. His books were mostly on philosophy, religion and history. But to my dismay, there was a total dearth of scientific and technical books in his study. There was only one book on the human body and another on tropical medicine. He had a complete set of Encyclopedia Britannica from which we could extract useful information and hard data. A large fraction of his books were authored by Swami Sivananda, a prolific writer from his Ashram in the Himalayas. Sivananda sent him every book he had written free of cost and corresponded with him regularly, even though they had never met each other in person to my knowledge. Publications from Sri Aurobindo's Ashram and Maha Bodhi Society among others also arrived regularly.

Father was an architect and a landscaper. Besides Cheena Bhavana, he designed and built several houses around it. Just as Gurudeva had added and appended rooms, corridors and floors to Uttarayan over the years, so did father to our residence behind Cheena Bbavana, albeit on a smaller scale. With the help of malis, he planted all the shade trees, flower trees and hedges around Cheena Bhavana which one sees today.

Father was a man of simple living and high thinking. He ate little and never smoked in his life. He had little desire of earthly possessions. The only luxury items he had was a Rolex watch which he wore constantly in his pocket and several Parker pens. In his early years in Singapore, he used to visit to ocean-front and wrote poems in his pastime. In his later years at Santiniketan, he practised Chinese calligraphy.

Father was an optimist and never dwelt in negatives. He was never afraid of disaster if financial situation was hard or a family member became sick. And he never panicked in a crisis. He always believed that "everything will be all right". Perhaps that belief stemmed from his own belief in a divine power.

And now about my mother. If father dedicated his entire life to the cause of Sino-Indian relations, so did mother indirectly by standing on his side throughout her life. Her life was a model study of the silent partner in the shadow. She, like father, came from an educated family in Hunan Province of China and was the principal of a school in Malaya before she met father. In addition to her duties as the principal, she also taught science and mathematics. My own scientific and mathematical interests must have come from her side.

Mother was a hard-working parent, who took the brunt of the daily life and successfully raised seven children besides taking care of father. A tireless worker, she toiled from dawn to dusk in those days when daily amenities were hard to come by at Santiniketan. In later years facilities improved in Bolpur and Santiniketan, but the number of visitors to our house increased steadily and mother had the additional burden in providing food and shelter for them. She had no break; no vacation that I can remember of. Yet she still managed to write articles for a Chinese daily in Singapore. She also attended the "Mahila Samiti" until it disbanded.

Mother was very different from father. Father was a Gandhian, while mother considered Gurudeva as a better model for the average person. Whereas father was an idealist and philosophical, mother was practical and down-to-earth. While father believed in self-healing, mother was a firm believer of modern medicine. Father believed in prayers but mother believed in practical solutions to problems. But different as they might have been, their natures were complementary to one another which served the family well.

There was a general division of labour in the family and the harder part of carrying out domestic chores fell entirely on the shoulders of mother. She raised a vegetable garden that was deserving of winning awards. She gave away her produce to friends and neighbours. All this she did for others. She never demanded anything for herself. "Sacrifice" is one word that characterised her entire life.

Both of our parents were loving and caring individuals, who did not exhibit their feelings in accord with the great tradition of the eastern cultures. Both wanted the best in their children and both were impartial as far as practicable. Father wanted his children to reach lofty heights in whichever profession they chose. Mother wanted her children to purpose endeavours which would be useful to mankind.

When their youngest sons were migrating to America, mother broke down in tears not knowing when she would see them again. But to father, they were joyous occasions. I learned later that when the plane was airborne, father raised his hand in the air and held it there for a prolonged while as if to send a blessing for a brighter life! I have carried that blessing with me ever since.

20

TAN YUN-SHAN LIVES IN OUR HEARTS FOREVER

I heard about the feat of Tan Yun-shan more than half a century ago. After I joined the Department of Eastern Studies of Beijing University to learn Hindi in 1951. I developed more interest in India and in Sino-Indian cultural exchange, hence there was an additional concern on my part for the activities of my academic senior, Prof. Tan Yun-shan. Whatever he had achieved was noticed by me with hearty admiration and inspiration.

Prof. Tan was an outstanding scholar, having dedicated his entire life to the inquiries about the religions, philosophies and literature of India, leaving behind abundant writings which are treasures for posterity.

Prof. Tan was also a diligent desseminator of Chinese culture, under taking research in Visva-Bharati on the one hand, teaching Chinese and lecturing on Chinese culture on the other — his indefatigable dedication nursed a permanent base for rearing up those who had shown an inclination to study China, and for their mutual exchanges. The Chinese People's Political Consultative Conference [China's equivalent of the Rajya Sabha of Indian Parliament] elected Prof. Tan as a Specially Invited Member in 1957 in recognition to his contributions. In 1979, he was confered *Deshikottam* — The highest academic honour by Visva-Bharti.

Furthermore, Prof. Tan was a messenger of amity and friendship between the two nations — India and China. Long since 1930s he had been Shuttling between China and India, meeting various leaders Like Gandhi, Nehru, Chiang Kai-shek, Mao Zedong, Liu Shaoqi, and Zhou Enlai etc., making real input to Sino-Indian friendly relationship.

During my student career I was all admiration for Prof. Tan, and longed for a visit to India, to Visva-Bharati in order to pay my respect to Prof. Tan, and to benefit from his teaching. However, uncertainty dominated the International Scene. Soon after I started working after graduation the singing of "Hindi-Chini Bhai Bhai" which had one time made me intoxicated suddenly stopped. In 1959, tension appeared on the Sino-Indian border which was followed by a brief war in 1962. It all seemed that the hope I had cherished in my student days would fall into a vacuum. I felt endlessly frustrated.

While I was studying I pondered upon things. On Sino-Indian relations Prof. Tan observed in his Yindu zhouyouji (A Tour Around India) that it was "specially important among the specially important". He added, "I firmly believe that whether we talk of world peace or world revolution, whether human civilization or human amity, we won't achieve our goal if the two nations, China and India, do not really unite and struggle with joint endeavours."How confident, how correct are these words. I wonder, Since Sino-Indian relations are of such great importance, would the little episode of the 1962 war create, a permanent obstacle in the way for our two great nations to join our hands towards the great goal of world place and joint development ? Of course not. Sino- Indian relations are bound to improve.

Indeed, history develops according to its own rhythm. In 1976, the two countries restored their diplomatic relations to the ambassadorial level. In the 1980s bilateral relations greatly improved. In the beginning of February 1988, I realized my dream and landed on the soil of India — the land of my longing. I then, visited the Visva-Bharati Campus which was evergreen. But , I lost the opportunity of meeting Prof. Tan and receiving his teachings. Yet, when I sauntered on the clean, spacious university complex of Santiniketan I felt it reverberating with the gentle smile of Prof. Tan. From the lofty teaching block of Cheena-Bhavana emitted out laud conversations in Chinese language which all the more made me feel deeply that Prof. Tan was still alive in our midst.

It is gratifying that since the China visit by Mr. Rajiv Gandhi in 1988, Sino-Indian relations have grown substantially. The border dispute is frozen, no longer affecting the overall improvement of bilateral relations. Exchanges in various fields are increasing. Trade volumes double every few years. President Jiang Zemin visited India in November 1996, resulting in a Sino-Indian agreement to build up a constructive co- operative partnership toward the 21st century. If Prof. Tan hears ail this in his Heavenly abode, he would definitely feel happy.

Facing with such a happy development of Sino-Indian relations what should we do? Once again, I remember the words of Prof. Tan. He said, "If we want the two nations (of China and India) to really unite, we must have them to understand each other. If we want the two nations to understand each other, we must study each other's national culture." This is enlightening. In order to have a closer co-operation between the two nations in the next century so as to create new splendours for humankind, the academia of China and India must leave no stone unturned to strengthen "Studies of each other's national culture" in order to achieve "Mutual understanding between the two nations".

During the birth centenary of Prof. Tan Yun-shan this would be the best course of action for us to remember our outstanding senior and pay our great respects to him.

21

TAN YUN-SHAN: AN ATTRIBUTE

Two brilliant megastars shine upon the horizon of the long river of the history of Sino-Indian cultural interface. One was the celebrated Buddhist Master Xuanzang of the ancient times; the other Prof Tan Yun-shan of the modern times. Both of them share many commonalities. In the first place, both of them were top class — of the national level. During his stay at the Nalanda Monastery, Xuanzang studied under the most famous scholar Shilabhadra. His academic achievements were commended first in India by King Harshavardhana then by the Tang Emperor, Tai Zong after his return to the country. The latter accorded VIP treatment to him. Prof. Tan Yun-shan worked together with Cai Yuanpei and Ravindranath Tagore, and other renowned cultural personalities and also maintained cordial relations with eminent political leaders, Chiang Kai-shek, Mao Zedong, Mahatma Gandhi and Jawaharlal Nehru. In the second place, both Xuanzang and Tan Yun-shan had made outstanding contributions to the cause of Sino-Indian cultural exchanges. As Xuanzang is a household word I need not dwell upon here. The most outstanding monument erected by Prof. Tan Yun-shan was the imposing Cheena-Bhavana standing on the Campus of Visva-Bharati. But there are also dissimilarities in the Comparisim while Xnanzang was an eminent Buddhist monk, great traveller and translator, Prof. Tan inspite of his profound learning in Buddhism was essentially an educationist and a cultural ambassdor. Hence, they had distinguished themselves in different light. Apart from that, the historical background in which they lived was also very different. Xuanzang lived in a very peaceful and prosperous time of Tang dynasty. During his stay of seventeen years in India, there was no war. But, the major activities of Tan Yun-shan were dogged and overshadowed by World War II. Xuanzang had hardly involved himself in political activities while Prof. Tan had contributed a lot to the common Sino-Indian anti Japanese struggle. Prof. Tan, therefore, was also a political activist. Viewing from the above fact while treading the foot-steps of Xuanzang, Prof. Tan has le left a deep imprint of his own in history.

I first came to know about Prof. Tan Yun-shan in the Summer of 1951. At that time, I was standing English in the Department of Western languages of Beijing University and was planning to move to the field of Hindi in the Department of Oriental Languages. In order to understand India I went to the Cai Yuanpei Library in search of books on India. A book on the shelf caught my attention. It was *Yindu Zhouyouji* (An account of my tour around India) — authored by Prof. Tan Yun-shan. After realising that Prof. Tan was a Hunanese an affinity was immediately created between me and the author. Prof. Tan's style had a great flow with vivid narratives that made me finish reading the book almost in one go. I learnt a lot from it. I must say that Prof. Tan was the first guide to escort me into the ranks of researchers in Sino-Indian cultural interface.

After graduating from the Department of Oriental Languages in 1955, I was appointed as the teaching assistant in the University Next year in October, I had the honour of personally meeting Prof. Tan, the man whom I had been admiring for a long time. I remember, it was a pleasant autumn morning. Prof. Ji Xianlin, Head of the Department of Oriental Languages, Prof. Jin Kemu, Director of Research of the Department and myself (I was the Secretary in the Research Division) received Prof. Tan in the Linhuxuan pavilion wearing a yellow overcoat a Napoleonic hat , he was a little reduced, but very energetic. Standing behind him was his daughter Ms. Tan Wen. She was wearing a green skirt but not a saree seeing them, I was reminded of Nehru and his daughter, whom we had met two years earlier. Prof. Jin Kemu informed me that, Tan Wen had topped the Bengali language examination in India. Tough,she was younger than me by a few years, I had developed some regards for her. Conversation was carried on among three elders mostly on Sino-Indian Cultural exchange and about their old acquaintances. Being a junior I listened to them in rapt attention without butting in. After the meeting, I took Prof. Tan and his daughter to go around the campus. The distinct impression I gathered was that such a celebrity was after all a man of easy access.

In Feb. 1983, Prof. Tan left for his Heavenly abode. When the sad news reached Beijing, many of those who had been working for Sino-Indian cultural exchange were in deep grief. During October in the same year, I went to India to participate in the Third International Hindi Conference. After the Conference, I went to the house of Prof. Tan Chung and conveyed my heartfelt condolence when the holy mountain Tai shrank, sages would wither [as the Chinese saying goes]. Though no more he has left an extremely rich and valuable spiritual heritage. Being a junior in the field of Sino-Indian cultural interface, I shall march forward along the path carved out by Xuanzang and Prof. Tan Yun-shan. (Translated by Yukteshwar Kumar.)

22

MY FIRST LESSON IN INDIAN STUDIES: READING TAN YUN-SHAN'S *TRAVEL ACCOUNT*

The first time I came to know the name of Prof. Tan Yun-shan was over ten years ago. I had reached Beijing from Sichuan, and was a post-graduate student at the Institute of South-Asian Studies of Beijing University. Partly because of academic requirements and partly because of my own personal idiosyncracy, I spent most of the time in the university library, looking for books and reading books. I wanted to find out all books related to India that were in the library, and at least flip them over. Among the books I was searching for was one *Yindu Zhouyouji* (An Account of My Tour Around India) by Mr. Tan Yun-shan.

The copy of *Yindu Zhouyouji* in our university library was a 1933 edition (22nd year of the Republic of China), published from Nanjing. The title of the book is enshrined by the calligraphy of Cai Yuanpei. It was a very old book with characters vertically printed and pages already turned brown. Evidently, it had been used by many readers.

My deepest impression about this book was its photographs one of which was that of Mahatma Gandhi. In the photograph, Gandhi was sitting cross-legged on the ground, his face lean, upper body uncovered, with a piece of white cloth girdled around the loin. Below the photograph was an observation by Prof. Tan Yun-shan:

"Mr. Gandhi was from a rich family, but has no connection today with property or family. His wife and son have joined his other followers in toiling, from place to place without warming their seats for the cause of national revolution and reconstruction of the society. All his clothes are self-spun and self-woven with hardly any work of the tailor. In summers, he only girdles a piece of cloth (i. e. dhoti) around the loin; during winter he covers a shawl over his upper body. Wherever he travels to, he carries the "Charkha" (spinning wheel) along with him. All Indians into the "Gandhian attire" before paying him a visit; none appears before him in western apparel. Even European and American visitors follow such a convention. His diet is simple and frugal, mainly of goat milk and vegetables. Slaughtering animals and consuming meat is a total taboo."

The dust of the "Cultural Revolution" had just settled down by then. Although I knew about Gandhi, but not much. In the books and article which I had read about Gandhi till then, there was more criticism than commendation. This book, however, was the only one I came across which was totally in approbation of Gandhi, in spite of the fact that it had been published so many years ago. It took me by surprise, but at the same time roused my interest in going ahead in reading the book. To use a current parlance of those times, I wanted to "liberate my mind" a bit.

It was the book of Prof. Tan Yun-shan that had enabled me to know a lot about Gandhi the man and his feat from a very different angle altogether. Here was freshness in my feeling. I still remember the impression which one chapter of the book left in me. While describing his own visit to Gandhi, Prof. Tan wrote what Gandhi had to say to him:

"Since my own country faces so many problems, I don't have the opportunity to study China's affairs. But I am aware of the fact that China has a very ancient and rich history and culture, the people of China are great and peace-loving. Such a great and peaceful nation can surely shoulder the great responsibility of safeguarding peace on behalf of the world.

If only China could harmonize its internal conflict and tackle her national problems through peaceful means, inbibing the spirit of Truth, I believe China can obtain salvation immediately".

Frankly speaking, what Gandhi had said appeared to me a bit naive although the beginning paragraph was very aptly put, and the second paragraph was also well said. However, later I gradually understood that in total contrast with other so-called "Statesmen" or "politicians", Gandhi was a truly towering personality in the history of India and also that of the world. His ideas, his spirit, his character and charisma, all were great. A part of such greatness lay in his naivity. But, unfortunately, this world of our's is crowded with hypocrites or naive people who are frauds while the genuinely naive are far too scanty. History recognises heroes only by success, hence many think that naivity is worthless.

This travelogue was the first of its kind that I read about India. In the book, Prof Tan Yun-shan had accounted what he saw and heard during his travels in India, in addition to a description of India's past, and present. He also dealt with the traditional friendship between China and India. All this helped me greatly to gain a concrete understanding of India.

Later, I came across many more books on India. I realized that what Prof. Tan Yun-shan had contributed to the revival and promotion of the friendly relations between China and India far exceeded a mere "travelogue". Through many decades, he had tirelessly shuttled himself between China and India, for the promotion of Sino-Indian friendship, in the endeavour of uniting China and India in their common struggle against imperialism, and aggression. He launched the Sino-Indian Cultural Society and built up the Cheena-Bhavana through which he contributed a lot to the cultural interface between the two countries.

Later, I had the pleasure to know Tan Chung, the honourable son of Prof. Tan Yun-shan. We have met a number of times, either in Delhi or Beijing. Every time we met, pondered over the inescapable topic of Sino-Indian friendship and Sino-Indian Studies and derived immense pleasure from our conversations. I was also fortunate enough to have travelled to Bengal, and to Santiniketan to visit the Cheena-Bhavana of Visva-Bharati. I can never forget the shady bowers and lush lawns of the campus. Even more unforgettable is the warm reception recorded to me by my Indian friends. The teachers and students of Cheena-Bhavana specially organized a meeting on the occasion of our visit and cordially invited me to speak. In my speech I mentioned about Prof. Tan Yun-shan. Like our Indian friends in Santiniketan, we have not forgotten all what Prof. Tan did for Sino-Indian friendship, just as we can never ever forget Faxian, Xuanzang and Yijing. We are all happy to see the happy state of the Sino-Indian relations today and we wish that it will grow from strength to strength.

Prof. Tan Yun-shan's birth centenary would be marked next year. On this occasion I quote a passage from his book here:

"Yes, China and India are two sister countries. This is what I have read from my childhood — a firm impression which can never be erased from my mind. I always feel that this land of India must be visited and the nation of India can never be ignored. That apart, her relations with China rates the highest among the things of highest importance. Leaving out the relations between the two countries in culture and history and focussing on just the current situation, I firmly believe that be it international peace or international revolution, be it the human civilization or the amity within the entire humanity, if China and India do not cooperate sincerely, do not make a common cause in their struggle, there would be no achievement whatsoever."

Sixty six years have elapsed since Prof. Tan Yun-shan had penned these words. Enormous changes have taken place in these sixty six years both in global development and in China and India. We have not only achieved independence, but have also obtained substantial progress in all fields. We now live together in a new era. The prospects of the twenty first century project peace and development as the main currents of the world. All of us who wish to see Sino-Indian friendship, be they Chinese or Indians are, to quote Yu Youren's "Foreword" in Tan Yun-shan's above-mentioned book, the "intermediaries between the peoples and cultures of China and India". I think if we close our ranks in work and struggle, and fulfil our duty of improving the friendship between China and India, it would be the best way of commemorating Prof. Tan Yun-shan.

Beijing
Dec. 18, 1997.

(Translated by Bijoy Das)

INDIA AND CHINA

23. Tagore: Pioneer in Asian Relations
Kalidas Nag

24. Tagore and Confucian China
Sampson Shen

25. On Theories of Nationalism for India and China
Prasenjit Duara

26. Colonialism and the Discourse in India and China
Manoranjan Mohanty

27. Friendship-In-Need between Chinese and Indian People in Modern Times
Lin Chengjie

28. Tan Yun-shan: The Pioneer of Indo Chinese (Sino-Indian) Studies and Cultural Bridge between India and China
H.P. Ray

23

TAGORE: PIONEER IN ASIAN RELATIONS

Moving amongst the delegates of the Asian Conference, I was agreeably surprised to notice how many of them remembered our national poet Rabindranath not only as the greatest luminary in the literary horizon of Asia, but also as a pioneer in reviving inter-Asian relations in modern times. I propose to recount here briefly some of the specific contributions of Rabindranath to the cause which found such glorious vindication in the Delhi Conference.

The earliest so-far-traced reference to Tagore's interest in Asian affairs is to be found in his Bengali article on Death Traffic in China protesting vigorously against the inhuman Opium trade of the European merchants. The article was published in 1881 before the foundation of the Indian National Congress, and it should be re-translated into Hindi, Urdu and other Indian vernaculars. Rabindranath's saintly father, Maharshi Debendranath Tagore, undertook, in an advanced age, a sea-voyage to China; though, unfortunately, his diary of that voyage is now lost, fragments were published in his famous Bengali journal *Tattva Bodhini Patrika* 1875-76 which printed articles on Taoism, Confucianism and other systems of Chinese philosophy as well as some vivid description of the temples of Canton which was apparently the terminus of his China tour.

Rabindranath naturally inherited from his father a deep appreciation of Chinese culture and it will be news to many that in his later years, when he read that brilliant vindication of Eastern idealism by Professor Lowes Dickinson in his Letters of John Chinaman, Tagore was the first to popularise the'book in Bengalii through his essay, *Chinamaner Chithi* (1905-06).

The Republic of China was established in 1911 and Tagore, after his 50th birthday, started on his momentous tour with the English version of his *Gitanjali* which brought the first Nobel Prize to Asia (1913). In his third foreign tour of 1912-13, the Poet came in contact with many oriental students and some of the early translations of the *Gitanjali* were in Chinese and Japanese.

In 1915, Mahatma Gandhi returned from South Africa and brought home to the Poet, at their first personal contact, the tragic history of race-hatred in South Africa. The Reverend C.F. Andrews and W. Pearson, two of the loyal British friends of the Poet, who were also professors at Santiniketan had already been to South Africa to help Mahatma Gandhi. Naturally, the Poet received with open arms the members of Mahatmaji's family and his disciples in Santiniketan.

In 1916, Tagore undertook a voyage through China and Japan to America and suffered humiliation from the Japanese for his trenchant criticism of nationalistic chauvinism which was the cause of the first world war. He repeated the same warning to Japan through his letters to the Poet Noguchi (1938).

In 1920, I had the privilege of travelling with him through France and other European countries. I saw how in his sixtieth year, Tagore plunged with the enthusiasm of a youth, into the planning of an Asian Research Institute at Santiniketan. He had already inspired Pandit Vidhusekhar Sastri to learn Tibetan with a view to restoring some of the forgotten Indian texts, luckily preserved in Tibetan translations. While in Paris, he came to learn from my venerable professor Sylvain Levi that a large number of valuable Indian scholars could be induced to learn Chinese. And although the financial resources of the Santiniketan School were very low in 1921, Rabindranath at once decided to invite Professor Sylvain Levi to inaugurate the department of the Sino-Indian studies at the cost of over ten thousand rupees. Thus Professor Levi spent some of the happiest months of his life in Santiniketan and the Visva-Bharati was founded in December, 1921, as the first institute of Asian

Culture, developing under the joint collaboration of the scholars from the East and the West.

In 1923 when I returned from the University of Paris to join the Post- Graduate Department of the Calcutta University, I had the rare fortune to be invited by Gurudeva to join his Visva-Bharati mission to China and the Far East. The poet had received a cordial invitation from eminent leaders of the Chinese Republic, led by the renowned Liang Chi Chao. Details of this memorable tour have already been published by me in many articles, and recently in the booklet, *Tagore in China*. His appearance in China opened a new chapter in the collaboration between China and India in modern days. Pandit Kshiti Mohan Sen explored the possibilities of organising a comparative study of Chinese and Indian religions and cultures. Acharya Nandalal Bose, who also was a member of the delegation, charmed artistic China by his magic brush and brought back to India valuable hints and suggestions regarding the assimilation of the techniques of Chinese and Indian arts. And I, in my humble way, hoped to integrate the studies of South-East Asian art and culture into our university curriculum; thanks to Dr. Tagore and to the support generously offered by the late Sir Ashutosh Mukerjee, I could organise the Greater India movement which completed its Silver Jubilee in the year of the Asian Relations Conference.

On my way back from China and Japan, I visited in 1924 our ancient culture colonies of Champa (Viet Nam) and Cambodia in Indo-China, as well as the islands of Java and Bali. In 1927 Tagore sailed for Indonesia .....on his return journey he spent some time in Siam, Malaya and Burma as well. Some of the significant poems that he wrote in this period should now be translated from original Bengali into different Asian languages. The entire East Asia with its rich legacies of Sino-Japanese art (mainly inspired by Indian Buddhism), the art and culture of Indonesia, Siam, Burma, in fact, of the whole of South-East Asia, was made for the first time real to our consciousness by the exploratory zeal and the creative genius of Rabindranath.

My friend Dr. Suniti Kumar Chatterji a pillar of our Greater India movement, who accompanied Tagore in 1927, has given a very valuable account of this cultural odyssey in his Bengali book *Dvipamoy Bharat*.

Another learned colleague and a dear friend at the University of Paris, the late Dr. Probodh Chandra Bagchi, opened a new chapter by proceeding to the National University of Peking as a visiting scholar; and he remembered, with gratitude, the fact that he got in touch with Professor Sylvain Levi for the first time in Santiniketan where he was initiated into the various branches of Sino- Indian studies in 1921-1922.

In 1930-31 I had again the privilege of travelling with the Poet through Europe and America. We watched how the venerable Poet, almost in his seventieth year, was still dreaming of exploring fresh fields of cultural collaboration. Visiting Soviet Russia in 1930, Tagore was deeply moved to find how eager were the rural folks of Russia, specially of Soviet Asia, to come to the aid of our unfortunate exploited rural population. Tagore's Letters from Russia written in Bengali (but not then permitted to be published in English), should now be published by Pandit Jawaharlal Nehru, pioneer of inter-Asian Relations, for the benefit of all those who cannot read them in the original, and specially for the numerous nations of Soviet Asia who sent such a large and brilliant delegation to the Asian Conference. When in 1931-32. I had the privilege of assembling and publishing The Golden Book of Tagore, messages flocked in from his admirers of Europe and America as well as from Soviet Russia, China, Japan, Indonesia, the Middle East and the Far East.

Tagore's relations with the Near Eastern countries were most cordial. He passed often through Egypt and King Fuad presented him with a set of valuable Arabic manuscripts for the Islamic Department of the Visva-Bharati. The celebrated Near Eastern poet Bustani personally visited Santiniketan; and I was glad to note that he completed the translations of some of our Sanskrit classics into Arabic. In 1932 the Poet received a personal invitation from the builder of Modern Iran, Reza Shah Pehlavi. Tagore then in his seventy-first year, flew to Teheran and to Baghdad and amidst the glorious roses of Iran, his birthday was celebrated with banquets and poetic recitals, evoking truly Iranian grace and glamour. The Shah also made gifts of enduring nature to the Poet by sending in his party to Santiniketan the celebrated poet and scholar Poure Daoud, together with some rare manuscripts from the Royal Library. Thus Iran also joined hands with India. And Iran and Iraq were the last foreign countries which the Poet could visit in his declining years. But even in his sick-bed, whenever he would hear about an Indian going to some outside country, specially to some Asian cultural zone, he would give enthusiastic blessings.

I remember vividly, in this connection, the evening when the venerable Poet was giving readings to us from his Bengali manuscript of *Chhelebela* (My Younger Days) and Pandit Jawaharlal Nehru quietly came into the lounge, had a few moments' conversation, and with his warm benidictions, started on his first voyage to the Chinese Republic. The Poet had the satisfaction of seeing firmly established, through the devoted zeal of Professor Tan Yun-Shan, Director of the Cheena-Bhavana, where a regular cultural exchange between China and India has been established. Scholars and students not only from China, but also from Japan and Java, Siam and Burma, Ceylon, Afghanistan and Iran and far-off Palestine, have been visiting the International University of Visva-Bharati. This account of Tagore's practically unaided efforts in reviving inter-Asian relations will, I hope, inspire us to undertake our responsibilities in a proper way and on an adequate scale in Free India.

(From Kalidas Nag, *Discovery of Asia*, Calcutta : The Institute of Asian African Relations, 1957, pp. 9-13.)

24

TAGORE AND CHINA

I

The relation between India and China has been unique in the history of the world. For thousands of years together, not a single conflict between two immediate neighboring countries is almost inconceivable, except the United States of America and Canada. More than that, instead of displaying brutal force, India and China exchanged their cultures and civilizations, religions and philosophies. Somebody may attribute this to the sky-pointing barriers of the Himalayas. But no explanation would be complete if it ignored the peaceloving nature of the two great peoples in the East, which is the real and fundamental reason underlying the fact. For aggression is the symbol of barbarism, which has long been cast away in these two nations; and without this brutal symbol, clash can never occur.

But the great days when Fa Hien, Hsuan Tsang and I Tsing went to India and Kasyapa Matanga, Kumarajiva and Bodhidharma came to China did not last long. As we have seen before, after the Sung Dynasty, in China the Buddhist culture was hampered by the interposition of superstition and degenerating force; while its existence on the other side of the Himalayas had long been discontinued. Since the link of the two countries at that time chiefly depended upon Buddhism, so when Buddhism died out in India, the one nation was severed from the other. The political development in the later centuries further prevented close intercourse. Frankly speaking, very little was known about each other in any respect in the last six or seven hundred years. This old friendship was not resumed until 1924 when Gurudeva Tagore came to China.

"The most memorable fact of human history is that of a path-opening, not for the clearing of a passage for machines or machine-guns, but for the helping the realization by races of their affinity of minds, their mutual obligations of a common humanity. Such a rare event did happen and the path was built between our people and Chinese in an age, when physical obstruction needed heroic personality to overcome it, and the mental barrier a moral power of uncommon magnitude. The two leading races of that age met, not as rivals on the battlefield, each claiming the right to be the sole tyrant on earth, but as noble friends glorying in their exchange of gifts. Then came a slow relapse into isolation, covering up the path with its accumulated dust of indifference. Today our old friends have beckoned to us again, generously helping us to retrace that ancient path, obliterated by the intertia of forgetful centuries and we rejoice.'

These words were included in Tagore's speech, "China and India", but it may not be absurd if the Chinese had used then, just changing the word Chinese into Indian, to welcome him when he came to their country.

Rabindranath came to China at the invitation of the Lecturer's Association of Peiping, which was organized by various universities and colleges in that city, with the late Prof. Liang Chi-Chao as its president. Starting from that ancient city, he toured all the big cities in China to the extreme south, and wherever he went, he was cordially welcomed and anxiously asked to deliver speeches on Indian culture and civilization. During this visit, he negotiated with Chinese cultural leaders on exchange of scholars and professors.

According to the plan mapped out at that time, Pandit Vidhushekhara Shastri and another scholar of Santiniketan were to be sent to Peiping to teach Sanskrit and to study the Chinese language. On the other hand, Liang Chi-chao and some others were to go to Santiniketan to help the institution in Chinese studies and to study Sanskrit. A lump sum of Rs. 20,000 had been donated by Seth J. K. Birla to Visva-Bharati to build a special guest house for the coming Chinese scholars. But due to the instability of the political situation in China, the scheme was unfortunately foiled.

But his visit was not in vain. He made a deep impression upon the Chinese mind. He loved China and was loved by the Chinese. Since then, almost all of his works in English have been translated into Chinese, one after another. He came to China just when the latter was beginning her Renaissance and his visit certainly gave a great impetus to this new movement. His poems of "Stray Birds" and "The Crescent Moon" have created new styles of prosody in the new Chinese poetry. A Crescent Moon Society (for poetry) and a Crescent Moon magazine were started immediately after this event by the late Mr. Hsu Chih-mo and Dr. Hu Shih. Dr. Hu was later hailed by some Americans as the counterpart of Rabindranath in China.

"As for the Poet's ideal and hope to unite Asiatic cultures and to revive the Indian and Chinese cultural relationship," a Chinese professor once said, "all of our Chinese scholars have the sincerest sympathy with him and our leading scholars and leaders have also cherished for long the same idea and are willing to co-strive for the common goal with joint endeavors. Now is the time for India and China to resume and strengthen their cultural relationship."

Actually, Tagore had been given a Chinese name, "Chu Cheng-tan" when he was in China.

After that, he became an ardent lover of China and understood China better than any foreigner of that time. Prof. Y. S. Tan, who was teaching at Santiniketan remarked:

"I found in the modern world two great savants who knew China and her people and culture best: one was Gurudeva, another is Bertrand Russell. But, after all, Russell is a Westerner and Gurudeva is an Easterner. A Westerner's comprehension of an old eastern country like China and her people and culture anyhow cannot be so deep, so intense, real and genuine as that of an Easterner."

How true this statement is needs hardly to be verified by the following words with which Tagore expressed his profound understanding of the Chinese culture:

"Can anything be more worthy of being cherished than the beautiful spirit of Chinese culture, that has made them love the things of this earth, clothe them with tender grace without turning them materialistic? They have instinctively grasped the secret of the rhythm of things — not the secret of power that is in science, but the secret of expression. This is a great gift, for God alone knows this secret. I envy them this gift and wish our people could share it with them."

Then the Sino-Indian Cultural Society came into existence in Nanking in the year 1933. The next year, Prof. Y. S. Tan was sent to India, and with the help extended by Tagore, set up the Indian headquarters of the Society in Santiniketan. Tagore, became its first president. Its charter stated: "The object of this Society shall be to study the Mind of India and China with a view to an interchange of their cultures and cultivation of friendship between the peoples of the two countries for the purpose of promoting peace and unity in the world." The program of the society include the following items: Organizing Indian cultural delegations to go to China, and Chinese delegations to come to India for conducting research work, and delivering lectures on Indian and Chinese cultures; recommending Indian students to study in China and Chinese students to study in India; establishing an Indian Institute in China and a Chinese Hall in India; publishing book and journals embodying the result of researches; etc.

At the time of the inauguration of the Society in Santiniketan, Tagore, as its first president, sent the following message to China:

"My friends in China,

"The truth that we received when your pilgrims came to us in India, and ours to you — that is not lost even now.

"What a great pilgrimage was that! What a great time in history! It is our duty today to revive the heroic spirit of that pilgrimage following the ancient path which is not merely a geographical one, but the great historical path that was built across the difficult barriers of race difference, and difference of language and tradition, reaching the spiritual home where man is in bonds of love and cooperation. "(April 23, 1934)"

In the last few years, the Society has done much for the revival of cultural intercourse between the two countries, its greatest achievement being the inauguration of the Cheena-Bhavana (China College), as a department of the Visva-Bharati (International University). Since then, Santiniketan has become the nucleus of Chinese studies under its research department Vidya-Bhavana, with Pandit Vidhushekhara Bhattacharya Shastri as its head.

After Tagore's visit to China, though Liang Chi-chao and others failed to come, time was ripening for the establishment of a separate department in Visva-Bharati to conduct Chinese studies. The first Chinese scholar holding regular classes in Santiniketan was a Mr. Lin, who stayed there for about two years. But the Cheena-Bhavana only came into being through the efforts of his successor, Prof. Y.S.Tan, who was also founder of the Sino-Indian Cultural Society, as already mentioned before.

Prof. Tan was editing a Chinese newspaper in Singapore when he met Tagore for the first time in that colonial capital. Being a devoted Buddhist, he had long been interested in the resumption of cultural and religious communications between India and China. When he saw Rabindranath and learned of his attitude toward China, he found it was a great chance and grasped it. He came to Santiniketan in the following year to teach Chinese, five students at first.

Prof. Tan returned to China in 1931, preparing for the organization of the Sino-Indian Cultural Society, and stressing the importance of setting up the Cheena-Bhavana before the Chinese public. With his zealous endevour, he won the sympathy of both the official and private circles, especially among the Buddhists, including such eminent persons as H. E., Mr. Tai Chi-tao, President of the Examination Yuan and the Rev. Tai Hsu, President of the Chinese Buddhist Association.

Prof. Tan returned to Santiniketan in 1934 to open the Indian Centre of the Cultural Society and went to Nanking, the then capital of China. Again in the latter part of the same year to raise funds and collect books for Cheena-Bhavana. These he brought over by sea when he came to India for the third time in 1936. The construction of the Chinese Hall followed soon afterwards. On April 14th, 1937, which was the Bengali New Year Day, the Hall was formally inaugurated by Rabindranath personally. Prof. Tan became its first Director.

The object of the Cheena-Bhavana, which is the official name of the hall, was "to establish and promote cultural exchange between China and India, for which purpose it will provide facilities for Chinese scholars to study Indian languages, religions and philosophies, — as well as for Indian scholars to study the Chinese languages, religions and philosophies, Buddhism being regarded as the nucleus of all such studies."

Since then, Santiniketan has had a special significance to China, and any party going from China and India, private or official, should not fail to pay a visit to this ideal University of Gurudev Tagore's. The Chinese Goodwill Mission headed by President Tai Chi-tao (which visited India some years before) and Cultural and Educational Mission headed by Vice-Minister Ku Yu-hsu (both in 1943) stayed in Santiniketan for a few days. The poet Hsu Chih-mo and artist Hsu Pe-on remained there for months.

During President and Madame Chiang Kai-shek's historical visit to India in 1942, Visva-Bharati was the only educational institution on their itinerary. Tagore, with his spirit of universal love, has established an ever-lasting friendship with the Chinese leaders and people. Though his body has gone, his spirit is still linking Chinese and Indian together.

Recently, through the efforts of Director Y. S. Tan, Prof. Wu Hsiao-ling, Pt. Vidhushekhar Shastri, Prof. Sujit kumar Mukhopadhyaya and others, the Cheena-Bhavana has attracted students not only from India and China, but also from Ceylon, Siam and Java. In 1944, Mr. Krishna Kinkar Sinha, an exstudent of that institution, was selected to go to Kunming in southwestern China to teach Indian language and culture. In view of its short history, what Cheena-Bhavana has achieved is not negligible and its future is promising. But it must be remembered that without the unreserved help given by the late Gurudev, there would have been no Cheena-Bhavana at all.

Of late much interest has been aroused both in China and in India for the revival of Sino-Indian cultural collaboration and not a few things have been done in this direction, both officially and privately, such as the exchange of research scholars between the two countries, the establishment of scholarships by the Chinese Government in India for Indian students to study Chinese history and culture, the opening of departments of Indian languages in at least three universities in China, Sir S. Radhakrishnan's visit to China at the invitation of the Chinese Govenment in 1945, and the exchange of missions of various subjects of science (notably, agricultural and medical). If one day the cultural relationship between our two countries can reach the same extent as in the glorious days when Buddhism entered China, let us not forget Gurudev, for he was the pioneer and the very symbol of this revival of international cultural collaboraion.

II

Tagore's "Religion of Man," or the Poet's Religion as he sometimes termed it himself, is actually the Religion of Love. For among millions of creatures, only Man is capable of realizing, possessing and attaining Love, the Universal Love. We get a clear idea of this Love from his view about the process of evolution. Being born at a time when science had already taken gigantic strides, Rabindranath had the opportunity to observe its successes and failures and could make out of them a systematic theory of the Religion of Love.

Regarding evolution, we can be sure that Tagore had never been satisfied with the theory of Darwin and Spencer. The world was there even before Man came, like the dancing of stars, flowing of rivers and roaring of thunder, but nobody knew its meaning. When life came to the world, the whole status changed. It was followed by a display of forces, yet there was no meaning. Fortunately, "before the chapter ended, Man appeared and turned the course of this evolution from an indefinite march of physical aggrandizement to a freedom of a more subtle perfection. This has made possible his progress to become unlimited, and has enabled him to realize the boundless in his power." So the world becomes full of meaning only when Man feels unity with the Universe. Scientists can explain the dancing of stars and atoms, but not the sorrow and joy of Man. To find the mystery of these things, we must advance a little further.

There are two different worlds now, one of meaningless forces, and another full of meaning. Of the forces, some you may reject, some you may accept. The display of them may be gigantic but may not satisfy you althogether. They are not what you want. They have no meaning. The appearance of Man changed the whole world. Man is the only creature who survives all others. Other creatures existed before men, but now only live in museums as skeletons.

It is Man who gives new ideas to the world. It is Man who makes a particular use of events. Strings were there before men, but they are used on the viloin only after Man came into the world. And men make it musical only because of its deep significance in the world which was not perceived before men were born. There were many other beautiful things in the world before Man appeared, but they were not appreciated until the appearance of Man. That proves that evolution has not been developing purely on the biological lines indicated by Darwin or Spencer.

It is true that Man had the habit of adapatation to his environment, when he first came into the world, but he did not submit long to this. On the contrary, he made the environment follow him. Man's evolution cannot be merely physical.He does not allow the environment to dominate. Man stands in an erect posture, as most animals cannot. Animals follow Darwin's principle, but Man does not. In the progress of evolution, Man makes the physical circumstance submit to him. What man does is to make the world subsidiary. In this way, Man exhibits the divine quality of evolution. If Man follows the process of evolution according to Darwin's theory, he would not be better than animals. So here lies the difference:

The development of intelligence and physical power is equally necessary in animals and men for their purposes of living; but what is unique in man is the development of his which gradually deepens and widens the realization of his immoral being, the perfect, the eternal."

Man has something besides this body of flesh and blood, while the beast has only a physical body. Man's greater body is in the Universe. Man should make use of this greater body. He can only live when he lives in the world. "My music is not in me," as Tagore put it, "but let me sing together with the Sun, Moon and Stars. The music is of the whole universe. For you are not merely a man of this body; you are the Moon, the Sun, and all. When you go out, dance together with the whole world." Man is not a man so long as he is limited to his body. Man cannot be separated from the Universe. Take him away from the world, and he is dead and the world also becomes meaningless. Therefore, Man is crying for union with the Universe.

"Alas, I cannot stay in the house, and home has become no home to me, for the eternal Stranger calls, he is going along the road.

"The sound of his footfall knocks at my breast; it Pains me!

"The wind is up, the sea is moaning.

"I leave all my cares and doubts to follow the homeless tide, for the Stranger calls me, he is going along the road.

"I am only waiting for love to give myself up at last into his hands. That is why it is so late and why I have been guilty of such omissions.

"They come with their laws and their codes to bind me fast; but I evade them ever, for I am only waiting for love to give myself up at last into his hands.

"People blame me and call me heedless; I doubt not they are right in their blame.

"The market day is over and world is all done for the busy.

"Those who came to call me in vain have gone back in anger. I am only waiting for love to give myself up into his hand."

Thus Man finds his salvation in union with the world. He must go out and meet the "Stranger." He must leave the limited home and plunge himself into the homeless world. Living together with the Universe, Man will never die. His personality cannot die. But he is one with it only when he comes to know how to love it. For then he must be able to feel freedom and unity. The Poet observed the difference between worldy pleasure and divine joy in the following passage:

"We have pleasure in the fulfillment of our necessity, —but this pleasure is of a negative nature. For necessity is a bondage, the fulfillment of which frees us from it. But there comes its end. It is different with our delight in beauty. It is of a positive nature. In rhythm of harmony, whatever may be its reason, we find perfection. There we see not the substance, or the law, but some relationship of forms which has its harmony with our personality. From the bondage of mere lines and matter comes out that which is above all limitations — it is the complete unity of relationship. We at once feel free from the tyranny of meaningness of isolated things — they now give us something which is personal to our ownself. The revelation of unity in its passive perfection, which we find in nature, is beauty; the revelation of unity in its active perfection, which we find in the spiritual world, is love. This is not in the rhythm of proportions, but in the rhythm of wills. The will, which is free, must seek for the realization of its harmony other wills which are also free, and in this is the significance of spiritual life. The infinite centre of personality, which radiates its joy by giving itself out in freedom, must create other centres of freedom to unite with it in harmony. Beauty is the harmony realized in things which are bound by law. Love is the harmony realized in wills which are free."

For the clash between the ideal and the real is everywhere. The ideal is Love; the real is War, an inevitable result of human desires racing after worldly pleasure. Men are always thinking of this clash and great thinkers feel it most acutely. But until the condition of perfect Love is obtained, war will never stop. On the other hand, these clashes also constantly remind Man of what he is able to do. So instead of rejecting these ideas, Man sticks to them, and gradually tries to raise the real to the level of the ideal. Thus Man goes ahead in spite of the pains the present condition may give. Along with this fundamental tendency, his actions may be converted into some thing higher. But these actions are real. Therefore the mainspring of human civilization cannot be separated from the real. Now, according to Darwin and Spencer, the adapted will live while the unadapted will be wiped out. Yet in fact, the secret of evolution is the real craving of Man for a higher condition, but not for the reason which Darwin thought. Man becomes the Man of today because he is not determined by environment. Spiritual revolution, therefore, is suggested by Tagore in place of Darwin's physical evolution.

Revolution means to adjust the real to the ideal but not by adapting oneself to the circumstance. Man becomes the man of today because of something different from what Darwin preached. Darwin would like Man to go all fours. When Man stood in the erect posture, he did not gain any advantage at first. But he has no weapons of his own and he had to use artificial instruments. Wasps have their stings, tigers their teeth. The fact that Man has to employ something which is not born with him is, according to Darwin, not advantageous at all. We can also imagine that at the very beginning, Man could not use his crude weapons adequately. But anyhow Man has risked and has been successful in handling them. That is why Man has succeeded in surviving.

Human beings are capable of attaining a much higher position than their present one and they are never content with the situation of today. This human aspiration, to desire something higher, constitutes a sharp difference between Man and animals. When the immediate object of human desire is obtained, another object stands out and thus is developed an unending circle. This discontent is the distinguishing and fundamental quality of Man. A man may get all kinds of worldly pleasure, but he will still not be content. Because these are not what he really wants.

What is it then, that really craves? Love, Unity with the Universe. As the Poet put it, the ultimate end of man is "to find the One which is in him; which is his truth, which is his soul; the key with which he opens the gate of the spiritual life, the heavenly kingdom. His desires are many, and madly they have the life and fulfillment. But that which is One in him is ever seeking for unity — unity in knowledge, unity in love, unity in purposes of will; its highest joy is when it reaches the infinite one within its eternal unity."

The human desire for immortality is a good example, which can never be attained by scientific researches. Religious leaders and philosophers have solved the problem by identifying themselves with the Universe. In the Bhagavad Gita, Lord Krishna told Arjuna to realize the world within his body and vice versa. Tagore told us "to be truly united in knowledge, love, and service with all beings, and thus to realise one's self in the all-pervading God." For this is "the essence of goodness, and this is the keynote of the teachings of the Upanisads: Life is immense!" When life is immense, naturally, there will be no question of death. Man becomes immortal.

From the foregoing paragraphs we have seen that the ultimate aim of the two great philosophers of the Orient is practically the same, Universal Love, to harmonize Man and the World, though the method which each employed to them emphasized the spiritual side of human civilization, which is in sharp contrast with the humanism of the West.

As Love is thus hailed as the paramount virtue of a human being, and the attainment of it is regarded as the ultimate goal of Man, the question naturally arises: Is it residing in the human soul or does it have to be borrowed from outside? Different answers will have different results. For if it is born along with man, then everybody has the ability to achieve salvation; otherwise, only those who know how to get it from outside can do so. This involves speculations about human nature. In this connection, as well shall see, both Confucius and Tagore are of the opinion that the quality of Universal Love is born with Man.

Confucius himself said very little about Human Nature. It is mentioned once in the Analects. "By nature, near together; by practice, far apart." Confucius meant that the nature of all men is almost the same, but he did not clearly define whether this nature is good or not. And this has been interpreted in three different ways: according to one school, Human Nature is good; according to another, it is bad; and a third school said it is neither good nor bad — it is rather neutral. Before discussing these views, we may quote another passage from the Analects:

"The Master said, I for my part have never yet seen one who really cared for Love, nor one who really abhorred wickedness. One who really cared for Love would never let any other consideration come first. One who abhorred wickedness would be so constantly practising Love that wickedness would never have a chance to get him. Has anyone ever managed to practise Love with his whole might even as long as the space of a single day? I think not. Yet I for my part have never seen anyone who gave up such an attempt, because he had not the strength to go on. It may well have happened, but I for my part have never seen it."

No doubt the Master meant that Universal Love is the supreme virtue and is difficult to be reached. But nobody has given up the attempt to reach it because of this difficulty. In other words, nobody belives it is impossible to get it. Certainly, this belief can only be established under the hypothesis of a good Human Nature. This throws light on the statement, "By nature, near together; by practice for apart." Obviously, the meaning of the Master is that Love is the basic Human Nature, which brings all Human Beings near together; but till now, inspite of frequent attempts, Man has not been able to practice it.

III

This confucianist theory of the goodness of human nature became manifest only after the appearance of Mencius, whose position in Confucianism is next only to that of the founder. We may conveniently put his arguements thus:

First of all, Nature, like the organs of the human body, is born with Man and there is a general resemblace among all human beings. This Nature, however, makes a difference between man and the animals. Aristotle states in his Ethics that the appetites and desires are shared in common by man and the animals, whereas that which differentiates man from animals is the fact that man possesses reason. Mencius meant the same thing when he said: "The faculty of the mind is thinking." A mind capable of reasoning is man's special prerogative and is what Heaven has given to us. And what the mind likes is reason and righteousness. So Mencius said:

"Thus all things which are the same in kind resemble one another. And why should we doubt this solely when we come to man? The Sage and ourselves are the same in kind. Therefore Lung Tzu said, "If a man make hempen sandals without knowing the feet (for which they are intended), yet I know he will not be making baskets of them." For sandals are all like one another because all men's feet are like one another.

"(The same way) with the mouths and flavors: all mouths have the same relishes. Yi Ya (a noted cook) only knew first what our mouths relish. Suppose that his mouth in its relish for flavors differed from that of other men, as is the case with dogs and horses which are not the same in kind with us, why should all men be found following Yi Ya in their relishes? In the matter of tastes the whole world models itself after Yi Ya: that is, the mouths of all men are like one another.

"And so also is it with the ear. In the matter of sounds the whole world models itself after the music-master K'ung; that is, the ears of all men are like one another.

"And so also is it with the eye. In the case of Tzu Tu (a man noted for his beauty), there is no man but who would recognize that he was beautiful. Anyone who would not recognize that he was beautiful. Anyone who would not recognize the beauty of Tzu Tu must have no eyes.

"Therefore I say: Men's mouths agree in having the same relishes; their ears agree in enjoying the same sounds; their eyes agree in recognizing the same beauty. Shall their minds alone be without that which they similarly approves? What is it, then, of which they similarly approve? I say it is the principle of reason and of righteousness. The Sages only apprehended ahead of us what our minds mutually approve of. Therefore the principles of reason and righteousness are agreeable to our minds just as the flesh of grass-fed and grain-fed animals is agreeable to our mouth."

In the second place, according to Mencius, there are four beginnings, namely, these of Love, Righteousness, Propriety and Wisdom, which are unquestionably good and possessed by all men. If these four beginnings are allowed to reach their complete development in a man, he becomes a Sage. A man's lack of Love does not come from the fact that his nature is basically opposed to that if the man of Love, but simply that he has not allowed these four beginnings inherent in him to develop fully. So Mencius said:

"In its (human nature's) reality, it is possible to be good. This is what I mean by saying that it is good. If men do what is not good, it is not the fault of their natural power.

"The feeling of commiseration belongs to all men: so does that of shame and dislike; that of reverence and respect; and that of right and wrong. The feeling of commiseration is Love: that of shame and dislike is Righteousness; that of reverence and respect is Propriety; and that of right and wrong is Wisdom. These are not fused into us from without. We originally are possessed of them. (We neglect them) simply because we lack reflection. Hence I say, "Seek and you will find them; neglect and you will lose them." (Men differ from one another)some twice as much as others, some five times as much, and some to an incalculable amount. It is because they cannot fully carry out their natural powers."

Note the sentence, "It is possible to be good." For what Mencius actually meant by saying that human nature is good, is that natures of all men have goodness, not that men's natures are all entirely good. In another passage, the great Confucianist scholar said:

"All men have a mind which cannot bear (to see the sufferings of) others... If today men suddenly see a child about to fall into a well, they will without exception experience a feeling of alarm and distress. This will not be as a way whereby to gain the favor of the Child's parents, nor whereby they may seek the praise of their neighbors and friends, nor that they are so because they dislike the reputation (of being unvirtuous).

"From this case we may perceive that he who lacks the feeling of commiseration is not a man; that he who lacks a feeling of shame and dislike is not a man; that he who lacks a feeling of modesty and of yielding is not a man; and that he who lacks a sense of right and wrong is not a man. The feeling of shame and dislike is the beginning of Righteousness. The feeling of modesty and yielding is the beginning of Propriety. The sense of right and wrong is the beginning of Wisdom. Man has these four beginnings just as he has his four limbs. When, having these four beginnings, he says of himself that he is incapable (of developing them), he is injuring himself. And when he says of his sovereign that he is incapable, he is injuring his sovereign.

"Since all men have these four beginnings in themselves, let them know to give them their full development and completion, and the result will be like fire that beings to burn, or of a spring which has begun to find vent. Let them have their complete development, and they will suffice to protect all within the four seas. Let them be denied that development, and they will not suffice to serve his parentswith."

When all men have a mind which cannot bear to see the sufferings of others, it means Man's nature is good.

Thirdly, all men have an intuitive knowledge and an intuitive ability. The epistemology of Mencius is practically a theory of knowledge a *priori*. That is why he said that the four beginings, "are not fused into us from without. We originally are possessed of them." Among these four beginnings, the feelings of commiseration, of shame and dislike, and of reverence and respect are real feelings while the so-called feeling of right and wrong is, in fact, some kind of knowledge. But Mencius himself might not have been conscious of this difference. It seems that he used the term of intuitive knowledge and intuitive ability to include the four beginnings, but there is still something more than these. He said:

"The ability possessed by men without having been acquired by learning is intuitive ability, and the knowledge possessed by them without the exercise of thought is their intuitive knowledge. Children carried in arms all know to love their parents, and when they are grown a little, they all know to love their elder brothers. Filial affection for parents is the working of Love. Respect for elders is the working of Righteousness."

It is clear that this ability and this knowledge are brought together with Man when he is born, and so they are one with the Human Nature. If a man can retain this original quality even after he has grown up, then, he is naturally good and is regarded as a great man. Mencius said, "The great man is a man who has not lost the infant's mind." Thus it is proved that Human Nature is good.

The chief contribution of the Sung school of Confucianism to the Chinese doctrine of Human Nature is to give a two-fold interpretation to the form. It is clearly expounded by them that in certain context, the term refers to the "Original and Essential Nature", while in others it refers to the "Physical Nature", that is, to the Essential Nature as conditioned by the physical element. "Mencius in his assertion that Nature is good speaks of it only in respect of its origin," said Chu Hsi, "making no reference to the physical nature." Yet in reality, while the real nature is the Original and Essential Nature, with which man is endowed by Heaven, it is never found except in conjunction with its material vehicle, and therefore any account of the Nature which treats of the one apart from the other must be inadequate, if not positively erroneous.

"Take light as an illustration, there must be some reflecting body, whether a mirror or a sheet of water, in order to have light. The light is the Nature; the mirror or water is the physical element; without the mirror or water the light is dispersed and lost."

This combination of the Essential Nature with its physical medium is termed the Physical Nature. It is to the inequalities in the physical element that the inequalities of virtue and vice, as well as the differences of species, are due; as in an old mirror which is marred by blemishes on its surface and so reflects the light unequally.

It must not be supposed, however, that there are two natures, the Essential and the Physical. There is only one nature; that is the Essential Nature. The Physical Nature is still the Essential Nature, but conditioned by the physical element. The physical element in and by itself can never be termed the Nature. It is the necessary medium for the individualization of the immaterial element by which the Essential Nature comes to be; and as that medium it conditions, impedes, and even distorts, the manifestation of the Essential Nature. It is the Essential Nature, as it is thus affected, that is called the Physical Nature.

This interpretation of the goodness of human nature is very similar to Tagore's conception, though not exactly the same. According to the poet there is a dualism in human consciousness.

"It is the dualism in his consciousness of what is and what ought to be. In the animal that is lacking, its conflict is between what is and what is desired; whereas, in man, the conflict is between what is desired; whereas, in man, the conflict is between what is desired and what should be desired. What we share with animals; but what should be desired belongs to a life which is far beyond it."

Obviously, the "what is" is the physical nature and the "what ought to be" is the Essential Nature.

Men do evil things because they do not realize the Universal Love which is the truth. They only know what is desired, but do not know what should be desired.

But "we must come to an end in our evil doing, in our career of discord. For evil is not infinite, and discord cannot be an end in itself. Our will has freedom in order that it may find out that its true course is towards goodness and love. For goodness and love are infinite and only in the infinite is the perfect realization of freedom possible. So our will can be free, not towards the limitations of our self, not where it is *maya* and negation, but towards the unlimited where is truth and love.... So in the freedom of our will, we have the same dualism of appearance and truth — our self-will is only the appearance of freedom, and love is the truth. When we try to make this appearance independent of truth, then our attempt brings misery and proves its own futility in the end. Everything has this dualism of *maya* and *satyam*, appearance and truth. Words are *maya* where they are merely sounds and finite, they are *satyam* where they are ideas and infinite. Our self is *maya* where it is merely individual and finite, where it considers its separateness as absolute; it is *satyam* where it recognizes its self, in *paramatman*."

Here *maya* is the same material element in Chu Hsi's theory while *satyam* is the real nature of human beings. The difference between a good man and a bad man in the ordinary saying is only due to the weaker or stronger appearance of *maya*. But *satyam* is always there, dwelling deep in the human soul. Whenever one realize its existence, one attains bliss and salvation.

This *satyam*, when manifest in our daily life, becomes the moral nature. But the question will be asked, What is this moral nature? or: What is goodness? Rabindranath's answer is:

"That when a man begins to have an extended vision of his true self, when he realizes that he is much more than at present he seems to be, he begins to get conscious of his moral nature. Then he grows aware of that which he is yet, to be, and the state not yet experienced by him becomes more real than that under his direct experience. Necessarily, his perspective of life changes, and his will takes the place of his wishes."

When a man reaches this status, he knows there is a life whose greater portion is out of his present reach, whose objects are not for the most part before our sight. He begins to distinguish between what he immediately desires and what is good. Thus the sense of goodness comes out of a truer view of his life, which is the connected view of the wholeness of the field of life, and which takes into an account not only what is present before us, but also what is not. And he feels for that life of his which is not yet existent, much more than for the life that is with him now. Then he is ready to sacrifice his present inclination for the unrealized future. In this he becomes great, for he realizes truth.

There is a passage in Sadhana, which states almost exactly what Mencius said about human nature:

"As he has a feeling for his future self which is outside his present consciousness, so he has a feeling for his greater self which is outside the limits of his personality. There is no man who has not this feeling to some extent, who has never sacrificed his selfish desire for the sake of some other person, who has never felt pleasure in undergoing some loss or trouble because it pleasure in undergoing some loss or trouble because it pleases somebody else. It is a truth that man is not a detached being, that he has a universal aspect; and when he recognizes this, he becomes great."

This universal aspect is peculiar to human beings. You cannot find it in other animals. A dog may lose its life when it comes to the rescue of a man, but it only does so when this man is its master, who feeds it. So the dog does this, for its own interest. But man may incur losses or troubles by doing something good for somebody who is a stranger to him, for whom he has no responsibility, He does it spontaneously and disinterestedly. This is the manifestation of human nature. Tagore further explained it as follows:

"For our moral faculty is the faculty by which we know that life is not made up of fragments, purposeless and discontinuous. This moral sense of man not only gives him the power to see that the self has a continuity in time, but it also enables him to see that he is not true when he is only restricted to his own self. He is more in truth than he is in fact. He truly belongs to individuals who are not included in his own individuality, and whom he is never even likely to know."

The word Dharma is also used by the poet-philosopher to interpret human nature.

"The Sanskrit word *Dharma*," he once remarked, "which is usually translated into English as 'religion' has a deeper meaning in our language. *Dharma* is the innermost nature, the essence, the implict truth, all things. *Dharma* is the ultimate purpose that is working in our self. When any wrong is done, we say that *dharma* is violated, meaning that the lie has been given to our true nature."

This *dharma* is the truth in us, but is inherent, not apparent. So much so that many people would mistake it and think that sinfulness is the nature of man, and only by the special grace of God can a particular person be saved. Tagore here gives the growing up of a seed into a tree as an example. Actually the appearance of the seed contradicts its true nature. When we take it for chemical (or any other kind) of analysis, we only find in it carbon and protein and a good many other things, but not the slightest idea of a branching tree. We get to know it *dharma* only when the tree begins to take shape. And it is the same with human beings:

"In the history of humanity we have known the living seed in us to sprout. We have seen the great purpose in us taking shape in the lives of our greatest men, and have felt certain that though there are numerous individual lives that seem ineffectual, still it is not their *dharma* to remain barren; but it is for them to burst their cover and transform themselves into a vigorous spiritual shoot, growing up into the air and light, and branching out in all directions."

Realizing this *dharma* in himself and attaining the moral nature, a man is thus symbolically described by Tagore as having a second birth. This second birth takes place when he knows that what should be desired belongs to a life which is far beyond the present one. When a man is born, "he still retains a good many habits and instincts of his animal life: yet his true life is in the region of what ought to be. In this, though there is a continuation, yet there is also a conflict. Many things that are good for the one life are evil for the other.

"This necessity of a fight with himself has introduced an element into man's personality which is character. From the life of desired it guides man to the life of purpose. This life is the life of the moral world.... This is the world of man's second birth, the extra-natural world, where the dualism of the animal life and the moral makes us conscious of our personality as man." It may be noted that when the poet said an element is introduced into man's personality, it does not mean that personaltiy is lacking in man and should be introduced from outside. Personality is *dharma* and is already there in man when he is born. The element introduced has only the function of helping discovers this inherent *dharma* so that he may come to realise it.

Religion is merely man's endeavor to cultivate and express those qualities which are inherent in the Dharma, and to have faith in it... Man begins his history with all the original promptings of his brute nature which helps him to fulfill those vital needs of his which are immediate. But deeper within him there is a current of tendencies which runs in many ways in a contrary direction, the life current of universal humanity. Religion has its function in reconciling the contradiction, by subordinating the brute nature to what we consider as the truth of Man, that is, by subordinating the physical nature to the essential nature.

But sometimes, "the contradiction between the two natures in us is so great that men have willingly sacrificed their vital needs and courted death in order to express their *dharma*, which represents the truth of the Supreme Man." In a word, Man becomes a man because he has this very *dharma* which is inborn and inherent. Though in many cases, it may be covered by different kinds of physical elements, yet it does not affect the fact that *dharma* is there, deep in the heart of everybody.

25

ON THEORIES OF NATIONALISM FOR INDIA AND CHINA

Whereas most nationalists believe that there is a continuous history of the nation from ancient times to the present, identifiable as the history of a self-same people, scholars of nationalism, particularly in the last fifteen or so years, have debunked all such notions of a continuous path as mythical. I am basically in agreement with the scholarly critique of nationalist myths, but the scholarly critique can be equally unhelpful when it denies any historical connection between the modern nation and the historical society from wence it emerges. In this article I want to suggest that these are both complex societies with distinct historical connections to the past, but these connections are not simple and continuous and nor are they singular. Modern Indians and Chinese are heirs to multiple narratives of political community which they have drawn upon and transformed.

Since at least Ellie Kedourie there has developed a tradition in the scholarship of nationalism which rightly debunks nationalist histories for their mythologies and suppressions of uncomfortable events. Alerting us to the self-consciousness of this exercise, Benedict Anderson has recently pointed out the unproblematic way in which Ernest Renan could write about being "obliged to having already forgotten" wars between different polities; and how these wars subsequently came to be written as "fratricides" among fellow Frenchmen (Anderson 1991, 200). While I am sympathetic with the critique of teleology in this literature, I am suspicious of the proposition which often accompanies it: that nationalism is a radically novel mode of consciousness. Suspicious (a) because this position ignores the complexity of the nature of historical memory and causality and (b) because it remains tied to the idea of self-consciousness as a uniquely modern phenomenon. In neither modern nor pre-modern society is it possible to sustain the notion of a unified consciousness presumed by the concept of nationalism.

Two of the most influential recent works on nationalism, by Ernest Gellner (1983) and Benedict Anderson (1983, revised 1991), emphasize the radically novel and modern nature of nationalist consciousness. Both are extremely fine studies and while I agree with many of their insights regarding the reproduction of nationalist ideology, I would like to challenge their interpretation of the nature and history of nationalist consciousness. Both analysts identify national consciousness conventionally as the co-extensiveness of politics and culture: an over-riding identification of the individual with a culture that is protected by the state. Both also provide a sociological account of how it was only in the modem era that such a type of consciousness—where people from diverse locales could "imagine" themselves as part of a single community—was made possible.

Gellner presents the following account of this discontinuity. Pre-industrial society is formed of segmentary communities, each isolated from the other, with an inaccessible high culture jealously guarded by a Gellner's general term for literate ruling elites. With the growth of industrialism, Society requires a skilled literate and mobile work force. The segmentary form of communities is no longer adequate to create a homogenously educated work force in which the individual members are interchangeable. The state comes to be in charge of the nation, and through control of education creates the requisite interchangeability of individuals. The primary identification with segmentary communities is thus transferred to the nation state as the producer of culture (1983). Thus a new type of consciousness, born of an homogenous culture and tied to the state, emerges in a industrial society.

In Anderson's view, nationalist consciousness was made possible with the breakdown of three defining characteristics of pre-modern society: sacred scripts, divine kingship and the conflation of history with cosmology. Together these had made for an unself-conscious coherence in society which broke down with the spread of print media through the engine of the capitalist market. Print capitalism permitted an unprecedented mode of apprehending time that was "empty" and "homogenous"— expressed in an ability to imagine the simultaneous existence of one's co-nationals. Travel and the territorialization of the faith relativized this community defining it as limited and the decline of monarchy transferred sovereignty to the community. To be sure, many of the characteristics of nationalism evolve historically through a succession of modular types of nationalist movements — one of Anderson's most interesting concepts. But he believes, nonetheless, that nationalisms have a defining systemic unity embodied in the unique type of self-consciousness of the people imagining themselves as one (1983, rev. 1991).

Consider first the argument empirically. The long history of complex civilizations such as that of China does not fit the picture of isolated communities and a vertically separate but unified clerisy. We now have considerable research about complex networks of trade, pilgrimage, migration and sojourning that linked villages to wider communities and political structures. We have also had a sense of how, through central place theory, these linkages worked to transmit resources and information though the society, as well as a differentiated picture of what areas, and when these areas, were more or less integrated with the central places of the empire (Skinner 1964, 1977). This was the case as well in Tokugawa Japan and 18th century India (Bayly 1983, Habib 1963). Moreover, even if the reach of the bureaucratic state was limited, notions of the culture-state indicate the widespread presence of common cultural ideas which linked the state to communities and sustained the polity.

It was not only, or perhaps even primarily, the print media that enabled Han Chinese to develop a sharp sense of the Other, and hence of themselves as a community, when they confronted other communities. The exclusive emphasis on print capitalism as enabling the imagining of a common destiny and the concept of simultaneity ignores the complex relationship between the written and spoken word. In agrarian civilizations this interrelationship furnishes an extremely rich and subtle context for communication across the culture. For instance, in pan-Chinese myths, such as that of gods Mazu and Guandi, not only were oral and written traditions thoroughly intertwined, but the myth provided a medium whereby different groups could announce their participation in a national culture even as they inscribed their own interpretation of the myth (through the written and other cultural media, such as folk drama and iconography) (Watson 1985, Duara 1988). As such, these groups were articulating their understanding of the wider cultural and political order from their own particular perspective. There were large numbers of people in agrarian societies who were conscious of their culture and identity at multiple levels, and in that sense were perhaps not nearly so different from their modem counterparts.

The point is not so much that national identity existed in pre-modern times; rather it is that the manner in which we have conceptualized political "identities" is fundamentally problematic. In privileging modern society as the only social form capable of generating political self-awareness, Gellner and Anderson regard national identity as a distinctly modern mode of consciousness: the nation as a whole imagining itself to be the cohesive subject of history. The empirical record does not furnish the basis for such a strong statement about the polarity between the modern and the pre-modern. Individuals and groups in both modern and agrarian societies identify simultaneously with several communities that are all imagined; these identifications are historically changeable, and often conflicted internally and with each other. As we shall see, whether in India or China, people historically identified with different representations of communities, and when these identifications became politicized they came to resemble what is called modern "national identities".

Behind this modern versus pre-modern polarity lies the assumnption of modern consciousness as a *unified* episteme marked by an epistemological break with past forms of consciousness. As modern subjectivity, the nation is *ipso facto* denied any credible links with the past. At the heart of this break is a deep confusion between the novelty and indeed revolutionary character of institutional arrangements in the modern world, and the radical novelty of consciousness, specifically of a cohesive and self-aware collective subject. Indeed, the self-consciousness of modern subjectivity in the writings of these analysts bears an unexpected resemblance to Hegelian epistemology. For Hegel the unfolding of Spirit (reason) through History culminates as man "stands in a conscious relation to his Spirit" (Hegel 1956, 103) and that nation-state, unlike other communities, possesses a self-consciousness because it involves the production of History in its very progress. But having attained self-consciousness it also stands at the end of History. Quite apart from the validity of such a characterization of "modem consciousness", we may also remind ourselves of the destructive side of this epistemology which justified domination of "unself conscious" societies and polities as the Other of the modern, rational self.

These modern analysts assume the cohesive collective subject of History as (a)possible and (b)possible only in the modern era. My alternative obliges me to reject both positions. In the strong sense, a cohesive self-conscious subject is an abstraction: as we have seen in the introduction, the meaning of the nation for the pluralities which inhabit and may identify with it—whether it be a denizen of New Delhi or an Assamese fisherman—are as different as they are themselves from each other. In a restricted and temporary sense, however, the nation may exist as a unified subjectivity: a provisional relationship, a historical configuration in which the national "self' is defined in relation to the Other. Depending on the nature and scale of the oppositional term, the national self contains various smaller "others"— historical others that have effected an often uneasy reconciliation among themselves and potential others that are begináing to forn this differences. Thus we must reject (b) in both the strong and the restricted senses and (a) in the strong, though not in the weaker, relational sense. But if we can salvage a unified subjectivity only in this weak sense, this subjectivity is by no means uniquely a product of modern society.

I will argue that there were totalizing representations and narratives of community with which people identified historically and with which they may continue to identify into the modern nation. Of course, pre-modern political identifications do not necessarily or telcologically develop into the national identifications of modem times and there are significant ruptures with the past. A new vocabulary and a new political system—the world system of nation-states — selects, adapts, re-organizes and even re-creates these older representations. But the historical memory of archaic totalizations does not always disappear and as this memory is periodically re-enacted, it often provides potent material along which to mobilize the new community. The real significance of the historical question lies in understanding that the relationship between the past and present is not a simple causal one, but a complex set of transactions in which the past remains materially and politically relevant in the present.

Historical Models of Political Community

In India and China, representations of community as a social totality are not new. Historical conceptions of political community have lived off a process of radical "Othering" and were periodically re-enacted, thus keeping them alive in historical memory. Of course, at different times, different social forces have seized this memory and turned it to their own needs, but the very process of its pursuit has enhanced the power of this historical memory. At the same time, it was an awareness of social totality that co-existed historically with other representations, including competing visions of community.

Let us first consider the case of imperial China. Before the advent of the modern nation-state there were several models of political community in China. One of these has been called "culturalism" and has been counter-posed to modern nationalism. Joseph Levenson was the most articulate advocate of the idea of cultualism which he saw as a mode of consciousness distinct from nationalism. Levenson observed a radical discontinuity between a nationalistic identity which he believed came to Chinese intellectuals around the turn of the 20th century, and earlier forms of Chinese. The high culture, ideology and identification of the literati, he believed, were principally forms cultural consciousness, an identification with the moral goals and values of a universalizing civilization. Thus the significant transition here is from a "culturalism" to a nationalistm to the awareness of the nation-state as the ultimate goal of the community (Levenson 1965). Culturalism referred to a natural conviction of cultural superiority that sought no legitimation or defence outside of the culture itself. Only when, according to Levenson, cultural values sought legitimation in the face of the challenge posed by the Other in the late 19th century, do we begin to see "decaying culturalism" and its rapid transformation to nationalism — or to a culture protected by the state (politicization of culture).

Levenson's notion of culturalism has enabled us to identify a particular conception or representation of political community that may have emanated from the literati (although, identification with this representation was not necessarily restricted to the literati). Where he is mistaken, I believe, is in distinguishing culturalism as a radically different mode of identification from ethnic or national identification. In order for it to exist as a pure expression of cultural superiority, culturalism would have to feel no threat from an Other seeking to obliterate these values. In fact this threat arose historically on several occasions and produced several reactions from the Chinese literati and populace. First, there was a rejection of the universalist pretensions of Chinese culture and of the principle that separated culture from politics and the state. This manifested itself in a form of ethnocentrism that we will consider in a moment. A second, more subtle, response involved the transformation of cultural universalism from a set of substantive moral claims into a relatively abstract official doctrine. This doctrine was often used to conceal the compromises that the elite and imperial state had to make in their ability to practise these values or to conceal their inability to make people who should have been participating in the cultural-moral, order actually do so. The universalistic claims of Chinese imperial culture constantly bumped up against and adapted to, alternative views of the world order which it tended to cover with the rhetoric of universalism: this was its defensive strategy.

Consider this second reaction first. The Jin and Mongol invasions of north China during the 12th century and their scant respect for Chinese culture produced an ideological defensiveness in the face of the relativization of the conception of the universal empire (*tianxia*). In the 12th and 13th centuries Confucian universalists could only maintain their universalism by performing two sleights of hand: connecting individuals to the infinite — rather than to a regime espousing universal values, thus severing theory from fact; and internalizing the determination of personal values — rather than making it contingent upon the traditional Confucian concern with an objective moral order (Trauzettel 1975). During the Ming ragine, a Han dynasty that succeeded the Mongols, Chinese historians dealt with the lack of fit between much of the known world and the Chinese world view simply by maintaining a silence. (Wang 1968, 45-46). When we look at the tribute trade system which is often cited as the paradigmatic expression of its universalistic claims to moral superiority, the imperial state adapted readily to the practical power politics of the day. For instance, in the early 19th century", the tiny northwestern khanate of Kokand successfully challenged the Qing tribute system (like the Jesuits, the Russians and several others before) and had established all but the formal declaration of equality with the Chinese empire. The Qing was forced into a negotiated settlement but it continued to use the language of universalism — civilizing values radiating from the son of heaven—to conceal the altered power relations between the two (Fletcher 1978b).

It seems evident that when the universalistic claims of this culture were repeatedly compromised and efforts were made to conceal these compromises, advocates of this universalism were operating within the tacit idea of a *Chinese* universalism — which is of course none other than a hidden form of relativism. We have tended to accept Chinese declarations of universalism at face value far more readily than we do other official doctrines. Is it perhaps because it plays a crucial role as the Other in interpretations of the encounter with the nation-states of the west?

Viewing "culturalism" (or universalism) as a "Chinese culturalism" is to see it not as a form of cultural consciousness per se, but rather to see culture — a specific culture of the imperial state and Confucian orthodoxy — as a criterion defining a community. Membership in this community was defined by participation in a ritual order which embodied allegiance to Chinese ideas and ethics centred around the Chinese emperor. While this representation of political community may seem rather distant from nationalism, one should consider the fact that the territorial boundaries and peoples of the contemporary Chinese nation correspond roughly to the Qing empire that was held together ideologically precisely by these ritual practices.

Just as significantly, during the Jin invasion of the 12th century, segments of the scholar class completely abandoned the concentric, radiant concept of universal empire for a circumscribed notion of the Han community and fatherland *guo* in which the barbarians had no place. This ethnocentric notion of Chineseness was, of course, not new. Chinese authors typically trace it to a quotation from the ancient classic, the *Zuozhuan*: "the hearts of those who are not of our race must be different" (Li Guoqi 1970, 20; Dow 1982, 353). Others (Langlois 1980, 362) find it still earlier in the concentric realm of inner and outer barbarians found in the; *Shang Shu*: pacific cultural activities were to prevail in the inner part whose inhabitants were not charaeterized as ethnically different, with militancy towards the outer barbarians who appeared to be unassimilable. Trautzell believes that in the Song, this ethnocentrism brought together state and "the people". The state sought to cultivate the notion of loyalty to the fatherland downward into peasant communities from among whom arose resistance against the Jin in the name of Han Chinese culture and the Song dynasty (1975).

While we see the representation of the ethnic nation rnost clearly in the Song, it re-appeared after the Manchu conquest in 1644. Its most explicit advocate in the late imperial period was Wang Fuzhi. Wang likened the differences between Manchus and Han to that between jade and snow, which are both white but different in nature, or more ominously, between a horse and a man of the same colour whose natures are obviously different (Li Guoqi 1970, 22). To be sure, it was the possession of civilization (*wen*) by the Han that distinguished them from the barbarians, but it did not stop him from the view that "it is not inhumane to annihilate (the barbarians) ... because faithfulness and righteousness are the ways of human intercourse and are not to be extended to alien kinds (*i-lei (yilet*) (in Langlois 1980, 364). Although Wang may have espoused the most extreme view of his generation, several prominent scholars of the Ming-Qing transition era held on to the idea of the fundamental unassimilability of the yi (barbarian) by the Hua (Chinese) (see Onogawa 1970, and Wu Weito 1970).

Despite the undoubted success with which the Qing made themselves acceptable as the legitimate sons of heaven, they were unable to completely suppress the ethnocentric opposition to their rule either at a popular level or among the scholarly elite. The anti-Manchu writings of Wang Fuzhi, Huang Zongxi and Gu Yanwu during the early period of Qing rule, together with collections of stories of Manchu atrocities during the time (*Mingji Yeshi:* Unofficial history of the late Ming) staged a re-appearance around the middle of the 19th century (Wu Weito 1970, 263). Zhang Taiyan, for instance, claims to having been nourished by a tradition both in his family and in wider Zhejiang society which held that the defense of the Han against the barbarians (*Yi : Xia*) was as important as the righteousness of a ruler (Onogawa 1970, 216). Certainly Han exclusivism seems to have reached a height by the late 18th century when the dominant Han majority confronted the non-Han minorities of China in greater numbers than ever before over competition for increasingly scarce resources (Naquin and Rawski 1987). Thus it is hardly surprising to find that, from at least the time of resistance to the increased foreign presence in south China after the Opium Wars through to the Boxer rebellion of 1898-1900, there existed a general expectation, not only among the elite, but also among the populace, that the state would protect the culture and the people of the empire (Wakeman 1966, Esherick 1987). Although not all segments of the population were affected by it, this representation of political community was sufficiently rooted to make it a powerful mobilizing force in the 19th and 20th centuries.

Thus we are able to discern at least two representations of political community in imperial Chinese society: the exclusive Han-based one founded on an ascriptive principle, and the other, based on the cultural values and doctrines of a Chinese elite. What has been described as culturalism was a statement of Chinese values as superior but, significantly, not exclusive. Through a process of education and imitation, barbarians could also become part of a community sharing common values and distinguishing themselves from yet other barbarians who did not share these values. Thus the cultural conception resembled the ethnic conception in that both periodically defined the distinguishing marks and boundaries of a politicized community; only the criterion of admissibility into the community differed.

In history, the two representations were *both* separate and related. As we have seen, at any point in time, the efforts to realize the one or the other could have very different effects — indeed, life and death effects — regarding who was to be considered inside and who outside the community. But as John Fincher has pointed out, "culturalism" and "racism" were also intertwined in such a way that the "historian's vocabulary has no very satisfactory definition of the strong sense of political community in 'traditional' China." (Fincher 1972, 69). Fincher looks at the writings of the anti-Mongol thinker, Fang Xiaoru (1357-1402) who in the face of general literati support of the Mongol dynasty, made a clear racialist distinction between the Mongols whom he likened to animals and Han Chinese. Yet, if the border between Chinese and barbarians was impermeable and based on biological fact, Fang was still only "half a racist" (Fincher 1972, 59), because he also believed that Chinese who enabled barbarians to rule couid themselves become barbarians. He thus invoked the culturalist principle, although in reverse: that birth among the Han did not ensure inclusion in the community. We will encounter several such examples of separateness and inter-penetration and we may invoke the concept of the "Supplement" to grasp the relationship between "culture" and "race" here. The supplement embeds the paradox of being separate from, yet necessary to the completion of a phenomenon. It thus complicates the binary opposition between "race" and "culture" which some of the historiography we have discussed above has found useful in its explanation of modern nationalism.

For Hegel, the ancient cultures of China and India each represented a lack in relation to the full development of Spirit which complemented the other. Spirit had made its progress through these cultures but found them wanting in the unity of the freedom of individual and state, of Unity and Difference, which made for true self-consciousness. China possessed objective rationality in the State but the state and its laws belonged to the One Individual (the Emperor). These laws ruled the individuals as of from outside and the individuals were like children obeying their parents without will or insight. In India, the contemplation of inner subjectivity led to the Negation of Reality — the Hindoo nature is Spirit in a state of Dream (Hegel 1956, 140) and thus awareness of State as the embodiment of Rationality was denied. Thus, "if China may be regarded as nothing but a State, Hindoo political existence presents us with a people, but no State" (Hegel 1956, 161). This complementarity of lack, as it were, plays the role of something like an archetype in the comparative historical sociology of India and China.

The notion of a lack of a state in India, or conversely, the overpowering role of society (read caste) is so deeply ingrained in both Indology and general understandings of India, that we tend to be especially suspicious about characterizations of totalizing political communities in pre-colonial India. Let us consider the cosmic ideology of Brahmanism because, in many ways, Brahmanic universalism (an obviously more specific and serviceable term than Hinduism) is interpreted similarly to Chinese culturalism. Ainslee Embree has summed up its core features: it includes the concept of the cosmic order and the role of the Brahmin in maintaining and interpreting this order; the concept of multi-levelled truth, of a hierarchical but rational order of society, of karma, of re-incarnation, and of the concept of dharma (religious or moral duty) (Embree 1985, 23-24). As in Confucianism, Brahmanic universalism is not dependent upon the wielding of state power, but rather exercises its control from outside and upon the state.

To be sure, a scholar like Embree believes that in some ways Brahmanism did provide a historical basis of a unifying ideology. Brahmanic texts became the source of political and social legitimacy for Hindu rulers since the 1st century B.C. Moreover, these texts showed some familiarity with the natural boundaries of the sub-contitent and an awareness of Aryavarta (land of the Hindus/Aryans) as a cultural region and a common heritage of language and value with others of their class throughout the sub-continent (Embree 1985, 27). But he believes that it is precisely this Brahmanism which prevented actual states from achieving a conflation of polity and community within the state because its universalism constantly directed the attention of Hindu rulers away from this goal and towards a de-territorialized, cosmic order (Embree 1985, 32). Thus the sum of Embree's argument appears to be that while Brahmanism provided the framework for a cultural community, it did not and could not produce that conflation of culture and polity so necessary to the emergence of nations.

More recent work, however, indicates that such a judgement of culturalist determinism may be premature. Just as cultural universalism was relativized (even while retaining its doctrine officially) as a result of the great Central Asian invasions in China, Brahmanic India was also so affected by the Central Asian invasions from the 11th to the 14th centuries. In a nuanced and detailed analysis of the Ramayana epic before and during this period, Sheldon Pollock, finds that this epic became the principal means of creating a representation of the politicized community in medieval Hindu India. Such was not the case with the other famous Indian epic, the Mahabharata, in which the problem of political power "man is slave to power, but power is slave to no man" — cannot be strictly said to be resolved because the *fratricidal* struggle is accompanied by a profound moral ambiguity. As Pollock puts it, not only is the antagonist not "othered" in the Mahabharata, but rather, they can never forget that they are indeed "brothered"(Pollock 1993, 281-3).

In contrast, the Ramayana responds to the problem of political power by a straightforward divinization of the king, Rama. According to Pollock the divine king is the only being on earth capable of combatting evil and evil itself is clearly othered", or more exactly, demonized. The period from the 11th to 14th centuries witnessed the Turkic invasions of India and Muslim political control came to be more or less established by the end of the period. This was also precisely the time when the divine political order of the Ramayana became historically grounded as numerous dynastic histories began to read the political world through the Ramayana narrative (Pollock 1993, 273-277). Although Pollock furnishes many examples, particularly clear is the explicit identification of the historical ruler, Prithviraja II (12th century), with the divine Rama and the explicit demonization of the enemy, the Turkic forces from Central Asia. The Ramayana enabled a totalizing conception of society built upon a radical distinction between self versus Other.

Thus, once again we discover that relativization finds its way into a cosmic ideology and creates a representation of political community — in this case, a Hindu political community — where culture and polity are conflated. Pollock also emphasizes that the Ramayana was repeatedly instrumentalized by Hindu elites of the medieval period to provide a "theology of politics and a symbology of otherness" (Pollock 1993, 286). To be sure, we are not referring to a real identification with this community among all who considered themselves Hindu, nor was it territorially coextensive with all of India. Rather, we are speaking of a representation of political community with which it was possible to identify and around which to mobilize. Migration, sojourning, and pilgrimage which often followed trading networks and which probably intensified during the medieval period, brought these ideas and rituals to a large community of believers Pilgrimage is perhaps the privileged means by which a religious community is both ritually and spatially delimited. In India, pilgrimage centres marked an inter-linked, sub-continent-wide territory not simply as a sacred space, but in the face of a demonized Other living in this territory, as the sacred space of Hindus.

While no Hindu power was able to successfully construct the politicized religious community across the sub-continent, we should not ignore the fact that it existed as a representation and several rulers, from Prithviraj II in the 12th century to the Marathas or Jai Singh of Jaipur in 18th century, did try to actualize it. At the same time, the drive towards the Brahmanical goal of a Hindu community, Bharatvarsha or Aryavarta, was countered by the urge to create the regional political community. The literature on regional states is most abundant for the 18th century successor states to the Mughal empire such as the Sikh and Maratha kingdoms. At one level, these 18th century polities were a product of state-building processes developing around emergent capital markets, professional service classes, modern European military technology and standing armies (Bayly 1983).

At another level, they were built around medieval devotional cults (Bhakti) which had integrated the regions linguistically. The syncretic impulses of these cults which created a popular literature of regional identification co-exited in some tension with the pan-Hindu model of political community we have outlined above. In the 18th century Maratha state, for instance, N. K. Wagle (1989) reveals how Maharashtrian Hindu chroniclers, Muslim saints and local judges sought ways to create a syncretic, regional tradition of adaptation and compromise even while the distinction between Hindus and Muslims was all too clear.

Finally, there existed a concept of political community which the Rudolphs have called the sub-continental empire. This appears to have been a regulative ideal among those who sought to rule South Asia as an empire. According to the Rudolphs, the sub-continental empire was a polity of ancient origins which recognized "ordered heterogeneity" — a polity which legitimated distinct cultural and functional communities, but who "lived as races apart" in their relations with each other (Rudolphs 1985, 43). In this conception, state power was limited by society's autonomous claims to self-regulation. Although this ideal was sanctioned by classical Brahmanical texts, it informed the ideals of the Moghuls and the British as well. The nature of this political conception is such that it is difficult to imagine it as the object of identification among ordinary people or collectivities. Nonetheless, to the extent that this tradition was articulated and kept alive in historical memory, it was perhaps an important influence upon the modern Indian nationalistic rhetoric of "unity in diversity".

To characterize pre-modern India and China simply as universal empires whose elites (mandarin or Brahmin) were concerned with cosmic values while the peasants lived with their noses to the soil misses the complex and dynamic nature of these societies. Individuals, strata or groups identified not only with one or more of the different representations of communities we have outlined above, but with others as well: provincial, linguistic and sectarian for example. We have also observed the unstable, intersecting and supplementary character of these representations and correspondingly, the identifications of people with them. Even while such a self-aware historical community may later disappear socially, the trace of it often lives on in historical memory and can return to haunt the present.

The Analytics of Community Closure

How do historical groups try to transform a society with multiple representations of political community into a single social totality? This process involves the hardening of social and cultural boundaries around a particular configuration of self in relation to an Other. Its analysis is important for my larger argument about history because this process of closure is relevant to both historical and modern communities; moreover, it reveals the role of existing historical and cultural resources in the transformation.

Sociologically, we may think of communities not as well-bounded entities but as possessing various different and mobile boundaries that demarcate different dimensions of life. These boundaries may be either soft or hard. One or more of the cultural practices of a group, such as rituals, language, dialect, music, kinship rules or culinary habits, may be considered soft boundaries if they identify a group but do not prevent the group from sharing and even adopting, self-consciously or not, the practices of another. Groups with soft boundaries between each other are sometimes so unself-conscious about their differences that they do not view mutual boundary breach as a threat and could eventually even amalgamate into one community. Thus, differences in dietary and religious practices may not prevent the sharing of a range of practices between local Hui muslim and Han communities. The important point is that they tolerate the sharing of some and the non-sharing of other boundaries.

An incipient nationality is formed when the perception of the boundaries of community are transformed: when soft boundaries are transformed into hard ones. This happens when a group succeeds in imposing a historical narrative of descent and/or dissent upon both heterogeneous and related cultural practices. I will permit myself a deconstructive excess and coin the word, *discent* to suggest the porosity of these two signifiers. It reveals how the tracing of a history is frequently linked to differentiating the self from an Other. The narrative of *discent* serves as a template by which the cultural cloth will be cut and given shape and meaning. When this narrative is imposed upon cultural materials, the relevant community is formed not primarily by the creation of new cultural forms — or even the invention of tradition — but by transforming the perception of the boundaries of the community. The narrative of *discent* is used to define and mobilize a community often by privileging a particular cultural practice (or a set of such practices) as the constitutive principle of the community — such as language, religion of common historical experience — thereby heightening the self-consciousness of this community in relation to those around it. Not only do communities with rigidified boundaries privilege their differences, they tend to develop an intolerance and suspicion toward the adoption of the other's practices and strive to distinguish, in some way or the other, practices that they share. In this sense, communities with hard boundaries will the differences between them.

Because the narrative succeeds in privileging certain cultural meanings as the constitutive principle of a community, it shapes the composition of the community: who belongs and who does not, who is privileged and who is not. Thus if common history (or Confucian ritual) is privileged over language and race, language and race always lie as potential counter-narratives: mobilizers of an alternative nation that will distribute its marginals differently. Thus within the hard community there will always be other soft boundaries which may potentially transform into hard boundaries, or new soft boundaries may emerge and transform into hard ones. A bifurcated history (see below) will be particularly attentive to these emergent narratives which are often effaced or appropriated by the dominant narrative.

This mode of analysis challenges the notion of a stable community that gradually develops a national self-awareness like the evolution of a species (History). Rather it asserts a deliberate mobilization within a network of cultural representations towards a particular object of identification. In the following essays, we will examine the role of various social actors — often different groups of intellectuals and politicians — who develop and deploy narratives to re-define the boundaries and identities of a collectivity with multiple identifications. But even when this closure is successful, it will unravel in time; the privileged practices that organize this identification will also change.

Consider the example of Manchu identity. The Qing dynasty (1644-1911) originated from a Manchu ethnic community which maintained an ambivalent attitude towards the dominant Han culture that it ruled. In the early stages of its rule it actively sought to maintain Manchu distinctiveness through a variety of means, including a ban on inter-marriage and Han migration to Manchuria, and the fostering of different customs. In time, however, not only was the ban on migration and inter-marriage ignored, but Manchu embrace of Chinese political institutions caused it to blur the distinctions between it and the communities it ruled. More importantly, and unlike the Mongols, the Manchus recognized early the roots of politics in culture and rapidly became the patrons not only of elite culture, but also of popular Han gods like Guandi and Mazu. Thus by the 18th century, in terms of their social and cultural relations, the Manchu communities resident in the hundreds of garrisons outside of their homeland in the northeast were losing their literacy in Manchu as well as contact with their folk traditions and melding into the general Han populace (Crossley 1990, 3,30; Kuhn 1990, 68-70).

At the same time, however, powerful counter-tendencies worked to shore up — or re-construct — a Manchu identity. Most noteworthy was the effort of the Qianlong emperor (1736-1795) to introduce a classic narrative of *discent* of the Manchus — the "Researches of Manchu Origins" discussed by Crossley (1987). "Researches" traced the descent of the Manchu clans to the first attestable peoples of the northeast thereby demonstrating a "racial" distinctiveness which Crossley defines as "immutable identity based on ancestral descent" (1987, 762). Moreover, it celebrated the Manchus as inheritors of the imperial tradition of the region which was independent of (dissented from) the Han Chinese imperial tradition and most closely associated with the Jin empire of the 12th century. To be sure, this narrative of *discent* played a part within a wider representation of power necessitated by the imperatives of ruling an empire which encompassed both Han Chinese and Central Asian politics (Crossley 1987; Kuhn 1990, 69). Confucian universalism was off-set by racial exclusivism, because as Crossley says, every "racial" group — Manchus, Mongols, Tibetans, Han and others — had their proper status according to their race. These races bore a relationship to the emperor set by the historical role of their ancestors in the creation and development of the state (Crossley 1987, 780). But this narrative which endorsed a conception of "race" as a constitutive principle of community, was also motivated by the fear on the part of the emperor of total cultural extinction of the Manchus. Thus, the Qianlong emperor took it upon himself to champion the Manchu language and values and punish those who forgot their roots (Kuhn 1990, 66-68).

Manchu identity flowered tragically in the late 19th century, both in response to Qianlong's efforts and also as a reaction to a Han ethnic exclusivism that became most evident during the years of the Taiping Rebellion. As early as 1840, in the days before the British attack on the lower Yangzi city of Zhenjiang during the Opium War, the tension in the city led to hostility between the Manchu soldiers in the garrisons and the civilian Han populace in which countless Han were slaughtered by Manchu soldiers on the allegation that they were traitors. Elliot shows that the entire event was interpreted as ethnic conflict both by survivors and by local historians (Elliot 1990, 64). This simmering tension culminated in the horrifying massacre of Manchu bannermen and their families during the Taiping Rebellion and again in the Republican revolution of 1911 (Crossley 1990, 130, 196-197). Manchus in the Republican era sustained their identity only by hiding it from public view and by quietly teaching the oral traditions to their children and grandchildren within their homes. Today Manchu identity finds expression not only in their status as a national minority in the PRC, but as Crossley observes, in such forms as the Manchu Association formed in Taipei in 1981 (Crossley 1990, 216).

The Manchu search for its own separate identity may be traced back to a narrative which privileged "race" as the definer of community. The tragedy of it was that this rhetoric forced a highly, if incompletely, assimilated people to turn their back on what had, after all, become their culture. And yet it would be wrong and untrue to the mode of analysis I have tried to establish here to posit an essentializing evolutionary trend in the growth of Manchu identity and the worsening of Han-Manchu relations. Crossley is sensitive to the ambivalences of Manchus towards this identity and important leaders of the Confucian intelligentsia were committed to a cosmopolitanism within their nationalism that included the Manchus as Chinese. Perhaps least understood in this regard are the Boxer "rebels" and various secret society groups in the last decades of the 19th century, who actually sought to support the Qing court — as the representative of Chinese culture — in the effort to expel the hated Westerner.

My effort to link narratives of *discent* to the self-definition of a group is relevant not only for ethnic nationalisms such as those of the Manchu or Mongols, but also for those less visible communities within. These include regional and provincial groupings within the Han such as the Cantonese, the so-called "sub-ethnic" groups such as the Tanka boat people, the Hui and Subei people. For example, the mid-19th century Taiping Rebellion was built up by the Hakka minority of south China who discovered a narrative of *discent* in a version of Christianity which depicted them as a "chosen people". This narrative gave them a mission as "god-worshippers" in their protracted, dreary battle against the earlier, and now, idolatrous settlers in south China and caused them to celebrate their own distinctive traditions over those of the larger Han community of which they were a highly ambiguous part. As the movement developed imperial ambitions, the Hakka coupled their anti-idolatrous message with appeals to an older rhetoric of the struggle of the Han against the Manchu (Kuhn 1977). The Taiping movement is instructive in showing how a community which had been successfully hardened by a redemptive narrative of *discent* was once again forced to re-negotiate its identity.

The process of community closure which we have analyzed here principally for a period before the establishment of modern nationalism is, as we shall see, also relevant for modern nationalism. Moreover, the conceptualization of a narrative of *discent* which I will apply to the later period as well, suggests that the process forging an exclusive or over-riding identity is not usually constructed *de novo*, but built from existing representations of community, although much is lost and transformed in the process. Finally, I wish to show that in both pre-modern and modern societies a plurality of representations and narratives continues to persist, even though the technical and institutional means of both closure and resistance differ in the two societies.

The Modern Nation-state System and the Question of History

We have observed that what is novel about modern nationalism is not political self-consciousness, but the world system of nation-states. Over the last century, this system, which sanctions the nation-state as the only legitimate form of polity, has expanded to cover the globe. Externally, the nation-state claims sovereignty within distinct, but not undisputed, territorial boundaries. Internally, the state claims to represent the people of the nation and through this claim, has steadily expanded its role in society, often at the expense of local authority structures. For instance, Children" have come increasingly under the jurisdiction of the state as the institutional rules governing childhood were diffused to all types of nation-states over the last hundred years (Boli-Bennet and Meyer 1978). It is important to grasp that the form of the nation-state is sanctioned by a battery of discourses generated from the system as a whole. We have seen how Social Darwinism joined race and History to the nation-state. Later, anti-imperialism and even socialism and Marxism would come to sanction the nation-state. At the same time, these nation-states also have to confront other alternative or historical representations from within the societies they govern.

The territorial conception of the nation also has a history which may be traced to what William McNeill has characterized as the system of competitive European states. From as far back as 1000 A.D., each of these states was driven by the urge to increase its resources, population and military technology over the others. In their competition, these states gradually became dependent on capital markets, both externally and internally, which further propelled the development of their economy and the competition between them (McNeill 1982). In time, the Church came to sanction some of these emergent regional states by endowing them with a theory of sovereignty without at the same time obliging them to achieve universalizing empire. This was possible because of the separation of temporal and spiritual authority, or, in other words, the source of legitimacy from actual exercise of power (Armstrong 1982). The culmination of this conception of the nation was first seen in the French revolution and exemplified in the idea of citizenship for all within the territory (Eley 1981).

However, no contemporary nation-state is a nation exclusively in this territorial sense. Even among the early modern European states, European dynasts had to combine the theory of territorial sovereignty with ethnicity to create modern nation states (Armstrong 1982). While most historical nations, defined as self-aware and even politicized communities, may have lacked the conception of themselves as part of a system of territorially sovereign nation-states, at the same time, modern nations seek the sources of their cohesion not in the territorial conception but from a narrative of the nation that privileges a particular principle defining community, say language, race, religion et al (and repressing the others). It is true, as Balibar (1991) and others point out, that territorial boundaries can themselves acquire a salience and develop powerful attachments for their citizens. Yet, even these territorial identifications have to be founded on an inherited, if contested, narrative of the "homeland" such as the “central plain” (Zhongyuan) or Aryavarta. The shape and content of national identities in the modern era are a product of negotiation between remembered historical narratives of community and the institutionalized discourses of the modern nation-state system.

How did modern representations of the nation engage with historical narratives in China during the years before the Republican revolution of 1911 when modern nationalism took hold among the Chinese intelligentsia? The constitutional monarchists, represented by Kang Youwei, inherited the Confucian culturalist notion of community. Although Kang was influenced by modern ideas, the conception of political community that he retained drew on culturalist Confucian notions. We see this in his lifelong devotion to the emperor (Protect the Emperor Society), which in the political context of the time meant more than a nostalgia for monarchy. Since the monarchs were Manchu and not Han it implied that he was convinced that community was composed of people with shared culture and not restricted to a race or ethnic group (imputed or otherwise).

In his debates with the anti-Manchu revolutionary Zhang Taiyan, Kang cited Confucius to argue that although Confucius had spoken of barbarians, barbarism was expressed as a lack of ritual and memory of the cultural community, Kang declared that during the Warring States, Wu and Chu had been different countries, but had become parts of China by the time of Han. Similarly, although Manchus were barbarians in the Ming, by now they had acquired Chinese culture and so had become Chinese. Kang asked whether it was necessary for China to get rid of the Manchus in order to build a new nation or whether the nation could embrace all ethnic groups on a harmonious basis, including the Manchus, Hans, Miaos and Moslems, as well as the Tibetans? (Onogawa 1970, 245,249).

The revolutionaries, such as Zhang Taiyan and Wang Jingwei, articulated their opposition to this conception by drawing on the old ethnocentric tradition that acquired new meaning in the highly charged atmosphere of the 1900s. To be sure, Zhang was a complex figure whose thought can scarcely be reduced to any single strain. But he and Wang Jingwei succeeded in articulating an image of the new community that was persuasive to many in his generation. At the base of this re-formulation of the old ethnocentrism was a dialectical reading of Wang Fuzhi's notions of evolutionism inter-woven with a new Social Darwinist conception of the survival of the fittest races. Thus each group was engaged in dialogue with disputed legacies which were, nonetheless, real and by no means completely reducible to modern discourses.

We can gain a deeper understanding of the complex transactions between the past and present through the discourse and the representations of the revolutionaries than through their elaborated theories. For instance, several scholars (Dikotter 1992, Price 1992) have pointed out the way in which the values of the Chinese lineage or descent line, perhaps one of the most important social institutions in late imperial China were "translated" to develop the modern concept of race. The transition from lineage to this conception of race as a community united by blood ties was enabled by the common semantic source, the signifier *zu*, which referred to the descent group and also to race or kind (a term also of greatest importance to Wang Fuzhi in the 17th century (Dikotte 291). Republican revolutionaries like Chen Tianhua, Zou Rong and Song Jiaoren were able to maneuver within the play of this signifier and, hence, with the emotions it evoked such as filiality. Thus Chen Tianhua pronounced: "The Han race is one big family. The [mythic] Yellow Emperor is the great ancestor, all those who are not of the Han race are not the descendants of the Yellow Emperor, they are exterior families. One should definitely not assist them" (cited in Dikotter 117). According to Dikotter, "race" became the "symbol of fictive biological cohesion that could link lineage loyalties in the face of foreign aggression (71). Donald Price believes that the representation of the nation embedded in the new conception of common descent from the Yellow Emperor was enabled by an extended and re-defined filial piety (*Xiao*). Racial vengeance against the Manchus was now an obligation one vowed to one's ancestors whether or not they were of one's immediate lineage (Price 1052-1053).

These notable contributions to our understanding of early 20th century anti-Manchuism have emphasized the manner in which historical ideas have enabled the transition to the new evolutionist conception of the racial-nation. By linking race to the more tangible cultural institution of lineage, the revolutionaries were able to deploy an unfamiliar narrative — which as we have seen in chapter I emphasized the strife between Historical and non-Historical races — as their narrative of *discent*. In this way they could mobilize existing cultural symbols to build the walls of a community without the Manchus. At the same time, the new evolutionist narrative of History also tried to re-cast and so to appropriate the dispersed meanings of existing symbols and practices. Ancestor worship, filial piety and kinship terminology which tended to be focussed within the lineage (*zongzu)* were now sought also to be turned outward to the race and nation (*Zongzu, minzu*). Thus, the mythic Yellow Emperor whose status as national symbol came to dominate nationalist discourse through the first few decades of the 20th century, continued to be officially revered as the originator of the race and the founder of the nation until 1941. In 1957, the religion of the Yellow Emperor was established in Taiwan with government approval (Dikotter 1 16-117). Neither the notion of simple continuity nor that of invention can do justice to the subtle transactions between the past and the present. The past does not shape the present simply by persisting in it. It enables the transformation of the present and in that transformation, is itself much transformed. Attention to the manner in which dominant narratives seek to inflect and mobilize the meanings of existing symbols and practices offers a more promising beginning to understanding history.

The revolutionary position also retained the capacity to invoke the oppositional culturalist model of community as its supplement. The revolutionary invocation of the racialist memory at the turn of the century could not confine the othering process to the Manchus alone. The construction of the Han Chinese self as the national subject necessarily threatened other non-Han groups, as Kang Youwei had warned it would. Most of the large minority communities had viewed their incorporation into the Qing empire as being on a par with the enforced incorporation of the Han; they did not equate the Qing empire with Zhongguo (China). The overthrow of the Qing in 1911 created for them the possibility of independence; the rhetoric of racialist nationalism made it urgent. Given their own equation of nation and race, the revolutionaries could hardly counter the growing Mongol independence movement, the establishment of an independent Mongolia in 1911 (Nakami 1984), and the threatening situation in Tibet and Xinjiang. It was in these circumstances that Sun Yat-sen and the leaders of the new Republic sought to supplement their racialist narrative with the culturalist narrative of the nation espoused by their enemies — the reformers and the Qing court itself. The Chinese nation was now to be made up by the "five races" (Manchu, Mongol, Tibetan, Muslim and Han) and so it happened that the boundaries of the Chinese nation came to follow the outline of the old Qing empire just as the Indian nation was sought to be made in the image of the British empire. Later, the narrative of race as constitutive of the nation would itself be dispersed, or perhaps, absorbed inside a larger nationalist narrative of the common historical experience against imperialism.

In India, several models of political community furnished the framework within which the modern nation was contested. We can find these historical conceptions within the motley body of the Indian National Congress itself which emerged in the late 19th century as the representative of Indian nationalism. Thus for instance, the secularist model of Jawaharlal Nehru and Rabindranath Tagore drew upon the idealized conception of the sub-continental empire. The Rudolphs (1985) point out that each of the empires in South Asia built upon the symbols of the classical idea of a universal ruler: Akbar restoring the Hindu idea of a *chakravartin* in the Persian idea of *shahanshah*; the British using Mughal ceremonies and language to re-vitalize the imperial state. Thus colonisers and conquerors reinforced a process of political formation whereby communities and regional kingdoms were incorporated (and not subsumed or obliterated) into an ordered heterogeneity.

Nehru may have been the first to narrativize a history of the sub-continental empire into what comes to be known as the secular History of India. In his view, what he considered India was the secular unity of different communities and religions, each of which had made distinctive historical contributions. The achievements of Hinduism, for him was merely one of the sources of India's greatness, together with those of Buddhism, the Turkic emperors, traditional science among other sources. For Nehru, the History of India was the most authentic testimony to the capacity (read necessity) of Indians to maintain a "unity among diversity". The high points of Indian history were the reigns of Asoka, the Guptas, Akbar and the great Moghuls all of whom attempted to develop a political framework to unite the cultural diversity of the sub-continent. While in contemporary India this idealized version is countered by a forceful process of state-building, nonetheless, the memory of ordered heterogeneity is perhaps visible in the notion of Indian secularism, which is not so much a strict separation of state and society, as it is the equal support of the state for all religions (Nehru 1960, 121-128).

The memory of Brahmanic universalism as the foundation of the new political community, filtered through Orientalist discourses of the 19th century, was appropriated in its split form as universalism and its supplement of closure. Its universal form was articulated by Sri Aurobindo (1872-1950) and others and influenced Mohandas Gandhi. Aurobindo emphasized Advaita Hinduism, a radically monistic faith which believes in the unity of all being and denies the reality of the many particular entities in the universe. In this highly abstract system, a communal framework was created to absorb or tolerate heteregenous elements domestically within an essentially Brahmanic universalism. Thinkers like Aurobindo and Gandhi had of course to develop strategies to square the circle: to contain their universalism within their terminal political community of the nation. One such strategy was to devise the Spiritual East/Material West duality whereby India remained the privileged locus as the origin and repository of true (Hindu?) Spirituality.

The supplement to Brahmanic universalism, which in recent times has threatened to overcome this universalism, is the historical memory of the nation-space as Aryavarta whose charter is traced to the medieval political readings of the Ramayana. Hindu nationalism has drawn much attention by its violent mobilization campaigns to recover the site of the alleged birthplace of Rama in Ayodhya from a Muslim shrine which existed there until Hindu nationalists destroyed it in December 1992. The Ayodhya destruction is only the most recent expression of a series of campaigns launched by Hindu nationalists since the end of the 19th century, such as the protection of the cow, the promotion of religious ceremonies to capture public spaces and the take over of other Muslim shrines. These nationalists, like the anti-Manchu revolutionaries, foreground atavistic revenge in their narrative of *discent*. Through this narrative of vengeance, they seek to re-invest local gods, local issues and local conflicts with national meaning. Hindu nationalism has no use for universalism and declares a homogenized Hinduness (Hindutva) to be. the sole or privileged criterion for inclusion in the political community of the nation. They thus seek to transform the relative porous boundaries of local communities into an over-arching hard boundary between a national community and its Muslim Other. It is a project that recalls the radical othering we found in representations of medieval Hindu community. Although on the face of it, the lofty universalism of Aurobindo and Gandhi seems far removed from such a thorough-going communalism, the supplement of Hindu nationalism could easily exploit the ambivalence towards outsiders within their thought.

I have described a multiplicity of historical representations of political community in China and Indian which may be seen as examples of complex agranian polities. This multiplicity includes the representation of totalizing communities that both resemble modern nations and continue to be relevant to them. As such, even in recent theories of nationalism, notions of differences between the modern nation and traditional empire turn out to be highly exaggerated. Moreover, these notions reflect and reproduce a highly suspect presumption of an epistemological gap between national consciousness as cohesive and self-aware and pre-modern consciousness as dominated either by universal cosmologies or parochial identities. The modern nation is formed through a process similar to that of its totalizing predecessors which deploys a narrative of *discent*-the tracing of a history which legitimates its difference from the Other — to fix and privilege a single identity from among the contesting multiplicity of identifications. In neither society can this closure prevent alternative narratives from challenging the hegemonic representation of political community. Contemporary theories of nationalism are fascinated by the ways in which nations "invent" or "imagine" their pasts. The old, literate, and what Asish Nandy has called "capacious" civilizations of India and China reveal that while these histories are by no means determinative and are often highly mediated modern nations still have to negotiate with the memories of past communities.

REFERENCES TO DUARA

Anderson, Benedict. 1991. *Imagined Communities: Reflections on the Origins and Spread of Nationalism* London. (Revised and expanded version of 1983 text).

Balibar, Etienne. 1991. "The Nation Form: History and Ideology" in Etienne Balibar and Immanuel Wallerstein eds. *Race, Nation, Class: Ambiguous Identities.* London: Verso Press. 86-106.

Bayly, Chris. 1983. *Rulers, Townsmen and Bazaars: North Indian Society in the Age of British Expansion.* Cambridge, UK: Cambridge University Press.

Boli-Bennet, John & Meyer John W. 1978. "The Ideology of Childhood and the State: Rules Distinguishing Children in National Constitutions, 1870-1970." *American Sociological Review 43:797-812.*

Crossley, Pamela. 1987. "Manzhou Yuanliu Kao and the Formalization of the Manchu Heritage." *Journal of Asian Studies 46.4:761-790.*

--1990a. "Thinking about Ethnicity in Early Modern China. *Late Imperial China* 11.1: 1-35.

- —— - —— 1990. *Orphan Warriors: Three Manchu Generations and the End of the Qing.* Princeton; Princeton University Press.

Dikotter, Frank. 1992. *The Discourse of Race in Modern China* Stanford: Stanford University Press.

Dow, Tsung-I. 1982. "The Confucian Concept of A Nation and Its Historical Practice". *Asian Profile* 10.4: 347-362.

Duara, Prasenjit. 1988a. *Culture, Power and the State: Rural North China, 1900-1942:* Stanford University Press.

--1988b. "Superscribing Symbols: The Myth of Guandi, Chinese God of War" Journal of Asian Studies 47.4:778-795.

Eley, Geoff. 1981. "Nationalism and social history" *Social History* 6.1:83-107.

Elliot, Mark. 1990. "Bannermen and Townsmen: Ethnic Tension in Nineteenth Century Jiangnan" *Late Imperial China* 11.1:36-74.

Embree, Ainslee T. 1985. "Indian Civilization and Regional Cultures: The Two Realities" in Paul Wallace ed. *Region and Nation in India* New Delhi:Oxford University Press. pp 19-39.

Esherick, Joseph W. 1987. *The Origins of the Boxer Uprising.* Berkeley: University of California Press.

Fincher, John. 1972. "China as Race, Culture, and Nation: Notes on Fang Hsiao-ju's Discussion of Dynastic Legitimacy" in David C. Buxbaum and Frederick W. Mote. eds., *Transition and permanence : Chinese History and Culture : A Festschrift in Honor of Dr. Hsiao Kung-Ch'uan* Seattle:University of Washington Press. pp 59-69.

Fletcher, Joseph. 1978a "Ch'ing Inner Asia c.1800" in John K. Fairbank ed., *The Cambridge History of China* vol 10, part 1. Cambridge UK: Cambridge Univ. Press. pp. 35-106.

—— 1978b "The Heyday of Ch'ing Order in Mongolia, Sinkiang and Tibet" in John K. Fairbank ed. *The Cambridge History of China* Vol. 10, Part 1. Cambridge UK: Cambridge Univ. Press. pp. 351-408.

Gellner, Ernest. 1983. *Nations and Nationalism.* Ithaca: Cornell University Press.

Habib, Irfan. 1963. *The Agrarian System of Moghul India 1556-1701.* New York: Asia Publishing House.

Hegel, Georg W.F. 1956 The *Philosophy of History* trans. by J.Sibree.New York : Dover Publications.

Kuhn, Philip A. 1977. "The Origins of the Taiping Vision: Cross Cultural Dimensions of Chinese Rebellions" *Comparative Studies in Society and History* 19.3:350-366.

—— 1990. *Soulstealers : The Chinese Sorcery Scare of 1768* Cambridge Ma.:Harvard University Press.

Langlois, John D Jr. 1980. "Chinese Culturalism and the Yuan Analogy: Seventeenth-Century Perspectives". *Harvard Journal of Asiatic Studies* 40.2:355-398.

Levenson, Joseph R. 1965. *Confucian China and its Modern Fate: A Trilogy* Berkeley and Los Angeles: University of California Press.

Li Guogi. 1970, "Zhonggno jindai minzu sixiang" (Modern Chinese Nationalist Thought) in Li Guogi ed. *Minzuzhuy;* 'Taibei: Shibao Chuban Gongsi. 19-43.

McNeill, William. 1982. The *Pursuit of Power* Chicago: University of Chicago Press.

Meyer, John W. 1980. "The World Polity and the Authority of the Nation State" in *Studies of the Modern World System* Albert Bergesen ed. New York: Academic Press. pp. 109-137.

Nakami, 1984. "A Protest against the Concept of the "Middle Kingdom": The Mongols and the 1911 Revolution" in Eto Shinkichi et al. ed. *The 1911 Revolution in China.* Tokyo: Tokyo University Press. pp. 129-

149.

Nandy, Ashis 1983. *The Intimate Enemy: Loss and Recovery of Self under Colonialism* Delhi: Oxford University Press.

—— 1987. *Traditions, Tyranny and Utopias: Essays in the Politics of Awareness* Delhi: Oxford University Press,

Naquin, Susan & Rawski Evelyn S., 1987. *Chinese Society in the Eighteenth Century.* New Haven: Yale University Press.

Nehru, Jawaharlal. 1960. *The Discovery of India* New York: Anchor Books.

Onogawa, Hidemi. 1970. "Zhang Binglinde paiman sixiang" (The anti-Manchu thought of Zhang Binglin) in Li Guoqi ed. *Minzuzhuyi* Taibei: Shibao Chuban Gongsi. pp. 207-260.

Pollock, Sheldon. 1989 'Mimamsa and the Problem of History in Traditional India" *Journal of American Oriental Society* 109.4:603-610.

—— 1993. 'Ramayana and Political Imagination in India" *Journal of Asian Studies* 52.2:261-297.

Price, Don C. 1992. "Early Chinese Revolutionaries: Autonomy, Family and Nationalism" in Academica Sinica, Modern History Institute ed. *Family Process and Political Process in Modern Chinese History* Part 2. Taipei: Academica Sinica Modern History Institute.

Rudolph Llyod I. and Susanne H. 1985. "The Subcontinental Empire and Regional Kingdom in Indian State Formation" in Paul Wallace ed. *Region and Nation in India* New Delhi. pp 40-59.

Skinner, G. William. 1964-65. "Marketing and Social Structure in Rural China" *Journal of Asian Studies* 24, nos. 1:3-43 and 2:195-228.

Trauzettel, Rolf 1975. "Sung Patriotism as a First Step toward Chinese Nationalism" in *Crisis and Prosperity in Sung China* John W. Haeger ed. Tueson: University of Arizona Press. 199-214.

Wagle, Narendra K. 1989. "Hindu Muslim Interactions in Medieval Maharashtra" in 0. D. Sontheimer and H. Kulke ed. *Hinduism Reconsidered* N. Delhi: Manohar. pp. 51-66.

Wakeman, Frederic Jr. 1966. *Strangers at the Gate: Social Disorder in South China. 1839-1861* Berkeley and Los Angeles.

Wang Gungwu. 1968. "Early Ming Relations with Southeast Asia: A Background Essay' in John K. Fairbank ed. *The Chinese World Order: Traditional China's Foreign Relations* Cambridge, Ma: Harvard University Press. 34-62.

Watson, James. 1985. "Standardizing the Gods: The Promotion of Tien Hou ('Empress of Heaven")

Along the South China Coast, 960-1960" in *Popular Culture in Late Imperial China* David Johnson et al. ed. Berkeley and Los Angeles: University of California Press. 292-324.

Wu Wei-to. 1970 "Zhang Taiyan zhi minzujuyi shixue" (Zhang Taiyan's historical studies of nationalism) in Li Guoqi ed. *Minzuzhuyi* Taibei: Shibao Chuban Gongsi. 261-271.

26

COLONIALISM AND THE DISCOURSE IN INDIA AND CHINA

This year is the birth centenary of Prof. Tan Yun-shan, the savant and pioneer in Sino-Indian studies. I had the privilege of seeing him when he visited the Centre for Chinese Studies of the University of Delhi in 1965, when the centre was under the charge of Dr. Tan Chung, the eldest son of Prof. Tan Yun-shan. As Dr. Tan Chung was my teacher, I can claim affinity with the senior Prof. Tan according to the traditions of both India and China. Furthermore, both Prof. Tan Chung (who has inherited his father's dedication to Sino-Indian studies) and I have been colleagues and friends, sharing a comradeship in promoting friendship and understanding between India and China in the last thirty years. In deference to his wishes, I contribute this article to the commemorative volume that he is editing in fond memory of Prof. Tan Yun-shan.

"China Can Say No" is the title of a book published in 1995 which challenges the West and records Chinese determination to withstand Western pressures. Even in the height of economic reforms in China and spread of Western technology as well as cultural forms in recent years the Chinese elite has emphasized "Chinese characteristics" on every front. On the other hand, the Indian elite has smoothly assimilated itself with the various waves of Westernization in the spheres of culture, economy and politics. The way the latest phase of liberalisation and globalization has been accepted in India confirms the trend of the last two centuries. A look at the cultural and intellectual responses to colonialism in Asia, especially in India and China shows this contrast to be conspicuous. Colonialism successfully determined the terms of discourse in India but failed to conclusively shape the discourse in China.

In this paper an attempt is made to explore the reasons behind this divergence in the struggle over terms of discourse in India and China. Why is it that the struggle was so easily won by the colonial forces in India who succeeded in institutionalising their values about civilization and human conditions which got consolidated after independence through the policies of the post colonial state. British rule in India claimed the role of a "civilizing mission". It established institutions of the state which included civil service, judicial magistrates, police and clerks for managing the organisation of society. It introduced European educational system to promote European ideas of arts and sciences. Imposition of English language through the educational institutions and operations of governmental machinery and especially in the realm of culture and media finally shaped the terms of discourse in favour of the interest of the colonial power. Indigenous institutions of politics, economy and culture were by no means ideal. They were also arenas of struggle as evident in course of many uprisings and cultural and religious reform movements. But colonial regime subdued these struggles and declared its view of the world as modern, scientific and rational, therefore bearer of advanced civilization. That it had a certain class, race and ethnic basis and was subject to struggle in Europe itself was not conveyed to the colonial society. The struggle against the colonial imposition continued to erupt from time to time in India but it lost the battle each time.

In China however the story was different. The early contacts between the European missionaries and traders on the one hand and the Chinese emperors and the officials on the other clearly recognised the high status of the Chinese. Even after China was defeated in the Opium War. in 1840, the Chinese rulers as well as masses consistently nurtured the idea of regaining China's honour. Each war, even when the Chinese were defeated produced greater nationalist consciousness of the Chinese. Even when they were influenced by Japan's modernization after Meiji Restoration of 1868, they made a distinction between techniques for use and basic values. "Taking Chinese tradition as the basis and applying Western techniques for application"

(*Zhongxue Wei Ti, Xixue Wei Yong*) was a perspective advanced by some Chinese thinkers in the late nineteenth century. In many ways the *Ti-Yong* perspective was modified during the May Fourth movement. The developments after 1919 during the Chinese Revolution proved that all foreign influences were discriminatingly integrated into the internal struggles producing unique Chinese strategies and experiments. The fifty years of the Communist Party rule in the People's Republic of China during the leadership of Mao Zedong and Deng Xiaoping have continued this trend of terms of discourse being mainly set by Chinese people themselves. Whether it was the Yan'an model of people's democratic revolution, the Chinese socialist experiments under Mao or socialism with Chinese characteristics under Deng, they had emerged through domestic struggles rather than as a result of colonial imposition. Even when the Chinese chose to adopt Western theories and techniques, ideas about society and nature they did it from a position of autonomy and self-confidence, in course of fair negotiations and objective evaluation rather than as a derivative from colonial knowledge which embody a relationship of political domination.

This contrast needs to be nuanced in several ways. But for our purposes in this exercise we can take the difference in the experience of the two countries as an assumption. Our main purpose is to seek explanations for this divergent pattern of intellectual responses and their consequences. That in turn will give some evidence to measure this contrast. It is argued here that the nature of the political movements in twentieth century in the two countries made the critical difference in the evolution of the terms of discourse in India and China. This is also significantly related to the distinct features of state formation in China since its unification in 221 B.C. as against India's dispersed political existence, the scholar bureaucrat class of the gentry as against India's caste based social order, the unifying role of the Chinese language as against the plurality of developed languages in the subcontinent and the fact that China was not a colony like India but a semi-colony under multiple domination by European powers and the Japanese.

Moving the centre in terms of discourse:

Let us identify the political question that we are dealing with. Attention is drawn here to the fact that frameworks of knowledge embody a political relationship; ideas, concepts and theories carry meanings which have a political history. Even when they seek to explain reality or truth about the world they do it from some vantage points. Thus terms of discourse like terms of trade are favourable to some and unfavourable to others[1]. Meaning systems are constructed in the context of power relationships.

Terms of discourse are used in two senses. Firstly, in the sense of terms as words which may be concepts and ideas. A great deal of literature exists on terms of discourse arising in different periods of history. "Social justice", "sustainable development", for example are terms of recent political discourse in India. In the second sense, and that is the sense in which it is used here, it means governing conditions of knowledge. To take an example, the discourse on freedom for a long time was limited to defending the rights of entrepreneurs and the upper classes. Terms of discourse on freedom changed with the emergence of worker's movement and later with the dalit movement in India and more recently with the women's movement. Thus the word may be the same but the concept evolved with the changes in the terms of discourse was different.

Ngugi wa Thingo has contributed a powerful concept which clarifies terms of discourse. He talks about the need for *moving the centre.* First "from its assumed location in the West and .... from its assumed location in the minority social stratum in all societies to its creative base among the people".[2] Ngugi has analysed in the African context how colonialism robbed the people of the colonies not only of natural resources and enslaved the human beings but "one of the worst robberies is that of the means of perceiving all that". It colonised the values of the local people by a variety of means including the most effective means of colonising the imagination by imposing the colonial language. Thus Africa was made speechless. A new class of elites with foreign tongues was nurtured as interpreters between Europe and Africa. The educational institutions produced this class to manage the new institutions of economy and the state. In the new markets and the courts the native turned into a foreigner in his/her own country. Even when the movements for change appeared on the scene often the peasantry did not know how they were being represented. Thus according to Ngugi the agenda of liberation has to contain the basic human right -- "the right to name the world".

Thus it is important to be conscious of the way the meanings of various notions came to be constructed. Colonialism snatched away the colonised people's right to imagination, rights to understand history in their own way, right to interpret nature from their vantage point. Upper class, upper caste, patriarchal, racial standpoints too denied similar rights. The struggle for liberation, therefore, entails removing the centre from Eurocentnic colonial vantage points to the Third World's own, and in theThird World itself from the dominant elite's to the vantage points of the oppressed people themselves. Thus the terms of discourse could change in favour of the oppressed only through the process of struggle.

In China the political movements evolved in such a way that colonial worldview did not get internalised by the Chinese people and the struggle to move the centre from the elite to the masses made serious advances. In India the Eurocentnic worldview was adopted by the Indian elite in course of a century of colonial policies and though there are some gains in the democratic movement in favour of the oppressed classes, castes, tribes and women the struggle continues in a zigzag course. This is because of some significant differences in the environment of struggle, historical processes and ideological trends involving the elites and political groups in the two countries.

State Formation and National Consciousness:

The fact that China was a unified political entity whereas India was not, had significant consequences for the Struggles taking place in India and China during the nineteenth century. Emperor Qin Shih Huang had defeated the feudal kingdoms and set up *Zhongguo* or Chinese state or the middle country in 221 B.C. Even though there were uprisings within inner China or invasions by Mongols, Manchu and others, the unified entity by and large continued. The emperor as the head of a bureaucratic state apparatus and an imperial army governed China for over two thousand years. It also performed certain welfare functions such as maintaining the grand canal for irrigation and narigation. When this imperial state was defeated in the Opium War and was forced to accept unequal treaties Chinese nationalism acquired a perspective to fight Western imperialism. A feeling of humiliation or hurting of national honour and the fast emergence of unequal relationship with the West were the fighting points which were built into Chinese nationalism. The Han elite also blamed the non-Han Manchu emperor's regime for this humiliation so the anti-imperialist consciousness was connected with a political campaign to overthrow the Manchu dynasty and establish a republic. Thus the concept of politics in the second half of the nineteenth century China centred on altering the power structure by defeating Western imperialism and Manchu monarchy.[3]

In India the picture was one of dispersed political power in eighteenth century when the East India Company expanded its influence. The Mughal empire had declined, some regions were under Maratha rule and there were numerous small and big kingdoms. The situation was very different from the political character of the subcontinent during Ashoka's rule in 4th Century B.C. or during Akbar's rule in the late 16th century. In the nineteenth century when the British evolved an integrated administration for maintaining their control and collecting revenue it was seen by the Indian elite as the first attempt at state formation. The British very cleverly maintained the princely states as separate entities with indirect control under the rule of paramountcy. After crushing the first war of independence in 1857 they set up direct administration making India part of the British empire in 1858. Thereafter started the step by step building of the state apparatus, the Indian civil service leading this process.

The two institutional interventions that had long term effects were introduction of the British education system and the legal system. The missionaries played a major role in setting up schools and colleges which were channels for introducing modern European knowledge system to India. Graduates from these schools and colleges were recruited as personnel in the offices of the government and companies. This was the beginning of the mass production of clerks at various levels. Since the economy had been plundered resulting in famines and destitution these were regarded as opportunities for making good in life. The introduction of the zamindari system and ryotwar system required an army of surveyors and record-keepers to demarcate agricultural land and legitimatise property rights so that the extent of revenue could be determined. This in turn required courts of law to settle property disputes hence the import of the British legal system. The new legal and judicial system gradually limited the operation of the prevailing systems of law in the Indian society. They were based on convention, customs as well as codes. Like the bourgeois system of law they too had discriminatory class, caste, and gender bias. But they also were based on centuries of experience and struggle.

The state formation in British India Military conquest, economic expropriation, educational and legal institution-building delegitimatized the local systems of knowledge. It shaped new terms of discourse about society and nature, what is good and what is bad. It moved the centre of discourse to Europe. Therefore, when reformers arrived on the scene, to begin with they saw these developments as positive for Indian people. They thought Indian people owed political unity to the British. They did not realise then that basis of state formation and its forms can vary and the fact of dispersed political power may actually be a positive heritage for building a decentralised, co-operative participatory and federal polity. Indian nationalists, discourse continues to debate these two perspectives on the legacy of state formation in India. The terms of discourse on nationalism shaped by colonial policies in the nineteenth century later on had the dominant section of the Indian National Congress subscribing to the centralistic view. Nehru's *Discovery of India* traced the roots of unity to Indus valley civilisation and Ashoka and unfurled a unitarian, centralistic perspective on state formation. This view was in its peak during Indira Gandhi's regime when India saw the glimpses of an authoritarian centralised state. Mahatma Gandhi represented the alternative view of decentralised federal or even confederal relationship among political regions in the subcontinent — a view that has echoed again and again in the politics of autonomy groups throughout the subcontinent since the 1970s.

Elite power and political movements:

China's gentry was a unique social stratum combining wealth, knowledge, status and power in one class. These were landowning families who trained their children with years of tutoring to take the imperial examination. So the officials of the imperial government, the provincial government as well as the county government came from the gentry class. No other class — the peasants, artisans and traders had the resources or the perspective which could afford decades of preparation for the public examination. The examination system was such that only the gentry's children had the family culture and environment to study and qualify. Therefore, they are called the scholar bureaucrats who mastered the literary techniques. They were based in the rural economy dominating over the peasantry and other classes. They were the official class which ran the state apparatus. The dominant ideology of Confucianism was internalised by this class which practised the "three guiding principles and five virtuous relationships". The economic, political and cultural dimensions of power reinforced one another. No doubt Confucianism had to contend with Taoism and Buddhism producing new elements of the value system, and value movement went on in Chinese history involving diverse trends often conflicting with one another. But on the whole the gentry determined the terms of discourse in imperial China.

When contacts with the West increased and ideas about Western science and democracy spread in China the gentry reacted sharply to their challenge. The first set of reactions belonged to the *Ti-yong* framework. The idea was to learns the enemy's techniques to fight the enemy. This developed into a new stage when attempts were made to reform the Manchu monarchical government since that was blamed for China's humiliations and weaknesses. After China's defeat in the Sino-Japanese War of 1894-95, there was a serious attempt for constitutional reforms in 1898. It was an internal response of the gentry to adjust with the new situation. Meantime Japan had emerged as an inspiration to China and the rest of Asia because of her modernising experience. Many Chinese students studying in Tokyo got together under the leadership of Sun Yat Sen's *Tong Meng Hui*. Gradually *Tong Meng Hui* became the rallying point for many revolutionary groups who sought to overthrow the Manchu monarchy, set up a republic and expel foreign powers who had by then controlled vast sectors of Chinese economy. Kuomintang under Sun Yat Sen's leadership represented a radical democratic element which grow out of the gentry framework. The 1911 Revolution was led by a section of the Han gentry, therefore. It had its limitations. Only under the impact of the Bolshevik Revolution when a stream of new youth emerged in China the domination by the gentry class was challenged. The new youth saw the relationship between the gentry class, old political institutions and colonialism through which it could enter and build up its presence with the help of the gentry. The May 4th movement in 1919 was the first major challenge to gentry domination as well as imperialism. The political struggle against gentry feudalism and Western colonialism thus got intensified. Meantime warlords had emerged in various parts of China presenting an unprecedented disintegration of the Chinese state. This too was attributed to manoeuvres of the gentry forces and colonial powers. Thus the agenda of reunification got built into the emerging democratic agenda. The Kuomintang under Chiang Kai-shek sought to defend Confucian ideology and assimilate Western science into it in collusion with the West. The Chinese Communist Party especially under Mao Zedong's leadership used Marxism-Leninism to fight feudalism as well as colonialism. It built upon Sun Yat-sen's Three People's Principles, namely, People's Nationalism, People's Rights and People's Livelihood to evolve its ideological perspective in course of a number of struggles with tials and errors. The CPC acquired mass support of the Chinese peasantry who were suffering the oppression of the gentry for centuries. Thus the people's democratic revolution significantly altered the terms of discourse. Mao Zedong's *on New Democracy* with its politics, economics and culture and the *Talks at the Yanan forum of art and culture* effectively initiated currents of new knowledge. The new discourse strongly repudiated feudal elements of Chinese culture but inherited the popular, democratic and humanist currents. It denounced exploitative, bourgeois and colonial elements of the Western culture but opened gates to democratic ideas and modern science. The power of evaluation was acquired.

In a sense, China had only a brief period when a section of the gentry had moved the centre of knowledge to the West during the first two decades of this century. Before that the gentry had stoutly guarded its centre of discourse and after the May 4th movement and especially through the writings of Lu Xun and others and through the political struggle during the anti-Japanese War, the centre of discourse was moved in the direction of the common people of China. Chinese nationalist discourse thus took a people's democratic turn with the help of Marxism. In other words, Marxism did not push Chinese discourse closer to dominant western discourse as was the case in India when Nehru and Indira Gandhi supported then by the CPI adopted Western industrialisation model and the knowledge system underlying it.

Indian elite had a disjunction between land, knowledge and political governance. They had no doubt complementary roles: Shudras cultivating land, Brahmins specialising in knowledge, Kshatriyas by and large ruling the kingdom and organising the army and Vaishyas doing trade. Together they exploited the majority of the people namely the service castes which included many lower castes and the so-called untouchables and the tribes were kept separate from the caste order. Much churning in the varna and later jati system took place through centuries. During the Mughal rule there was a certain standardization in upper caste elite formation. The British used them in the respective feudatory states and their administrative zones thus maintaining the caste system. In course of building the political and economic institutions they recruited from these upper castes. They added a legal economic basis through the zamindari and ryotwar systems so that these elites now came from land - owning families. Modern India's first wave of elite formation thus owed a great deal to the British initiative. It was now rooted in feudal agriculture and it was nurtured though modern schools and colleges. In the process the section of the elite which got trained in the traditional Sanskrit education systems, the gurukuls, ashrams, tols and Islamic institutions such as Madarsas and other centres slowly became the second class academics not needed by the modern state. This never took place in China. There was no great divide among the educated. Those who got education in Japan in the early part of the twentieth century, those who went to school in France and Germany in the 1920's did have some advantage in skills. But their privileges and their role in the national political and economic process were not comparable to the English speaking elite in India. The fact that India was colonised by one European power and China had several European countries and Japan indirectly controlling various sectors of economy, cultural society made a great deal of difference.

In the field of technical education this divide became more conspicuous in India. Western medical education entered India under colonial auspices, Western engineering knowledge replaced local knowledge very fast. The learning of English distinguished this section of the Indian elite from the rest. Whereas in China the Chinese language got simplified after the May Fourth movement and was made accessible to the ordinary Chinese. In India the local languages were pushed behind since the elite made English an instrument of power. In other words, the Indian elite now became the interpreters for the people of India who were rendered speechless, to use the words of Ngugi. But they interpreted it using Western theories and concepts. Because they had lost the moorings of local culture. They knew very little about their own history. They know more about the history of Western political thought than about Indian political thought. Whereas a Chinese child can recite the dynasties and their dates and the principles of Confucianism, Taoism and Buddhism with ease. Indian child's awareness of India's history and philosophy is almost non-existent. The Indian elite grew up with a colonised mind suitably permeated by the local class caste race patriarchal outlook. It is this elite which was put in charge of running independent India under Nehru and his successors. It is an elite which perpetuates the colonial terms of discourse.

The Struggle continues : New experiences of struggle in China and India no doubt present a contrast. The Chinese revolution created people's democratic terms of discourse. Whether the terms have been retained and further democratised or new sources of hegemonic terms have emerged in the context of the reforms of the past two decades has to be further examined[4]. Whether a new Chinese bourgeoisie has emerged which has opted for Western capitalist values in course of recent economic developments in China has to be investigated. The liberation (*Jiefang*) discourse of the people's democratic revolution in China which sought to gain liberation from alien rule as well as from class, ethnic, racial, patriarchal and other forms of oppression continues to be on the agenda of the Chinese people. Similarly the *swaraj,* (self rule) agenda that Gandhi had laid down for Indian people continues to acquire new meaning and in course of the many social struggles of peasants, workers, women, dalits and adivasis in recent decades continues to challenge the dominant terms of discourse which colonialism together with local power structures had laid down. Thus struggle of the Vasco da Gama epoch is not over.

1. Manoranjan Mohanty, 'Changing Terms of Discourse', *Economic and Political Weekly,* Vol. XXIV, No. 37 (September 16, 1989).

2. Ngugi wa Thiongo, 'Decolonising the Means of Imagination' in *Symphony of Freedom* (Hyderabad : AIPRF, 1996).

3. Gong Shuduo, 'Chinese Revolution and Culture' in Manoranjan Mohanty (ed) *Chinese Revolution Comparative Perspectives on Transformation of Non-Westen Societies* (Delhi: Ajanta 1992).

4. Manoranjan Mohanty, 'Swaraj and Jiefang : Freedom Discourse in India and China's in Neera Chandhoke (ed), *Understanding the Post-Colonial World- Theory, and Method* (Delhi : NMML & Sterling, 1994).

27

FRIENDSHIP-IN-NEED BETWEEN CHINESE AND INDIAN PEOPLE IN MODERN TIMES

The multi-faceted cultural contacts between China and India centred around the dissemination of Buddhism in ancient times. They were interrupted after the 15th or 16th century because of the drastic changes within the two nations and the gradual eastward expansion of Western colonialism. But, the tree of Sino-Indian friendship had been deep-rooted. In the period of modern history, the two peoples once again closed their ranks in their common struggle against colonialism. The two peoples extended their sympathy towards each other, offered their hands to each other. The old tree of friendship came to life with new blossoms. This friendship was struck in times of need. Although without the magnificence of the ancient cultural interface between two great civilizations, this was the friendship of great affection and depth.

I

India was subjugated by colonial powers during the 18th and 19th centuries, and China likewise became a semi-colony. The tyrannic rule of the Western imperialist powers cruelly exploited and looted India and China and the two peoples lived in abysmal suffering. When the Indian Mutiny triggered off in 1857, the Chinese people received the news with delight, and it was a great inspiration to them. The Mutiny forced the British authorities to withdraw the troops which were on their way to China. Their earlier schedule of launching the Second Opium War against China was disrupted. During the Taiping Rebellion (in China), many Indian soldiers in the British army were driven by their pure sense of justice to defect to the Taiping army, and turned their rifles back at the imperialists and the Manchu feudalist suppressors. During the Boxer Rebellion, one Indian soldier condemned the atrocities committed by the imperialists and expressed sympathy with the just cause of the Chinese people in his diary. These were the first signs of the shared opposition and common hatred against their enemies. However, because of their historical and social limitations, such mutual sympathies were devoid of class consciousness.

The newly emergent nationlist forces during the end of 19th and the beginning of 20th century marked a genuine theoretical realisation of the commonality of destiny between the two peoples, of the necessity to cooperate with each other in the anti-imperialist struggle, as well as putting into practice such cooperation. Such a realisation also got heightened in the process of anti-imperialist struggle by and by.

After the defeat of his bourgeois reformist movement, Kang Youwei, its leader, took refuge in Darjeeling. He toured many places (in India), met people of all walks of life, and then felt for the miserable sufferings of Indian people under the colonial rule with deep sympathy. He said that the British colonial rule was a system of racial discrimination and exploitation. A handful of colonial bosses trampled the Indians under their feet with tyrannic behaviours, treating Indians like dirt with "extreme cruelty". "No Indian can get a better place than that of a subject of the sixth class." Britons had in their possession all the best of wealth and resources while even the richest among Indians could only share some of the left-overs of the spoils. "The vast land of India is like a big prison.[1] He, then lamented with depression: "How sad is it to belong to a state that is dead!"[2]

Another leader of the same Reform Movement, Liang Qichao, had mentioned India in about 100 articles of his writings. He analysed the causes why India had become a colony, and strongly condemned the ruthless and tyrannic rule of British colonialism. While discussing the Indian problems, both Kang Youwei and Liang

Qichao would ponder over how China should not step into the Indian shoes. The common fate of the two peoples under the colonial rule was touched upon by them.

The early Indian nationalists and reformers were opposed to the opium trade (which Britain had imposed on China). Keshab Chandra Sen demanded as early as 1870 that the British government stopped the opium traffic. He pointed out that it was a "dirty trick in killing thousands of the pitiable Chinese".[3] An editorial of the *Amrita Bazar Patrika* in 1874 entitled "Chinese and British" listed the instances of how the British Colonialists had fleeced the Chinese,with such tricks including the opium trade. The editorial concluded by saying that it was fully justified when the Chinese looked upon the British as "devils".[4] When the famous poet, Rabindranath Tagore was only a lad of 20 years old, he already wrote articles condemning opium trade as a trade that manufactured death, as a behaviour of piracy. The famous activists of the Indian National Congress, Romesh Dutta and Gopal Krishna Gokhale also exposed and condemned with righteous indignity the shameful opium trade and the Opium War launched by Britain (against China).

Around the end of the 19th century and the beginning of the 20th century, a nationlist group led by Bal Gangadhar Tilak emerged in the Congress Party, while a bourgeois revolutionary group led by SunYat-sen also appeared in the Chinese scene. The nationalist movements of both the countries entered into the phase of nationalist revolution. From an identical revolutionary stand, the revolutionary groups of the two countries realised the need of mutual support and cooperation in their common struggle. They made great efforts along this direction. Thus the friendly relations between the two peoples entered into a new stage.

II

The pioneer of this new stage were Sun Yat-sen, Zhang Taiyan from China, and Borohan, Bose[5] and others from India. Sun Yat-sen referred to India a number of times in his writings and speeches. He was of the opinion that India's becoming a colony was due to the English East India Company's taking advantage of the internal split of the Indian feudal society. He thought that Britons were the most cunning conquerors. He pointed out: "What the colonialists expect the most is to get the colonies supply them raw materials and making them the markets of their indusrial manufactures."[6] For this purpose, they made "China and India bear the brunt".[7] According to him Britain had adopted economic and supra-economic measures in India to reach this target. She destroyed the traditional Indian textile industry and drained India's resources by levying heavy land revenues. All this resulted in economic decline, famines occuring in quick succession, people living in destitution, and skeletons bleaching the plains. He said: "Every year, Britain exacted huge quantity of food-grains from India for her own consumption, while in India nineteen million people died from hunger in ten years. It is not as if India is not producing grain, but the Indian produce is looted by Britain, hence India is made to starve".[8] He continued: "Though apparently Britain seems to mean no plundering in India, in reality it is a predatory tyrannic rule depriving Indians the means of survival, hence it is a plunder in a large scale."[9] Talking about the position of India within the British Empire, he pointed out: "It is India, not Britain itself that has made up the Empire." "In India lies the economic foundation of Britain, the life-line of Britain." "Without India the British Empire is but a third rate state." "Without India the British Empire is bound to disintegrate." He futher pointed out that since India was the life-line of Britain, the British authorities "would hold to India with no stone un-turned even to the extent of sacrificing everything else."[10] Therefore, the Indian revolutionary movement would not be a smooth sail. He advised the Indian people to treat unity with the foremost importance and persevere in their struggle.

In 1905, Sun Yat-sen went to Japan from Europe, he founded Zhongguo Tongmenhui (League of China) in Tokyo, and started Minbao (People's paper) as its mouthpiece. At that time, revolutionaries from many Asian countries, including India, stayed at Tokyo. Sun Yat-sen often gathered together with them and discussed with them the problems of anti-mperialist struggle and national liberation. He was the greatest inspiration for these revolutionaries. These were the earliest contacts between the revolutionaries of the two countries.

In 1906, an important thinker and activist of the Chinese bourgeois revolution, Zhang Taiyan, went to Tokyo. He was appointed the editor of *Minbao.* He had further contacts with the Indian revolutionaries, and started building an intimate relationship of close cooperation with them. In the same year, the Indian revolutionary, Borohan, went toTokyo from the U. S. A. and became the leader of the Indian patriots living in

Tokyo. The three easily established a sincere comradeship because of their identical revolutionary aspirations under identical circumstances. Zhang Taiyan wrote: "I was very happy in meeting these two gentlemen Borohan and Bose. We were first in high spirit, then all of us sank into a tearful mood. When they narrated about the decline of India and the plans of their revolutionaries. I was overtaken by a sense of grief and could not come out of it."[11] They briefed each other about the situation in their own country, also talked about the close contacts of the two nations in history, and expressed their desire for mutual support in their future struggles. Zhang Taiyan continued: "I think the two countries have been old bosom friends. We should consider the pros and cons and complement each other."[12] Afterwards Zhang became close friends of the two Indians. He said: "Though we are foreigners to each other there is rapport between us. We are good brothers."[13]

On April 20, 1907, Zhang Taiyan attended a function commemorating Shivaji, held in a girls' college at Toranomon, Tokyo, under the auspices of the Indian patriots. Zhang knew that the intention of the function was to propagate the idea of Swaraj. The meeting first went on very smoothly. Then, a Japanese politician named Ogama Shigenoba, who used to advertise himself as a friend of Asian peoples, began to compliment the British rule in India as one of "benevolence and love". He called upon the Indian people to concentrate their energies on "social reform", not to "put the blame on others, nor resort to violence". The atmosphere of the meeting was spoiled by his speech. Subsequently, Zhang Taiyan wrote an article in *Minbao* criticising the fallacy of Ogama Shigenoba. He observed: "What bullshit is this advice for Indian generosity! He was defending the British rule with an aim to hoodwink the Indians, like offering a lollipop to a crying child. This is too abominable to be tolerated!"[14]

At that time , the Indian patriots had no newspaper of their own. Zhang had spoken out what they wanted to but had no occasion to say. A minor sensation was created by Zhang's condemnation in Tokyo. Later on, Zhang not only wrote articles to introduce and commend the Swadeshi Movement in India, but also made *Minbao* carry more than ten articles translated from Indian revolutionary journals and the content of a leaflet put out by the Indian revolutionaries. He said that by doing so he wished to "make his Chinese comrades aware of this, and spread the just voice of the Indian nation all over the world."[15] His was the only non-Indian paper in Tokyo reproducing such large numbers of Indian writings.

Out of his brisk contacts with the Indian revolutionaries, Zhang Taiyan became the first person to put forward the idea of unity between China and India. In 1906, he propounded this idea in his articles on "Zhina Yindu lianhe fangfa" (The way of unity between China & India), and "Da Youmin shu" (A reply to You-min). He explained that his specifically advocating this Sino-Indian unity was because these two nations had had intimate contacts in history. They were "countries of affections" (*qinnizhi guo*), and should support each other "in view of the past affection and friendship".[16] Unity would benefit the struggles for independence and liberation in both the countries. China and India were the two great countries in Asia. They should shoulder the responsibility of safeguarding peace in Asia. He wrote: "Among the oriental civilizations, China and India are the only two greatest. They are endeared to each other as bosom friends. They should join hands to augment their strength. If they do not embrace each other and support each other, Asia will become protectionless."[17] He further suggested a two-phased course for achieving unity. First, the two peoples should support each other in their stuggle against imperialism, and should increase cultural exchanges to promote mutual understanding. Then, after the victories of their revolutions, the governments of the two nations should strike an alliance to jointly uphold peace in Asia. He said: "After China and India achieve their independence, they should form a holy alliance; then, Asia will be incident free."[18]

Both Borohan and Bose supported this idea. In 1907, they joined Zhang in establishing an "Association of Asian Affinity". The core of this organization was the revolutionaries of China and India, while it should also admit the revolutionaries of other countries. Its aim was "to oppose imperialism, to strive for the independence of all the subjugated nations of Asia". Members of the organization were under obligation "to render support to the members of other countries whenever revolution occurred there. The support should stretch to the maximum extent within the member's ability, either directly or indirectly."[19] This was the first organisational attempt on the part of Chinese and Indian revolutionaries. But soon after, this association was banned, *Min Bao* was also closed down by the Japanese authorities.

In the beginning of the 20th century, the leaders of the Indian radicals, Bal Gangadhar Tilak and Aurobindo Ghose, expressed their concerns about the Chinese national struggle. Tilak observed in an article that the boycott of American goods by the Chinese people in 1905 demonstrated that the people of a subjugated country could defeat an arrogant ruler by resorting to unity, with courage and determination. He used the example of Chinese struggle to stimulate the Indian people repeatedly. The boycott of British goods in 1905 by the Indian people against the British attempt to partition Bengal was, to an extent, the impact of the victory of the Chinese boycott of the American goods. The activities of the Chinese bourgeois reformists and revolutionaries at the end of the 19th and the beginning of the 20th century had inspired Aurobindo Ghose and Mahatma Gandhi who was, then, in South Africa. Aurobindo Ghose categorized the spread of nationalism as "the progress of China"[20], while Gandhi called it "the awakening of China."[21] The 1911 Revolution was a powerful booster of the morale of the Indian patriots. One of the important members of the Ghadar Party, Mula Singh said that the Indians must follow the path of China and that of other countries to reach the goal of Indian revolution.[22]

At the beginning of the World War I, Indian revolutionary organizations inside and outside India which advocated armed struggle often sent missions to the Far East to purchase arms. They often sought Sun Yat-sen's help. For example, Naren Bhattacharyya (later M. N. Roy), who was a member of a secret organization in Bengal, and the special envoy of the Ghadar Party in U. S. A., Sachindra Sen, Vishnu Ganesh Pingle, had all met Sun Yat-sen in China. Sun did what he could in helping them. When Sun Yat-sen was in Shanghai and Japan, he helped Rash Bihari Bose (who had made an abortive assassination attempt on Governor-General Hardinge in 1912, and had again engineered an armed uprising in Punjab and north India in February 1915 for which he was absconding) to escape arrest twice. Sun Yat-sen also maintained close contacts and established cooperation with the well-known Indian revolutionary Barkatullah. Indian revolutionaries greatly admired Sun Yat-sen. They also knew that Sun was an advocate for armed struggle. It was but natural that they would seek his help. Rash Bihari Bose recorded the unforgettable memory of how he had been helped by Sun in his book entitled *The Revolutionary India*. He mentioned the names of Mr. Toyama Mitsuru, Dr. Terao, and Mr. Miyazalei Tolenot as those Japanese friends of Sun Yat-sen who had rendered help to him to settle down in Japan without being harmed.[23]

When Gandhiji launched the non-cooperation movement Sun Yet-sen had assumed power in Guangzhou as the Extraordinary President of the provisional government, ready to launch his Northern Expedition against the war-lords. He hailed Gandhiji's movement as the "awakening of India". In 1921, he said in a speech: "The Indians have long been oppressed by the British. They have now reacted with a change in their revolutionary thinking... There is progress in their revolutionary spirit, they will not be cowed down by Britain."[24] Sun Yat-sen regarded the high tide of the Indian struggle as an integral part of the wave of national self-rule in the world after the World War I. He observed: "Since the European War, there has been a drastic change in the world situation." There emerged a new force. "What is the force? It is the great awakening of the oppressed section of humankind to form a massive resistance against the mighty powers." "Though India has gone under by the force of Britain, the common people stand opposed to the British."[25] Sun Yat-sen departed from his prepared text to specially commend Gandhiji's doctrine of non-cooperation while he was speaking and propounding the doctrine of his own Three People's Principles in 1924. He said: "What is non-cooperation? It is not to supply what the British are wanting. It is not to accept what the British are eager to supply. If the British need workers, no Indian would work for them; if the British bring up a lot of imported goods for the Indian consumption, the Indians should refuse to use them, and only consume their native products. In the beginning the British had taken this idea lightly. Through the passage of time non-cooperation organizations had mushroomed in India, and this greatly hurt the British economy, hence the British government throws Gandhi into prison." Sun, then, called upon the Chinese people to emulate the Indian example, become united and act, "sever economic ties" with the imperialists. He continued: "If all Chinese could emulate the Indian example of non-cooperation.....we will not be cowed down even if the foreign powers resort to the suppression of armed forces, economic measures, and the presence of their people."[26]

Apparently it looked strange that a champion of armed revolution like Sun Yat-sen would be favourably disposed for a non-violent and non-cooperation movement. But Sun had a wide vision to look at the strategies and tactics of the national struggle from various angles. He dwelt upon the active and passive ways in fighting imperialism: active, like awakening the national spirit, seeking the solutions of people's power and livelihood, and face to face against foreign aggression; passive, i.e. "non-cooperation, to weaken the role of imperialists, hence safeguarding the national position, avoiding the fate of total extinction."[27] While he thought that the non-cooperation movenient was an effective economic weapon in fighting the foreign rule the people will have to resort to armed struggle to overthrow it.

Sun Yat-sen also advocated Sino-Indian unification. He wrote in 1923 that "All the oppressed peoples should unify their efforts to fight against the tyranny of foreign aggressors." "India and China are the backbone of the oppressed peoples in Asia."[28] In deference to Sun's wishes, the Guangdong revolutionary government and the Kuomintang Party adopted as one of their foreign policies the unification with all the oppressed peoples, especially with India.

III

During the period of Northern Expedition, the mutual support and cooperation between the nationalists of the two countries in their anti-imperialist struggle reached a climax, unfolding in a wider dimension and demonstrating a refreshing form. I may like it to the first crop of fruits from the tree of Sino-Indian friendship which the two peoples had nurtured in modern history. After the "May 30" atrocity in 1925, the British government despatched large contingents of troops from India to suppress the Chinese people's anti-imperialist struggle. The Commissioner of Foreign Affairs in the Guangdong revolutionary government sent a telegram to Gandhiji, leader of the Indian Congress, calling upon him and his Party to use their influence to stop the British imperialists' using the Indian troops to massacre the Chinese people. Gandhiji immediately published this letter in the journal *Young India* which was run by him, and condemned the British authorities for sending troops to China. In September 1925, the All Indian Commitee of the Congress discussed the China issue, and passed the unprecedented resolution in the Congress history on China. The resolution expressed sympathy for the Chinese people in their struggle against foreign domination, and also strongly protested against the Indian government's despatch of Indian soldiers to suppress the Chinese freedom movement.[29] This was followed by meetings held at various places in India, voicing a wide spread demand for the withdrawal of Indian troops from China.

The Northern Expedition won victories in battle after battle, and the world was shocked. Jawaharlal Nehru, who was in Europe, at that time, actively campaigned for moral support for it among the leading circles of the Congress Party. At the end of January, 1927, the Working Committee of the Congress Party passed a resolution on the "China issue", expressing fraternity with the struggle of Chinese people. The Indian workers, students and people of all walks of life held meetings to celebrate the victory of the advancing troops of the Expedition. The protest movement against sending Indian troops to China gathered greater momentum. Gandhi wrote another article condemning the British. The nationalist press in China quickly reported the news of Indian people's support with expressions of gratitude. On March 2, 1927, *Minguo Ribao* (Republican Daily) at Guangzhou carried at a prominent space the news of Gandhi's condemnation with a bold heading reading: "The Indian reader condeming British militarism". Some of the resolutions passed by the Congress Party and other organizations were translated into Chinese and published. On April 13, 1927, Minguo Ribao at Hankou published a resolution of the Ghadar Party with the headline: "The great unification of the revolutionary forces of China and India".

On February 10, 1927, a world conference of the oppressed nations was held in Brussels, which provided an excellent opportunity for the revolutionary organizations of China and India to establish direct contacts and a relationship of collaboration. The leaders of the Chinese delegation were Liao Huanxing representing Kuomintang, and Xiong Guangxuan representing the Guangdong revolutionary government. Nehru participated in this conference as the representative of the Congress Party. The delegations of two countries fully utilised this opportunity to exchange ideas and experience. They expressed their common desire for direct cooperation between Kuomintang and the Congress Party. Nehru said in his speech: "The noble example of the Chinese nationalists has filled us with hope, and we earnestly want as soon as we can to be able to emulate them and follow in their footsteps (long applause)."[30] Both parties decided to take some concrete measures, including establishing a news bureau and having a permanent representative from China in India. Kuomintang invited a Congress delegation to visit China. The All China Trade Union invited its Indian counterpart and the Congress Party to send delegates to participate in the international trade union conference to be held in China. The Indian National Congress invited the Kuomintang to send delegates to its annual conferences. The two delegations also issued a joint declaration on behalf of the two peoples to reiterate the importance of strengthening Sino-Indian cooperation in their common struggle against imperialism. Both the Declaration and the collaborative measures worked out at the Brussels Conference were later endorsed by the leadership of both the parties.

In March 1927, Xiong Guangxuan wrote serial articles in the Hankou Minguo Ribao, reporting about the Conference. Three of these articles introduced the Indian nationalist organizations to enable the Chinese people to further understand the Indian national movement. Nehru, after the conference, reiterated the great significance of the Chinese revolution and its vital interest to India, in his report to the Working Committee.

Some of the collaborative measures started to move. Kuomintang decided to send a delegation consisting of Madam Soong Ching-ling (i. e. Madam Sun Yat-sen), Wang Jingwei (President of Kuomintang) and Gu Mengyu to visit India. Nehru and other leaders of the Congress Party were elated by the coming visit of Madam Sun Yat-sen. However, the British government refused to issue a visa to her for fear of a powerful impact to be created by her visit. Madam Sun Yat-sen expressed indignation in her letter addressed to the Indian Congress, saying that though the British colonialist authorities could stop her from going to India so ungracefully, they could not prevent her from expressing her sentiments through letters. She assured the Indian people that all the loyal followers of Dr. Sun Yat-sen would continue in paying attention about and expressing sympathy for the Indian independence struggle. She also wrote a letter to the women of India. Nehru told her in his reply that her two letters were read and warmly welcomed and highly appreciated in the annual convocation of the Congress Party. He continued: "It is humiliating for us that a foreign power should prevent one whom India honours from visiting our country. We trust however that the time is not far distant when you will be able to come to this country as the honoured guest of the nation."[31]

Another avenue of cooperation between the nationalists of the two countries, during the period of Northern Expedition, was the cooperation between the Chinese branch of the Ghadar Party and the Chinese nationalists. The Gadar party had their branch in China as early as the World War I. The Party had an expansion during the Northern Expedition. It passed many resolutions in support of the Chinese people's struggle, and hailed the victory of the Chinese revolutionary army. One resolution maintained that British imperialism was the common enemy of the two peoples. It called the countrymen of India, wherever they were, not to support or participate in the sinful activities of the British in waging war against China.[32] The leader of the Ghadar Party, Munsha Singh, was of the view that the political atmosphere in China was very favourable to the function of the Ghadar Party. While pushing forward the revolutionary movement in India at the same time, it could help the Chinese revolution, the two were complimentary. Some experienced political workers were sent to China. The main places where Ghadar Party was active were: Shanghai, Beijing, Guangzhou, and Hankou. The party established a publishing house and started their newspaper. Many posters were secretively distributed among the Indian soldiers. One article written by Inder Singh appealed to the Sikhs and all Indians who stayed in China not to serve the British imperialists and not to oppose the Chinese national struggle. The article said that the true sons and daughters of China were fighting for the freedom of their motherland. The freedom of China was closely linked with that of India. If China won her freedom, it would bring about the Indian freedom in the near future. The task of the Indians was to help the Chinese nationalist force.[33]

For the sake of mutual coordination and support, the revolutionaries of India, Korea, and Vietnam who were in China, along with their Chinese counterparts, formed an organization called "Association of Oppressed Nations" in 1925. The Indians who joined this organization were the members of Ghadar Party. Leaders of the party, Deshandra Singh and Charan Singh, were elected as members of the executive committee of this organization which may be regarded as the extension and development of the "Association of Asia Affinity" founded by Zhang Taiyan, Borohan and others in Tokyo. The new Association immediately plunged into activities, such as secretly distributing leaflets, instigating the Indian soldiers and Sikh policemen not to be the British tools to enslave other nations, it called upon the expatriates from India and other nations in China to stand by the Chinese people. It even suggested the recruitment of volunteers among Indian expatriates in Hankou to form a military force to join the Northern Expedition under the command of the Chinese military authorities. This suggestion did not materialise due to some practical difficulties. At the beginning of 1927, Deshandra Singh went to Shanghai which was under the control of the war-lords to convene secret meetings of the Ghadar Party. Unfortunately he was arrested along with 12 core members of the Ghadar Party. The Association suffered a great setback, yet still survived.

IV

During the period of Anti-Japanese War (1937-45), collaboration between the nationalist forces of China and India reached a greater climax. There were many reasons behind it. First, the Indian Congress Party, Indian Communist Party and many other parties of India all condemned the Japanese aggression on China and Fascist expansion of Germany, Italy and Japan in the world. They sympathised with the Chinese people's determination to resist aggression. Jawaharlal Nehru, the left wing leader of the Indian Congress, even publicly criticised the non-resistance policy of Chiang Kai-shek; for this he was greatly respected by the Chinese people. Secondly, the Chinese Communist Party which stood for fighting against Japan appealed to all the oppressed nations in the world, including the Indian people and nationalist forces to support China's Anti-Japanese War. After China had begun an all out war against Japan, the Kuomintang led by Chiang Kai-shek also appealed for help from the Indian Congress. After the Pacific War broke out, America and Britain formed an alliance with China and established the relationship of military cooperation. Thirdly, the Chinese people of all walks of life maintained close rapport with the development of Indian national movement. The Chinese people supported the nationalist demands put forward by the Indian National Congress.

On July 7, 1937, a full scale Anti-Japanese War broke out in China. The Indian masses rose to the occasion by creating a warmth of enthusiasm in support of the Chinese War. Gandhi, Nehru, and Tagore, in their speeches and writings, pointed out the just cause of Chinese resistance against Japan. They appealed to the Indian people to do their best in aid of the Chinese struggle for national honour and survival. Nehru, as the President of the Congress that year, solemnly declared on behalf of the Congress: "Our attitude is one of complete opposition to Japanese aggression and of sympathy to China."[34] Acting on his suggesion, India held the first "China Day" on September 26, 1937. The Indian masses responded with enthusiasm by holding meetings condemning the Japanese aggression. The Congress, following Nehru's suggestion, appealed to the people to boycott Japanese goods to express solidarity with the Chinese people. A nation-wide boycott movement was created. Businessmen pledged not to sell Japanese goods. Those who did not, got their shops picketed by volunteers who persuaded customers not to enter them. On December 24, 1937, on received an appeal for help from Chu The [Zhu De], Commander-In-Chief, Eighth Route Army, China. Chu Thé, it will be remembered, was the chief of the famous army which performed the prodigious feat some years ago of marching 8,000 miles in spite of almost insuperable difficulties. The feat is unique in military annals."[35] Having complimented the firm determination of the 8th Route Army and the Chinese people, he suggested that on January 9, 1938 India would mark another "China Day", and appealed for donations to help the Chinese soldiers fighting on the anti-Japanese frontier get provisions of medicines and other supplies. The "China Day" proposal was widely supported by various nationalist organizations, groups, and people from all walks of life, including the Indian Communist Party. Tagore took a lead in giving donation. This was followed suit by the broad masses. Even the Indians abroad extended their hands of help. The famous dancer, Shankar, held a charity performance in London, and donated all the proceeds to the cause of the Chinese people. This aid was like the life-giving wind and rain in spring which nourishes the hearts of people. Major Chinese newspapers carried timely reports and described the Indian support as "brotherly help" and "friendship in need".

In 1938, Subhas Chandra Bose became the President of the Indian Congress. He pushed up the aid-China wave from strength to strength. On June 12 a third "China Day" was observed. The central theme was to stand by the Chinese people when they faced the most difficult times. Meanwhile, the anti-Japanese boycott movement and the donation collection did not slacken, the Japanese trade with India suffered a drastic decline. Yet, the most memorable event was the Congress decision to send a medical team to China, which was initiated by Nehru during his tenure as the Congress President. The Medical Team was composed by five doctors. Atal, Cholkar, Kotnis, Basu and Mukherjee. When they arrived in China they volunteered to go to North China to treat the wounded soldiers behind the enemy lines, braving great hazards and risks. Kotnis and Basu worked in the frontier for some time. Their diligence and valuable service demonstrated before the Chinese people the warmth of the Indian support for China, and won admiration among all who had come across the Indian doctors. Dr. Kotnis died in China because of overwork. He personified the symbol of everlasting magnificence of Sino-Indian friendship. Mao Zedong mourned his death by observing that "The army has lost a helping hand, the nation has lost a friend. Let us always bear in mind his internationalist spirit.."[36] The story of the Indian Medical Team had become a household word in China. When Dr. Basu was finally leaving China,

Mao Zedong, Zhu De, gave a high evalution of the work of the Team, and extended a hearty gratitude for the Indian Congress and Indian people in their letters addressed to the Indian Congress Party.

The Chinese people would always remember with gratitude Mahatma Gandhi and Gurudeva Tagore who criticised the Japanese militarists in international fora. Gandhi wrote an open letter to the Japanese people, while Tagore denounced the malice of the Japanese poet, Noguchi Yonejiro. They demonstrated their expansive righteousness, upheld humanism, and showered their friendship for the Chinese people.

In August 1939, Nehru visited China which pushed the fighting-comradeship between the people of China and India to a new high. Nehru was honoured as "the great leader of the Indian people" and "an intimate friend of China". He was warmly received by Chiang Kai-shek, other high ranking officers of the Kuomintang Party and its government, the representatives of the Communist Party in Chongqing, and also people of all walks of life. Earlier, Nehru had written to Mao Zedong, hoping to visit Yan'an. He got Mao's invitation telegram after he reached Chongqing. The telegram read : "I hear that you have reached Chongging, which will further close the ranks of the two nations in unity in their struggle for national independence, freedom and liberation. I send you my warm regards on behalf of the Chinese Communist Party and people. I invite you to visit Yan'an, so that I can listen to your admirable views in person."[37] Nehru who had earlier been eager to see Yan'an was jubilant that his cherished wish would be realised. But, with the flare up of the World War II, he had to rush back home. He sent a telegram to Mao Zedong before leaving China expressing his gratitude for the invitation, regretting his inability to visit Yan'an, and hoping to fulfil his wish in a future trip. He also hoped that this short visit of his to China would strengthen the contacts between the two countries which would fight together hand in hand in their courses of liberation.[38]

When Nehru was in China, he conceived a seven point programme of how to strengthen contacts between China and India. These included the set up of "an efficient and regular service of information", exchange visits by specialists to study each other's cottage industries and cooperatives, "cultural contacts between universities", direct contacts between "the two national movements", Chinese delegates to the annual sessions of Indian Congress, developing "a common outlook and policy on major international issues", and the organizations of industrial cooperatives getting "into direct touch with the All India Village Industries Association" etc.[39] The Kuomintang side also put forward identical suggestions. These plans for strengthening cooperation went a step further than what had been proposed during the Brussels Conference. Most of these plans were implemented later.

China, on her part, did her best to support the Indian struggle for independence. After World War II broke out, the Indian Congress passed a resolution demanding that Britain, which flaunted the banner of fighting for freedom, should apply this very principle to India in the first instance, and the Congress would decide their attitude towards the War only according to the British attitude towards India. The mouth-piece of the Chinese Communist Party, *Xinhua Ribao* (New China Daily), carried this resolution with a headline to the news: "The Indian Congress issued a declaration, stood opposed to the imperialist war, exposed the British duplicity about their fighting for freedom and democracy, adhered to the struggle for national liberation and the realisation of democratic politics". This was coupled with an editorial said: "The Indian people do not wish to join this imperialist war. They do not want to be common fodder of the British imperialism. They do not believe that Britain is genuinely fighting for democracy and freedom. Their stand is correct." The editorial concludes: "We salute our Indian brothers, and wish them march forward with vigour."[40] A little later, all the Chinese newspapers reported the anti-war attitude of the Indian people as well as the non-cooperation movement led by Gandhi, expressing their support for the struggle of the Indian People.

On October 31, 1941, when the news of the arrest of Nehru was known, the Chinese people of all walks of life expressed their concern. On Novermber 2nd, the leaders of the Chinese Communist Party, Mao Zedong, Zhou Enlai, Chen Shaoyu, Qing Bangxian, Ye Jianying, sent a joint telegram to Nehru expressing concern. The telegram reads: "The Chinese people have been grateful for your warm kindness in campaigning for support for their cause of war against Japan. We deeply believe that you and the national leaders who have been struggling for the Indian people's liberation will soon be released and carry on your struggle now that all the people of India and the progressive personalities of the world are demanding your freedom."[41] *Xinhua Ribao* issued an editorial to support Nehru and condemn the British authorities. It wrote: "What crime had Nehru committed? Perhaps it is that he was against India joining the war, because he was for the independence of India. In other words, probably he is sent to jail because he is not able to sing: "Long live British imperialism."[42] In Chongqing, the China Defence League also sent a telegram to Nehru expressing their solidarity. Wang Yunsheng, member of the Standing Committee of the National Association for Foreign Affairs, also sent a similar telegram along with 30 others.

The British authorities wanted to entice the Indian Congress Party to support the War, but refused to concede to the just demands of the Congress. The issue was deadlocked. After war broke out between Germany and the Soviet Union, the Chinese Communist Party advocated the establishment of a world-wide anti-Fascist united front, but, at the same time, reiterated the necessity of the colonial rulers' adopting measures to: "materialize independence and equality among all nations."[43] Accordingly, Xinhua Ribao issued an editorial on January 20, 1942, urging the British policy-makers to convert the empty words of the Joint Declaration of Roosevelt and Churchill into reality. The editorial appealed to the British authorities to give the Indian people "democracy, freedom and the right for arming themselves." It said: "The time has come that the British government change their [Indian] policies."

After war broke out in the Pacific area, Chiang Kai-shek became the Commander-in-Chief of the Allied Forces in the China theatre. He too wanted to break the deadlock in India. In February 1942, he was invited to India by the British-Indian Viceroy for discussion of matters of military cooperation. Madam Chiang, and more than ten high-ranking military and government officers accompanied him. In this visit, Chiang Kai-shek met Nehru many times. He also met Gandhi, the leader of the Muslim League, Jinnah, and the Indian women leaders, Mrs. Pandit, and Mrs. Naidu and others. He exchanged views with them on the situation of the Indian national movement and how to strengthen the contacts between India and China. Chiang also visited Visva-Bharati, and paid homage to the late lamented poet Tagore. One of the aims of Chiang's visit was to help break the Indian political deadlock. Before his departure, Chiang issued an open letter to the Indian people in which he reiterated the necessity for the British authorities to "quickly grant political power to the Indian people' to enable the Congress Party to fully support the War.[44] The Congres Party and the Indian people took all this as a powerful support for the India national movement. Nehru said in a speech later: "Although it is not customary for the head of one state to interfere in the internal affairs of another state, yet Chiang Kai-shek, the head of the Chinese state, who recently toured India, expressed himself in unmistakable terms on the question of India's freedom."[35] Chiang's open letter was widely appreciated in China. *Xinhua Ribao* said in its editorial : "Indeed, Britain should put into practice what is said in the Joint Declaration of Roosevelt and Churchill, granting political power to the Indian people on the basis of allowing the Indian people freedom and liberation."[36] A tremendous political pressure was built up by Chiang's open letter. Churchill was visibly annoyed, but had to put up a gesture of willing to compromise.

In reciprocating the "China Day" activities held annually in India in many years since 1938, an "India Day" was observed under the auspices of many cultural groups under the Central Committee of Cultural Movement in Chongqing. The day was observed by holding a photo exhibition, screening movies, delivering lectures, giving radio talks, publishing a special volume, and other activities to popularise information about the Indian national movement and expressing friendly sentiments and gratitude of the Chinese people for the Indian people.

In the first half of 1942, Japanese troops occupied South East Asia, and began to bombard the cities in India. In view of the British unwillingness to break the political stalemate, Gandhi launched the "Quit India" movement and the Indian Congress unfolded an uprecedented large scale non-cooperative movement. The British authorities resorted to pre-emptive arrest of Gandhi and almost all the leaders of the Congress Party on August 9th. When this news reached China, a wave of protest was organised by the Chinese political circles and the press. Every major newspaper issued an editorial condemming the British suppression. *Jiefang Ribao* (Liberation Daily), the mouth-piece of the Chinese Communist Party commented that the Bombay Resolution to urge Britain to quit India was just and correct, "it should be supported by all the people who are opposed to aggression, and should be accepted by Britain." It said that the British violent response to a non-violent movement was responsible for the deteriorating situation in India which only "saddens our near and dear, and gladdens our enemies."[37] *Ta Kung Pao*, the progressive liberal daily, commented in its editorial: "The aim of the Indian freedom struggle conforms to that of the Allied Nations fighting the Fascists. There is not a single Chinese who does not support the Indian cause."[38] When the news of Gandhi's indefinite fast in jail reached China, thirteen Chinese celebrities, Shen Junru, Zhang Yilu, Zuo Shunsheng, Huang Yanpei, Guo

Moruo, Zhang Shenfu, Mao Dun, Tao Xingzhi, Luo Longji, Zhang Bojun, Liu Qingyang, and Shi Liang sent a joint telegram to the British-Indian Viceroy, urging him to immediately release Gandhi. Chiang Kai-Shek also sent telegram after telegram to the US President, Roosevelt, urging him to put pressure on Britain to break the deadlock. Soong Ching-ling, Soong Mai-ling, and Tai Chi-tao (who visited India in 1940) maintained their correspondence with Nehru when he was in prison.

The Chinese people were not only concerned with the Indian national movement, but also with the sufferings of the Indian people. When famine broke out in Bombay, Bihar and other places in 1943, major Chinese newspapers published articles severely accusing the British authorities for their indifference towards the people's sufferings. Donations were collected from all walks of life in China for relief to their Indian brothers and sisters.

At the end of World War II and the victory of China's Anti-Japan War, both Nehru and the President of the Congress Party, Maulana Azad, sent telegrams of congratulations to China. The All Indian Committee of the Congress also passed a resolution to express their heart-felt joy over the victory of the Chinese people.

After the World War II, the Indian Congress began to build up a nationalist country while China opted for a new democratic revolution. This new development created complexity for Sino-Indian relations. Yet, strengthening the friendship between the two countries remained their common desire. Nehru, leader of the Congress, sincerely hoped that China would be united to reconstruct the nation and play an important role in safeguarding peace in Asia and the world. He adopted a non-intervention policy towards China's civil war. He also quickly came to terms with reality. After the founding of the People's Republic of China, India was the second country among the non-communist countries to recognize it.

On September 3, 1946, a provisional Indian government was established. On August 15, 1947, India won independence. The Chinese Kuomintang government maintained diplomatic relations with India. The Kuomintang ambassador participated in the Independence Celebrations. The Chinese press warmly congratulated the Indian independence.

After the Indian Republic and the People's Republic of China established diplomatic relations, India actively advocated on the restoration of China's UN seat, and increased her cooperation with new China in the struggle against colonialism, and pursuance of independent foreign policy. The Chinese side continued to strengthen her friendship which China had built with India during the past anti-colonial struggle. On January 26, 1951, the great leader of the Chinese people, Mao Zedong, attended the celebration of Indian Independence Day in Beijing and said: "Indian nation is a great nation, Indian people are good people. The friendship between the two nations and the two peoples was very good in the past lasting for several thousand years. Today, when we celebrate the national day of India, we hope our two nations, China and India, will continue to be united to work hard for peace."[39]

V

Cultural interaction is an important means to promote the mutual understanding to thicken mutual affection between the peoples of India and China, and also the stones and also the macadem to sustain political cooperations between the two countries. The pioneers and leaders of national movements of both China and India have time and again reiterated the importance of cultural interaction. When he moted the idea of Sino-Indian fraternity, Zhang Taiyan said: "About the means of unity the best way is to disseminate culture into each other."[50] Nehru exhorted in 1937 that both the countries should enhance understanding towards each other, drawing inspirations from the past and present. He regarded understanding each others cultural and ideological background as the foundation of real understanding.[51]

The resumption of cultural exchange between the two countries began in the beginning of the 20th century. But the real builder of the golden bridge of Sino-Indian cultural interaction was Rabindranath Tagore. His winning the Nobel Literature Prize in 1915 created a great sensation in China — when the Chinese intellectuals were highly frustrated under the arrogant repression of Western cultural supremacy. That an Asian (and also a non-white), like Tagore, could obtain the highest laurel in world literature. His writings began to be translated into Chinese. In 1924, he responded to the invitation of Jiang Xue She (The Lecture Society) to visit China. Several famous Indian scholars accompanied him. They made wide contacts with personalities of Chinese circles of literature, drama, painting, education, philosophy, religion etc. and started a real meaningful interaction in many realms.

After Tagore's visit cultural interactions between the two countries gained substantial developments both in dimension and in depth. In the first place, Indian studies in China expanded to philosophy, history, society, language and other fields. A large number of paper and special studies were published. Universities began to have curricula in such subjects. Secondly, Chinese scholars and students began to visit India, studying and doing research on India. They included Zeng Shengdi, Tan Yun-shan, Xu Zhimo, Xu Dishan, Gao Jianfu, Hai Weiliang etc. about whom we have obtained information. Thirdly, the most outstanding fruition was the establishment of the Sino-Indian Cultural Society and Visva-Bharati Cheena-Bhavana.

October 10, 1998 is going to be the Centenary of Tan Yun-shan. I wish to use this opportunity to highlight his contribution to the friendship-in-need between Chinese and India in modern times. Tan Yun-shan was invited in 1927 by Tagore to go to India to teach in Visva-Bharati. The Sino-Indian Cultural Society was conceived by Tagore, but it came into being in Nanjing, China, in 1933, and at Santiniketan in India in 1934, after Tan Yun-shan had busily shuttled himself between the two countries. Encouraged by Tagore, Tan continued to appeal for donations and obtained a sufficient sum to build the Cheena-Bhavana on the campus of Visva-Bharati with a plot allotted by Tagore for the purpose. In April1937, the Cheena-Bhavana was established, and Tan was appointed as its director. After its establishment, many famous Indian scholars came to teach there. Even more Chinese scholars visited and stayed in it who included Tao Xingzhi, Xu Beihong, Xu Fancheng, Chang Renxia, Wu Xiaoling, Jin Kemu etc. Many more Chinese students and young teachers went there for higher studies. Cheena-Bhavana became the first important base for Sino-Indian cultural interaction with scholars of China and India staying together and learning from each other, in addition to a journal and many special writings published by it. Tao Xingzhi exchanged experience of educational reform with Tagore and Gandhi. He also obliged Gandhi and wrote an article on "The popular education movement in China" which was published in *Harijan*. Gandhi wrote an "Introduction" to the article, and pointed out that it had important reference value to the educational reform in India. Xu Beihong exchanged notes with Tagore on painting, and held painting exhibitions at Santiniketan and Calcutta, an idea noted by Tagore who wrote the "Introduction" for the exhibition.

1939, two years after the establishment of Cheena-Bhavana, saw Nehru visiting China on the invitation of the Chinese government. The actual agency which was instrumental to this visit was Sino-Indian Cultural Society the Chinese chapter of which was now headed by Zhu Jiahua (also spelled as Chu Chia-hua) who was the chief secretary of the Kuomintang. Tan Yun-shan was the Indian representative of the Sino-Indian Cultural Society and was in close touch with Zhu Jiahua. That Nehru's visit was arranged by Tan Yun-shan and the Sino-Indian Cultural Society can be proved by the following telegram sent by Tan:

"To ChungKing [Chongqing] Chief Secretary of Kuomintang Central Office, Chu, also addressed to the Party chief, Chiang [Kai-shek], President [of the Examination Yuan], Tai [Chi-tao], Education Minister, Chen [Li-fu], also attention of President [of the Executive Yuan], Kung [Hsiang-hsi], Minister Yeh.

Indian leader Nehru is scheduled to fly to China on the 20th. I have already accorded welcome to him on your behalf. Kindly extend hospitality after he arrives.

Obediently,

Tan Yun-shan

August 18."[52]

Nehru's 1942 visit to China resulted in furthering cultural interactions between the two countries, after his talks with Chinese leaders, Chiang Kai-shek and others. The two countries began to exchange visiting groups for studying each other's Socio-politico-economic problems, visiting scholars between China and India also increased.

Tan Yun-shan and the Sino-Indian Cultural Society were also instrumental to the China visit of famous Indian philosopher, Dr. S. Radhakrishnan in 1944 which was a lecture tour. His lectures in Kunming and Chongqing not only contributed to enhanced Chinese understanding of Indian tradition, philosophy and culture, but also aroused keen interest among young Chinese intellectuals in Indian studies. Dr. Radhakrishnan was a member of the Sino-Indian Cultural Society and had been a friend of Tan Yun-shan for many decades. After returning to India from his China lectures, he developed an interest in Sino-Indian cultural interaction, and wished to emulate Tagore to develop the Benares Hindu University — to which he was the Vice-Chancellor - into a strong base of Sino-Indian cultural interaction like the Visva-Bharati. On September 19, 1946, he wrote to Tan Yun-shan thus:

"The University has decided to confer the Degree of Doctor of Letters on His Excellency Dr. Tai Chi-Tao, President of Examination Yuan of the National Government of India, honoris causa, and we will be pleased to hear that His Excellency has kindly consented to accept the Degree.

It is our intention to build up a Chinese Library in this University and to have, if possible, a Professor of Chinese if the National Government of China is so pleased as to endow a Chair in the University for the purpose."[53]

To this letter, Tan Yun-shan replied on October 10, 1946 thus:

"I felt indeed very glad that the Benares Hindu University has decided to confer the Degree of Doctor of Letters, honoris causa, on His Excellency Dr. Tai Chi-Tao, President of Examination Yuan of the National Government of China. I have cabled and written to His Excellency advising him to accept the honour which you have so kindly offered to him ... I am sure he will gladly [come over to India development of China will not prevent him from coming.

I am also very glad to learn that you intend to build up a Chinese Library and to have a Professor of Chinese in your University. Would you please let me know whether you intend to have a separate Chinese building together with Chinese books or simply to have some Chinese books in the University Library? If you intend to have a separate building, together with books, may I suggest that a full Chinese Department be established in The University for Sino-Indian Studies....[same] as the Cheena-Bhavana in Visva-Bharati at Santiniketan... As the Benares Hindu University of India, is the first and biggest National University of India, and the relaionship between India and China has become... closer day by day, I think it is very necessary for the University to have such a Department. It will not be very difficult for the National Government of China to endow a Chair and some scholarships for this purpose. If you so desire, I shall try my humble best to help you in materialising the project."[54]

These two letters have reflected the close contacts between Tan Yun-shan and Radhakrishnan. However, the Benares Hindu University did not establish a second Cheena-Bhavana in India. Not that there was no possibility to realize such a plan, but Radhakrishnan was himself posted to Paris as the Indian representative of UNESCO. Later, he was India's Ambassador to the USSR, then, returned to India to become the Vice-Chancellor of Delhi University, then was elected as the Vice-President, and finally, the President of India. The change of leadership in the Benares Hindu University left no one to implement Radhakrishnan's original plans.

As Tan Yun-shan frequently shuttled between China and India, he become a messenger among the leaders of the two countries. For instance, before his departure for China in 1938, he received a letter from Nehru asking him to convey the Indian people's support for China's Anti-Japanese War efforts. The President of National Congress, Subhas Chandra Bose, also wrote to him, asking him to convey the support of Indian National Congress for China's fighting against the Japanese aggression. Tagore gave him a lettler to be presented to Chiang Kai-shek which he handed over to Chiang at Wuchang. In 1939, Tan Yun-shan was leaving China for India, the Vice-President of the Executive Yuan, Kung Hsiang-hsi (H. H. Kung) asked Tan Yun-shan to carry a letter to Mahatma Gandhi,wanting to strengthen friendship between China and India. In 1940, when Tan Yun-shan returned to China from India, he carried Gandhiji's reply to H.H. Kung in which Gandhiji heartily appreciated Kung's emphasis on Sino-Indian friendship. The letter was published by the Chinese press and made a great impact in China.[55]

In 1945, when Gandhi heard about China's victory over Japan, he sent a telegram from Poona to Tan Yun-shan, expressing the warm congratulations and affection for the Chinese people. Every time When Tan Yun-shan returned to China he would tell the Chinese public about the Indian people's support for China's war efforts through lectures, articles, as well as special pamphlets. The information conveyed by him was a great encouragement to our people while acknowledging the real affection and friendship from the Indian people. Through the intermediary of Tan Yun-shan the public leaders of India and the Indian people also had a better understanding of the justice of China's Anti-Japanese war and China's determination in fighting it which, inturn, further strengthened their support for China.

Tan Yun-shan had carried out a lot of activities in molilizing support for the Anti-Japanese war while he was in India. Through lectures and writings he made publicity of the bravery of Chinese soldiers in fighting the Japanese aggressors, and the atrocities of the latter committed on Chinese soil. His vantage position prevented the Japanese propaganda machine from penetrating into Santiniketan and reaching the Gurudeva. In 1938, Tagore exchanged letters with the Japanese poet, Yone Noguchi, which completely demonstrate China's gaining an upper hand in international morality. Tagore was a great admirer of Japanese culture and art, and had visited Japan a number of times. He told Noguchi, "Believe me, it is sorrow and shame, not anger, that prompted me to write to you. I suffer intensely not only because the reports of Chinese suffering batter against my heart, but because I can no longer point out with pride the example of a great Japan."[56]

Tan Yun-shan definitely had his personal input in Tagore's unreserved condemnation of the Japanese aggression on China. As Tagore wielded a tremendous influence in international circles, his historic debate with Noguchi become banner news in the world media which registered a tremendous blow on the morality of the Japanese aggressors, and constituted a powerful moral support to the Chinese people.

Tan Yun-shan had maintained a warm personal relationship with Nehru from 1930s onwards when the latter was but an ordinary politician, but was frequent visitor to Santiniketan. This lasted the entire duration of Nehru's prime-ministership — making the two old friends for more than three decades. Nehru was also one of the Honorary Presidents of the Sino-Indian Cultural Society. When he was the Prime Minister of India (and later the Chancellor of Visva-Bharati), and when he visited Santiniketan he would make it a point to go to Cheena-Bhavana to see Tan Yun-shan.

Tan Yun-shan maintained deep friendship with Indian leaders on the one hand, while on the other hand, he first had had intimate contacts with the National Government of China, and, then, established mutual respect and trust with the leaders of the People's Republic of China, particuarly Premier Zhou Enlai. This enabled him to play the rate of an intermediary — a faceless role in promoting friendship and understanding. In 1942 when Generalissimo and Madam Chiang Kai-shek visited India to have talks with the leaders of the Indian independence movement, Tan Yun-shan was associated with this significant international affair. The Chiang couple made a point to visit Cheena-Bhavana (that time Tagore was no more), and was received by Tan Yun-shan. They also met Nehru who was there to welcome the Chinese leader. Tan Yun-shan helped to arrange Chiang's talks with Nehru. They talked from Santiniketan upto Calcutta in the company of Tan Yun-shan. This talk enabled Nehru to deepen his understanding of and close affection with China. Later, when Gandhi was ready to launch the "Quit India" movement, he was mindful of Chiang Kai-shek's worries (that it would disturb the strategic deployment of the Allied Forces and would benefit Japan). Gandhi talked to Nehru and then signed a letter addressed to Chiang Kai-shek (which might have been drafted by Nehru), declaring solemnly: "To make it perfectly clear that we want to prevent in every way Japanese aggression, I would personally agree that the Allied Powers might, under treaty with us, keep their armed forces in India and use the country as a base for operations against the threatened Japanese attack... I shall take no hasty action. And whatever action I may recommend will be governed by the consideration that it should not injure China, or encourage Japanese aggression in India or China."

This pledge by Gandhi and Nehru was vitally important to ensure the victory of China's Anti-Japanese War and to the entire Asian theatre of the Allied Forces. This was also the biggest achievement of Chiang Kai-shek's talks with Nehru. We should recognize Tan Yun-shan's contribution in it.

The Cheena-Bhavana headed by Tan Yun-shan not only attracted a visit by Chiang Kai-shek, but, once again, welcomed Premier Zhou Enlai in 1957. A small institution of a university having been visited by two highest leaders of China at different times is an extreme variety. This proves that the Chinese leaders gave great importance to Sino-Indian friendship and cultural interaction. Needless to say that this was also meant to be a full appreciation of the hard labour put in by Tan Yun-shan.

The two great nations and the two great peoples are now greeted by the twilight of the dawn, after spending a long crucifying dark night. Both countries are marching forward, developing their own economies. Let us always remember those years when we shared with each other our sorrows and joys, that history of our friendship in need. Let this precious historical memory for ever inspire us to maintain our fraternity generation after generation so that we put in our common endeavours to strive for a greater, newer, prosperous future.

---

1. See *Kang Youwei zhenglun ji* (Collected works of Kang Youwei on politics), vol. 1, p. 621; vol. 2, p. 812.
2. Kang Youwei, *Wanmucaotang yigao* (Manuscripts left behind from the study of exuberant plants), p. 168.
3. Birendra Prasad, *Indian Nationalism and Asia*, Delhi.1979, p. 28.
4. *Ibid*, p. 29.
5. Both were not the full names of the persons who cannot be identified.
6. *Sun Zhongshan quanji* (Collected works of Sun Yat-sen), Beijing,1984, vol. 3, p. 82.
7. *Ibid.*
8. *Ibid*, vol. 4, p. 42.
9. *Ibid.*
10. *Ibid*, pp. 66-72.
11. *Minbao*, photolithographic edition. Beijing: Science Publishers, 1957, vol. 2, No. 13, p. 97.
12. *Ibid.*
13. *Ibid*, p. 98.
14. *Ibid*, p. 97.
15. *Ibid*, vol. 4, no. 21, p. 107.
16. *Ibid*, vol. 3, no. 20, p. 38.
17. *Ibid*, no.19, p.100
18. *Ibid*, no. 20, p. 38.
19. *Xueshu yuekan* (Academic monthly), 1979, No. 6.
20. *Sri Aurobindo*, vol. 2, p. 230.
21. *Collected Works of Mahatma Gandhi*, vol. 5, p.172.
22. Manmathanath Gupta, *History of the Indian Revolutionary Movement*,Bombay1972, p. 1.
23. Chinese translation of Rash Bihari Bose's *The Revolutionary India*, 1933. p.1.
24. *Sun Zhongshan quanji*, vol. 6, p. 14.
25. *Ibid*, vol. 9, p. 223.
26. *Ibid*, vol. 9, p. 240.
27. *Ibid*, p. 241.
28. *Ibid*, p. 241.
29. A. M. Zaidi & S. Chand (eds), *Encyclopaedia of Indian National Congress*, New Delhi, 1980, vol. 9, p. 43.

30. *Selected Works of Jawaharlal Nehru*, vol. 2, p. 276.

31. *Ibid,* vol. 4, p. 85.

32. D. Biteli, *Communism in India*, Calcutta, 1972, p. 180.

33. *Ibid,* pp. 209-210.

34. *The Selected works of Nehru*, vol. 8, p. 719, Nehru's letter to V. K. Krishna Menon, Allahabad, August 30, 1937.

35. *Ibid,* vol. 8, p. 733.

36. Sheng Xiangong et al, *An Indian Freedom fighter in China: A Tribute to Dr. D.S. Kotnis, Beijing*: Foreign Language Press, 1983, p. 174.

37. *Xinhua Rihao* (New China Daily), Sept. 5, 1938.

38. *Ibid.*

39. Nehru's note "On the development of contact between China and India" which he wrote in Chongqing for the benefit of the leaders of the Kuomintang government. See *Selected Works of Jawaharlal Nehru*, vol. 10, pp. 102-108.

40. *Xinhua Ribao* (New China Daily), Sept. 26, 1941.

41. *Ibid,* Nov. 3,1941.

42. *Ibid,* Nov. 5, 1939.

43. *Ibid,* Jan. 1, 1942.

44. *Zhongyang Ribao* (Central Daily), Feb. 23, 1942.

45. *Selected Works of Jawarharlal Nehru*, Vol. 12, p. 247, Nehru's speech in New Delhi on April 7, 1942.

46. *Xinhua Ribao*, Feb. 24, 1942.

47. *Jiefang Ribao* (Liberation Daily), August 27, 1942.

48. *Ta Kung Pao*, August 12, 1942.

49. *Renmin Ribao* (People's Daily), Jan. 27, 1951.

50. *Minbao*, vol. 4, no. 22, p.131.

51. *Selected Works of Jawaharlal Nehru*, vol. 7, pp. 709-10.

52. This telegram was carried in a story by *Yindu Bao* (Indian Journal), a Chinese language newspaper published in Calcutta, August 18, 1939, p. 3, "local news".

53. Letter now preserved in the family archives of Prof. Tan Chung.

54. Same as above.

55. *Xinhua Ribao (Xinhua Daily)*, Feb. 13, 1940.

56. The entire correspondence was published by Tan Yun-shan as "Poet to Poet", a copy of which is preserved in the family archives of Prof. Tan Chung.

57. *Collected Works of Mahatma Gandhi*, vol. 76, pp. 224-25.

28

TAN YUN-SHAN : THE PIONEER OF SINO-INDIAN STUDIES AND A CULTURAL BRIDGE BETWEEN INDIA AND CHINA

As one proceeds from Bolpur to Santiketan along the roads that are lined by *palash* and *ashok* and *muchkunda* trees on the road to Ratanpalli, you are in a different world altogeher inspite of the changes that have over taken Visva-Bharati . An institution that was to represent India where she her wealth of mind and where the whole world found its shelter, has today become a mere centre of Bengali culture with its Tagore-Nama. It is only the world, to be specific, with China, the largest country of Asia and a major power in the world.

The French Sino-Indologist Sylvain Levi declined an offer to go to Harvard to teach at Santiniketan, Stella Kramrisch and Witernitz taught at this University. C.F Andrews and William Pearson gave their lives to this place. When Pearson died he left all his money to Santiniketan.

Tan Yun-shan helped set up Cheena-Bhavana whose buliding is the most impressive structure in the Ashram. As per the late professor's statement, twelve teacher's quarters were built near the Bhavana with the munificense of foreign donors mostly Chinese.

An extremely significant and unique feature of India-China relations is that while India has enriched the world with her philosophical and other intellectual wealth, with her vastly rich resources of folk, animal and strange tales, Cosmology and divinity, China has taken upon herself to preserve these priceless treasures for the benefit of Asia and the world. While India concentrated on unravelling the mystery of the universe, epistemology and the magic of rhetoric and prosody, China discoverd the beauty in nature, and the material needs of human beings, like paper, printing, compass and explosives. China also showed the world the need of recording the history of one's own country and the neighbours so as to draw lessons from the success and failure of the ancestors and also to show that commoners and elites outside the court are as important as the royalty. Whatever the material aspirations of the rulers, the historians and other writers depicted the world outside China under inspiration of the adage, "the whole world is our home" (Tianxia yiria), like our own ancestoys who considerde the whole world as their own relatives

We find the same Principle being materialized in the case of Cheena-Bhavana. Nowhere has the dreams of Gurudeva been so magnificently manifested than in the handiwork of Tañ Yuns-han and Prabodh Chandra Bagchi, that is, the Cheena-Bhavana.

While talking about Cheena-Bhavana we must take into account the immortal contribution of three great men. The fountain-head, the inspiration and the soul was of course Gurudeva. Next come both professors Tan Yun-shan and P.C. Bagchi. While Tan built the edifice, the body, the crossbars, the sound and solid structure, the canopy and the like, with an eye to the ecology of the entire complex, Bagchi consolidated the edifice through constant study and discovery of the very foundation of our common civilization based on Buddhism. He gave a very scholarly and comprehensive survey of this phase of India China brotherhood.

The greatness of Tagore lies not only in his writings, but also in the undying impact that he made on the youths of India and China. No one was so deeply moved by the spirit of India-China brotherhood based on Buddhism as the Gurudeva. He endeavoured to bring back the golden period of what Tan-Chung has called the Buddhist twinhood. In doing so, he was presumably inspired by his vision to usher in an Asian material and cultural regeneration. His consciousness about this ideal was reflected long ago in 1881 (Bengali year 1288) when as youngman of twenty he wrote a carping criticism of the British in a review entitled "Death Traffic in China" in *Bharati* (May 98 number) it was a review of the English translation of Theodore Christlieb's German book The Indo *British* opium Trade". It shows deep interest he took in China even in his very early days . In the last part of the article he quoted the Chinese emperor, Dao Guang as saying, I can never stoop so low as to make money out of the sin and suffering of my subjects.

Tagore's conclusion was vastly devastating and exposed the meanness of the then British Christians. He concludes, "It is written in the Christian scriptures:" If anyone smite you on one cheek, turn to him the other. "When the English Christians tempted the Chinese Emperor with a big revenue to be obtained by killing his subjects, the Emperor refused. He would not do thing so despicably mean. Doubtlessly, what this non-Christian Emperor did was a slap on the face of the Christian English. Unfortunately it had no effect"

Tagore regarded China as India's lost brother, and it was to know and understand that lost brother that he visited China affer a lapse of a thousand years after the golden period of Sino-Indian brotherhood. The first thing he did after reaching Beijing In April, 1924, was to convey India's deep love and shraddha (respect) to China.

We all know how much deep faith did the Chinese intellectuals like *liang Qichao Xu Zhimo, Zheng tuo* and many others reposed on Tagore for the new message of resurrection and progress. I need not dilate on that. Sisir Das and Tan Wen's *Vitarkita Atithi* (The Controvessial Guest) and some other writtings on the same subject have dealt in detail the ramifuaction before and after the visit. We have two convincing examples of how Gurudeva changed the lives of disillusioned Chinese youths. The first one I am talking about is Guo Muoruo, new China's leader on the cultural front for decades and life president of the Chinese Academy of Sciences. He was indeed a disenchanted Chinese student in Japan during the second decade of this century, and was inclined either to become a Buddhist monk or to commit suicide, and the more he sought encouragement from ancient Chinese writings the greater was his pessimism, until he discoverd a new message from the poems of Tagore in the English version *The Crescent Moon.* These poems changed him into a new man.

Tan Chung has written in a number of places (including a passing reference in this volume) that, Guo Monuo recoved his courage and optimism in life, after learning how to look at life's challenges with a calm and counageous heart.

Another remarkable scholar whose life was given a new direction was Tan Yun-shan. According to his eldest son, Tan Chung, Tan Yun-shan also fell into a mood of disillusionment similary to that of Guo Monuo after his arrival in Singapore in 1924. He used to go to the seashore and both his country's future and his own personal career appeared to him as an endless turmoil as the sea. He became a totally changed man affter he met Gurudeva in 1927 in Singapore during Tagore's Southeast Asian tour.The next year, Tan arrived at Santiniketan, and new leaf in his life started. All told, Tagore seems to have exercised a magical spell on young Chinese minds when they lived in the age of turbulence."

Tan Yun-shan was a bunch of contradictions and complex mentality before the crucial meeting with Poet Tagore. All the patriotic and ambitious contemporary intellectual youths of his country (and Tan was no exception) trained their eyes on the direction of the Far West in the quest of a solution to save the country from the rot. There was a voice calling him to go to Europe exactly as Zhou Enlai, Zhu De, Deng Xiaoping, and many other future leaders of the Chinese communist movement was doing. Singapore was just his first stop on his long-distance travel. Meanwhile, he was a man also deeply imbibed in traditional oriental values. To him the ancient pilgrimage between China and India was far from dead. Tagore's lectures in China in 1924, and the warm welcome of him by eminent Chinese such as Liang Qichao and others had Kindled a revival of his great fancy for that pilgrimage. What he had regretted was that while Tagore's boat was sailing towards Shanghai, His boat was leaving Shanghai for the "South Seas" alsmost at the same time. But, suddenly, the one he had longed to meet -- Rabindranath Tagore -- was presenting himself within easy reach -- in Singapore where he had just begun his wanderer's life. While he immediately went to Tagore's hotel as if climbing the Tai Mountain, he discovered to his pleasant surprise that the Tai Mountain was opening its arms to embrace him. Tagore was keen to look for someone who could help him to resurrect the "Great pilgrimage" from oblivion, and convert his Visva-Bharati into the modern version of a Nalanda University of ancient times, and even something more than that to re-enact the historical friendship and interface between India and China. It was as if destiny had arranged their historic meeting in Singapore.

After arriving in India in 1928, he started equipping himself for the historic task enjoined on him by delving deep into Indian philosophy, literature and culture with the help of the famous scholars at Santiniketan, and conducting Chinese classes at the same time for Indian scholars. During the vacations, he toured the various Buddhist shrines and the historical relics, and the impressions he gathered were put together in his travelogue *Yindu Zhouyou Ji* (Travels in India) with the hope of creating interest about India among the Chinese youth.

Around 1931, both the poet and the professor felt the urgent need of setting up a permanent institution of Chinese studies and promote exchange of scholars between the two countries wiithout which revival of old ties would remain a chimera. Tan carried this realization of the Gurudeva and his colleagues as well as his own sense of urgency and left for China after stenjing for 3 years at Santiniketan. His visit to China was highly successful, the Sino-Indian Cultural Society was founded at Nanjing in 1933 through which donations of books and funds for the establishment of Cheena Bhavana were raised in China. An imposing building was erected and about a hundred thousand books in the form of traditional Chinese blockprints, modern printed editions of ancient classics and dynastic histories, journals and cllectanea enriched the library. It took several years of hard work before the fateful day for realization of the Gurudeva's dream. Cheena-Bhavana was inaugurated by Gurudeva in 1937 (on the Bengali New Year's Day). The building and the library were gifts of love from China, said Gurudeva. Donation of books continued till late fifties when Prime Minister, Zhou Enlai, after his visit to Visva-Bharati, gifted such valuable collections as *Congshu Jicheng* and *Wanyou Wenke* and many other rare collections.

Cheena-Bhavana is the most prominent and beautiful structure in the Ashrama complex of Santiniketan where people come to see the rich collection and to enjoy the sight of the immortal artistic creations of such talented artists like Nandalal Bose and Vinod Behari Mukhopadhyaya whose defictions of the life and legend of Buddha enshrine the Cheena-Bhavana hall and corridor. These geniuses have done these murals not for material benefit but out of their sheer love for China, and for their passion to preserve our heritage and to inspire the posterity for building a permanent bridge of friendship between India and China.

On the front side of the building is engraved the four Chinese characters *Zhongguo Xueyuan*, the Cheena-Bhavana -- beautifully calligraphed by Lin Sen, the then president of the Republic of China. Outside the conference room on the ground floor, a bronze slab is fixed on the wall with exquite handwriting of Tai Chi-tao. The text is his essay on Sino-Indian cultural Interface, and his impressions on Buddhist shrines visited by him, as well as his hope for the future improvement of India-China relations. The keen interest shown by prominent scholars and statesmen invests this institution with an importance that should inspire the younger generation in the study of Cultures and civilizations of India and China and Sino-Indian interface and Synergy.

Prof. Tan was a unique personality who combined the Confucian ethic with Buddhist teachings highlighting the values of *Ren* (perfect virtue, benevolence) and *Yi* (righteousness) of the Confucian way of self-cultivation in *synthesis* with *karuna* (compassion,) *Prajana* (wisdom) and *Ksanti* (forbearance)and other traits of Buddhism, thus upholding the highest value of both the countries. He emphasised the spiritual basis of our culture and ardently hoped that the two peoples set in this strife ridden modern world good examples so that other nations are inspired to emulate them. This was the best way of eliminating conflict and war of ushering in lesting world peace. In this way humankind would bring about *datong* (mahasamata) utopia in this globe where greed, insecurity, hatred and conflict would disappear, and the world itself would become a *sukhavati dhame* (abode of happiness) — a vision that embraces the happiness of all humanity.

Tan Yun-shan's views on history and philosophy were akin to that of the early Chinese historians and philosophers a view based on life cycle analogy. Men have their periods of birth, growth, maturity, senility and death. The dynamics behind this process is moral, and the lessons to be drawn from the study of dynastic rise and fall are the moral lessons.Thus, Tan remarks, when things get into one extreme, they are sure to get a reversal. Therefore, all the civilizations of the world must have their vicissitudes, and they evolve in rotatory motions, not in straight lines.

The period of 1942-43 was very critical for India with the launching of Quit India Movement when almost all the political leaders of India were either arrested by the British government or were in hiding against the interest of the war effort by the Allied Power against the Axis Powers. China bore the brunt of enemy attacks against the Allied Powers in the Eastern Hemisphere, but the main rear of the China Theatre, the lifeline of Anti-Japanese War was India. The Chinese leadership as well as the public were terribly worried about the Indian situation while their sympathies lay on the side of the Independence Movement. It was a crucial life-and-death moment for China against the Axis Powers. Tan Yun-shan realised the urgency of the situation and took a very bold and upright, "Appeal to conscience" on 24th September, 1942, he observed:

"The present political deadlock and situation in India cannot be allowed to last longer. It will do good to nobody but help the common enemy. He appealed to his Indian brethren to abandone the path of violence, and then, pleaded with the British to grant independence to India and in support of his arguments, he even quoted Confucius who says, "If names be not rectfied, words will not be in accordance with the truth of things, and affairs cannot be carried on to success. He then told Britain: "when you declare India independent and free, the name of India and the present war will be immediately rectified and the present deplorable situation of India as well as of the war will be entirely changed for the better. If you declare India independent and free just now, you will not only gain the heart of the 400 million Indian people, but also obtain the praise, enthusiam and admiration of the United Nations." Such a courageous yet risky step could be taken only by a person of Tan Yun-shan's calibre who had deep love for the country, and who had indetified himself with the weal and woe of the people of India.

Tan Yun-shan's relation with Gurudeva was exactly like our *Guru Shishya Parampara* (The preceptor and disciple) relationship, a relation of complete submission and surrender. He has adimitted in his writings that whenever he met Gurudeva, he "always felt a kind of divine light mingled with love, mercy bliss abd joy, pouring out from him upon me". He was so much enchanted by Tagore's personality that as per his own words "whenever I saw him, I always almost forgot everything, either bitter or sweet, happy or unhappy, good or bad.I really could not and like to put him any question or to request him to do anything for me." This is the true spirit of an *antevasin* (student disciple) of our ancient times.

Tan Yun-shan was quick witted and had a keen sense of humour. Once Tagore asked him, how different people of differnt nations viewed thing of beauty. In reply, Tan referred to a saying of Mengzi (Mencius) which runs as, thus "all men's mouths agree in having the same relishes, all men's ears agree in enjoying the same sounds, all men's eyes agree in recognizing the same beauty." Tagore smiled and said, "No, it is not always so.The young Chinese poet Susima (Xu Zhimo, the name is poetically rendered into Bengali by Tagore) who came here, you know, was quite a handsome person. I asked our girls if they appreciated his beauty. All of them said No." Tan Yun-shan interrupted: "Gurudeva, you may not believe your girls more than the Chinese sage. The girls might have felt shy to tell you that they appreciated the beauty of a young Chinese poet."

Tan Yun-shan can rightly be called the Xuanzang of modern China, Visva-Bharti for him was the modern Nalanda with Tagore Personifying the combined personality of Silabhadra and Kalidasa. Tan was responsible for reviving the broken intellectual bonds between India and China after an Inteerragnum of nearly one thousand years. Unlike Xuanzang who came to India to learn and carry her wealth of learning and philosophy back to China for the benefit of his countrymen, Tan Yun-shan not only drank deep into the fountain of Indian culture, but imbued with the thoughts of benevolence and charity like a true Confucian,. He made India his second home, and settled down at Santiniketan for teaching Indians the cream of Chinese culture and civilization. An ardent Buddhist scholar, deeply religious, unassuming and reticent, he represented all that is best in Chinese civilization. The Poet's true disciple and friend, collaborator and co-worker, Tan was not a visionary but a man of action. He was undoubtedly one of the most fascinating personality in Visva-Bharati. In the course of a message, Mahatma Gandhi had described Cheena-Bhavana as the symbol of the living contact between India and China. Looking at Tan Yun-shan, one could rightly say that he symbolised Mahatma's ideal of that living contact in human form. In addition to the Buddha, Confucius and Tagore, he was also greatly influenced by Mahatma Gandhi and Sri Aurobinda, and tried to evolve a synthesis of their teaching.

Although the unhappiest in the wake of the deterioration of Sino-Indian relations during the early sixties, Tan Yun-shan and his family never thought of leaving India (but most of the educated Chinese from calcutta and Delhi had left India or were expelled by our government). He always wanted that his endeavour should be perpetuated even when he was no longer there, and for this task he had selected his eldest son Tan Chung, a highly accomplished scholar both in classical and modern Chinese, a poet, and a dedicated savant with a vision for future India-China relations.

The greatest contribution of Tan Yun-shan to Bengal and to India is, to my mind, the priceless treasure that he had collected for the Cheena-Bhavana from different sources in China. In arranging such a gift he hoped that Indian scholars would be encouraged to study Chinese and to contribute towards advancing Sino-Indian studies and promoting mutual understanding. The Cheena-Bhavana owes its birth and growth to Professor Tan's herculean efforts. It consists of more than 100, 000 volumes of different collections, many of them rarely to be found even in China today. They include the Sung edition (10-14th century AD) and the reproduction of what is known as the Dragon edition (1936 reprint) of the Buddhist Tripita along with many separate volumes of important Buddhist treatises. Ten set of the Shanghai edition of the Chinese Buddhist Tripitakas were presented to the library by the Chinese people, nine sets of which were presented by Professor Tan to different universities and institutions in India. This edition of the Tripitakas contains 1916 different work in 8416 fascicles most of which were translate into Chinese from Sanskrit. The Sanskrit originals of these treatises are unfortunately lost in India now. It took nearly a thousand years of hard labour to translate them into Chinese by translators numbering more than a hundred at a time, most of them great scholars, both indian and Chinese.The emperors patronized them and spent lavishly for this noble cause. Other collections vary from several voumes to over 800 volumes comprising such rare collections as *Sibu Beiyao, Sibu Congkan, Congshu Jicheng, Wanyou Wenku, Gujin Tushu Jichen, Cefu Yuangui, Shuofu,* the 24 dynastic histories in various editions, and so on. It is a pity that such a rich collection remains *neglected* on the shelves without being frequently consulted.

While addressing the annual convocation of Visva-Bharti on 7th 1989, the late Prime Minster Rajiv Gandhi remarked "Rabindranath's ideals should not be turned into fossil to be kept in museums but should be interpreted in modern light." He further said, "Visva-Bharati cannot be allowed to degenerate into a minor provincial university." I dont know if he had Cheena-Bhavana in mind or not, if so, then it is only the inmates of Cheena-Bhavana who can turn this fossil into a blooming plant bubbling with life. It is these inmates who can act as the bridge between man and man, institution and institution, nation and nation, and as Mahatma Gandhi said in his message for the first issue of the now defunct Sino-Indian Journal in 1947, "I long for the real friendship between China and India based not on econmics but on irresistible attraction. Then will follow real brotherhood of man". But Alas! That real brotherhood is yet to begin because it is encomics that dominates all spheres of international relations today and not human sentiment.

In a private meeting with the Chinese intellectuals like Liang Qichao, Xuzhimo and others on 25th April, 1924 in Beijing, in reply to a question on the west's allegation against China's exclusive nationalism, (in other words sinocentrism) Tagore had made a very apt remark. I quote a few sentences. He said, "China is not merely a geographical country. China means a culture and a civilization. It represents a fulfilment and progress of many social and human ideals. And surely the Chinese can expect from others freedom in that field, so that they can offer the results of their *Sadhana*, as their best gift to humanity."

We the Sinologues and the Sinologists are in the most advantageous position to understand the value of this gift, assimilate its essence and disseminate it.

Chinese is now a tool for research on both modern, medieval and ancient Indo-Chinese relations. What is more, Chinese records are the most authentic, continuous and comprehensive sources for reinterpretations and discovery of new data on Indian history, ancient and medieval. It also provides bread and butter to many who aspire for nothing more than introduction into modern Putonghua, the official vehicle of expression. The Defence, the Cabient Secretariat, the differnt Universities, the numerous prospering tourist agencies, the Business Houses, INSDOC and NISTADS of the CSIR, and so on, are too eager to utilise the knowledge of suitable linguists on handsome payments. And for all this, the people of Eastern India will remain forever grateful to Gurudeva and to Professor Tan Yun-shan for providing us with an excellent infrastructure and suitable milieu.

WRITINGS OF TAGORE, NEHRU AND TAN YUN-SHAN

29. China and India
Rabindranath Tagore

30. India and China
Jawaharlal Nehru

31. Cultural Interchange between India and China
Tan Yun-shan

32. My Devotion to Rabindranath Tagore
Tan Yun-shan

33. My First Visit to Gandhiji
Tan Yun-shan

34. Ahimsa in Sino-Indian Culture
Tan Yun-shan

35. Tagore-Noguchi Correspondence on Japanese Aggression, 1938
Poet to Poet

36. An Appeal to Conscience
Tan Yun-shan

29

ADRESS AT THE OPENING, CEREMONY OF VISVA-BHARATI CHEENA-BHAVANA ON APRIL 14, 1937 INDIA AND CHINA

The most memorable fact of human history is that of a path-opening, not for the clearing of a passage for machines or machine guns, but for helping the realisation by races of their affinity of minds, their mutual obligation of a common humanity. Such a rare event did happen and the path was built between our people and the Chinese in an age when physical obstruction needed heroic personality to overcome it and the mental barrier a moral power of uncommon magnitude. The two leading races of that age met, not as rivals on the battle-field, each claiming the right to be the sole tyrant on earth, but as noble friends, glorying in their exchange of gifts. Then came a slow relapse into isolation, covering up the path with its accumulated dust of indifference. Today our old friends have beckoned to us again, generously helping us to retrace that ancient path obliterated by the inertia of forgetful centuries, and we rejoice.

This is, indeed, a great day for me, a day long looked for, when I should be able to redeem, on behalf of our people, an ancient pledge implicit in our past, the pledge to maintain the intercourse of culture and friendship between our people and the people of China, an intercourse whose foundations were laid eighteen hundred years back by our ancestors with infinite patience and sacrifice. When I went to China several years ago I felt a touch of that great stream of life that sprang from the heart of India and overflowed across mountain and desert into that distant land, fertilising the heart of its people. I thought of that great pilgrimage, of those noble heroes, who, for the sake of their faith, their ideal of the liberation of self that leads to the perfect love which unites all beings, risked life and accepted banishment from home and all that was familiar to them. Many perished and left no trace behind. A few were spared to tell their story, a story not of adventurers and trespassers whose heroism has proved a mere romantic excuse for careers of unchecked brigandage, but a story of pilgrims who came to offer their gifts of love and wisdom, a story indelibly recorded in the cultural memory of their hosts. I read it when I was received there as a representative of a revered race and felt proud as I traced the deep marks our ancestors had left behind on their achievements. But I also felt the humiliation of our long lasting evil fate that has obscured for us in an atmosphere of insanity the great human value of a noble endeavour, one of the most precious in the history of man.

I told my Chinese hosts on that occasion: "My friends, I have come to ask you to re-open the channel of communication which I hope is still there; for though overgrown with weeds of oblivion, its lines can still be traced. I have not the same voice that my ancestors had. I have not the wisdom they possessed. My life has not attained that consciousness of fulfilment needed to make this message fruitful. We in India are a defeated race; we have no power, political, military or commercial; we do not know how to help you or injure you materially. But, fortunately, we can still meet you as your guests, your hosts, your brothers and your friends. Let that happen. I invite you to us as you have invited me. I do not know whether you have heard of the institution I have established in my land. Its one object is to let India welcome the world to its heart. Let what seems a barrier become a path, and let us unite, not in spite of our differences, but through them. For differences can never be wiped away, and life would be so much the poorer without them. Let all human races keep their own personalities, and yet come together, not in a uniformity that is dead, but in a unity that is living".

That has happened and friends are here from China with their gift of friendship and co-operation. The Hall which is to be opened today will serve both as the nucleus and as a symbol of that larger understanding that is to grow with time. Here students and scholars will come from China and live as part of ourselves, sharing our life and letting us share theirs, and by offering their labours in a common cause, help in slowly re-building that great course of fruitful contact between our peoples, that has been interrupted for ten centuries. For this Visva-Bharati is, and will, I hope, remain a meeting place for individuals from all countries, east or west, who believe in the unity of mankind and are prepared to suffer for their faith. I believe in such individuals even though their efforts may appear to be too insignificant to be recorded in history.

It might be supposed that in a world so closely knit by railways, steamships and air lines, where almost every big city is cosmopolitan, such special invitations for contact are superfluous. But, unfortunately, the contacts that are being made today have done more to estrange and alienate peoples from one another than physical inaccessibility ever did. We are discovering for ourselves the painful truth that nothing divides so much as the wrong kind of nearness. People seem to be coming in each other's way, dodging and trapping one another, without ever coming together. We meet others, either as tourists when we merely slide against the surface of their life, entering hotels only to disappear from their land, or as exploiters in one disguise or another. We are living in a world where nations are divided into two main groups those who trample on others' freedom, and those who are unable to guard their own; so that while we have too much of intrusion on others' rights, we have hardly any intercourse with their culture. It is a terrorised world, dark with fear and suspicion, where peaceful races in dread of predatory hordes are retreating into isolation for security.

I am reminded of my experience as we were travelling up from Shanghai to Nanking along the great river, Yang Tse. All through the night I kept on coming out of my cabin to watch the beautiful scene on the banks, the sleeping cottages with their solitary lamps, the silence spread over the hills, dim with mist. When morning broke and brought into view fleets of boats coming down the river, their sails stretching high into the air, a picture of life's activity with its perfect grace of freedom, I was deeply moved and felt that my own sail had caught the wind and was carrying me from captivity, from the sleeping past, out into the great world of man. It brought to my mind different stages of the history of man's progress.

In the night each village was self-centred, each cottage stood bound by the chain of unconsciousness. I knew, as I gazed on the scene, that vague dreams were floating about in this atmosphere of sleeping souls, but what struck my mind more forcibly was the fact that when men are asleep they are shut up within the very narrow limits of their own individual lives. The lamps exclusively belonged to the cottages, which in their darkness were in perfect isolation. Perhaps, though I could not see them, some prowling bands of thieves were the only persons awake, ready to exploit the weakness of those who were asleep.

When daylight breaks we are free from the enclosure and the exclusiveness of our individual life. It is then that we see the light which is for all men and for all times. It is then that we come to know each other and come to co-operate in the field of life. This was the message that was brought in the morning by the swiftly moving boats. It was the freedom of life in their outspread sails that spoke to me; and I felt glad. I hoped and prayed that morning had truly come in the human world and that the light had broken forth.

This age to which we belong, does it not still represent night in the human world, a world asleep, whilst individual races are shut up within their own limits, calling themselves nations, which barricade themselves, as these sleeping cottages were barricaded with shut doors, with bolts and bars, with prohibitions of all kinds? Does not all this represent the dark age of civilization, and have we not begun to realize that it is the robbers who are out and awake?

But I do not despair. As the early bird, even while the dawn is yet dark, sings out and proclaims the rising of the sun, so my heart sings to proclaim the coming of a great future which is already close upon us. We must be ready to welcome this new age. There are some people, who are proud and wise and practical, who say that it is not in human nature to be generous, that men will always fight one another, that the strong will conquer the weak and that there can be no real moral foundation for man's civilization. We cannot deny the facts of their assertion that the strong have their rule in the human world: but I refuse to accept this as a revelation of truth.

It is co-operation and love, mutual trust and mutual aid which make for strength and real merit of civilization. New spiritual I and moral power must continually be developed to enable men to assimilate their scientific gains, to control their weapons and machines, or these will dominate and enslave them. 1 know that many will point to the weakness of China and India and tell us that thrown as we are among other ruthlessly strong and aggressive world peoples, it is necessary to emphasize power and progress in order to avoid destruction. It is indeed true that we are weak and disorganised, at the mercy of every barbaric force, but that is not because of our love of peace but because we no longer pay the price of our faith by dying for it. We must learn to defend our humanity against the insolence of the strong, only taking care that we do not imitate their ways and, by turning ourselves brutal, destroy those very values which alone make our humanity worth defending. For danger is not only of the enemy without but of the treason within us. We had, for over a century, been so successfully hypnotised and dragged by the prosperous West behind its chariot that, though choked by the dust, deafened by the noise, humbled by our helplessness, overwhelmed by speed, we yet agreed to acknowledge that this chariot-drive was progress, and that progress was civilization. If we ever ventured to ask, however humbly: Progress towards what, and progress for whom? It was considered to be peculiarly and ridiculously oriental to entertain such doubts about the absoluteness of progress. It is only of late that a voice has been heeded by us, bidding us take account not only of the scientific perfection of the chariot, but of the depth of ditches lying across its path. Today we are emboldened to ask: what is the value of progress if it make a desert of this beautiful world of man? And though we speak as members of a nation that is humiliated and oppressed and lies bleeding in the dust, we must never acknowledge the defeat, the last insult, the utter ruin of our spirit being conquered, of our faith being sold. We need to hear again and again, and never more than in this modern world of head-hunting and cannibalism in disguise that: - By the help of unrighteousness men do prosper, men do gain victories over their enemies, men do attain what they desire, but they perish at the root.

It is to this privilege of preserving, not the mere body of our customs and conventions, but the moral force which has given quality to our civilization and made it worthy of being honoured, that I invite the co-operation of the people of China, recalling the profound words of their sage, Lao-tze [Laozi: Those who have virtue attend to their obligations, those who have no virtue attend to their claims. Progress which is not related to an inner ideal, but to an attraction which is external, seeks to satisfy endless claims. But civilization, which is an ideal, gives us power and joy to fulfil our obligations.

Let us therefore abide by our obligation to maintain and nourish the distinctive merit of our respective cultures and not to be misled into believing that what is ancient is necessarily outworn and what is modern is indispensable. When we class things as modern or old we make a great mistake in following our calendar of dates. We know that the flowers of Spring are old, that they represent the dawn of life on earth, --- but are they therefore symbols of the dead and discarded? Would we rather replace them with artificial flowers made of rags, because they were made "yesterday"? It is not what is old or what is modern that we should love and cherish but what has truly a permanent human value. And can anything be more worthy of being cherished than the beautiful spirit of the Chinese culture that has made the people love material things without the strain of greed, that has made them love the things of this earth, clothe them with tender grace without turning them materialistic? They have instinctively grasped the secret of the rhythm of things, --- not the secret of power that is in science, but the secret of expression. This is a great gift, for God alone knows this secret. I envy them this gift and wish our people could share it with them.

I do not know what distinctive merit we have which our Chinese friends and others may wish to share. Once indeed our sages dedicated themselves to the ideal of perfect sympathy and intellect, in order to win absolute freedom through wisdom and absolute love through pity. Today we cannot boast of either such wisdom or such magnanimity of heart. But I hope we are not yet reduced to such absolute penury of both as not to be able to offer at least a genuine atmosphere of hospitality, of an earnestness to cross over our limitations and move nearer to the hearts of other peoples and understand somewhat of the significance of the endless variety of man's creative effort.

30

INDIA AND CHINA

(Address at the Sino-Indian Cultural Society General Body Meeting at Santiniketan on December 23, 1945)

It was, I think eight and a half years ago that Prof. Tan Yun-Shan asked me to come here to open the Cheena Bhavana. I gladly agreed, but a very unusual thing happened on the day of my starting. I fell suddenly ill and was unable to come and had to be content with sending a message with my daughter, Indira. The last occasion I visited the Cheena Bhavana was when I came here in the company of the illustrious leader of China, Generalissimo Chiang Kai-shek.

I am very happy today to be able to participate in the meeting of the Sino-Indian Cultural Society. I have listened with pleasure and attention to the report of your activities. And yet I have felt how much more could be done in respect of increasing the contact between China and India, having due regard to the numerous bonds that bind these two vast countries. Like all members of your Society I am anxious to develop all manner of contacts, cultural and otherwise between them, both intensively and extensively. I would like to see branches of the Society in a large number of places in India and China, so that its activities might extend beyond a few specialists, to the common man in both the countries.

Perhaps the conditions created by the war during the last five or six years have come in the way of developing this contact, as they have come in the way of much else. And yet the war has certainly brought us nearer and closer to China than ever before, both physically and psychologically. The war has made China look to the west of her rather than to the east of her. The centre of activities in China came nearer to India with the development of communications by road and air. Today it is possible to be in the heart of China after a brief day's journey. All these factors, which might have taken place in course of time, but which have been expedited by the war, have led to the closest associations and approximations between China and India. That association should have a greater and wider effect on the public mind, rather than be limited to our small Society of experts specialising in research. By that I do not mean to say that their work is without value. The scholars can do much by way of guiding popular enthusiasm, by providing data for them and by canalising their feelings.

It seems obvious to me that in the future India and China will necessarily come nearer to each other. By that I do not mean mere continuation of the ancient bonds, although they will of course be there. Taking an objective view of world situation as it seems to develop, it seems inevitable that in their own interests, China, India and some other countries of South East Asia will have to hang together and develop together, not only culturally but economically as well, through the contacts of trade and commerce. They will not be able otherwise effectively to resist the aggression of the so-called Western Powers. Mutual contact and agreement are essential for their self-preservation.

The tempo of the world changes rapidly today and it is foolish to prophesy anything. But one thing is patent to everybody and that is that although the war has just ended, even now we see signs of trouble and conflict. Even among the victors in this war there are already dark hints of further wars on a far more extensive scale.

Whether another war is likely or not I connot say. But nobody can ignore the possibility of such a thing happening. We should put our own house in order before that fear materialises. India and China, which have played a different part in world affairs, are passing through some kind of turmoil today. In China it has taken the obvious course of a civil war and in India the trouble is deep-seated. These differences among our own people result in a certain weakening of our ability to influence the world which is extremely unfortunate. Now that hostilities have ceased in the Pacific Theatre, India and China should have had the privilege of directing the future course of events. Instead we have helplessly to watch things happening which are not only injurious and detrimental to our interests but which are positively hateful. It is hateful to think, e. g., of the recent events in South East Asia.

Things would certainly have improved if China could take a hand in the South East Asian affairs. China undoubtedly is one of the principal powers of the world today. Naturally therefore many eastern countries look to China today with the hope that she would give a lead to Asian affairs, that she would play as vital a role in peace as she has done during these eight years of war. It is therefore a matter of deep anguish for many of us who think of China that there should be so much internal trouble there at the present moment. You have rightly passed a resolution congratulating China. What she did and what she passed through during these eight years is something which is difficult for us even to imagine. The sufferings the Chinese have undergone and the heroic courage they have shown are something unparalleled. It is right therefore that we should congratulate them and send our best wishes to the great leaders of the Chinese people, and notably to Generalissimo Chiang Kai-shek. In the midst of a great deal of civil conflict in China I do not think there is anybody who challenges the right of the Generalissimo to be the leader of China. Even those critics who might differ from him have to acknowledge that in the present circumstances he is the only possible leader, the one man to lead China out of chaos and confusion. It is right that you should wish him success in his attempt at uniting the different elements in China.

Let us hope that the present state of affairs in China will end soon and give place to a strong feeling of unity and solidarity. A strong and united China and a strong and united India must come close to each other. Their amity and friendship will not only lead to their mutual benefit but will also benefit the world at large. There are in China and India certain elements and traditions, which the West does not have, elements which are essential for world equilibrium.

However that may be, one thing seems to be dead certain and that is this: There is going to be no equilibrium in this world unless there is equilibrium in India. China and South East Asia. There is not going to be harmony or peace even for a short time, and much less for a long time, unless the problems of Asia are settled satisfactorily, unless aggression and interference by western countries in Asian affairs cease once for all.

Tremendous power has been unleashed in the closing stages of the war by the Atom Bomb. It may he that this discovery relating to atomic energy may give such resources for physical might to certain nations that they might ignore with impunity the claims of other nations. It may be that success in the last war has made some nations feel that they have no obstacles left and they can do whatever they like with the rest of the world. But I imagine that, it such be their feeling, they will very soon find that they are exceeding by mistaken. Whatever the atomic energy might not do, even this mighty source of power is not going to enable the countries who possess it to go on imposing their will on the countries of Asia for all time to come.

Those who desire peace for the world must know once for all that there can be no equilibrium or stability for either the East or the West unless all aggression, all imperialist domination, all forced interference in other countries' affairs end completely. This is the lesson which the East still has to teach the West, which China and India have to teach, and it is this lesson which your Society has to teach as well, if it is to live up to its ideals worthily.

31

CULTURAL INTERCHANGE BETWEEN INDIA AND CHINA
An Address

Gurudeva and Friends,

I am glad to come back to India and stay with you once again. I have carried no gifts for you from beyond the seas; I have with me merely my enthusiasm and the sympathy of my heart and the enthusiasm and sympathy of my people which I offer to you in all humility.

Time flies as fast as the darting arrow. It has been three long years since I left India for my Fatherland. But during this long interval, there was not a day when I did not think of India, specially not a moment when I did not think of this beautiful beloved Visva-Bharati at Santiniketan. I left Santiniketan just like a bee leaving its hive. I love Santiniketan as much as my native village; I love India also as much as my Fatherland. This time, when I left my native village and my Fatherland for India and for Santiniketan a second time, it is just the same to me as if I returned from India and Santiniketan to my Fatherland and my native village three years ago. The objective facts are opposite, but my sentiments are the same. Hence my pleasure to be here is really beyond the expression of the symbolic words which I can use.

India and China are naturally a pair of sister countries. Their similarities and their associations are great, numerous, and intimate. Looking over the geography and history of all the nations in the world, we find there are not any other two nations that can be compared to our two countries. This is true from every respect and from every standard of observation and judgment.

Our two countries, both situated in the bright and glorious continent of Asia. India to the south-west and China to the north-east, spread out lordly in different directions but yet are linked up at the main line, just like the two wheels of a carriage or the two wings of a bird, and, even better to say, like the two hands and feet or the two ears and eyes of a person. And the Himalayas, gigantic and majestic, brilliant and magnifieent, exactly resemble the common backbone, or the shoulders, or the neck, and also the nerve system of theirs. Though their boundaries are marked off, yet the physical shape is similar.

A Chinese proverb speaks of "an extensive land with a multitudinous people."Both India and China have actually possessed them. Besides, the soils of our two countries are fertile, beautiful and productive; the peoples honest, frugal and industrious. The products of soils and the outputs of labour are sufficient not only to maintain our own national existence but also to contribute to international prosperity.

Our civilizations started from the misty, ancient times, that is, many thousands of years ago. According to the orthodox historic accounts in Chinese, the formal estabilishment by Huang-Ti of a United Empire in China was accomplished in 2697 B.C., so that this present year 1934 is the year 4631 in the Chinese calendar of orthodox history. But the pre-historic periods must have been long and full of events. Some old books assert that Chinese civilization began about eighteen thousand years before Huang-Ti; others even go so far as to say that our rudimentary culture appeared fifty thousand years prior to the formation of Huang-Ti's Empire. Such remarks may be true, but the recorded facts are a little too remote to be reliable. It is only after the reign of Huang-Ti that and verified, so that there is no more room for any doubt at all. About India, the historical records of very ancient times are rather insufficient but according to references in Chinese books on Buddhism, the condition of ancient India was roughly similar to that of ancient China.

Modern scholars have proved from investigations that the date of the first appearance of the Vedas cannot be less than 2,000 B.C. to 3000 B.C., and consequently no one can be sceptical of the early civilization of India. The invention of the written language is the most essential element of civilization, and a knowledge of such invention is a clue to the understanding of the history of civilization of any nation. The system of Chinese written language came into perfect existence at the time of Huang-Ti; so it follows that such language must have budded and evolved for a long time before that period. Arguments and proofs are found in abundance in old Chinese books and classics, so numerous that I have no space here to quote them all. In a Chinese book by the name of "Fa-Yuan-Chu-Lin" or "Pearls of Buddhist World", written by a famous monk named Tao-Shih in the Tang Dynasty, we find a beautiful passage about the system of Indian written language. It says briefly:

In ancient times, there were three great inventors of written languages: the first was Brahma, whose way of writing was from the left to the right; the second was Kharu, whose way of writing was from the right to the left; the third was Ts'ang-Chia, whose way of writing was from top to bottom."

What is here meant by Brahma is the inventor the inventor of Chinese words, who was also an official in the government of Huang-Ti. In reality, Ts'ang-Chia was not the man who created, but the man who edited and compiled the Chinese written language. It is also stated in the book just quoted that:

Brahma was the eldest; Kharu the next: both living in Tienchu (India); and Ts'ang-Chia the youngest, living in the Middle Kingdom (China)."

Now then, the time for the creation of Indian written language must be undoubtedly far earlier than the age of Asoka, or at least corresponding to the period where Ts'ang-Chia compiled the system of Chinese written language. Recently, archaeologists have made considerable discoveries in India, and I hope what I have just mentioned may be verified by some new concrete evidences. It is now very clear that the ages and facts of the beginning of Indian and Chinese civilizations are somewhat similar to each other.

The true old civilized nations of the world are four in number. Egypt and Babylonia, India and China. But ancient Egypt and Babylonia have become at present mere vague terms in history. Not only have their original peoples dwindled away, but also their civilizations paled into the twilight of the dim past; their lands and their cities are afording only materials for archaeologists to dig out, and only a subject-matter for scholars and poets to sing and mourn for ever. There are also many othery younger nations which come and go, rise and fall. Only our two countries, India and China, have stood up firm and high from the very beginning to the present day for thousands of years already. Though our lands have many times been trampled down, devastated and usurped by foreign people politically and economically, yet our superior traditions, teachings, systems, and customs have often assimilated. the wild, barbarous. Invaders and made them educated and cultured, so that our two countries are able to survive others and shine permanently. Such are the great singular- characteristics in the histories of India and China only.

Again the elementary spirit of the Chinese national character is "Benevolent love" and "Polite deference", which may be represented by the word "jen" or perfect virtue. The essential spirit of the Indian national character is mercy and "peace" which may be represented by the word "Ahimsa". These four terms, " benevolent love" and "polite deference", "mercy" and "peace," though different in form, are yet fundamentally the same in sense. The life of the Chinese adheres to the "Golden Mean", so their attitude towards Nature is a process of harmonization. The life of the Indians lays stress upon Continence so their attitude towards Nature is a process of assimilation. The Chinese have a custom of worship of their ancestors, and love of their kinsmen, so that the System of big families is able to exist generation after generation. And this is the case with the Indian people too. The Indians have the inclination to stick to their native land, honour their teachers and respect their elders. And this is the case with the Chinese people too. In social intercourse the Chinese emphasize "justice" and "uprightness"despise "advantage" and "disadvantage." And so do the Indian people. In relationships between man and woman, the Indians observe "chastity " and prize" modesty And so do the Chinese people. In addition to such moral ;standards, the teaching of our sages at different times are very much similar on the whole. Confucius set up the "Wu-Chiang" or Five ethical laws: first, "jen" or benevolence; second, "Yi" or uprightness; third, "Li" or propriety; fourth, "Chih" or wisdom; fifth, "Hsin" or faithfulness. Varadhamana Jina and Sakyamuni Buddha both preached five ascetic rules or " Pancha Silani" those ,of Jina are first, " speak the truth"; second, " live a pure, poor life; third, "non-killing fourth," "non-stealing" fifth, "observe chastity", and those of Buddha are first, "non-killing"; second, "non-stealing"; third, "non-adultery"; fourth, "non-lying"; fifth," non-drinking". Besides, the Chinese people generally regard "Chin-TeYung" or wisdom, benevolence, and courage as three sublime moral laws of the universe; the Indian people observe " Sila Samadhi and Prajna" or asceticism, meditation and wisdom as the guiding lamps of human life. Principles of such a moral nature are too copious to be enumerated in detail.

So much for the similar features in our national life. As for the interchange of cultures between India and China, it has taken place for more than two thousand years in the book of "Buddhacharita" or the classical biography of Lord Buddha, it is stated that Buddha once learnt from Visvamitra Acharin, who told him of many books among which one was a " Book of China". In another book called Ratnakutha or the great classics of Buddhist treasures, we also find the names of some Chinese feudal states, such as "Wu, "shu", "chin". Such records as appear in Chinese books are even far more in quantity. At a time when most of the modern strong nations had no shadow of existence yet, and when their peoples were still in a primitive State of life over an uncultivated land, our Countries India and China, had already achieved glorious and brilliant civilizations, and our wealth and prosperity had reached a stage really superior to what the European and American Powers have attained to - day in the true sense of life. The essence of the present Western civilisation of which the white races are so proud and for which the common people have so much envy and admiration is science. India and China possessed even in ancient times the beginnings of some sciences. Long, long ago, India had what we call in Chinese "Wu-Min" the Five sciences or " Pancha-Vidya" : first, the science of sound or " Sabdavidya"; second, the science of crafts or " Silpakarmasthana-vidya"; third, the science of medicine or " Chikitsa-vidya"; fourth, the science of cause or " Hetu-vidya" fifth, the science "Liu-Yi" or introspection or "Adhyatma Vidya". In China, we had what we call now "Liu-Yi" or the six Arts; first, " Li" or propriety, second, uya" or music; third, "Sheh" or archery; fourth "Yu" or Coachmanship of fifth "Shu" or writing; sixth, "su" or Mathematics. Besides, there existed what were styled " Lu-Shu" the six writings and " Lu-Ching" the six classics, and many other studies of medicine, surgery, astronomy, astrology, pottery, architecture and the like. It is only of such things of the modern West as steamers, trains, air-planes and battleships, submarines, cannons, guns, bombs, tanks, poison gases, death rays and many other brutal weapons of bloodshed and massacre, that our two countries, India and China had really had none.

The early facts concerning Indian and Chinese relation ship of culture are found in various Chinese books, such as "Lieh-tsu", "chou-shu-dui-yi" or the Book of Wonders of Chou, " Lie-Sien-Chuan" or the biography of fairies, Shih-Laoh-Chih "or Sketches of Buddha and Laotzu. "Tsi-Lu" or the Seven Records, Ching-Lu or the Classical Records, and " Fu-Tsu-Tung-Chi" or the Accounts of Buddha, etc. but this is only a bare enumeration, not any adequate, systematic description. This is of course due to the remoteness of time and the complexity of circumstances. Any momentous event which happened in the world, and any intercourse which took place between the nations must first have a long period of growth before any clear and detailed records could be made about them. So the actual his torical facts of our cultural interchanges are available only after the influx of Buddhism into China. The formal date for the first introduction of Buddhism into China is generally recognized to be the Yung-Ping tenth year of Min-Ti of Han Dynasty (67 A.D.) when the Emperor himself accorded Buddhism his royal welcome to the Capital Lo-Yang. But in fact, it is certainly not the Yung-Ping tenth year. when Buddhism first entered China it is also certainly not after the Chinese acceptance of Buddhism that our cultures began to have interchange. We can only say that Buddhism was first formally welcomed by a Chinese Emperor in Yung-Ping tenth year, and that the cultural interchange between. India and China became more intimate and prevalent after the royal recognition of Buddhism. After this great. Indian sages and scholars came to China and learned Chinese monks and scholars travelled to India in large numbers at diffefent times, carrying on the real work of Cultural exchanges through the medium of Buddhism. According to the records of a Chinese book called " Li-Tai-Kao Seng-Chuan" or the biographies of great monks in various ages, there were two hundred Chinese monks who studied in India with great success, and twenty-four Indian sages who preached in China with marvellous achievement. But it must be bered that there must have been many, many more monks and scholars who either perished on the way or disliked to leave their earthly names to posterity. In another book called "Tang-Kao-Seng-Chuan" the biographies of the great monks of Tang Dynasty, there is a poem of two lines read as below.

Away from Chang-An monks go West to learn.

Out of a hundred no ten do return.

From this we see that many are they who went to India but few are the fortunate who could return to China. This must also hold good with the Indians who toured in the East. At that time, those people had to pass on foot through Central Asia; there were difficult deserts to cross, dense forests to pass, snowy mountains to climb, wild animals to encounter, terrible hunger and cold to suffer; it took years of hardship for them to reach their destination through such difficulties. Such terrific trials and difficulties can easily be imagined, but their pious souls made them defy: every trial and every difficulty. This brave, strenuous and persevering spirit to our ancient sages naturally commands our heartiest reverence and worship and consequently stimulates and increases our mental powers to strive on for. the same cause.

With regard to the influence of Indian culture on the Chinese civilization, it is almost inexpressible, in words. From the point of view of philosophy, the thoughts of Confucianists and Taoists had been closely intermingled with Indian thoughts since the dynasties of Wei (220-264 A.D.) and Tsin (265-419 A.D.) ; the process of assimilation was gaining momentum especially during the Tang Dynasty (678-906 A.D.) and in the subsequent age of the " Five Dynasties" (907-956 A.D.) till there was evolved in the, philosophy called Sung Dynasty (960-1276 A.D.) a new Li-Hsio" or New Rationalism. From the point of view of literature,the prose and poetry of Tsin and Tang Dynasties, the Records of philosophical discourses in the Sung and Ming (1368-1643 A.D.) Dynasties, had a striking tint and tay our of Indian literature inform and inquality. Even the system of Chinese written language was affected by Indian influence a certain Buddhist named Shou-Wen of the, the Dynasty formulated thirty-six alphabets purely on the basis of Sanskrit words and then created a revolution in the pronunciation, sounds, and rhymes of Chinese words. And China learned from India many methods, such as the building of pagodas, the making of statues, and the practice of fresco, etc. As for the translations into Chinese Of Indian classical works, they may be regarded as a rare wonder in the world history of civilization, as far as perfection and quantity are concerned. No translation works of any modem nation can be a match for that Chinese treasury of abundance and superiority. In addition to a complete translation of the most important classics of Buddhism, there were also translated into Chinese many other classical works of ancient India. Let us take, for example, just a few of such best known books as were recorded in the catalogue of classical works of the history of the Sui Dynasty, namely: Brahman Astronomy Brahman, Mathematics Brahman, Medicine Brahman, Astrology, Calendar and Mathematics Jiva: Rishi's Fatalism. "Gandhari : Mythology and Necromancy" All these books and some others amounted to tens of kinds and above a hundred of volumes. The only pity is that such valuable masterpieces are either unseen or lost at the present time. 'Even in the translated works of Buddhist classics, mention was occasionally made about the social and cultural affairs of India in addition to the religious philosophy, religious ceremonies and ascetic rules In short, all the learnings, thoughts, systems, religious practices, social usages, and popular customs and habits of India have appeared more or less in the translated works of Chinese, and accordingly affected Chinese life to a considerable extent. The theory of cause and effect, the belief in the cycle of life and death, and the faith in the wheel of reward and punishment have especially left vivid impressions deeply rooted in the hearts of the general masses of the Chinese people and become a firm, potent social force.

But on the other hand, the influence of the Chinese culture over the Indian civilization seems to be comparatively meagre and insignificant. In China, we can see everywhere things and objects of Indian style or model; but in India we can hardly see anything of Chinese origin. Some minutes ago I made an allusion to Visvamitra Acharin who once told Buddha of many books including one called " A Book of China". Whether there is any such book still in India I don't know. It is also said in same Chinese book that the great Buddhist Hsuan-Tsang had translated into Sanskrit the Chinese classical book of "Tao-Te-Ching" or the Classics of Virtue by Lao-Tse, but again my limited knowledge of Sanskrit prevents me from knowing if there is still existent any such text in Sanskrit today here is therefore a question worthy of our attention; Since the Indian influence.over Chinese culture has been so great why is the Chinese effect upon Indian culture so little? If we consider the merits of these two cultures, the religion and Philosophy of India are, of course, supreme and unparalleled in human history, but the ethics and arts of China are also superior and matchless. And the Chinese classical works are capable of being translated and many of them should be translated, too; why were there so many Indian classical books transalted into Chinese and yet none of Chinese great works rendered into Sanskrit? I have often sought for the reasons and I think there may be three of them; first, India might have been influenced by Chinese culture for some time but such influences dwindled away with the long lapses of time; secondly, the religious sentiment of the Indian people was rich and strong, so strong that they were behaving as all religious peoples do, only actively to teach their gospel to others but not passively to receive any gospel from others; thirdly, the Chinese mentality might be receptive and sensitive to absorb and assimilate any other good civilization but shy and reluctant to propagandize their own culture among others. At any rate, I feel China has received too much from but returned too little to India; she must, therefore, have the sense of gratitude and do the duty of reciprocation towards India.

Something, however, has China gratefully done for Indian culture though not directly but indirectly. It is that she has taken great care and made much effort to preserve, to cherish, to cultivate, and to magnify what she has got from India at different ages. Those translated works, quoted in the foregoing paragraphs, are really a precious treasury of parts of ancient Indian culture, and greatly deserve our patient investigation, if we want to understand dear old India thoroughly today. Some original works written by Chinese visitors to India, such as "Eu-Kuo-Chi" or Records of The Buddhist Nations by Fa-Shien, "Si-Yu-Chi" or Records of the Western Kingdoms by Hsuan-Tsang, and "Nan-Hai-Kuei-Chuan" or Messages from the South Sea by afford us typically valuable materials for the study of ancient India. These books of travels have been now translated into several magnification languages and are being studied by scholars and historians who take much interest in the research of the ancient history of India. What a great service have these books done to the preservation and fication of Indian culture! But perhaps the greatest service China has rendered to Indian civilization is her work in relation to Buddhism. It may be said that Buddhism was born in India, enriched in China, and then scattered over the whole world. I once metaphorically asserted that Buddhism was a beautiful young lady of India who was married to China, enjoyed a happy life, and has had a comfortable family of children, grand-children and great grand-children. In order to do homage to her motherland, this lady must revisit her old home of India. Sastri Mahasaya and Professor Kshitimohan Sen kindly added." She must come toget with her husband and all her children too". How interesting and significant is this remark of these learned Professors! It is, therefore, the duty of China to send her back and the duty of India to welcome her home.

So far I have related some true facts about the old intimate relationship between the cultures of our two great sister countries. But for the last few centuries it is deplorable to say, that friendly relationship has somehow dwindled and even stopped, probably on account of vicissitudes of life and changes in circumstances. At the same time the modern science of Europe rose so much in power and materialism roared so loud for force that the so-called Industrial Revolution was brought about in the turbulent tide of the human sea. As the history of European civilization is short, their philosophy, their religion and their ethical thought are not mature and effective enough to control this raging tide; then, woe to all, their means of production have turned out to be tools of destruction ! Their greed for gain and thirst for blood lead to the invention of sinful and murderous arms and weapons which, in turn, give rise to deadly wars and struggles. Every nation is mad, everything is wrong, and every place is disturbed. The last Great World War is only the first outburst of this materialistic insanity. Not only the West is troubled but also the East is suffering. Especially. I our two oldest civilized countries, India and China fell into the whirlpool of disasters and difficulties. The better the culture, the fiercer the attack. Our civilizations are now misunderstood; our national systems, broken; our social lives, distressed, and our peoples, despised. Consequently we are so busy with our own national concerns and strifes to deal with this mad tide of materialistic currents that we have no leisure to look after our old important and intimate national relationship of the past.

But spiritually, our national love for and sympathy with each other have never been cold though the apparent formal connection is somewhat severed in course of time. As soon as opportunity comes, we shall snatch it and renew our old relationship at any cost. Fortunately in 1924, just ten years ago, Gurudeva Rabindranath Tagore, the Poet, accompanied by Professor Kshitimohan Sen, Professor Nandalal Bose and Professor Kalidas Nag paid a visit to China; it is this visit that marks the resumption of our old national friendship. The impression Gurudeva Rabindranath Tagore gave us during his sojourn is even greater than what our sages did in the past. The Chinese generally regard Gurudeva Rabindranath Tagore and Mahatma Gandhi as the modern Buddhas of India. Gurudeva's works in English have been mostly translated into Chinese and the poems of "Stray Birds" and "The Crescent Moon" have created a new style of prosody in Chinese poetry at present. And there are in China now a Crescent Moon Society and a Crescent Moon Magazine, both of which, founded and directed by Dr. Hu Shih, are dedicated to the memory of the Great

Poet-philosopher's visit to China. As for the Poet's ideal and hope to unite Asiatic cultures, and to revive the Indian and Chinese cultural relationship, all of our Chinese scholars have the sincerest sympathy with him and our leading scholars and leaders have also cherished for long the same idea and are willing to co-strive for the common goal with joint endeavours. Now is the time for India and China to resume and strengthen their cultural relationship.

Bearing in mind the importance of this point, I, in my humble way have initiated a movement to organise the Sino-Indian Cultural Society. The object of the Society will be to link up the learnings of our two countries, to interchange our cultures, to cultivate friendship between our people and lastly, to work for universal peace and human fraternity. In China, a good number of friends and well wishers, most of whom, I may add, are our leading scholars and Buddhists, have already joined the Society. In India, I confidently hope your leaders of thought and culture will readily respond to our invitation and under the guidance of our revered Gurudeva Rabindranath Tagore will work for the common goal.

The present world is in a state of confusion and chaos and the brewing mischievous storms are even beyond our power of imagination. The more nations talk of love and peace, the deeper they envy and hate one another; the more they seek for friendship, the fiercer they brandish their swords. It is terrible even to think of the fact that armaments are both openly and secretly being prepared, mysterious weapons of slaughter are being invented, day and night. The scholars of politics and statesmen say, it is all a political problem, the students of economics and financiers say, it is all a problem of economy, but really it is only a cultural problem of all the world. If the ultimate remedy is not sought from culture it is impossible to cure the current malady and to avoid the future catastrophe. The Powers of Europe and America have come to the end of their wits in the labyrinth; it is then urgently necessary for the Easterners, especially Indians and Chinese, to shoulder this duty of human salvation. I make this remark not because I have the least prejudice against or look down upon Europe and America; but I am convinced that the misuse of the modern Western sciences and materialism is responsible for the imminent crisis and tribulations of the world. So a new outlet to a human life must be researched out from the Eastern civilizations, especially from the cultures of India and China.

I do not mean that all the modern Western sciences should be thrown away, but that the application of such, science must be controlled, directed, modified, and adjusted by the benevolent and harmonious spirit of Indian and Chinese cultures, so that a new civilization will be brought about for the constructive benefit and betterment of all humanity. The enlightened persons of Europe and America who have been aware of the shortcoming of their own cultures are now all making efforts to find the healing medicine from the cultures of India and China. Hence, needless to say, we Indians and Chinese must wake up at once, and restore our old national relationship. By the interchange of our cultures we shall achieve our cultural renaissance; by cultural renaissance we shall create a new world civilization; and by the new civilization we shall relieve all mankind. Our two countries having made a glorious world in the past, can't we make again a glorious world in the future?

32

MY DEVOTION TO RABINDRANATH TAGORE

I

The editor of the Bengali Women's Magazine has been so kind as to ask me to write something about Rabindranath Tagore for its special number to celebrate Rabindranath's 81st Birthday. What shall I write? I feel rather diffident. I cannot merely praise him nor can I criticise him. For firstly, he is my Guru, and my eulogy and worship can best be kept in my heart and mind rather than be expressed by words; secondly, a man like him needs no verbal and superficial praise. He himself very often expressed that he is imperfect, but to me he is perfection personified. Then what shall I write and what can I write about him? But as I could not refuse the eager and earnest request of the editor, I shall simply pen a few words about my own devotion to him.

When he visited China in 1924, i was just coming out from my country. I could only meet him for the first time at Singapore in 1927. When I saw him, I immediately loved him and offered my humble self to him if he could make any use of me. But my admiration for him did not start there and then. Before that, I had watched all the news about him when he was in China and read all the speeches and lectures he delivered there. I had also read all the translations of his works in Chinese and some of them in English. All these had inspired me very deeply. Moreover, being a student of Buddhism, I had a great love for India which was the cradle of Buddhism and had been regarded by the Chinese Buddhists for centuries as a heavenly kingdom. When I saw Rabindranath, I at once found in him the very representative and symbol of the Buddha's country.

Since my first stay at Santiniket in 1928, I have continually read more about him and saw more of the things done by him. The more I read and saw, the greater became my admiration for him. Then I gradually devoted myself more and more to him as well as to the cause that he had undertaken. My own humble idea was that these two great sister nations, India and China, should be brought together once again in order to work for universal peace and human fraternity through their cultural contribution and co-operation. We should, on the one side, revive our old historical relationship which had unfortunately lapsed into isolation for centuries; and on the other side, form new cultural contacts and friendship in the hope of bettering the present world which is full of brutal hostilities and deadly conflicts; if need be, only by showing an example of the amity and harmony existing between our two countries. Rabindranath Tagore has been the emblem of this hope and the focus of these ideas. I therefore devoted myself to him and made Santiniketan my second home. I do not think that my humble devotion can add anything to his greatness but I congratulate myself for having had the fortune, opportunity and privilege of living near to him. Now, I am sitting at his feet and working under his spiritual guidance and leadership. He is not only the Gurudeva of Santiniketan and India but also the Gurudeva of humanity and the world.

Recently, quite recently, some unnecessary questions were put to me by some thoughtless people. I have been asked more than once by some Indian friends: "What do you think will become of Santiniketan when Rabindranath Tagore is no more?" This was really a very sad, if not a very unfortunate question and I felt very very sorry for it. I did not know how to answer but said to my questioners:

"Dear friends, why should you ask me such a question and how can you ask me such a question? Rabindranath Tagore may live hundred years and more. But he has to leave this world some day as all other human beings do and as all the other sages did in different times past. But his soul, his ideal, his works and his achievements will ever remain.

The Lord Gautama Buddha passed away more than two thousand years ago, but his teachings still remain and will for ever remain in this world; and those places where he was born, where he lived, preached and died, although only ruins today, are still great sacred spots for pilgrims from countries far and near. Today the Maha Bodhi Society is even going to establish an International Budhist University at Sarnath, the spot where Lord Buddha turned the Chakra of Dharma for the first time."

Now, Rabindranath Tagore has himself founded the Santinikentan University of world-fame and reputation, and he has breathed his life into it as Gandhiji once said. How can there be any doubt about its future, even when Rabindranath Tagore is physically no more? Indeed, we should not think of such questions and such questions especially should not come out of the lips of our friends. We can only and should only pray for his long life and good health, and try our best to support the work that has been undertaken by him. As Mahatma Gandhi very recently appealed in the newspapers: "Indeed, the Gurudeva himself should command all the monetary help he needs. He has brought lustre to India. Many men have derived signal assistance from him and his institution. Their children are receiving instruction in Santiniketan. His art decorates many an Indian home. His poetry, his novels, plays and his art enrich the minds of thousands of boys and girls, men and women." I should say that Gurudeva has brought lustre not to India alone but to the world at large. He has indeed given a new splendour to human history. His Asrama, the Santiniketan University has not only been an educational institution for Indian children but also a great centre of world culture and civilization. Therefore, we, especially Indian friends, should not think anything else about it, but try our best to help it, to support it and to develop it.

Lastly I may also tell my Indian friends, men and women, that in my daily morning and evening prayers, I do pray for Gurudev's long life and sound health. I most sincerely hope all Indian friends, men and women, will do the same. On the auspicious occasion of the 81st birthday of Gurudeva I would like to join with the Bengali women as well as all the Indian people twice to pray in this manner. May Gurudeva live with us for many years to come! May Santiniketan become more and more prosperous and more and more successful!

April 3, 1941

Santiniketan

II

Rabindranath Tagore needs no words of eulogy and praise from me. In fact I can hardly find out sufficient and suitable words which can be used either to describe him or to praise him adequately from my poor vocabulary. Human language is yet very often an insufficient instrument to express our ideas. Rabindranath Tagore has long been well-known to the world as the greatest poet of modern times. But, I think he was much more and much greater than a mere poet. His songs are perhaps of greater emotional appeal to his own people than his poetry. His poetry undoubtedly rank with the rhymes of the other greater-than-mere poets. His songs are perhaps of greater emotional appeal to his own people than his proetry.His poetry undoubtedly rank with the rhymes of the other great poets of the world, not merely of today but also of the past. But there is hardly a match to his songs from the very begining of civilisation up to now. Besides these he ws also a great educationist, a great philosopher, a great novelist, a great dramatist, a great painter, a great singer, a great orator and what not. He could really be called " all in one", "all in all", and "all and all". To my humble self, he was more of a perfect saint and a supreme Gurudeva than anything else. He was and still is and will ever be, a supreme Gurudeva not only of Santiniketan and India but also of China and the whole world.

In China Rabindranath Tagore together with Mahatma Gandhi had long been regarded as the Buddhas of modern India. Rabindranath's visit to China in the year 1924 had been a great event in Chinese cultural history. He had awakened the dormant conscience of the Chinese nation which had been intoxicated and doped by the modern splendours and glories of materialistic west for over a hundred year. It was this visit of Rabindranath Tagore that had given a momentous impetus to the new national movements of the awakening of China. China had conferred on him a Chinese name called "Chu Chen-Tan". "Chu" was the old Chinese name for India, also called "Tien-Chu", meaning heavenly kingdom. "Chen-Tan" was the old Indian name for China, according to a Buddhist book. "Chen" means thunder, "Tan" means sun-rise; "Chen-Tan" when put together, as in the old Indian name for China, it means the country that is situated where the sun rises, i.e., the

Eastern Country. But here, as in the Chinese name for Rabindranath, it may be translated into English as "Thunder-Voiced Rising Sun". Therefore, "Chu Chen-Tan", with three characters joined together, has a double significance : first, the "Thunder voiced Rising Sun of India"; second, the "Symbol of Unity and Combination of India and China". Historians and Biographers may consider such a thing as merely a tiny trifle in Rabindranath's life. But it indicates China's love, respect, reverence and veneration for him. Immediately after his visit, there was formed the "Crescent Moon Society" by the late young Chinese poet, Mr. Hsu Chih-mo and Dr. Hu Shih and other friends, just to commemorate this historical event. Later on the Sino-Indian Cultural Society initiated by my humble self was founded entirely under his noble inspiration and it will surely ever remain as a concrete and living memory of his noble ideas.

I, my humbie self, met the late Gurudeva for the first time in 1927 at Singapore. When he was visiting China in 1924, I was just coming out from my country. When I saw him, even for the first time, I immediately loved him. But my admiration of him did not just start from that time. Before that, I had watched all the news about him when he was in China and had read all the speeches and lectures he delivered there. I had also read all the few Chinese translations of his works and some of his English books too. All these inspired me very much. Moreover, being a student of Buddhism, I had naturally a great love for India which is the cradle of Buddhism and had been regarded, as above mentioned, by the Chinese people as a heavenly kingdom throughout past centuries. When I saw Rabindranath Tagore I found immediately in him the very representative and symbol of India. I came to Santiniketan for the first time, a year later in 1928. Since then I read more about him and saw more things done by him; and gradually devoted myself more and more to him as well as to the cause which he had undertaken. My own humble idea was that these two great sister nations, India and China, should be brought together once again in order to work for universal peace and human fraternity through our cultural co-operation and contribution. We should, on the one hand, revive our old historical contact which had unfortunately been lost for centuries; and on the other hand, create a new cultural relation in the hope of bettering the present world which is full of brutal hostilities and deadly and atrocious conflicts, by showing an example of the amity and harmony of friendship between our two countries. Rabindranath Tagore, the Gurudeva, was exactly the emblem of this hope and the focus of these ideas. I, therefore, offered my humble self to him and worked under his auspices and guidance since then till the very end of his life. And I shall continue my devotiom to him and work under his spiritual light till the very end of my life.

We all know and understand well that death is the natural consequence of life, and that death and life are necessities in Nature's course. One has come to live in this world, and one has to die in this world. There is nothing to be grieved at or mourned over. But this is merely philosophy. Human beings cannot live without feelings and sentiments. This has been specially evident in the death of the world-beloved Gurudeva, Rabindranath Tagore. Especially those of us who had personal contact with him, we cannot but feel deeply grieved and bereaved by his demise as Pandit Jawaharlal Nehru said in his condolence message to Sri. Rathindranath Tagore, Gurudeva's only surviving son : "Gurudeva's passing away has left us all, who have grown up in the shadows of his towering genius and mighty personality and enveloped by his great tradition, forlorn and in the dark." Therefore, the whole of India mourned for him: nay, the whole world mourned for him too. But mere mourning will not be sufficient. Neither the holding of memorial services nor the publishing of special numbers of newspapers and magazines.

33

MY FIRST VISIT TO GANDHIJI

I first visited Gandhiji at Bardoli in April, 1931. But I had my first glimpse of him about three years ago at an annual session of the All-India National Congress held in Calcutta in December, 1928. Before going to Calcutta to attend the Congress session, I took leave of Gurudeva Tagore. Gurudeva advised me that I should meet Gandhiji there. ``Would you give me a line of introduction?" I asked. ``There's no need, Gandhiji will be very glad to meet you," Gurudeva replied.

Calcutta was then quite a strange place to me, for I had only passed through it once a few months back when I came to Santiniketan and to India for the first time. I could hardly find out Gandhiji's whereabouts. Moreover,I thought that it might not be right to intrude upon his time on such an occasion when he was so busy with the Congress affairs. I then dropped the idea of meeting him for the time being and only saw him from a little distance at the inaugural meeting of the Congress session. It was indeed a gigantic view. The people, numbering more than a lakh, shouted thunderously when Gandhiji entered the Congress Nagar but quieted down immediately when he began to address them. His figure appeared rather frail but his face was shining and the eyes sparkling. He spoke slowly in a rather low voice but with clear accent and beautiful tone. I was quite happy with this distant darshan and came back to Santiniketan satisfied in spirit.

Later on I frequently met friends coming from Gandhiji. All of them asked me to go and stay with him for some time. I told them about my long-cherished hope of visiting Gandhiji and requested them to convey to him my respect and admiration. As a matter of fact, I had even contemplated before coming to this country that I would first stay with Gurudeva at Santiniketan for some years and then go to Gandhiji to stay with him at the Satyagraha Ashram at Sabarmati for two or three years or even to follow him for ever, if possible. But destiny often plays with our plans in a strange manner. After having been at Santiniketan for little more than two years, I went to Tibet in the winter of 1930 quite accidentally, an event which need not be related here. When I returned to India from Tibet, again I was called back home for certain family affairs. My original plans were altogether upset. However, I could not leave India without meeting Gandhiji.

While in Tibet, staying in the Residential Palace (Noblingone) of the "Living Buddha" (the Dalai Lama) outside the city of Lhasa, I had to answer many questions put by the late Dalai Lama, the 13th one, and his ministers about India. By the way, I used to tell them what Gurudeva and Gandhiji were doing in India and how their inspiration was going to change India's destiny. His Holiness, the late Dalai Lama, was especially interested in Gandhiji's way of living and his Satyagraha movement. He therefore asked me to convey his personal message to Gandhiji when I was returning to India. This sense of a special mission was a further fillip to my eagerness to visit Gandhiji.

Immediately after my return to Santiniketan from Lhasa, I wrote to Gandhiji informing him of my longing to visit him and requesting him to grant me a darshan. He responded very promptly and asked me to meet him in New Delhi on any near date which might be convenient for me. On my way to Delhi, I availed myself of the opportunity of making a pilgrimage to all the important sacred places of Lord Buddha along the Ganges, such Buddha Gaya, Rajagiri, Nalanda, Sarnath, Kushinagara, Lumbini, Sravasti and Sankisa. But after visiting these places. I was somewhat delayed and when I arrived in Delhi, Gandhiji had already gone back to his Satyagraha Ashram at Sabarmati. I then followed him there. As I have mentioned before, a stay of some years at the Satyagraha Ashram has been part of my plans, and I felt happy that, although I could not realize this long cherished idea, I could at least see the place now. But when I arrived at the Ashram, Gandhiji had gone on to Bardoli for some urgent and important meetings. The Secretary of the Ashram, Sri Narandas K.

Gandhi, was very kind to me; he showed me everything in the Ashram and treated me just as a brother. He lost no time to send a wire to Gandhiji who replied immediately that I was welcome to Bardoli and that he would be staying there for a few days more. So I followed him to Bardoli.

On my way from Sabarmati to Bardoli, a very interesting incident happened which has left a vivid impression on my mind even now. It occurred at the Surat station where I had to change and take another train. As I had just entered the waiting room, a " C.I.D." followed me and made some inquiries as to who I was, where I came from, what I was doing in India and what was my purpose in visiting Gandhiji. I told him all the truth and he was satisfied and left. I then had a wash and prepared myself for a little rest. But as soon as I came out of the bathroom, another gentleman suddenly greeted me and asked: " Are you going to Bardoli to see Mahatma Gandhi?" I was quite embarassed by such an unexpected query and thought that he might be another " C.I.D." But he did not await my reciprocation and went on: " I am also going there to pay homage to the Mahatma. I have only recently come back from America where I stayed for more than ten years. I went there first as a student and later on started on a business career there after finishing my course of studies. My name is Dua. Let us go together." He also showed me some letters of introduction. I felt much relieved and happy to have him as companion. We then went together. In the train, he took off his American dress and put on Indian Kurta and Dhoti. He was feeling a little shy of doing this and explained to me. "I bought these clothes from Bombay especially for visiting Mahatma Gandhi." At the same time he looked at the "Gandhi Cap" on my head and asked: ``You also bought this cap for the same purpose?" No, it was presented to me yesterday by the Secretary of the Satyagraha Ashram at Sabarmati", I answered him "but unfortunately I have not got any Kurta and Dhoti." We laughed and talked and reached Bardoli in no time.

From Bardoli station we took a horse carriage to the Swaraj Ashram where Gandhiji was staying. We were received at the gate by some Ashramites and put in a very neat and tidy guest room but without any furniture. Only a few minutes later came Sri Devadas, Gandhiji's youngest son. He asked us how long we could stay there. Mr.Dua said that he had some urgent business in Bombay and intended to leave by the afternoon or the next morning train if he could see the Mahatma immediately. Sri Devadas told him that Bapu was having a meeting at the moment and also had several engagements in the afternoon, however, he would see if Bapu could spare some time in the evening. He then turned to me: " May I know your programme? Gandhiji has been expecting you for some time past. Can you stay with us for some days?" I said. Yes. I am not in a hurry and would see Gandhiji when it will be convenient for him." He said: " That's very good," and left. After about half an hour, Devadas came again and told us that Gandhiji would see Mr. Dua in the evening and meet me the next morning, but I could also see him in the evening if I would like to do so. He added that there were prayers everyday early in the morning and late in the evening and asked whether I would like to attend these prayers, which Gandhiji himself conducted. I told him: " I would certainly attend the prayers, but would like to meet Gandhiji next morning as appointed by him."

On the next day, the 27th April, 1931, I got up very early and attended the morning prayer which began exactly at 4 a.m. and ended in less than half an hour. As it was still dark and I was a little bit tired after a long pilgrimage, I returned to my room after the prayer and slept again. And Mr. Dua left for his destination. At half past ten, Sri Devadas came and took me to Gandhiji. He was staying in the upper storey of a building. The room was as neat and tidy as the guest room in which I was put up and also without any furniture excepting a big square mattress and a long pillow both covered with white Khaddar. Gandhiji was sitting and spining on the mattress, supported by the pillow; and the pillow and the mattress were backed by the wall. As soon as I came to the door of his room, he beckoned me with a gracious call : "Come in ! Come in !" I paid him my profoundest adoration and salutation. He took the precedence of me and said:

"I have been expecting you for a long time, first in Delhi, then at Sabarmati. I was quite anxious whether anything had happened to you. Now, I am very glad that at last you have come here.

"Many thanks for your kindness" I said, I am extremely sorry that I have been much dalayed on the way. But the delay was due to my pilgrimage to the Sacred Places of the Lord Buddha. For this, I hope, you will pardon me."

"Certainly", he quickly interjected. "You need not be sorry for that. Now, tell me how long can you stay here?"

"I have come specially to pay my homage to you. As this is done, I may take the first train for Bombay either this afternon or tommorrow morning", I answered.

"And then?" he interrupted me.

"Them from Bombay I shall go to Madras; from Madras, Culcutta; and from Calcutta, back to China."

"Have you already booked your tickets for all these places?" He joked. "But I am told by Devadas that you are not in a hurry. Fortunately I did not see you yesterday, otherwise you might have gone this morning." We all burst into laughter.

"Then, may I stay with you for ever?" I asked.

"So much I do not expect from you. You only stay here as long as I shall stay and leave when I leave."

"This is a great privilege for me and I shall certainly do so", I said,

"This morning I wanted you to have a walk with me but found that you were asleep", he told me.

I was abashed by this unexpected revelation and could not know how to express or explain myself. I regretfully asked: "Why did not wake me up?"

He immediately understood my awkward position and came to my relief, saying; ``You need not worry about that. It was better for you to have some rest after such a long pilgrimage, journeying in the hot summer of India. You might also have some sweet dreaming in the dawn. That's why I did not wake you up."

We all again burst into laughter. I then solemnly presented him the letter which I had brought from His Holiness, the late Dalai Lama, and told him how I had brought it and what was my communion with His Holiness. He was very much delighted at the matter and asked: "What has His Holiness written? Is it written in Tibetan?"

"I do not know what His Holiness has written. But it might have been written in Tibetan. For, His Holiness does not know any foreign language and the letter was written by himself with his own hand. To be faithful to him and to you, as a messenger, I did not and could not see it."

"Very well, you can see it now." He laughed and opened the letter. "Oh, you are right. It is exactly written in Tibetan. Can you translate it for me?"

"No, I have no knowledge of the Tibetan language and only learnt the alphabets while at Lhasa."

"Then it will never be understood by me." We all broke into laughter once again.

The letter was written on a typical Tibetan paper in long shape, bearing two seals in vermillion ink, one of big size, the official one, and the other of smaller size, the personal one. It was wrapped with a long piece of pure white cloth, called "Cartar" in Tibetan. The "Cartar" is an emblem of love, affection and respect. In Tibet, when people meet for the first time or on some special occasion, they exchange their " Cartars" as we exchange our cards. When they receive or visit elderly and respectable persons, they first offer their " Cartars" as we offer our garlands. The Tibetans also do their worship with " Cartars" as we do with flowers. Although Gandhiji could not read the letter, yet he appreciated and enjoyed it much. I asked him whether he would be so kind as to acknowledge receipt of and reply to the letter. He quickly responded: " Oh, yes, I shall write to him, but not the reply, because I, do not know the contents of his letter. Since I do not know Tibetan, I shall write in Gujrati so that he may also not understand it but enjoy it as I do." He said joyfully?

"But you certainly understand each other without knowing each other's language. As Lord Buddha said, all Buddhas understand each other by heart and not by speech. Don't you think so?"

He looked at me smiling. We then talked about China and India, about the religious and cultural contacts, the old and intimate friendship in the past, and the importance of reviving these contacts and friendship today, between the two countries. He told me that he had great admiration for Chinese culture and civilization, and love for the Chinese people. When he was in South Africa, he had many Chinese friends there and many of them had even joined his Satyagraha Movement there. I told him that the Chinese people had the greatest respect and profoundest love for two great persons of modern India, namely himself and Gurudeva, and regarded them as the living Bodhisattvas of the Buddha country. There had been a long-cherished desire among the Chinese people for his visit to China as they had Gurudeva's in 1924.

It is also my earnest desire to visit that great country" he said, " but there is one thing always standing in my way. I cannot leave and will not leave India until she is free. However, I hope I shall be able to go to your country at least once in this life of mine."

"'Yes, you will certainly be able to do so. India will soon be free. I most earnestly pray for your long life."

As the meeting had been sufficiently long, I took leave of him and said good-bye.

"What! Leave and Good-bye? Are you going away immediately? Will you not stay here for some time more?"

"Yes, I am staying."

"Then, take leave when you leave, and say good-bye when you go away." He gave his blessing in joke once again. In the evening, there was a mass meeting in a distant village. Gandhiji sent Sri Davadas to me asking me to accompany him and to attend the meeting. We went together half the way on foot and half the way by car. It was Gandhiji's habit to have a walk in the morning and in the evening everyday. But as the village where the meeting was held was a little too far away and he could not walk all the distance, a car was waiting for him at halfway. While walking along the road, he was interested in talking about the Chinese way of living.

"Your people are very artistic. They lead even their daily life artistically. But one thing I do not like much, that is that they take too much meat. Is it not so?" He remarked. I ``No, it is not quite true, Mahatmaji. Most of the Chinese people do not take much meat. Especially the village people of China are almost pure vegetarians. They may have meat only on a few special occasions in a year, such as the New Year and other seasonal festivals or when they have important guests. Moreover, cow-slaughter is usually prohibited. Your conclusion is drawn perhaps only from the habit of the few Chinese friends living in the big cities of India such as Bombay and Calcutta or some such place." I explained to him.

"I am very glad to hear your explanation." He intervened: "Are you a vegetarian?"

"No, I have not yet been. But I prefer vegetarian diet to meat." I told him frankly.

"Then, I would advise you to give up all non-vegetarian food and be a pure vegetarian. Can't you?" He persuaded me.

"Yes,I can." I boldly answered and agreed : "I have been contemplating for some time past to take only pure food. Now, as you have so graciously advised me, I will certainly try to be a vegetarian and will regard this as a happy memory of our meeting."

He was much pleased with my undertaking of the pledge and wished me all success.

By the time we had already come to the place where the car was waiting the — place was surrounded by hundreds of people including men and women, old, young and children. They gathered together there simply for a darshan of the Mahatma. When they saw Gandhiji, they shouted in one voice " *Mahatmaji Ki Jai*!" Then they made *Pranama* to him and took the dust of his feet. The men offered him money, some with big notes, some with a few rupees, some with a few annas. The women offered him yarn spun by themselves, and children gave flowers. Similar incidents occurred at several places on the way and it took us quite a long time to reach the venue of the meeting. I was deeply moved by the scenes. I bad never seen such a thing before a simple man with no authority behind him having such great influence over his people and held in such profound reverence by them. I was reminded of the Chinese sage Mencius' saying: " A man who influences people with virtue gets the heart of people." Also I remembered the saying of the great Chinese philosopher, Lao-Tzu. " The more one does for others, the more the other will do for him; the more one gives to others, the more the others will give to him." These words uttered by the Chinese sage and philosopher more than two thousand years ago were proved by Gandhiji that day.

The meeting lasted for about two hours and we returned to the Ashram late in the night.

The next day was Gandhiji's silence day. Although he did not speak, he worked as usual. His programme had been suddenly changed by some urgent important affairs. He had to go to Surat in the afternoon. I too, therefore, prepared to leave Bardoli. I saw him once again in the morning and requested him to bless the Chinese students with a message. He answered me in writing saying that he would send me the message and his reply to the Dalai Lama after some time and asked me to give my Calcutta address to him. He also asked me to go by the same train if I were so prepared, for I had to change my train again at Surat for Bombay.

We left Bardoli at 5-45 p.m. and arrived at Surat about one and a half hours later. The station was already flooded with thousands of people. They shouted at the arrival of Gandhiji Some local leaders of the Congress came up to the train to receive him. But Gandhiji was still observing silence. He answered the continuously thunderous hail of the people and returned greetings to the leaders with a smiling face and folded hands. I intended to take leave at this juncture, but those friends very affectionately asked me to go to their place with Gandhiji for a while and told me that there was still ample time for me to get my train for Bombay. So I went with them. Such was the rush of visitors that we could hardly get out of the station.

I stayed there for about two hours and had dinner with them. After that, Sri Devadas and two other friends took me round the ancient city of Surat and accompanied me to the station. Before leaving, I again paid Gandhiji my profoundest salutation and adoration, and asked him: "May I take your leave and say good-bye to you know !" He grasped my hands, nodded, smiled and looked at me just as a father grasping the hands of his child. I almost wept at his boundless Maitri and Karuna, and felt great sadness at leaving him. All friends there said in one voice: "you must come again", and I bade them all "Farewell !"

After touring through Bombay and Madras, I came back to Calcutta on 6th May, 1931. Gandhiji's message to the Chinese students along with his reply to His Holiness, the late Dalai Lama, had already reached my Calcutta address. His reply to the late Dalai Lama was really written in Gujrati with his own hand as he had said at Bardoli, but his message to the Chinese students, which was attached in a short letter addressed to me, was in English and this also with his own hand. I posted the Gujrati letter to His Holiness, the late Dalai Lama, without knowing the contents. I took the other message to China, which was widely published in almost all the important Chinese journals and was appreciated, not only by the students, but by the whole people of my country. This was his first message to China.

I quote this message below, not only as a loving memory of my first meeting with Gandhiji but as an emblem of the long, great and intimate friendship which started two thousand years ago and will continue for ever between China and India :—

"Dear Friend,

You must come again whenever you like. My message to the Chinese students is :— Know that the deliverance of China is through Ahimsa pure and unadulterated.

Yours sincerely,

M.K. Gandhi

As at Sabarmati. 4-5-31,"

Reprint from The Sino-Indian Journal, Vol. I--Part II, Edited by Profesor Tan Yun-Shan.

34

AHIMSA IN SINO-INDIAN CULTURE

"Sino-Indian Culture" is a new term coined by myself about fifteen years ago. It has come into current use since the foundation of the Sino-Indian Cultural Society in both the countries, India and China, in 1934 and 1935 respectively.

Culture, in my humble opinion and to put it in a very simple way, is the cultivation of the whole of human life, and not only of the spiritual side of civilization as is usually regarded. It is the compass, as well as the pilot, of the progress of human society. It gives significance to human life and distinguishes human life from that of plants and animals. It helps man to realise at the first stage the real meaning and value of life, and ultimately to reach its real goal, in which alone there is eternal peace, love, joy, freedom and blessing. In this respect, there is not only much similarity but much identity between the culture of India and that of China. The most striking feature and analogy of these two cultures is the spirit of Ahimsa.

Ahimsa is a word negative in form but with a positive sense. Mahatma Gandhi translated it into English as "Nonviolence". The ancient Chinese Buddhist scholars translated it into Chinese as "Pu-Hai" meaning "Non-hurting". Its positive form is "Love", "Universal Love". That is "Maitri", in Sanskrit; "Jen", in Chinese. These couples of words, Ahimsa and Maitri, or Non-violence and Universal Love, or Pu-Hai and Jen, were born married. And they could never and would never be divorced or separated. They always carry the same message and disseminate the same gospel together. But the Chinese prefer to use the positive form rather than negative, while Indians on the other hand prefer to use the negative one. Therefore the Chinese and the Indians have also become an unseparated couple in culture.

Why was the negative word preferred by the Indians? Gandhiji once explained this by saying :--

"All life the flesh exists by some violence. Hence the highest religion has been defined by a negative word, Ahimsa. The world is bound in a chain of destruction. In other words, violence is an inherent necessity for life in the body. That is why a votary of Ahimsa always prays for ultimate deliverance from the bondage of the flesh."

(C.F. Andrews*: Mahatma Gandhi's Ideas, p. 138.*)

The Chinese sage, Mencius, put it in another way. He said :--

"Men must be decided on what they will not do, and then they are able to act with vigour in what they ought to do."

If a man wants of do things good, he must first not do things evil. So also if a man wants to love people and other beings he must first not hurt them. If a man preaches Love or Maitri or Jen but does not practise Ahimsa, or Non-violence or Pu-Hai, then his Love is no reality. It is merely a false expression or hypocricy. Therefore almost all the great religions in the world uphold a set of precepts to govern the acts of their followers.

Ahimsa in Sino-Indian culture is not only a very prominent feature but also an ancient tradition. It is as ancient as the culture itself. Or as Gandhiji said:--

"Truth and Non-violence are as old as the hills."

(The Harijan, 28-2-36)

In India, Ahimsa is one of the most cardinal virtues and doctrines of almost all the religions and philosophical sects. It had been repeatedly taught and expressly stated by the Rishis in the ancient scriptures, such as the Aitreya Brahmana, the Satapatha Brahmana, the Chandogya Upanishad, the Vamana Purana and Manu's Book of Law. Therefore it was thus declared in the Mahabharata :—

"Ahimsa is the supreme Religion."

And Gandhiji did recite the same words on several occasions.

(C.F. Andrews : *Mahatma Gandhi's Ideals.*)

But the gospel of Ahimsa was first deeply and systematically expounded and properly and specially preached by the Jain Tirthankaras, most prominently by the 24th Tirthankara, the last one, Mahavira Vardhamana. Then, again by Lord Buddha. And at last it was embodied in the thoughts, words and deeds and symbolized by the very life of Mahatma Gandhi.

As Ahimsa is one of the cardinal virtues and doctrines of almost all the philosophical and religious systems in India, so also it is in China. The only difference is, as mentioned above, that instead of using the negative word Ahimsa, the Chinese preferred to use the positive word Jen.

Jen has a vast volume of meanings and a lot of diversities of interpretations. Different scholars of different schools have explained it at different times. Even the greatest saint of China, Confucius, gave it a good many different explanations to different persons on different occasions. Once asked by his disciple named Fan-Chieh: What about Jen? The Master said :—

"It is to love all people."

(Confucian Analects.)

At another time asked by another disciple called Yen-Yuan, about the same, he said :—

"To subdue one's self and return to propriety; this is Jen."

(Confucion Analects.)

Again answering the same question asked by another disciple, named Chunk-Kung, the Master said:-

"Don't do to others what you would not wish done to yourself."

(Confucian Analects.)

Again at another time another disciple, called Tzu-Chang, asked the Master about the same topic, and he answered saying :—

"To be able to practice five things everywhere under heaven constitutes Jen."

When asked what they were, the Master said:—

"Gravity, generosity, sincerity, earnestness and kindness."

(Confucian Analects.)

Confucius also said on several other occasions :—

"A man of Jen will always rest in perfect virtue."

"Only the Man of Jen can always love people."

"A man devoted to Jen will have no hatred."

(Confucian Analects.)

In Yi-Ching, the Book of Change (the Vedas of China) it has been said :—

"The superior gentleman realized in the virtue of Jen will nurture people."

"The great virtue of Heaven and Earth is life. The great jewel of the saint is his position. How to maintain his position? It is by Jen."

In Shu-Ching, the Book of History, it is written :—

"The people have no fixed affection, but always think of the virtuous of Jen."

In Chung-Yung, the Doctrine of the Golden Mean, it was said thus :—

"Jen is the characteristic element of humanity and the great exercise of it is in loving all people, especially relations."

Such passage in ancient Chinese scriptures are rather too many to be quoted one by one here. In general, Jen means Universal Love. Some European savants rendered it into English as Benevolence and Perfect Virtue. The Chinese classical scholars of Sung Dynasty also explained it as: "The entire virtue of the heart." I think the Sanskrit word Maitri as understood by Buddhist religion and philosophy is the nearest enquivalent to it.

This Gospel of Jen was first properly taught and preached in China about twenty-five centuries ago by the greatest Chinese saint Confucius (551-479 B.C.). Then again it was more profoundly and systematically expounded and disseminated by the great Chinese sage Mencius (372-289 B.C.). Afterwards almost all the classical scholars of all the dynasties of China's long history cherished, promoted and propagated the same message but explained and interpreted it according to their own ways. In modern times, Dr. Sun Yat-sen, the Father of the Chinese Republic had scientifically explained the lofty ideal of Jen in his San Min Chu Yi, the Three People's Principles, for his national movement of Chinese emancipation and the renaissance of Chinese culture.

Mencius was the first sage who attempted to apply this perfect doctrine ot practical politics. When he first met King Hui of the Leang State, the King asked : "Venerable Sir, since you have not counted it far to come here, a distance of a thousand miles, may I presume that you are likewise provided with counsels to profit my kingdom?" He replied : "Why must your Majesty use that word 'profit'? What I am 'likewise' provided with, are counsels to Jen and Yi or benevolence and righteousness, and these are my only topics. If your Majesty says. What is to be done to profit my kingdom?' The great officers will say, 'What is to be done to profit our families? and the inferior officers will say, 'What is to be done to profit our persons?' Superiors and inferiors will try to snatch this profit, the one from the other, and the kingdom will be endangered....... There never has been a man trained to Jen or benevolence who neglected his parents. There never has been a man trained to Yi or righteousness who made his sovereign an after consideration. Let your Majesty also say, Jen and Yi or benevolence and righteousness and these shall be the only themes. Why must you use that word 'profit'?"

(The Works of Mencius.)

With this noble mission, Mencius went from state to state and preached to and discussed with the Kings one after another. Although none of them did actually act on his wise advice and made real avail of his presence, he had left behind an inextinguishable spirit of love, mercy and benevolence in the Chinese polity through all the long centuries. A few passages from his exhortations to the heads of the different states and his discoureses with his disciples will illustrate a little more his lofty ideals.

"The man of Jen has no enemy."

"Treat with the reverence due to age the elders in your own family, so that the elders in the families of others shall be similarly treated; Treat with the kindness due to youth the young in your own family, so that the young in the families of others shall be similarly treated."

"The carrying out of his kindly heart by a prince will suffice for the love and protection of all within the four seas, and if he does not carry it out, he will not be able to protect his wife and children."

"Jen or benevolence is the most honourable dignity conferred by Heaven and the quiet home in which man should dwell."

"Benevolence is the tranquil habitation of man, and righteouness is his straight path."

"The benevolent man loves others. The man of propriety shows respect to others."

"Jen or benevolence is man's heart, and Yi or righteousness is man's path."

"Benevolence subdues its opposite just as water subdues fire. Those, however, who now-a-days practice benevolence do it as if with one cup of water they could save a whole wagon-load of fuel which was on fire, and when the flames were not extinguished, were to say that water cannot subdue fire. This conduct, moreover, greatly encourages those who are not benevolent."

(Above : *The Works of Mencius.*)

Lao-Tsu, another of the greatest saints of China, elder than Confucius, was perhaps the only Chinese sage who preferred to use the negative rather than the positive phraseology in discourses on his principles. He would like to lay stress more on the passive side of things rather than on the active side. For instance, the Confucianists used to say : "the heart of Heaven is Benevolence and Love," but he said :—

"Heaven and Earth are not benevolent ; they treat all created things like straw dogs we use at sacrifices. The saint is not benevolent; he looks upon the people in the same way."

(Lao-Tzu : *Tao Te Ching.*)

Again he said :—

"Tao is eternally inactive, and yet it leaves nothing undone. If kings and princes could but hold fast to this principle, all things would work out their own reformation. If having reformed, they still desired reformation. If having reformed, they still desired to act, I would have them restrained by the simplicity of the nameless Tao. The simplicity of the nameless Tao brings about an absence of desire. The absence of desire gives tranquility. And thus the Empire will rectify itself."

(Lao-Tzu : *Tao Te Ching.*)

Lao-Tzu was also perhaps the first sage, not only in China but in the world at large, who openly and strongly opposed the use of violent force and weapons and condemned war. He said :—

"He who serves a ruler of men in harmony with Tao will not subdue the Empire by force of arms. Such a course is wont to bring retribution in its train."

"Where troops have been quartered, brambles and thorns spring up. In the track of great armies there must follow lean years."

"The good man wins a victory and then stops ; he will not go on to acts of violence. Winning, he boasteth not; he will not triumph; he shows no arrogance. He wins because he cannot choose; after his victory he will not be overbearing."

"Weapons are instruments of ill omen, hateful to all creatures. Therefore he who has Tao will have nothing to do with them."

(Lao-Tzu : Tao Te Ching.)

He went even so far as to say :—

"The violent and stiff-necked die not by a natural death."

"The best soldiers are not warlike; The best fighters do not lose their temper. The greatest conquerers are those who overcome their enemies without strife."

(Lao-Tzu : To Te Ching.)

Another great Chinese saint who preached the same gospel of Ahimsa or Non-violence as Lao-Tzu and of Jen or Love as Confucius and Mencius but in a different way from them all, was Mo-Tzu.

Mo-Tzu lived a little later than Lao-Tzu and Confucius but earlier than Mencius. He was born about 500 B.C. The mode of his life, his ideals and works are very similar to that of the ancient Indian Buddhist Bodhisattva Ksitigarbha and that of Gandhiji. I therefore, have sometimes called Mo-Tzu the ancient Mahatma of China and Gandhiji the modern Mo-Tzu of India. Mencius described him by saying : "If there is benefit for the world, he will, do it even by grinding away his body from crown to heel."

Mo-Tzu preached the gospel of non-violence and opposed war not only by words but also by action. Once when he heard of the news that the Ch'u State was to attack the Sung State, he immediately went from his native State Lu, walked for ten days and ten nights, to see the King of Ch'u and persuaded him to stop the aggression, and he succeeded in his efforts.

According to Mo-Tzu's philosophy, all people should only love one another, should not fight and hurt anybody; this is the will of Heaven. He said :—

"Heaven wishes people to love and benefit each other, and does not want people to hate and hurt each other. Why ? Because He loves all and benefits all."

"How do we know that Heaven loves all and benefits all? Because He possesses all and feeds all."

"How to follow the will and wish of Heaven? That is to love all people and Heaven."

(Works of Mo-Tzu.)

He thought that Non-Loving is the only cause of chaos and calamities; and attacking a country and killing people are the greatest sins in the world. Thus he said :—

"How were chaos and calamities caused? They were caused by people not loving each other. A thief loves his own house and does not love the others' house, he therefore steals the others' house for the benefit of his own house. A murderer loves his own body and does not love the others' body, he therefore murders the others' body for the benefit of his own body ....Officers, each loves his own family and does not love others family, they therefore exploit others' families for the benefit of their own families. The state kings, each loves his own country and does not love others' countries, they therefore attack others' countries for the benefit of their own countries ....If all look upon others' houses as their own house, who will steal? If all look upon others' body as his own body, who will murder? If all look upon others' family as his own family, who will exploit? If all look upon others' country as his own country, who will attack?........................Therefore, when all love each other, there will be peace; and when all hate each other, there will be chaos and calamity."

(Works of Mo-Tzu.)

Again :—

"To killl one man is called wrongful and must receive one death punishment. Accordingly to kill ten men is ten times wrongful and must receive ten death punishments. And to kill hundred men is hundred times wrongful and must recive hundred death punishments........................Now the greatest wrong is to attack a country but receive no punishment........................Is this right?"

(Works of Mo-Tzu.)

Again :—

"Which are the greater ones among the evils of the world? They are those actions of the big countries attacking the small countries, of the big families disturbing the small families; and those deeds of the strong robbing the weak, of the group of many oppressing the group of few, of the clever deceiving the dull, of the high class scorning the low. These are the greatest evils of the world.

(Works of Mao-Tzu.)

The foregoing paragraphs have dealt at sufficient length with the ideals and messages of the Chinese saints and sages. Now, come to India again.

In India, Mahavira Jaina and Sakyamuni Buddha preached almost the same gospel in the same way. The fundamental principles and teachings of both of them, such as the "Pancha Silani" or the five rules are nearly the same. Those of Buddha are: first, non-killing; second, non-stealing; third, non-adultery; fourth, non-lying; and fifth, non-drinking. And those of Jaina are: first, speaking the-truth; second, living a pure and poor life; third, nonkilling; fourth, non-stealing and fifth, observing — chastity.

The Three Jewels (Triratna) of Jaina, namely: (1) Samyag-Darsana, right conviction, faith and perception combined; (2) Samyag-Jnana, right knowledge; (3) Samyak-Charitra, right conduct; are all included in the Eightfold Noble Path (Aryamarga) of Buddha, namely, (1) Samyag Dristi, right views; (2) Samyak-samkalpa, right thought; (3) Samyag-Vac, right speech; (4) Samyak Karmanta, right conduct; (5) Samyag-Ajiva, right livelihood; (6) Samyag-Vyayama, right effort; (7) Samyak-smriti, right remembrance and (8) Samyak-Samadhi, right meditation. Both of these sets of items are right ways leading to the same goal Nirvana.

Besides, both, Mahavira Jaina and Sakyamuni Buddha believed in the doctrine of Karma and Samsara. They both denied the omnipotent and omniscient God; and believed that only one's own zeal and effort could work out one's own salvation.

The similarity between the two religions, Jainism and Buddhism, is so great that some Western savants mistook them for one and the same. The real facts are that from the religious point of view they were indeed very similar to each other, but from the metaphysical point of view they are quite different.

But the most striking feature of the two religions is the same teaching, the same gospel of Ahimsa in both its positive and negative senses; in its negative sense of "absolute and perfect harmlessness towards all living beings", and its positive sense of "absolute and eternal happiness for all living beings."

As Love is the indissoluble partner of Ahimsa as stated before, Truth is another inseparable companion of Ahimsa. As Gandhiji once said:--

"Ahimsa, and Truth are so intertwined that it is practically impossible to disentangle and separate them. They are like the two sides of a coin, or rather a smooth unstamped metallic disc. Who can say, which is the obverse, and which the reverse ?"

(From Yeravada Mandir, 13)

Ahimsa, Love, and Truth are the trinity of One which we may call the Supreme, or God, or Heaven, or Brahma, or any other name we like. In carrying out their mission this Trinity have again a number of allies or comrades such as Charity, Sacrifice, Selflessness, Fearlessness, Forgiveness, etc. Thus Gandhiji said :-

"In its positive for, Ahimsa means the largest love, greatest charity. If I am a follower of Ahimsa, I must love my enemy. I must apply the same rules to the wrong-doer who is my enemy or a stranger to me, as I would to my wrong-doing father or son. This active Ahimsa necessarily includes truth and fearlessness."

(Speeches and Writings of Mahatma Gandhi, 346.)

"Ahimsa is the extreme limit of forgiveness. But forgiveness is the quality of the brave. Ahimsa is impossible without fearlessness."

"Let us now examine the root of Ahimsa. It is uttermost selflessness. Selflessness means complete freedom from a regard for one's body. If man desired to realise himself, i.e., Truth, he could do so only by being completely detached from the body, i.e., by making all other beings feel safe from him. That is the way of Ahimsa."

(Young India, 4-11-1926, 348-385.)

Now, what is the truth of Ahimsa? The truth is this. All living beings in the world have the same life and the same soul. They belong to the same mother, come from the same origin and will return to the same home. It is like a tree of which the stem, branches, leaves, flower, and fruits all came into being from one and the same roots. It is also like an ocean, of which all individual beings are but its separate drops. We therefore belong to all, and all belong to us. Thus the Chinese sages said :---

"Heaven, Earth and I were born at the same time and all beings are one and the same with me."

(Chuan-Tzu : Tsi-Wu Lun.)

"All things are one" and "Love all beings; Heaven and Earth are one and the same body."

(Hui-Tzu : Quoted by Chuan-Tzu.)

"All things are already complete in me."

(Mencius : Books of Mencius.)

"All people are my brethren and all things are my fellows".

(Chang-Tsai : Si-Ming.)

As such, we therefore should love not only all people but all living beings. We must treat all of them as ourselves and must not hurt any of them, causing them pain, following the Golden Rule in the great Epics taught by the ancient Indian sages: "Do naught to others which if done to thee would cause thee pain." Jesus Christ and Confucius also gave us exactly the same message. Jesus Christ said in His Sermon on the Mount: "Whatsoever ye would that men should do to you, do ye even as to them." Confucius said in answer to a question as to "What is the most simple way one may follow for his whole life time?" Put by his disciple. "What you do not want done to yourself, do not do to others."

Lord Mahavira illustrated this message in an even more lucid way in the following passages :--

"The man also, who still lives in the house, should in accordance with his creed, be merciful to all living beings; we are bidden to be fair and equal with all."

"Towards your fellow-creatures be not hostile that is the Law of Him who is rich in control."

"All beings hate pain: therefore one should not kill them."

"A man who insults another will long whirl in the cycle of births; to blame others is not good."

"A cruel man does cruel acts and is thereby involved in other cruelties but sinful undertaking will in the end bring about misery."

(Sutra Kratanga, S.B.E. Series.)

"In happiness and suffering, in joy and grief, we should regard all creatures as we regard our own self, and should therefore refrain from inflicting upon others, such injury as would appear undesirable to us, if inflicted upon ourselves."

(Yogasastra.)

This is the reason why most Hindus, especially the Jainas and the Buddhists, would refrain from taking any flesh for their food. The Jain Sadhus and Sadhwis would even refrain from taking fresh vegetables, because they are living, and to hurt any living thing is in Jainism a deadly sin. They go even so far as to drink only boiled water or even breathe with a cloth across their mouth to avoid insects and unseen Jivas inhabiting the air. They would also sweep their path lest they may tread on insects. According to them, under the law of Ahimsa, killing of vermin is also forbidden, so that asylums have been established for decrepit animals rather than that they should be put out of their misery by the destruction of life.

People may think that the way which the Jains preach and follow is rather impracticable and therefore unreasonable. This is a wrong notion. It may be impracticable but is not absolutely unreasonable. It is impracticable because humanity has not yet progressed enough. When humanity has sufficiently developed and reached a certain higher stage this law of Ahimsa should be and would be followed by all.

From what has been said above we can have an outline of the spirit of Ahimsa in Sino-Indian Culture. The facts related and the passages quoted are only those which came readily to my mind and were easily available. Similar facts and passages of the same kind and too numerous in Chinese and Indian literature and scriptures to be quoted in full. It is even difficult to make the best adequate selection of them. These facts and passages were not merely religious ideals or ethical principles but actual and real events in history. Looking over the histories of India and China, from the very begining to the present day, these two countries have never attacked or invaded any other country, never exploited any other people, though they have often been attacked, invaded and exploited by other warlike peoples. But those who invaded India and China were often assimilated and absorbed by Indian and Chinese cultures, and have enjoyed with the Indian and Chinese people their national wealth and harmony of life.

It has been therefore my firm belief, and also my humble mission, that we Chinese and Indians, the two greatest peoples of the world, should culturally join together and mingle together to create, to establish and promote a common culture, called Sino-Indian Culture, entirely based on Ahimsa. By creating, establishing and promoting this common Sino-Indian Culture, we shall further create, establish and promote a common World Culture on the same basis. By creating, establishing and promoting a common World Culture, we shall create and establish a great union of the World. And by creating and establishing a great Union of the World, we shall lead the world to real and permanent peace, love, harmony and happiness !

Visva-Bharati Cheena-Bhavana,

Santiniketan, 10-9-49.

35

POET TO POET

(Full text of correspondence between Yone Noguchi and Rabindranath Tagore on the Sino-Japa nese Conflict.)*

41 Sakurayama,
Nakano, Tokyo.
July 23rd, 1938

Dear Rabindranath,

When I visited you at Shantiniketan a few years ago, you were troubled with the Ethiopian question, and vehemently condemned Italy. Retiring into your guest chamber that night, I wondered whether you would say the same thing on Japan, if she were equally situated like Italy. I perfectly agreed with your opinion and admired your courage of speaking, when in Tokyo, 1916, you censured the westernization of Japan from a public platform. Not answering back to your words, the intellectual people of my country were conscious of its possible consequence, for, not only staying as an unpleasant spectacle, the westernization had every chance for becoming anything awful.

But if you take the present war in China for the criminal outcome of Japan's surrender to the West, you are wrong, because, not being a slaughtering madness, it is, I believe, the inevitable means, terrible it is though, for establishing a new great world in the Asiatic continent, where the "Principle of live-and-let-live" has to be realized. Believe me, it is the war of "Asia for Asia." With a crusader's determination and with a sense of sacrifice that belongs to a martyr, our young soldiers go to the front. Their minds are light and happy, the war is not for conquest, but the correction of mistaken idea of China, I mean Kuomingtung government, and for uplifting her simple and ignorant masses to better life and wisdom. Borrowing from other countries neither money nor blood, Japan is undertaking this tremendous work single-handed and alone. I do not know why we cannot he praised by your countrymen. But we are terribly blamed by them, as it seems, for our heroism and aim.

Sometime ago the Chinese army, defeated in Huntung province by Hwangho River, had cut from desperate madness several places of the river bank; not keeping in check the advancing Japanese army, it only made thirty hundred thousand people drown in the flood and one hundred thousand village houses destroyed. Defending the welfare of its own kinsmen or killing them, — which is the object of the Chinese army, I wonder? It is strange that such an atrocious inhuman conduct ever known in the world history did not become in the West a target of condenmation. Oh where are your humanitarians who profess to be a guardian of humanity? Are they deaf and blind? Besides the Chinese soldiers, miserably paid and poorly clothed, are a habitual criminal of robbery, and then an everlasting menace to the honest hard-working people who cling to the ground. Therefore the Japanese soldiers are followed by them with the paper flags of the Rising Sun in their hands ; to a soldierly work we have to add one more endeavour in the relief work of them. You can imagine how expensive is this war for Japan. Putting expenditure out of the question, we are determined to use up our last cent for the final victory that would ensure in the future a great peace of many hundred years.

I received the other day a letter from my western friend, denouncing the world that went to Hell. I replied him, saying : "Oh my friend, you should cover your ears, when a war bugle rings too wild. Shut your eyes against a picture of your martial cousins becoming a fish salad ! Be patient, my friend, for a war is only spasmodic matter that cannot last long, but will adjust one's condition better in the end. You are a coward if you are afraid of it. Nothing worthy will be done unless you pass through a severe trial. And the peace that follows after a war is most important." For this peace we Japanese are ready to exhaust our resources of money and blood.

Today we are called under the flag of "Service-making," each person of the country doing his own bit for the realization of idealism. There was no time as today in the whole history of Japan, when all the people, from the Emperor to a rag-picker in the street, consolidated together with one mind. And there is no more foolish supposition as that our financial bankruptcy is a thing settled if the war drags on. Since the best part of the Chinese continent is already with us in friendly terms, we are not fighting with the whole of China. Our enemy is only the Kuomingtung government, a miserable puppet of the west. If Chiang Kai-shek wishes a long war, we are quite ready for it. Five years ? Ten years ? Twenty years? As long as he desires, my friend. Now one year has passed since the first bullet was exchanged between China and Japan ; but with a fresh mind as if it sees that the war has just begun, we are now looking the event in the face. After the fall of Hankow, the Kuomingtung government will retire to a remote place of her country; but until the western countries change their attitude towards China, we will keep up fighting with fists or wisdom.

The Japanese poverty is widely advertised in the West, though I do not know how it was started. Japan is poor beyond doubt, — well, according to the measure you wish to apply to. But I think that the Japanese poverty is a fabricated story as much as richness of China. There is no country in the world like Japan, where money is equally divided among the people. Supposing that we are poor, I will say that we are trained to stand the pain of poverty. Japan is very strong in adversity.

But you will be surprised to know that the postal saving of people comes up now to five thousand million yen, responding to the government's propaganda of economy. For going on, surmounting every difficulty that the war brings in, we are saving every cent and even making good use of waste scraps. Since the war began, we grew spiritually strong and true ten times more than before. There is nothing hard to accomplish to a young man. Yes, Japan is the land of young men. According to nature's law, the old has to retire while the young advances. Behold, the sun is arising, be gone all the sickly bats and dirty vermins ! Cursed be one's intrigue and empty pride that sin against nature's rule and justice.

China could very well avoid the war, of course, if Chiang Kai-shek was more sensible with insight. Listening to an irresponsible third party of the West a long way off, thinking too highly of his own strength, he turned at last his own country, as she is today, into a ruined desert to which fifty years would not be enough for recovery. He never happened to think for a moment that the friendship of western countries was but a trick of their monetary interest itself in his country. And it is too late now for Chiang to reproach them for the faithlessness of their words of promise.

For a long time we had been watching with doubt at Chiang's program, the consolidation of the country, because the Chinese history had no period when the country was unified in the real meaning, and the subjugation of various warlords under his flag was nothing. Until all the people took an oath of co-operation with him, we thought, his program was no more than a table talk. Being hasty and thoughtless, Chiang began to popularize the anti-Japanese movement among the students who were pigmy politicians in some meaning because he deemed it to be a method for the speedy realization of his program; but he never thought that he was erring from the Oriental ethics that preached on one's friendship with the neighbours. Seeing that his propagation had too great effect on his young followers, he had no way to keep in cheek their wild jingoism, and them finally made his country roll down along the slope of destruction. Chiang is a living example who sold his country to the West for nothing, and smashed his skin with the crime of westernization. Dear Rabindranath, what will you say about this Chiang Kai-shek?

Dear poet, today we have to turn our deaf ears towards a lesson of freedom that may come from America, because the people there already ceased to practice it. The ledgerbook diplomacy of England is too well known through the world. I am old enough to know from experience that no more worse than others. Though I admit that Japan is today ruled by militarism, natural to the actual condition of the country, I am glad that enough freedom of speaking and acting is allowed to one like myself. Japan is fairly liberal in spite of the war time. So I can say without fear to be locked up that those service-crazy people are drunken, and that a thing in the world, great and true, because of its connection with the future, only comes from one who hates to be a common human unit, stepping aside so that he can unite himself with Eternity. I believe that such a one who withdraws into a snail's shell for the quest of life's hopeful future, will be in the end a true patriot, worthy of his own nation. Therefore I am able to disgrace the name of poet, and to try to live up to the words of Browning who made the Grammmarian exclaim:

"Leave Now for dogs and apes! Man has Forever",

Yours very sincerely,
Yone Noguchi.

"Uttarayan,"
Santiniketan,Bengal.
Sepember 1, 1938.

Dear Noguchi,

I am profundly surprised by the letter that you have written to me: neither its temper nor its contents harmonise with the spirit of Japan which I learnt to admire in your writings and came to love through my personal contacts with you. It is sad to think that the passion of collective militarism may on occasion helplessly overwhelm even the creative artist, that genuine intellectual power should be led to offer its dignity and truth to be sacrificed at the shrine of the dark gods of war.

You seem to agree with me in your condemnation of the massacre of Ethiopia by Fascist Italy but you would reserve the murderous attack on Chinese millions for judgment under a different category. But surely judgments are based on principle, and no amount of special pleading can change the fact that in launching a ravening war on Chinese humanity, with all the deadly methods learnt from the West, Japan is infringing every moral principle on which civilisation is based. You claim that Japan's situation was unique, forgetting that military situations are always unique, and that pious warlords, convinced of peculiarly individual justification for their atrocities have never failed to arrange for special alliances with divinity for anihilation and torture on a large scale.

Humanity, in spite of its many failures, has believed in a fundamental moral structure of society. When you speak, therefore, of "the inevitable means, terrible it is though, for establishing a new great world in the Asiatic continent" — signifying, I suppose, the bombing on Chinese women and children and the desecration of ancient temples and Universities as a means of saving China for Asia—you are ascribing to humanity a way of life which is not even inevitable among the animals and would certainly not apply to the East, in spite of her occasional aberrations. You are building your conception of an Asia which would be raised on a tower of skulls. I have, as you rightly point out, believed in the message of Asia, but I never dreamt that this message could be identified with deeds which brought exaltation to the heart of Tamer Lane at his terrible efficiency in manslaughter. When I protested against "Westernisation" in my lectures in Japan, I contrasted the rapacious Imperialism which some of the Nations of Europe were cultivating with the ideal of perfection preached by Buddha and Christ, with the great heritages of culture and good neighbourliness that went to the making of Asiatic and other civilisations. I felt it to be my duty to warn the land of Bushido, of great Art and traditions of noble heroism, that this phase of scientific savagery which victimised Western humanity and had led their helpless masses to a moral cannibalism was never to be imitated by a virile people who had entered upon a glorious renascence and had every promise of a creative future before them. The doctrine of "Asia for Asia" which you enunciate in your letter, as an instrument of political blackmail, has all the virtues of the lesser Europe which I repudiate and nothing of the larger humanity that makes us one across the barriers of political labels and divisions. I was amused to read the recent statement of a Tokyo politician that the military alliance of Japan with Italy and Germany was made for "highly spiritual and moral reasons" and "had no materialistic considerations behind them". Quite so. What is not amusing is that artists and thinkers should echo such remarkable sentiments that translate military swagger into spiritual bravado. In the West, even in the critical days of war madness, there is never any dearth of great spirits who can raise their voice above the din of battle, and defy their own warmongers in the name of humanity. Such men have suffered, but never betrayed the conscience of their peoples which they represented. Asia will not be westernised if she can learn from such men : I still believe that there are such souls in Japan though we do not hear of them in those newspapers that are compelled at the cost of their extinction to reproduce thier military master's voice.

"The betrayal of intellectuals" of which the great French writer spoke after the European war, is a dangerous symptom of our Age. You speak of the savings of the poor people of Japan, their silent sacrifice and suffering and take pride in betraying that this pathetic sacrifice is being exploited for gun running and invasion of a neighbour's hearth and home, that human wealth of greatness is pillaged for inhuman purposes. Propaganda, I know, has been reduced to a fine art, and it is almost impossible for peoples in non-democratic countries to resist hourly doses of poison, but one had imagined that at least the men of intellect and imagination would themselves retain their gift of independent judgment. Evidently such is not always the case ; behind sophisticated arguments seem to lie a mentality of perverted nationalism which makes the "intellectuals" of today to blustering abcut their "ideologies" dragooning their own ``masses" into paths of dissolution. I have known your people and I hate to believe that they could deliberately participate in the organised drugging of Chinese men and women by opium and heroin, but they do not know; in the meanwhile, representatives of Japanese culture in China are busy practising their craft on the multititudes caught in the grip of an organisation of a wholesale human pollution. Proofs of such forcible drugging in Manchukuo and China have been adduced by unimpeachable authorities. But from Japan there has come no protest, not even from her poets.

Holding such opinions as many of your intellectuals do, I am not surprised that they are left "free" by your Government to express themselves. I hope they enjoy their freedom. Retiring from such freedom into "a snail's shell" in order to savour the bliss of meditation "on life's hopeful future", appears to me to be an unnecessary act, even though you advice Japanese artists to do so by way of change. I cannot accept such separation between an artist's function and his moral conscience. The luxury of enjoying special favouritism by virtue of identity with a Government which is engaged in demolition, in its neighbourhood, of all salient bases of life, and of escaping, at the same time, from any direct responsibility by a philosophy of escapism, seems to me to be another authentic symptom of the modem intellectual's betrayal of humanity. Unfortunately the rest of the world is almost cowardly in any adequate expression of its judgment owing to ugly possibilities that it may be hatching for its own future and those who are bent upon doing mischief are left alone to defile their history and blacken their reputation for all time to come. But such impunity in the long run bode disaster, like unconsciousness of disease in its painless progress of ravage.

I speak with utter sorrow for your people ; your letter has hurt me to the depths of my being. I know that one day the disillusionment of your people will be complete, and through laborious centuries they will have to clear the debris of their civilisation wrought to ruin by their own warlords run amok. They will realise that the aggressive war on China is insignificant as compared to the destruction of the inner spirit of chivalry of Japan which is proceeding with a ferocious severity. China is unconquerable, her civilisation, under the dauntless leadership of Chiang Kai-Shek, is displaying marvellous resources ; the desperate loyalty of her peoples, united as never before, is creating a new age for that land. Caught unprepared by a gigantic machinery of war, hurled upon her peoples, China is holding her own. No temporary defeats can ever crush her fully aroused spirit. Faced by the borrowed science of Japanese militarism which is crudely western in character, China's stand reveals an inherently superior moral stature. And today I understand more than ever before the meaning of the enthusiasm with which the big-hearted Japanese thinker Okakura assured me that China is great.

You do not realise that you are glorifying your neighbour at your own cost. But these are considerations on another plane : the sorrow remains that Japan, in the words of Madame Chiang Kai-Shek which you must have read in the spectator, is creating so many ghosts. Ghosts of immemorial works of Chinese art, of irreplaceable Chinese institutions, of great peace-loving communities drugged, tortured, and destroyed. "Who will lay the ghosts ?" she asks. Japanese and Chinese people, let us hope, will join hands together, in True Asian humanity will be reborn. Poets will raise their song and be unashamed, one believes, to declare their faith again in a human destiny which cannot admit of a scientific mass production of fratricide.

Yours sincerely,
Rabindranath Tagore.

P.S. — I find that you have already released your letter to the Press ; I take it that you want me to publish my answer in the same manner.

41, Sakurayama,
Nakano, Tokyo.
Oct. 2nd, 1938.

Dear Tagore,

Your eloquent letter, dated Sept. 1st. was duely* received. I am glad that the letter inspired me to write you once more.

No one in Japan denies the greatness of China, — I mean the Chinese people. China of the olden times was great with philosophy, literature and art, — particularly in the T'ang dynasty. Under Chinese influence Japan started to build up her own civilization. But I do not know why we should not oppose to the misguided government of China for the old debt we owe her people. And nobody in Japan ever dreams that we can conquer China. What Japan is doing in China, it is only, as I alreay said, to correct the mistaken idea of Chiang Kai-shek; on this object Japan in staking her all. If Chiang Kai-shek ; on this object Japan is staking her hands for the future of both the countries, China and Japan, the war will be stopped to once.

I am glad that you still admire Kakuzo Okakura with enthusiasm as a thinker. If he lives to-day, I believe that he will say the same thing as I do. Betraying your trust, many Chinese soldiers in the front surrender to our Japanese force, and join with us in the cry, "Down with Chiang Kai-shek !" Where is Chinese loyality to him?

Having no proper organ of expression, Japanese opinion is published only seldom in the west; and real fact is always hidden and often camouflaged by cleverness of the Chinese who are a born propagandist. They are strong in foreign languages, and their tongues never fail. While the Japanese are always reticent, even when situation demands their explanation. From the experiences of many centuries, the Chinese have cultivated an art of speaking for they had been put under such a condition that divided their country to various antagonistic divisions ; and being always encroached by the western countries, they depended on diplomacy to turn a thing to their advantage. Admitting that China completely defeated Japan in foreign publicity, it is sad that she often goes too far and plays trickery. For one instance I will call your attention to the reproduced picture from a Chinese paper on page 247 of the Modern Review for last August, as a living specimen of "Japanese Atrocities in China : Execution of a Chinese Civilians." So awful pictures they are — awful enough to make ten thousand enemies of Japan in a foreign country. But the pictures are nothing but a Chinese invention, simple and plain, because the people in the scenes are all Chinese, slaughterers and all. Besides any one with commonsense would know, if he stops for a moment, that it is impossible to take such a picture as these at the front. Really I cannot understand how your friend-editor of the Modern Review happened to published them.

It is one's right to weave a dream at the distance, and to create an object of sympathy at the expense of China. Believe me that I am second to none in understanding the Chinese masses who are patient and dilligent, clinging to the ground. But it seems that you are not acquainted with the China of corruption and bribery, and of warlords who put money in a foreign bank when their country is at stake. So long as the country is controlled by such polluted people, the Chinese have only a little chance to create a new age in their land. They have to learn first of all the meaning of honesty and sacrifice before dreaming it. But for this new age in Asia, Japan is engaging in the war, hoping to obtain a good result and mutual benefit that follow the swords. We must have a neighbouring country, strong and true, which is glad to co-operate with us in our work of reconstructing Asia in the new way. That is only what we expect from China.

Japan's militarism is a tremendous affair no doubt. But if you condemn Japan, because of it, you are failing to notice that Chiang's China is a far more great military country than Japan. China is now mobilizing seven or eight million soldiers armed with European weapons. From cowardice or being ignorant of the reason why they had to fight, the Chinese soldiers are so unspirited in the front. But for this unavailability you cannot forgive Chiang's militarism, if your denial is absolute and true. For the last twenty years Chiang had been trying to arm his country under the western advisers ; and these western advisers were mostly from Italy and Germany, the countries of which you are so impatient. And it should be attributed to their advice that he started war ;

though it is too late to blame the countries that formally provided him with military knowledge, it is never too late for him to know that the western countries are not worthy of trust. There is no country in the world, that comes to rescue the other at her own expense. If you are a real sympathizer of China, you should come along with your program with she had to do, not passing idly with your condemnation of Japan's militarism. And if you have to condemn militarism, that condemnation should be equally divided between China and Japan.

It is true that when two quarrel, both are in the wrong. And when fighting is over, both the parties will be put perhaps in the mental situation of one who is crying over spilt milk. War is situation of one who is crying over spilt milk. War is atrocious, - particularly when it is performed in a gigantic way as in China today. I hope that you will let me apply your accusation of Japanese atrocity to China, just as it is. Seeing no atrocity in China, you are speaking about her as an innocent country. I expected something impartial from a poet.

I have to think (sic) you that you called my attention to the "Modern intellectual's betrayal of humanity," whatever it be. One can talk any amount of idealism, apart from in reality, if he wishes, and take the pleasure of one belonging to no country. But sharing patriotism equally with the others, we are trying to acquit the duty of talk Heaven when immediate matter of the earth is well arranged.

Supposing that we accept your advice to become a van-guard of humanity according to your prescription, and supposing that we leave China to her own will, and save ourselves from being a "betrayal of the intellectuals," who will promise us with the safety of Japanese spirit that we cultivated with pairs of thousand years, under the threat of communism across a fence? We don't want to barter our homeland for an empty name of intellectuals. No, you musn't talk nonsense ! God forbid !

Admitting, that militarism is criminal, I think that, if your humanity makes life a mutilated mud-fish, its crime would never be smaller than the other. I spent my whole life admiring beauty and truth, with one hope to lift life to a dignity, more vigorous and noble ; from this reason, I face in madness, with three wild eyes, promised me with a forthcoming peace. And also at Elephanta Island ; near Bombay, I learned from the Three-headed Siva a lesson of destruction as inevitable truth of life. Then I wrote :

"Thy slaughter's sword is never so unkind as it appears.

Creation is great, but destroying is still greater,

Because up from the ashes new Wonder take its flight."

But if you command me to obey the meekness of humanity under all the circumstances, you are forgetting what your old Hindu philosophy taught you. I say this not only for my purpose, because such reflection is important for any country.

I wonder who reported to you that we are killing innocent people and bombing on their unprotected towns. Far from it, we are trying to do our best for helping them, because we have so much to depend on them for co-operation in the future, and because Bushido command us to limit purnishment to a thing which only deserves it. It was an apt measure of our Japanese soldiers that the famous cave temples of the 5th century in North China were saved from savage repacity of the dereated Shinese (sic) soldiers in fight. Except Madame Chiang with frustrated brain, no one has seen the "ghosts of Chinese institutions and art, destroyed". And if those institutions and art, admitting that they are immemorial and irreplacable, had been ever destroyed it is but the crazy work of Chinese soldiers, because they want to leave a desert to Japan. You ought to know better since you are acquainted with so many Japanese, whether or not we are acquainted with so many Japanese, whether or not we are qualified to do anything barbarous.

I believe that you are versed in Bushido. In olden times soldiery was lifted in Japan to a status equally high as that of art and morality. I have no doubt that our soldiers will not betray and tradition. If there is difference in Japanese militarism from that of the West, it is because the former is not without moral element. Who only sees its destroying power is blind to its other power in preservation. Its human aspect is never known in the foreign countries, because they shut their eyes tight. Japan is still an unknown existence in the West. Having so many things to displease you, Japanese militarism has still something that will please you if you come to know more about it. It is a excusable existence for the present condition of Japan. But I will leave the full explanation of it to some later occasion.

Believe me that I am never an eulogist of Japanese militarism, because I have many differences with it. But I can not help accepting as a Japanese what Japan is doing now under the circumstances, because I see no other way to show our minds to China. Of course when China stops fighting, and we receive her friendly hands, neither grudge nor ill feeling will remain in our minds. Perhaps with some sense of repentence, we will then proceed together on the great work of reconstructing the new world in Asia.

I often draw in my mind a possible man who can talk from a high domain and act as a peace-maker. You might write General Chiang, I hope, and tell him about the foolishness of fighting in the presence of a great work that is waiting. And I am sorry that against the high-pitches nature of your letter, mine is low-toned and faltering, because as a Japanese subject I belong to one of the responsible parties of the conflict.

Finally one word more. What I fear most is the present atmosphere in India, that tends to wilfully blacken Japan to alienate her from your country. I have so many friends there, whose beautiful nature does not harmonise with it. My last experiences in your country taught me how to love and respect her. Besides there are in Japan so many admirers of your countrymen with your noble self as the first.

Yours sincerely,
Yone Noguchi

"Uttarayana",
Santiniketan, Bengal.
October, 1938.

Dear Noguchi,

I thank you for taking the trouble to write to me again. I have also read with interest your letter addressed to the Editor, Amrita Bazar Patrika, and published in that journal.* It makes the meaning of your letter to me more clear.

* The following is the text of the letter referred to :

"Dear Editor,

Dr. Tagore's reply to my letter was a disappointment, to use his words, hurted me to the depths of my being. Now I am conscious that language is an ineffective instrument to carry one's real meaning. When I wanted an impartial criticism he gave me something of prejudiced bravado under the beautiful name of humanity. Just for a handful of dream, and for an intellectual's ribbon to stick in his coat, he has lost a high office to correct the mistaken idea of reality.

"It seems to us that when Dr. Tagore called the doctrine of "Asia for Asia" a political blackmail, he relinquished his patriotism to boast quiescence of a spiritual vagabond, and wilfully supporting the Chinese side, is encouraging Soviet Russia, not to mention the other Western countries. I meant my letter to him to be a plea for the understanding of Japan's view-point which, in spite of its many failures, is honest. I wonder whether it is a poet's privilege to give one whipping before listening to his words. When I dwelled on the saving of the people of Japan at the present time of conflict, he denounced it as their government's exploitation "for gun running and invasion of a neighbour's hearth and home." But when he does not use the same language towards his friend China his partiality is something monstrous. And I wonder where is his former heart which made us Japanese love him and honour him. But still we are patient, believing that he will come to senses and take a neutral dignity fitting to a prophet who does not depart from fair judgment.

"Living in a country far from your country, I do not know where Dr. Tagore's reply appeared in print. Believing that you are known to his letter, I hope that you will see way to print this letter of mine in your esteemed paper.

Yours sincerely
Yone Noguchi."

I am flattered that you still consider it worthwhile to take such pains to convert me to your point of view, and I am really sorry that I am unable to come to my senses, as you have been pleased to wish it. It seems to me that it is futile for either of us to try to convince the other since your faith in the infallible right of Japan to bully other Asiatic nations into line with your Government's policy is not shared by me, and my faith that patriotism which claims the right to bring to the altar of its country who sacrifice of other people's rights and happiness will endanger rather than strengthen the foundation of any great civilization, is sneered at by you as the "quiescence of a spiritual vagabond".

If you can convince the Chinese that your armies are bombing their cities and rendering their woman and children homeless beggars — those of them that are not transformed into "multilated mud-fish", to borrow one of your own phrases —, if you can convince these victims that they are only being subjected to a benevolent treatment which will in the end "save" their nation, it will no longer be necessary for you to convince us of your country's noble intentions. Your righteous indignation against the "polluted people" who are burning their own cities and art treasures (and presumably bombing their own citizens) to malign your soldiers, reminds me of Napoleon's noble wrath when he marched into a deserted Moscow and watched its palaces in flames. I should have expected from you who are a poet at least that much of imagination to feel, to what inhuman despair a people must be reduced to willingly burn their own handiwork of years', indeed centuries', labour. And even as a good nationalist, do you seriously believe that the mountain of bleeding corpses and the wilderness of bombed and burnt cities that is every day widening between your two countries, is making it easier for your two peoples to streatch your hands in a clasp of ever-lasting good will ?

You complain that while the Chinese, being "dishonest", are spreading their malicious propaganda, you people, being "honest", are reticent. Do you not know, my friend, that there is no propaganda like good and noble deeds, and that if such deeds by yours, you need fear no "trickery" of your victims? Nor need you fear the bogey of communism if there is no exploitation of the poor among your own people and the workers feel that they are justly treated.

I must thank you for explaining to me the meaning of our Indian philosophy and of pointing out that the proper interpretation of Kali and Shiva must compel our approval of Japan's "dance of death" in China. I wish you had drawn a moral from a religion more familiar to you and appealed to the Buddha for your justification. But I forget that your priests and artists have already made sure of that, for I saw in a recent issue of "The Osaka Mainichi and The Tokyo Nichi Nichi" (16th Septernber, 1938) a picture of a new colossal image of Buddha erected to bless the massacre of your neighbours.

You must forgive me if you words sound bitter. Believe me, it is sorrow and shame, not anger, that prompt me to write to you. I suffer intensely not only because the reports of Chinese suffering batter against my heart, but because I can no longer point out with pride the example of a great Japan. It is true that there are no better standards prevalent anywhere else and that the so-called civilized peoples of the West are proving equally barbarous and even less "worthy of trust." If you refer me to them, I have nothing to say. What I should have liked is to be able to refer them to you. I shall say nothing of my own people, for it is vain to boast until one has succeeded in sustaining one's principles to the end.

I am quite conscious of the honour you do me in asking me to act as a peace- maker. Were it in any way possible for me to bring you two peoples together and see you freed from this death-struggle and pledged to the great common "work of reconstructing the new world in Asia", I would regard the sacrifice of my life in the cause a proud privilege. But I have no power save that of moral persuasion, which you have so eloquently ridiculed. You who want me to be impartial, how can you expect me to appeal to Chiang Kai-Shek to give up resisting until the aggressors have first given up their aggression ? Do you know that last week when I received a pressing invitation from an old friend of mine in Japan to visit your country, I actually thought for a moment, foolish idealist as I am, that your people may really need my services to minister to the bleeding heart of Asia and to help extract from its riddled body the bullets of hatred ? I wrote to my friend :

"Though the present state of my health is hardly favourable for any strain of a long foreign journey, I should seriously consider your proposal if proper opportunity is given me to carry out my own mission while there, which is to do my best to establish a civilised relationship of national amity between two great peoples of Asia who are entangled in a desolating mutual destruction. But as I am doubtful whether the military authorities of Japan, which seem bent upon devastating China in order to gain their object, will allow me the freedom to take my own course, I shall never forgive myself if I am tempted for any reason whatever to pay a friendly visit to Japan just at this unfortunate moment and thus cause a grave misunderstanding. You know I have a genuine love for the Japanese people and it is sure to hurt me too painfully to go and watch crowds of them being transported by their rulers to a neighbouring land to perpetrate acts of inhumanity which will brand their name with a lasting stain in the history of Man."

After the letter was despatched came the news of the fall of Canton and Hankow. The cripple, shorn of his power to strike, may collapse, but to ask him to forget the memory of his mutilation as easily as you want me to, I must expect him to be an angel.

Wishing you people whom I love, not success, but remorse,

Yours sincerely,
Rabindranath Tagore.

36

AN APPEAL TO CONSCIENCE

Before making my appeal, I must make myself clear to those to whom I shall appeal. All my friends know that I am a pure and simple Chinese Buddhist scholar. Though occupying the position of a University Professor, I regard myself a pilgrim to India. My humble ideal and mission is to bring these two great nations, India and China, together through cultural intercourse and co-operation, not only for the good of our two countries but for the good of the whole world. I have nothing to do with any kind of politics. I also do not know much about politics. But the present situation in India has prompted and compelled me to make this appeal although this seems to involve political problems. However my motive is pure and unadulterated, conscientious and humanitarian, not at all political but humanitarian.

The present political deadlock and chaotic situation in India cannot in any case be any more prolonged and should not be allowed to last longer. It would do good to nobody but help the common enemy. It will serve neither the purpose of Great Britain nor the purpose of India but will be a tempting invitation to the Japanese Militarists. It is just like the kingfisher and the clam in Chinese story. When a clam exposed itself to the sun, a kingfisher struck its beak into it. The clam immediately closed its shell and caught the beak of the kingfisher. The kingfisher said to the clam: Today it will not rain, tomorrow it will not rain,then you must die." The clam retorted: "Today you will not get out, tomorrow you will not get out, then will die the kingfisher." Then came a fisherman who caught both the kingfisher and the clam. Therefore both of them became the victims of the fisherman. Now the Japanese fisherman is watching at the gate of India with vigilant eyes and a mind made malicious by the cult of militarism. He will surely avail himself of every opportunity to catch both the clam and the kingfisher. If that happens, it will be most unfortunate and tragic, not for India alone but for the United Nations and human decency. A Chinese proverb says: " Don't let your Kinsmen feel pain and your foes feel pleasure". The present situation in India cause great anxiety to India's friends, but makes Hitler, Mussolini and Tojo laugh so loudly in their broadcast. Therefore I make this appeal.

First I must appeal to my Indian brethren.

All of you know that I am a lover of India. I love and regard your country just as much as my own; used to claim the privilege for myself of being half Indian and half Chinese. Your aspirations for the freedom and independence of India have all my sympathy and enthusiasm. In fact, your aspirations are also mine. But your present actions and movements, especially the ways and methods of your actions and movements such as looting shops, derailing trains, burning post-offices, raiding government offices, and killing govermnent officials, are not at all desirable and advisable. So far as I understand, such actions and movements are not included in the programme of the All-India National Congress and such methods and ways of movements and actions are hated by Mahatma Gandhiji. Mahatmaji has declared several times that India should not embarrass the British and the United Nations in their prosecution of the war against the Axis. He also said very often that India should sacrifice herself for a greater cause.

Now the present war is not merely a war between the British and the Germans. It is a war between the United Nations and the Axis. In other words, it is a war between the Democratic powers and the Aggressive Forces. It is a war between freedom and slavery, between justice and injustice, between good and evil, between morality and immorality, between humanitarianism and brutality. Therefore, India not only should not impede and harass the British and the United Nations in their effort in prosecuting the war, but also should join them to fight the Axis, especially the Japanese. For the Japanese have already knocked at the door of India and will be your most dangerous, ruthless and cold-blooded enemies when they get into your country. Of course, I quite understand your bitterness caused by the recent happenings in India. You say that you cannot fight with the British who have denied freedom to India; that until India is independent you cannot join the war with anybody or declare war against anybody; that this war is also merely a war among the hypocritical imperialists for their power, and the mastery of their colonies; and that if you join the war unconditionally at this stage it will only help the British Imperialists to perpetuate their grasp on India. If this is really the case and if the present war is really so simple, you are right to say so. But the problems in the present war are not so simple and the future of India will not be simple either. When the war is over and the United Nations have won it, India will surely be independent and free. There will be no power on earth which could refuse the right to India to regain her independence and freedom, provided only India joins the war. The British cannot and will not, in any way deny or delay India's freedom and independence. But if, unfortunately, the United Nations lose the war, there will be no such thing as independence or freedom not only for India but for the whole world. There will be only the terrible tyranny of Germany, Italy and Japan, most probably of Germany alone. All the other nations and peoples will be trampled under Hitler's iron heel; even Duke Mussolini and General Tojo will be only Herr Hitler's obedient jacks.

So I most earnestly appeal to you, my dear and respected Indian brethren, for the sake of India's own defence, for the sake of the United natiions common cause, and for the sake of peace, justice and humanity; you must cease the present mass movement against the British Government, and turn the present movement into a fighting campaign against the Japanese invasion. If you do not like, for certain reasons, to join hands with the British, you can join the war shoulder to shoulder with the United Nations. There are United States troops in India. You may also join the war in various ways. If you do not all of you like to fight with the United Nations in arms, you can fight non-violently by organising the people and giving them necesary information and instructions about the war, by telling the people about the danger of a Japanese invasion and training them how to resist it, and by doing nothing which may be considered harmful to the United Nations and helpful to the enemy. You must realise the rultlessness and mercilessness, the atrocities and brutalities, and the immorality and inhumanity of the Japanese Militarists. You must not listen to Japanese propaganda which is merely deceit and lie. You must not think of having a change of Master as Mahatmaji once said. If unfortunately the Japanese ever come to be India's master it will be worse for you, worse than any other imperialist power. You can easily see this from what the Japnese have done and are doing in Korea, Formosa and in occupied China. Moreover, you must not be disappointed and dismayed by the present situation. The future of India is very great, hopeful, bright and glorious. You have only to fight for it now by joining the United Nations in this war. My dear and respected Indian brethen, cease your present mass movement against the British Government, join the United Nations, and fight the aggressive Axis, especially the Japanese invaders!

Now, let me appeal to our great ally, the British Authorities :

For everybody's sake and for many reasons you must first declare India independent and free immediately, then form an Indian National Government as soon as possible. This is the aspiration not only of the Indian people but also of the people of the United Nations. Even your own British people, most of them, I dare say, have the same desire too. Perhaps only our common enemies would not like you to do so; because if you declare India independent and free, their propaganda will be useless and they will lose their hope of getting the Indians on the their side. Otherwise, Hitler may cry loudly again and again: ``If Mr. Churchill can set India free I will kneel down before him;" the Japs may daily broadcast to the Indian people: "The British would not give you freedom and we shall come to relieve you." I therefore, most humbly and earnestly pray to you farsighted British statesmen, to declare India free and independent immediately. Let Hitler kneel down before Mr. Churchill, let the Japs shut their evil mouths and may their day-dreams evaporate !

I say you must first decalre India independent and free immeditely because this is the first and most urgent thing to do. This is what we call "Cheng Ming", in Chinese, meaning 'to rectify names'. Once the greatest Chinese saint Confucius was asked by his disciple Tsu-Lu what he would do first if he had to administer the government. Confucius answered: ``First, I would rectify names."He again said : "If names be not rectified, words will not be in accordance with the truth of things. If words be not in accordance with truth of things, affairs cannot be carried on to success." When you declare India independent and free, then the name of India and the present war will be immediately rectified, and the present deplorable situation of India as well as of the war will entirely be changed for the better. Then you can very easily form an Indian

National Government. To declare India independent and free needs not much time. But to form an Indian National Government will take a little more time. Still I hope you will accomplish this work as soon as possible. For the Indian National Government will help and join us to carry on the war against the Axis. The sooner this Indian National Government be formed the better will it be for us all. By declaring India independent and free, you will lose nothing; by forming an Indian National Government, you will get everything not only for yourselves but also for the United Nations.

You may say that you have promised India freedom and independence already, but this is not the time to declare it; and that you are ready to grant India Self-Government, but until the Indians themselves settle their internal quarrels you cannot do it. If we only think of one side and look at it from one standpoint, it is quite right to say so. But if we also think of the other side and look from the other standpoint, we shall have quite a diffrent view. I am fond of quoting proverbs. Another Chinese proverb says : "The onlooker is always more clear than the man who is inside the affair." As an onlooker and outsider as well as a well-wisher, I think this is the best and most favourable time to declare India independent and free. This is a golden opportunity to declare India independent and free. For the desire and demand for India's freedom and independence has never been so eager, so great and so urgent. You should not miss this golden opportunity. If you declare India independent and free just now, you will not only gain the heart of the 400 million Indian people, but also obtain the praise, enthusiasm, appreciation and admiration of the United Nations. You will not only win the war but will write a glorious page in the history of mankind. When you declare India independent and free, the Indians will naturally settle their internal quarrels and come together to form a National Government. Although there are discordancies and controversies among the different rections and parties in India, the desire and demand for India's freedom and independence are the same everywhere. Even if the Indians cannot settle their internal quarrel and form a National Government after your Declaration, the blame and fault will be theirs not yours. Then you have done your duty and justice is on your side, your Government will remain here, and it will only increase your dignity and strengthen your hold on India.

There is no need of fearing that, when India becomes independent and free and has her own national government, she may make peace with the Japanese, or she may not join the war, or she may oppose the United Nations to carry on the war in India. It will be exactly the opposite. When India becomes independent and free, she will totally and whole-heartedly join the war with us. The Indians will neither make peace with the Japs nor oppose the war to be carried on in India. For the All-India National Congress, and other parties have declared more than once that if they have their independence and freedom they will join the United Nations and fight the Axis at all cost. It was because they had not got their freedom and independence, they said, that they could not join the war. We may not believe in anybody else but we must believe in the sincerity, the honesty, the truthfulness and the sublime personality of Mahatma Gandhi. We may not trust other people but we must have trust in the zeal, the eagerness, the great effort and enthusiasm of Pandit Jawaharlal Nehru to fight against the Italian Fascists, the German Nazis and the Japanese Militarists. As a matter of fact the Indians also cannot make peace with the Japanese or oppose the war even if they liked to do so. For the power is still in your hands and the United Nations troops are here. But if they cannot get their independence and freedom they may be deadly disappointed and may despair. Great disappointment and despair may compel them to do anything and everything to harm not only the British authorities but also the common cause of the United Nations.

Again, you need not also fear that when India becomes independent and free you will lose your relationship with and your advantage, profit and benefit in this country. It will again be just the contrary. You will not only not lose all these things but will gain more and more. The truth is that human feelings are reciprocal and mutual, and the natural law is relative and respondent. When there is a sound, there must be an echo; when there is an action, there must be a reaction; when there is a movement, there must be a response; and when there is a cause, there must be an effect. So far as I know, most of your intellectuals and scholars do not read much of other Chinese philosophers but like to read Lao-Tsu. If your statesmen also read Lao-Tsu, you will understand all the things I have said above. It is a very small book, only about five thousand words in Chinese and there are several English translations. So you can read it very easily. Lao-Tsu told us: "The more you do for others, the more you give to others, the more you will gain." He said again: "If you want to gain it, you must give it first." Again he said : "If you want to hold it, you will lose it." The Indian people are a very philosophical and sensible, hospitable and benevolent, friendly and thankful people. If you give them freedom and independence, they will surely ever reciprocate your kindness, your goodness, and your greatness. So also will be your benefit, your advantage and your profit. Then neither Hitler nor Mussolini nor the Japanese can break the link between your two great nations. Nor can they interfere with your benefit, advantage, and profits in India. But it will be better for you not to think in those old terms, Dominion, Autonomy and Self-government. Let India be completely independent and free, make her your equal and true ally. After this war, there must be a great Union of all the free nations ; there should be no Empire either like the old German, Italian and Japanese or as the French, the Dutch or your own Empire. It will be very good for you to take the lead and start this movement just now in India. If you can take the lead and start this movement just now in India, you will surely be crowned with success. And the whole world will really bow to you.

Moreover, you have declared again and again that you and the United Nations are fighting this war for freedom, for peace, for justice, for democracy and so on. How can we deny the very freedom to India whose population consists of one-fifth of the whole world? If such a great number, as the Indians are, do not join us or unfortunately side with the Axis, how can we be sure to win the war ? Even if we can win the war without setting India independent and free what will be the significance of the war? To fight to win the war or to defeat the Axis is not enough for us. We must fight and destroy the very cause of war. Hitler might have thought that if the British could dominate such a large country as India in Asia, why we Germans could not dominate such small countries as Austria, Czecho-Slovakia, Poland, etc., in Europe? Therefore Hitler said at the very beginning of the war : ``If Mr. Churchill can set India free, I shall kneel down before him." The Japanese might think that if Great Britain could rule such a great nation as India from so far away, why could not the Japanese conquer China and thereafter the whole of Asia from so near by? So the late Tanaka made the world-famous ``Memorial". Of course the real cause of the war is not due to your domination of India. But by settting India free and independent, you will break the excuse and pretext of the Axis for their aggression and thereby remove one of the causes of war. At least you will set a noble example to them and relieve your responsiblity for causing further wars. Until the cause of war be removed there will be no peace, no freedom, no justice; even after this war. Therefore, I most earnestly and humbly appeal and pray to you far-sighted British statesmen, for everybody's sake and for many reasons, to declare India independent and free, and to form an Indian National Government, enabling the Indian people to join the war totally and to finish wholeheartedly and the Axis as soon as possible.

The above appeal to both, my dear and respected Indian brethren and our great and honourable ally, the British Authorities, comes from the depth of my heart. It is from my conscience that I appeal to your conscience. As an admirer and lover of you both, my words are very frank and simple. I hope both of, you will not misunderstand me. Anyhow, I must wish you both well and pray for peace and an earliest settlement between you both!

Santiniketan,

September 24,1942

SELECTED CORRESPONDENCE BETWEEN TAN YUN-SHAN AND INDIAN LEADERS

1. C. Rajagopalachari to Tan Yun-shan (and message), July 7, 1948
2. Dr. Rajendra Prasad to Tan Yun-shan, January 4, 1957
3. Message from Dr. Rajendra Prasad, September 3,1948
4. Pandit Jawaharlal Nehru to Tan Yun-shan, August 26, 1948
5. Pandit Jawaharlal Nehru to Tan Yun-shan, August 15, 1959
6. Dr. S. Radhakrishnan to Tan Yun-shan, September 19, 1946
7. Dr. S. Radhakrishnan to Tan Yun-shan, February 17, 1960
8. Shri Lal Bahadur Shastri to Tan Yun-shan, July 31, 1964
9. Shri Lal Bahadur Shastri to Tan Yun-shan, January 2, 1966
10. Mrs. Indira Gandhi's Condolence Message on Prof. Tan Yun-shan's Demise, February 22, 1983

GOVERNMENT HOUSE,
NEW DELHI.

7th July 1948.

The culture and philosophy of the ancient people of Asia have again reached a point in the revolution of time when they have a very particular and urgent office to perform. The vanities which were taken for some time past to be civilization have been exposed and the West, through the voice and thoughts of its distressed people, turns for truth once again to the East. May China and India respond to this call.

C. Rajagopalachari

No: 11 - G/4

GOVERNMENT HOUSE,
NEW DELHI

7th July 1948.

Revered Friend,

I am grateful for your felicitation. I esteem it very greatly, coming as it does from a philosopher and scholar of your standing. I have received good wishes from good men throughout the world as well as from friends in this country. May these good wishes have some potency in maintaining my courage and helping me in such work as falls to me. Kindly convey to the Generalissimo and Madame Chiang and His Excellency Dr. Tai Chi-Tao my gratitude for their kind thoughts about me and for their good wishes for India.

It gives me great pleasure to note the renewal of your office of culture in India as representative of China.

I am enclosing a small message, beyond which I am unable to do anything, for your Gandhi Memorial Number.

With kind regards and great respect,

Yours sincerely,

C. Rajagopalachari

Professor Tan Yun-Shan,
Director,
Visvabharati Cheena-Bhavana,
SANTINIKETAN,
West Bengal.

No. 101- G/57.

18/1/57

RASHTRAPATI BHAVAN,
NEW DELHI.

4th January, 1957.

My dear Shri Tan Yun-Shan,

I have received your letter dated the 26th December, 1956.

It is a pleasure to note that your visit to China has been successful in enhancing mutual understanding between the two countries and in furthering cultural relationship between them.

I am grateful to His Excellency Chairman Mao Tse-Tung for his very kind enquiries about my health and I hope and pray that His Excellency the Chairman may for long continue to guide the destinies of his great country.

With my best wishes,

Yours sincerely,

Rajendra Prasad

Shri Tan Yun-Shan,
Principal & Professor,
Visva-Bharati Cheena-Bhavana,
Santiniketan, West Bengal.

Message

India and China have been on most friendly terms for many centuries. This has been possible because neither had any political ambition against the other and each was anxious to derive and imbibe the best that the other could offer. We have thus a cultural link between the two countries which is stronger than any political link and has been able to stand the ravages of time. Mahatma Gandhi was one of those souls who created such bonds and it has been our good fortune to witness the most remarkable scenes of how the world revered him and reacted to his teachings. He has thus forged another link between China and India and I hope our relations will grow more intimate and more fruitful in the days to come.

Rajendra Prasad

3.9.48

PRIME MINISTER,
INDIA.

AIRMAIL.

No. 1223-P.M.

New Delhi,
The 26th August, 1948.

My dear Professor,

Thank you for your letter of the 17th August and your telegram.

I am glad to learn that the Education Ministry of China have appointed you to act as China's Cultural Representative in India. I hope that with your assistance and advice we shall develop further cultural contacts with China.

I am very grateful for the good wishes of the Generalissimo and Madam Chiang and Dr. Tai Chi-Tao. It is very good of Dr. Tai Chi-Tao to send me a new photograph of his which I shall treasure.

I have received the first issue of the Sino-Indian Journal.

I am glad that my book "Discovery of India" has been translated into Chinese. I am afraid I have no time at all to write a fresh preface for it. I hope that its publication will not be delayed because of me.

It is possible that I may go to England in October next. I shall not be going to America this year. I can only spare a few days to go abroad and I shall return from England to India. I am afraid, therefore, that I cannot go to China on that occasion much as I would have liked to do so. I hope to do so some time later.

Yours Sincerely

Jawaharlal Nehru

Professor Tan Yun-Shan.

PRIME MINISTER'S HOUSE
NEW DELHI

No.1651-PMH/59

August 15, 1959

My dear Professor Tan,

Thank you for your letter of the 11th August. I am indeed myself distressed at many recent developments which have resulted in some strain on the friendly relations between India and China. As you know, I have always attached great importance to these friendly relations both in the present and for the future. We are two great countries, neighbours of each other, and it would be a tragedy if we do not have those friendly relations.

I am glad you are going to China. I am sure your talks there will be helpful. Should you wish to come to New Delhi, I shall gladly meet you.

Yours sincerely,

Jawaharlal Nehru

Professor Tan Yun-Shan,
Visva-Bharati Cheena-Bhavana,
Santiniketan.

Sir S. Radhakrishnan

Vice-Chancellor

BENARES HINDU UNIVERSITY

19th Sept. 1946.

My dear Professor Tan Yun Shan,

Thank you very much for your kind letter of the 17th September.

The University has decided to confer the Degree of Doctor of Letters on His Excellency Dr. Tai Chi-Tao, President of Examination Yuan of the National Government of China, honoris causa, and we will be pleased to hear that His Excellency has kindly consented to accept the Degree.

It is our intention to build up a Chinese Library in this University and to have, if possible, a Professor of Chinese if the National Government of China is so pleased as to endow a Chair in this University for the purpose.

Trust you are keeping well.

With kindest regards,

Yours sincerely

[signature]

Prof. Tan Yun-Shan,
Director, Cheenabhavan,
Santiniketan. (Bengal)

3.73.
30/9/46

No VP-6/4687

VICE-PRESIDENT
INDIA

NEW DELHI

17th February, 1960.

My dear Professor Tan Yun Shan,

Thank you for your letter of the 14th instant and your kind words.

I am glad to know that you had an interesting time in Peking.

You must have followed the proceedings in our Parliament and the latest communication which our Prime Minister has sent to Premier Chou En-lai. I hope if and when the Prime Ministers meet, the situation will get clarified and improved.

With kind regards,

Yours sincerely,

(S. Radhakrishnan)

Professor Tan Yun Shan,
C/o. Shanti Niketan,
West Bengal.

प्रधान मंत्री भवन
PRIME MINISTER'S HOUSE
NEW DELHI

8/8/64

NO. 623-PMO/64.

31st July, 1964.

Dear Prof. Tan Yun-Shan,

I thank you for your letter of the 30th June. As I said in my last letter, it is indeed unfortunate that these differences should have developed between two great countries like India and China which have had so much in common. One is naturally impressed and moved by your reference to the historical and spiritual ties between them.

2. As you know, after the late Prime Minister's statement in Bombay, I sent a letter to the Prime Minister of Ceylon. Let us see how things shape. It is better to wait awhile. I would not like to trouble you to come over to Delhi at present but if at any time I feel the need for your help, I shall gladly avail of it. How wonderful it would be if what you have suggested in your last but one para could be made a reality! In fact neighbours should have that kind of relationship, if there has to be peace in the world.

With renewed thanks,

Yours sincerely,

Lal Bahadur

(Lal Bahadur)

Prof. Tan Yun-Shan,
Director,
Visva-Bharati Cheena-Bhavana,
Santiniketan
(West Bengal).

No. 4 - PMO/65

प्रधान मंत्री भवन
PRIME MINISTER'S HOUSE
NEW DELHI

8/1/66

January 2, 1966.

Dear Tan Yun-Shanji,

I have read your letter which you handed over to me in Santiniketan. I am indeed thankful to you for the kind sentiments you have expressed.

I feel sorry that the gulf between India and China should get wider. I know it is not easy to find a solution to our problems and perhaps it would be better for us to allow some time to pass and then give further thought to it.

I am sorry I had very little time at my disposal during my visit to Santiniketan this time. However, I was glad to see and meet you.

Yours sincerely,

Lal Bahadur

(Lal Bahadur)

Shri Tan Yun-Shan,
Professor & Director,
Visva-Bharati Cheena-Bhavan,
Santiniketan.
West Bengal.

प्रधान मंत्री भवन
PRIME MINISTER'S HOUSE
NEW DELHI

February 22, 1983

Dear Prof. Tan Chung,

I am deeply grieved to learn that Prof. Tan Yun-Shan is no more. He was a great scholar and a man of true culture. Gurudev Tagore and my father had affection and regard for him. He identified himself with Santiniketan and contributed immensely to a better understanding between the civilisations of India and China.

It is a fitting close to his life of devotion that he should die at Bodhgaya. My sympathy and condolences to you and other members of your family.

Yours sincerely,

Indira Gandhi

(Indira Gandhi)

Prof. Tan Chung,
C/o Cheena-Bhavana
Santiniketan
West Bengal - 731 235

SINO-INDIAN CULTURAL SOCIETY

1. Introduction by Tan Yun-shan
2. Membership.

INTRODUCTION

The cultural relationship between India and China is indeed a rare thing in human history; it has no parallel in any other two countries of the world ; and it is really a wonder in the history of human contacts and international intercourses. We have seen from the very beginning of human history that between nations and nations and between countries and countries there were more of diplomatic quarrels, political conflicts, military invasions, economic exploitations, commercial struggles and so on than of any cultural intercourses, neighbourly contacts and friendly relationships. But it was quite different with India and China. From times immemorial these two ancient nations approached each other with love, affection and respect. They exchanged their greetings and gifts just as noble friends would do. They had "traded in ideas, in art, in culture, and grown richer in their own inheritance by the other's offerings": (Pandit Jawaharlal Nehru's words). There never happened such things as diplomatic quarrels, political conflicts, military invasions, economic exploitations, commercial struggles and so on between these two great countries, India and China. Who would dare say that such amicable contact and noble relationship between China and India is not a rare thing and wonder in the history of human society and international relations ?

But unfortunately, very unfortunately, this contact and relationship between India and China, later on, relapsed into forgetfulness, probably on account of vicissitudes of life and changes of circumstances. For the last few centuries, the path between these two countries had been filled with deep darkness and was covered up with the accumulated dust of indifference. Nevertheless, from a spiritual point of view our national love and sympathy for each other have never ceased, though the formal relationship has been somewhat suffered in course of time. As soon as the opportunity arises, we shall ever be ready to take hold of it and renew our old relationship at any cost. Let me quote the late Gurudeva Rabindranath Tagore's message which he sent through my humble self to China ten years ago, and which has inspired us all so much and so deep :

"My friends in China,

The truth that we received when your pilgrims came to us in India, and ours to you, -- that is not lost even now.

What a great pilgrimage was What a great time in history! It is our duty today to revive the heroic spirit of that pilgrimage, following the ancient path which is not merely a geographical one but the great historical path that was built across the difficult barriers of race difference and difference of language and tradition, reaching the spiritual home where man is in bonds of love and co-operation."

Rabindranath Tagore,
Santiniketan, 23rd April, 1934.

Yes, it is our duty today not only to revive the old friendships and associations but also to create new contacts and relations between our two great countries, India and China. It is our duty not only to discover the ancient path and follow it but also to make our own way and a way for others to follow in the future. But how and what to do? First of all some strong and sound organization must be formed. Hence, the Sino-Indian Cultural Society.

The Sino-Indian Cultural Society was first initiated in China in 1933, then initiated in India in 1934. But it was inaugurated in India first in 1935 and then in China in i935. Therefore, China has had the privilege of taking the leading part in initiation, but India, in inauguration. From this we can see the urgent need of and the genuine zeal for the Society in both the countries, and both countries emulated each other in the formation of the society. Now the society has its formal existence already for ten years in India and nine years in China. Although the unfavourable and unfortunate situation of the world, specially the war in China, has hampered to a very great extent the work and growth of the Society, yet it has been going on quite well, especially in India. For this, our due tribution must go first to the supreme inspiration and auspice of the late Gurudeva Rabindranath Tagore, then to the wise guidance and keen interest of the present President of the Society, Dr. Abanindranath Tagore, and to the greatest enthusiasm and tireless effort of Sri Rathindranath Tagore, the illustrious son of the late Gurudeva and the General Secretary of The Sino-Indian Cultural Society in India, as well as to other co-workers.

The object of the Society, as prescribed in the General Constitution, is "to study the Mind of India and China with a view to an interchange of their cultures and cultivation of friendship between the people of the two countries for the purpose of promoting peace and unity in the world". This may be analysed in a more plain manner into six items: firstly, to study Indian and Chinese learnings; secondly, to have a cultural intercourse between India and China; thirdly, to develop mutual understanding of Indian and Chinese feelings; fourthly, to start associations of Indian and the Chinese people; fifthly, to establish love and peace among human beings; and lastly, to bring about a great union and harmony in the world.

In accordance with the above object and in order to carry it out the following General Programme has been made :

1. To organise Indian cultural delegations to go to China and Chinese cultural delegations to come to India for reasearch work respectively.

2. To organise delegations to deliver lectures on Indian and Chinese cultures in both countries.

3. To recommend Indian students for studying Chinese culture in China and Chinese students for studying Indian culture in India.

4. To establish a Sino-Indian or Indian Institute for Indian and Chinese students and scholars to study in China. If the Society is unable to build an independent institute there for the time being, the Society shall affiliate it to some well-known Chinese university.

5. To establish an Indian-Chinese Institute or Chinese Hall for Indian and Chinese students and scholars to study in India. The Institute and the Society itself may in the first instance be affiliated to the International University at Santiniketan.

6. To publish books and journals containing the results of researches in Indian and Chinese cultures, and revealing the spirit and content of the same.

7. To open in both the countries a Sino-Indian Publishing House for publishing and circulating books on India and China.

8. To found in both countries a Sino-Indian Library and Museum first on a small scale within the scope of the Society and the Institute, which shall be gradually developed and expanded into an independent library and museum.

9. To make arrangements for the purpose of receiving, guiding and accommodating Indian visitors to China and Chinese visitors to India.

As mentioned before, the unfavourable circumstances of the world and the war in China have handicapped a great deal of the work of the Society, and have even retarded its very growth ; the above programme has not been fully and satisfactorily carried out. In China, immediately after the formation of the Society, we had acquired quite a large and new building for the Society as its headquarters at Nanking. We intended to make out of it an institute together with a library for our regular Sino-Indian studies. But before we could hardly complete our plan and just start the work, the Sino-Japanese War broke out. The wanton Japanese invasion of China had not only upset the country but also our Society. The Japanese indiscriminate bombardment of Nanking did not only destroy the city, but also our Society building. Later on, the location of the Society along with the city of Nanking, the then capital of China, had been very painfully lost to and very ruthlessly occupied by the merciless Japanese soldiers and invaders. Since then, the members of our Society in China have been scattered over the interior of the country. They could hardly have the chance of having a formal meeting. And the circumstance of the country compelled them to concentrate every energy and effort upon fighting the enemy out not only for the independence and freedom of their own country but also for the preservation of peace, justice and decency of the whole world. They could not naturally do any obvious work for the Sino-Indian Cultural Society. But this does not mean that they have forgotten or neglected the work of the Society. Nor is it that the Society has died away or ceased to exist. The Society will never die and will exist for ever. Despite the absolutely difficult conditions of the country, the members of the Society in China have tried and are always trying their best to promote the ideals and to further the cause of the Society either individually or jointly. Whenever and wherever there was any chance and opportunity they would never fail to carry on the work of the Society either directly or indirectly or both. There have been successive visits of several Chinese Missions to India in recent years : first, the Buddhist Mission led by His Holiness Tai Hsu, President of the China Buddhist Accociation, which visited India in January-February, l940; second, the Good will Mission led by His Excellency Tai Chi-Tao, President of the Examination Yuan of the National Government of China, which visited India in December, 1940; third, the Cultural and Educational Mission led by Dr. Y. H. Ku, Vice-Minister of Education, which visited India in March-April, 1943; all these Missions had been more or less encouraged by the Society, and all the members of these Missions are members of The Sino-Indian Cultural Society in China. Although the historical visit of the supreme Chinese leader and personality Generalissimo Chiang Kai-Shek and his heroic consort Madame Chiang to India in February, 1942, was more political and military in purpose than cultural, yet it has given great impetus to the Society and both the Generalissimo and Madame Chiang are the Society's best patrons and benefactors. Very recently the Society has again constructed a new and large building at Chungking. Meetings and lectures have been occasionally arranged in the new building. Plans for starting a library and an institute are under preparation. Arrangements for Sino-Indian studies have been made for members both inside and outside the Society. It is hoped that as soon as the War will be over the Society will without doubt be ready to carry on its programme in full swing in China.

In India the condition is different from that of China. Immediately after the inauguration of the Society, a scheme for establishing a Chinese Hall at Santiniketan was drafted and it had soon been carried out very successfully. Hence the establishment of the Visva-Bharati Cheena-Bhavana, I think, many friends would like to hear and to know; mentions, references and remarks have been very often made by different persons in different publications; several articles have been written and published by several scholars and writers in several languages; and great attention has been focussed from and generous enthusiasm has been given by numerous friends in every walk of life, specially in the cultural and educational fields of both the countries, India and China. The Visva-Bharati Cheena-Bhavana is a department of the Visva-Bharati University as the very name indicates, forming an integral part of the same world-known International University at Santiniketan. But it, at the same time, is also the centre of the Sino-Indian Cultural Society in India. The work of the Society in India has been concentrated on this Cheena-Bhavana during the last few years. It has a big two-storied building together with two hostels and two family quarters for the time being; the main building consists of a large hall and ten spacious residential rooms down-stairs, and a large Library, four big research rooms and several offices, working and reading rooms upstairs. The Chinese Library of the Cheena-Bhavana is not only magnificent and unique in India but also rare and unusual in all countries outside China. It contains about two hundred thousand fascicles of Chinese books, most of which deal with Chinese Buddhism, Chinese Classics, Chinese Philosophy, Chinese History, Chinese Literature and Chinese Art, and are very important and valuable. I am afraid that owing to the indiscriminate and criminal Japanese bombardments on Chinese institutions, museums and libraries, many of these books might have been lost in China and shall be found only in the Visva-Bharati Cheena-Bhavana. The main work of the Cheena-Bhavana is Sino-Indian studies and research, for which we have provided the following courses :—(1) Languages-including Chinese, Tibetan, Sanskrit, Pali, Hindi, Bengali and other modern Indian languages ; (2) Buddhism-including Chinese, Indian and Tibetan, (3) Other Religions-including Hinduism, Jainsim, Confucianism and Taoism; (4) Philosophy - including Indian and Chinese; (5) Literature-including Chinese and Indian ; (6) History - including Chinese and Indian ; (7) Cultural Studies-including Chinese and Indian, both ancient and modern. (8) Restoration of lost Sanskrit works from Chinese and Tibetan scriptures; (9) Translation of Chinese, Sanskrit, Pali and Tibetan scriptures; (10) Editing of Sanskrit, Chinese and other works ; and so on. These items and subjects open before us a very vast sphere of work and give us the opportunity of cultivating many rich fields. It needs much labour and it will take long time to accomplish the end. At present we have one and half-a-dozen of workers in the Cheena-Bhavana, including the staff-members, research scholars and students, both Indian and Chinese, of whom we may specially mention one of the most celebrated Indian savants in modern time, Maha-mohapadhyaya Pandit

Vidhushekhara Bhattacharya Shastri, who had been a very intimate friend and co-worker to the late Gurudeva for more than thirty years, who had been the former principal of the Research Department of Visva-Bharati for more than ten years and the Head of the Sanskrit Department of the Calcutta University for eight years, and now has taken charge of directing research studies in the Cheena-Bhavana. The Sino-Indian Cultural Society in India has already published a number of pamphlets and bulletins. Several books are ready for publication. An annual journal is also under preparation. But owing to the problem of paper, we have to postpone these publications for the time being.

The preceding two paragraphs have only given a very short account in a general way of the works done by the Sino-Indian Cultural Society in both countries, China and India. Besides these, the Society from the very beginning has been sending from time to time students and scholars from China to India and from India to China for studies. Among those who went to China from India, special mention should be made of Shri Krishna Kinker Sinha, who was a research scholar of the Visva-Bharati Cheena-Bhavana and has been sent to China at the request of the Oriental Languages College, established by the Ministry of Education of the national government of China, as professor of Hindi to that College. Shri Sinha is also a Life Member of the Society. He is not only a good scholar of Hindi Literature but also an ideal, active worker along cultural and educational lines. A man with a simple mind, sincere heart and religious nature, he has no hankering after any thing else but love for and devotion to Sino-Indian studies as well as to the common cause of the Sino-Indian Cultural Society. He has already written a number of articles on Chinese subjects in Hindi, has translated Dr. Sun Yat-Sen's "San Min Chu Yi" into Hindi for the first time, and now is translating the Generalissimo's "China's Destiny" into Hindi. Such men and workers like him are really needed and have proved themselves extremely helpful to the Society. Hence these few remarks. The Oriental Languages College of China has also invited another Indian professor, Dr. D. N. Roy of Gwahati, Assam, whose name is already well known both at home and abroad, and who is also a member of the Society. Besides these, the recent idea of the exchange of Indian and Chinese students between the Government of India and the Government of China has also come from the project of the Sino-Indian Cultural Society. And the recent visit of the most outstanding exponent of Indian Philosophy, Sir Sarvapalli Radhakrishnan, Vice-Chancellor of the Benares Hindu University, to China in May this year (1944), and the most memorable and historical visit of the great Indian National leader Pandit Jawaharlal Nehru to China in August, 1939, have given great impetus to the Society ; the former is an elected member of the Central Committee of The Sino-Indian Cultural Society in India and the latter is an elected Honorary President of The Sino-Indian Cultural Society in India.

The most important and characteristic feature of the Sino-Indian Cultural Society is that we have gathered under the Society almost all the leading scholars, educationists, culturalists, religionists, writers, artists, etc., of both the countries, India and China. The Society also enjoys the great courtesy, countenance and patronage, though without any material support, of both the Government of India and the Government of China; and many Government high officers of both the countries have joined the Society as its members. It has also had the greatest sympathy, enthusiasm, encouragement, good wishes and blessings of all the National leaders of India and China, and the best wishes of the Indian and Chinese people as well as of peoples over the world. But one sad thing is that shortly after the institution of the Society, many of its-members have left the Society as well as the world forever without witnessing any accomplishment of the aim of and of the works taken by the Society. The most mournful event in the history of the Society is India is the inopporture demise of the Gurudeva Ravindranath Tagore, the founder — President, the spiritual Guide and the sponsor of the Society. It was due to his inspiration, that my humble self has taken, the intial step in organizing the Society and had devoted my humble self to the common cause of the Society. The most tragic event of the Society in China is the unexpected death of the late Dr. Tsai Yuan-Pei, the first Chief Director of the Executive Committee of the Society in China. Dr. Tsai was one of the greatest cultural leaders of modern China, the Founder-President of Academia Sinica, the highest Chinese National Institute for learning, the sponsor of the New-Culture Movement in China, and Patron of many educational and cultural institutions both national and international. He was also one of the best friends and co-workers of the late Dr. Sun Yat-Sen. He was a typical old Chinese scholar of simple ideals and noble spirit. His ideas, however, were those of the young and the active and he possessed a large heart, combined with a rare farsightedness. His interest in and hope for the Society were so deep and so great that during the last years of his life he gave up all offices of other institutions, but kept the only one . of the Sino-Indian Cultural Society in China as its Chief Director of the Executive Committee. It was mainly owing to his patronage together with the patronage of His Excellency Dr. Tai Chi-Tao, President of the

Examination Yuan of the National Government of China who is already very well known to India, that the Society owes its existence in China. To those two great souls, the late Gurudeva Rabindranath Tagore and the late Dr. Tsai Yuan-pel, we, the members of the Sino-Indian Cultural Society in India as well as in China, especially my humble self, will remain in debt for ever and will ever pay our highest homage. At last, I would like to point out another very salient and important feature of the society, which needs and deserves special mention and explanation. We have especially preseribed General Constitution that the Society may cooperate with others cultural or literary organizations of diffeent countries but it shall strictly keep away from any political movement, and shall never participate in any work against any State or Race or Government. Why should we have made such a particular restriction which no other organization of the same kind would have even. There are several reasons: First, as I have mentioned at the very beginning, the relationship between India and China from time immemorial had been purely cultural and religious and not political. Therefore we have had no quarrel or conflict of any kind between us but love and respect for each other. We should not only always follow and maintain such noble traditions ourselves, but should also help it to spread all over the world. Secondly, all political movements so far as we have seen are based on either narrow nationalism or communalism or sectarianism. They care only for their own interest or the interest of a particular nation or a particular community or a particular sect, and they cannot help taking recourse to all kinds of evil means, especially in the unhealthy atmosphere of the present world politics. They also can not go without hatred, anger, wrath enmity, hostility and all kinds of ill will.

The only exception may be Mahatma Gandhi's movement. But according to me Gandhiji's movement is rather more religious than political. All these things are not only aganist the aim and object of our Sino-Indian Cultural Society, but also against our Hindu-Chinese cultural tradition. The ultimate aim and object of our Society is not only the good of our own countries and peoples but also the good of the whole world and all mankind. We should not have any kind of ill will for any one but should only have the best wishes for everybody, and our good will and motive should he absolutely Sincere and unselfish. Thirdly, the life of a political movement is always short and it changes like a Chamelion. There is no in the association of politicians and in the poltical raletionship between countries. Today they are friends and tomorrow they can be ememies, or today they are enemies and tomorrow they can turn into friends. Such unfair and undesirable things must naturally be avoided by our society, and the life of our society and the relationship between our two great countries must be long and permanent. Fourthly, when we say, we shall never participate in any work against awy State or Race or Government, it is not because we are afraid of any State or Race or Government, but because we have got nothing to do with such work, and Such work is absolutely not our business and is also against the aim and object of our society. As we have no evil design of any kind, we have naturally no fear. The aim and object of our society, when carried out, will only help every State or Race or Government. Fifthly, a cultural society, like ours should always keep up its lofty dignity and maintain its high prestige. We should and must only work within the limit of our duty and according to the scope of our programme. Of course, there were people who did utilise such organization as custody for all kinds of mean works ; but we should absolutely not only avoid this kind of things but also condemn the same. Otherwise, we shall not only lose our dignity and damage our prestige and shall do no good to any body but harm to our own society. As we have taken our stand on this ground, I believe we shall surely achieve our aim which is our sacred duty as well as our holy responsibility, not only to our own selves, to our own countries and to our own peoples, but also to the whole world and all mankind !

Santiniketan
1944

TAN YUN-SHAN

MEMBERS

PERSONNEL OF THE SINO-INDIAN CULTURAL SOCIETY IN CHINA

(A) Directing Committee

Chief Director:

1. Dr. Chu Chia-hua
President, Academia Sinica, & President of the Chinese League of Nations' Union.

Vice-Chief Director

2. Mr. Ku Meng-yu
President, National Central University of China.

Standing Director (in -charge)

3. Mr. Chang Tao-fan
Dean, National Central Political School.

Standing Directors:

4. Mr. Ch'en Li-fu
Minister of Education, China.
5. Mr. Shen Shih-hua
Commissioner to India.
6. Mr. Shen Tsung lien
Councillor, Supreme National Defence Council.
7. Mr. Ch'en Ta-chi
Chairman, Examination Commission of the Examination Yuan.
8. Prof. Ju Pe'on
Professor, National Central University.
9. Mr. Wang Tseng-shan
Councillor, the Legislative Yuan.

Directors:

10. Prof. Tan Yun-Shan
Founder of the Society & Directory Cheena-Bhavana, Visva-Bharati.
11. Venerable Tai-Shui
President, China Buddhist Association.
12. Mr. Tseng Jung-p'u
Administrative Vice-Minister, Ministry of Foreign Affairs.
13. Mr. Hollington K. Tong
Vice-Minister, Ministry of Information.
14. Mr. Mai-she-wu-to
Member of the Central committee of Kuomintang.
15. Dr. Yieh Ch'i-sun
Secretary-General, Academia Sinica.

16. Prof. Ch'en Yin-K'o
Professor, National South-west Associated University.
17. Mr. Shen Shih-yuan
Vice-Chairman, Examination Commission of Examination Yuan.
18. Rev. F'a-tsun
Director, The Sino-Tibetan Buddhist Institute.
19. Prof. Tsung Po-Hua
Professor, National Central University.
20. Prof. Chang Hsu
President, The National Western-Boundary Cultural Institute.
21. Prof. Li Cheng-kang
Professor, National Central University.
22. Venerable Lama Hsi-Jao-Chia-Chno
Tibetan Representative, The People's Political Council.
23. Prof. Tang Yung-ting
Professor & Chairman, Philosophy Department of National Peking University.
24. Prof. Feng You-lan
Acting Dean, College of Arts of National South-west Associated University.
25. Mr. Shih Shang k'uan.
26. Mr. Chen Tien-hsi
Secretary, The Examination Yuan.
27. Prof. Ma Tsung jung
Professor, The Fu Tan University.
28. Mr. Chang Chia-sen.
29. Prof, Ku. Chen-kang
Professor, The Cheloo University.
30. Prof. Chan Chi-chun
Professor, National Central University.
31. Prof. Chang Yi
Professor, National Central University.
32. Dr. Fu Ssu-nien
Director-General, Research Institute of History and Philology, Academia Sinica.
33. Dr. Li Sze-kuang
Director-General, Research Institute of Geology Academia Sinica.
34. Mr. Chiang Fu-tsung
Director, National Central Library.
35. Dr. Chiang Meng-lin
President, National Peking University.
36. Mr. Li Shou-houa
President, The Sino-French University.
37. Dr. Wang Hsing-kung
President, The National Wuhan University.
38. Dr. Chu Ke-Chen
President, National University of Chekiang.
39. Mr. Ch'eng Tie'n-fang
Former Ambassador to Germany.
40. Mr. Wei Chuo-min.
41. Prof. Ma Fu
President, National Academy.
42. Prof. Lu Ch'eng
Professor, The Chinese Adhyatma Vidya Institute.
43. Dr. Lo Chia-lun
Former President, National Central University.

44. Mr. Yang Chih-fu.
45. Mr. Hin Shu-chih.

(B) Supervisory Committee

Chief Supervisor:

1. Mr. Tai Chi-tao
   President, The Examination Yuan.

Vice-Chief Supervisor:

2. Mr. Ch'en Poo-lei
   Secretary-General to the Generalissimo.

Standing Supervisor:

3. Dr. Wang Ch'ung-hui
   Secretary-General, Supreme National Defence Council.
4. General Pai Ch'ung-hsi
   President, Chinese Muslim Association.
5. General Shang Chen
   Formerly Governor of Shansi Province.
6. Dr. Wang Shih-Cheh
   Minister, Ministry of Information.

Supervisors

7. Mr. Wu Ching-heng
   State Councillor, National Government State Council.
8. Mr. Ma Lin
   State Councillor, National Government State Council.
9. Mr. Chang Chia-nao.
   Minister, Ministry of communication.
10. Mr. Yeh Chu-ts'ang
    Vice-President, The Legislative Yuan.
11. Dr. C. J. Pao
    Consul-General for the Republic of China in Calcutta.
12. Mr. Ma Ho-tien
    Director, Commission of Mongolian & Tibetan Affairs.
13. Mr. Lui Wen-huei
    Concurrently Chairman, Sikiang Provincial, Government,
14. Mr. Ouyang Tsien
    President, The China Adhyatman Vidya Institute.
15. Mr. Lui Wei-Chih
    Minister, Ministry of Overseas Chinese Affairs.
16. Mr. Hsu Shih-ying
    Acting Chairman, The National Relief Commission
17. Mr. Li T'ieh-cheng.
18. Mr. Hsu Chung-hao
    Formerly Secretary-General, The Examination Yuan.
19. Dr. Chiang Ting-fu
    Director of Political Affairs Council.
20. Dr. Quo Tai-Ch'i
    Chairman, National Foreign Affairs Council
21. Dr. Ku Yu-hsiu
    Political Vice-Minister, Ministry of Education.
22. Prof. Wu Tsun-sheng

Director, Department of Higher Education of Ministry of Education

23. Mr. Wu T'ieh-Cheng
Secretary-General, Central Committee of Kuomintang.

PERSONNEL OF THE SINO-INDIAN CULTURAL SOCIETY IN INDIA

I Founder-President

1. Gurudeva Dr. Rabindranath Tagore

II. Honorary Presidents

1. Mahatma Gandhi
2. Marshal Chiang Kai-Shek
3. Sri Aurobindo Ghose
4. President Tai Chi-Tao
5. Pandit Jawaharlal Nebru
6. Madame Chiang Kai-Shek
7. Madame Sarejini Naidu

III. President

1. Dr. Abanindranath Tagore

IV. Patrons

1. Seth Jugal Kishore Birla
2. Raja Sahib of Awagarh

V. Central Committee

(1) SANTINIKETAN

1. Sjt. RathindranathTagore
General Secretary, Visva-Bharati.
2. Sjt. Surendranath Kar
Santiniketan Secretary, Visva-Bharati.
3. Pandit Kshiti Mohan Sen
Principal, Vidya-Bhavana, Visva-Bharati.
4. Sjt. Nandalal Bose
Director, Kala-Bhavana, Visva-Bharati.
5. Sjt. Anil Kumar Chanda,
Principal, College, Visva-Bharati.
6. Sjt. Krishna R. Kripalani,
Rector, School Department, Visva-Bharati.
7. Sjt. Prabhat Kumar Mukherjee,
Librarian, Visva-Bharati.
8. Sjt. Charu Chandra Bhattacharya,
Secretary, Publishing Dept. Visva-Bharati.
9. Madame Indira Devi,
Honorary Director, Sangit-Bhavana, Visva-Bharati.
10. Madame Pratima Devi,
Director, Sangit-Bhavana, Visva-Bharati.
11. Sjt. Gurdial Mallik,
Visva-Bharati.
12. Sjt. Kshitish Roy,

Asst. General Secretary. Visva-Bharati.

13. Pandit Hazari Prasad Dwivedi Sahitya Sastri
Director, Hindi-Bhavana Visva-Bharati.

14. Sjt. Kanti Ghose
Author & Asst. Editor, "V. B. Patrika".

15. Sjt. Sujit Kumar Mukhopadhyay,
Sanskrit Professor, Cheena-Bhavana, Visva-Bharati.

(2) CALCUTTA

1. Maulana Abul Kalam Azad.
President, All-India National Congress.

2. B. C. Roy,
Vice-Chancellor, Calcutta, University.

3. Sjt. Ramananda Chatterjee,
Editor, "Modern Review"

4. Dr. Surendranath Das-Gupta,
Principal, Sanskrit College & Professor, Calcutta University.

5. Dr. Suniti Kumar Chatterjee,
Professor & Head of Dept. of Comparative Philology, Calcutta University.

6. Dr. Prabodh Chandra Bagchi,
Lecturer, Calcutta University.

7. Dr. Kalidas Nag,
General Secretary of the Royal Asiatic Society & Professor of Calcutta University.

8. Dr. Mahendranath Sircar,
Professor of Philosophy, Presidency College.

9. Dr. Benoy Kumar Sarkar,
Professor, Calcutta University & Author.

10. Dr. Amiya Chakravarty,
Lecturer, Calcutta University & Author.

11. Dr.. Shyamaprasad Mukherjee,
Ex-Financial Minister, Bengal ; Ex-Vice-Chancellor & now President, Post-Graduate Council, Calcutta University.

12. Mahamahopadhyaya Vidushekhara Sastri,
Head of the Sanskrit Department, Calcutta University.

13. Sir Jadunath Sarkar,
Formerly Vice-Chancellor, Calcutta University.

14. Prof. Humayun Kabir,
Professor, Calcutta University.

15. Dr. Nihar Ranjan Ray,
Chief Librarian, Calcutta University.

16. Sjt. Atul Chandra Gupta,
Advocate, Calcutta High Court & Author

17. Sjt. Bhagirathi Kanodia,
Leading Industrialist, Calcutta.

18. Seth B. M. Birla,
Leading Industrialist, Calcutta.

19. Sjt. Hiran Kumar Sanyal,
Jt. Editor, ``Parichaya"

20. Professor Sushobhan Sarkar,
Professor, Presidency college.

21. Sjt. Suhrid Chandra Sinha,
Landlord, Calcutta.

22. Dr. Ramesh Chandra Majumdar,
Formerly Vice-Chancellor, University of Dacca.

23. Dr. P. N. Banerjee,
M. L. A. (Central); Leader, Congress Nationalist Party.
24. Sjt. Tushar Kanti Ghosh,
Editor, "Amrita Bazar Patrika".
25. Sjt. Hem Chandra Nag,
Editor, "Hindusthan Standard"
26. Sjt. B. Sen Gupta,
Managing Editor, United Press.

(3) DACCA

1. Dr. Khan Bahadur Mohamud Hassan,
Vice-Chancellor, Dacca University.

(4) PATNA

1. Babu Rajendra Prasad,
Formerly President, now Member, Working Committee, All-India National Congress.
2. Dr. Satchidananda Sinha,
Vice-Chancellor, University of Patna.
3. Sjt. Rahula Sankrityayana,
Orientalist &.Social & Political Worker.
4. Dr. Subimal Sarkar,
Principal, Patna College.

(5) BENARES

1. Sir S. Radhakrishnan,
Vice-Chancellor, Benares Hindu University.
2. Dr. Bbagavan Das,
Author & Formerly M. L. A. (Central)
3. Babu Siva Prasad Gupta,
Author & Landlord.
4. Babu Sriprakash,
M. L. A. (Central) & Editor, "Aj".
5. Pandit Iqbal Narayan Gupta,
Pro-Vice-Chancellor, Benares Hindu University.

(6) SARNATH

1. Mr. Devapriya Valisingha,
General Secretary, Maha Bodhi Society of India.
2. Prof. Dharmanand Kofiambi,
Formerly Professor of Bombay University & Author.

(7) ALLAHABAD

1. Mrs. Vijaya Lakshmi Pandit,
President, All-India Women's Conference & M. L. A. ;
formerly Minister, U. P. Government.
2. Dr. Amarnath Jha,
Vice-Chancellor, University of Allababad.

(8) LUCKNOW

1. Raja Bisheshwar Dayal Seth
Vice-Chancellor, University of Lucknow.
2. Prof. Dhurjati Prasad Mukherjee,

Professor, University of Lucknow.

(9) ALIGARH

1. Sir Ziauddin Ahmed,
   Vice-Chancellor, Muslim University.
2. Dr. Hadi Hassan
   Professor, Muslim University.
3. Prof. Habib
   Professor, Muslim University.

(10) AGRA

1. Mr. J. C. Chatterjee
   Vice-Chancellor, University of Agra.

(11) DELHI

1. Sir Maurice Gwyer,
   Formerly Chief Justice, India ; Vice-Chancellor, University of Delhi.
2. Mr. John Sergeant,
   Educational Adviser to the Government of India.
3. Mr. H. Prideaux-Brune
   China Relation Officer, Delhi
4. Dr. Shaukat Ansari,
   Congress Leader, Delhi.
5. Shri Raghunanda Saran,
   Congress Leader, Delhi.
6. Dr. Zakir Hussain,
   Principal, Jamia Millia University.
7. Shri Devadas Gandhi,
   Managing Editor, "Hindusthan Times".
8. Mrs. Satyen Roy,
   M. L. A. (Central) & Member, Central Board of Education.
9. Dr. Dhirendra Mohan Sen,
   Technical Assistant, Education, Health & Land Dept., Government of India.
10. Dr. Sudhir Sen,
   Formerly Secretary to the Commerce Member, Government of India.

(12) LAHORE

1. Mian Afzal Hussain
   Vice-Chancellor, Punjab University.
2. Sir Bakshi Tok Chand,
   Judge of the Lahore High Court.
3. Dr. Raghu Vira,
   Director, International Academy of Indian Culture.

(13) BOMBAY

1. Madame Sophia, Wadia,
   Secretary, P. E. N. Club, India Centre.
2. Sir R. P. Masani,
   Formerly Vice-Chancellor, University of Bombay.
3. Shri E. M. Munshi.
   Formerly Home Minister, Government of Bombay.
4. Dr. Manilal Patel,
   Director, Bharatiya Vidya-Bhavana.

5. Mrs. Lilavati Munshi,
M. L. A., Formerly Parliamentary Secretary, Government of Bombay.
6. Mr. Yusoof Mehar Ali,
Sometime Ex. Mayor, Bombay; General Secretary, Congress Socialist Party.
7. Shri B. G. Kher,
Formerly Prime Minister & Minister of Education, Government of Bombay.
8. Mr. B. J. Wadia,
Vice-Chancellor, Bombay University,

(14) POONA

1. Dr. Vasudev Gokhale,
Professor & Rector, Forgusson college.
2. Dr. R. N. Dandekar.
Secretary, Bhandaskar Oriental Research Institute.
4. Dr. S. M, Katre.
Director, Deccan College Research Institute.

(15) NAGPUR

1. Shri T. J. Kedar,
Vice-Chancellor, University of Nagpur.

(16) HYDERABAD DECCAN

1. Nawab Sir Mehdi Yar Jung Bahadur
Vice-Chancellor, Osmania University.

(17) MYSORE

1. Shri N. S. Subba Rao
Vice-Chancellor, Mysore University.

(18) ANNAMALAI NAGAR

1. Mr. M. Rathnaswami,
Vice-Chancellor, Annamalai University.

(19) TRIVANDRUM

1. Sir C.P. Ramaswami Iyer
Prime Minister Travancore & Vice-Chancellor, Tranvancore University.
2. Dr. James Cousins.
Curator, Art Museum Professor, Travancore University.
3. Mrs. Margaret Cousins,
Author and Social Worker

(20) WALTAIR

1. Sir. C.R. Reddy
Vice-Chancellor, Andhra University.

(21) MADRAS

1. Dr. A. Lakshmanaswami Mudaliar
Vice-Chancellor, Madras University.
2. Shri. C. Rajagopalachariar
Formerly Prime Minister, Government of Madras
3. Shri. G. A. Natesan
Editor, "Indian Review".
4. Shri. K. Srinivasan
Editor, "The Hindu".
5. Srimati Rukmini Devi
President, Kalashetra, Adyar.
6. Rev. Bhikkhu Arya Asanga

Librarian, Adyar and Author.

(22) TIRUPATI

1. Dr. M. Krishnamachariar
Director, Sri Venkateswara Oriental Institute.
2. Pandit Aiyaswami
Professor, Sri Venkateswara Oriental Institute.

(23) PONDICHERRY

1. Sjt. Nalini Gupta
Author and Secretary , Sri Aurobindo Asrama.

(24) CEYLON

1. Sir Baron Jayatillake
Ceylon Representative to the Government of Indlia.
2. Mr. Wilmot Perera
Founder Sripali Academy.
3. Dr. G. P. Malalasekara
President, Buddhist Congress and Professor, University of Colombo.
4. Mr. L. H. Mettanand
Principal, Dharmaraja College, Kandy

(25) HONORARY MEMBERS

1. Mr. S. H. Hua,
Chinese Commissioner, New Delhi.
2. Dr.C. J. Pao,
Chinese Consul-Ganeral, Calcutta.
3. Prof. Tan Yun-Shan,
Director, Viisva-Bharati, Cheena-Bhavana, Santiniketan

(V1) WORKING COMMITTEE.

1. Dr. Abanindranath Tagore (President), President, Visva-Bharati.
2. Vidushekhar Sastri, Professor, Calcutta University.
3. Kshitimohan Sen, Principal, Vidva-Bhavana, Visva-Bharati.
4. Nandalal Bose, Principal, Kala-Bhavana, Visva-Bharati.
5. Dr. Kalidas Nag, Lecturer, Calcutta University.
6. Dr. Amiya Chakravarty, Lecturer, Calcutta University.
7. Dr. Prabodh Chandra Bagchi, Lecturer, Calcutta University.
8. Indira Devi, Authoress.
9. Gurdial Mallik, Curator, Rabindra Museum, Santiniketan.
10. Hazariprasad Dwivedi, Editor, Visva-Bharati Patrika, (Lecturer, Visva-Bharati)
11. Rathindranath Tagore, (General Secretary) Visva-Bharati.
12. Dr. D. M. Bose, (Treasurer) Treasurer, Visva-Bharati & Director, Bose Institute, Calcutta.
13. Anil K. Chanda, (Joint Secretary), Principal, Siksha-Bhavana, Visva-Bharati.
14. Surendranath Kar, (Joint Secretary) Secretary, Santiniketan.
15. K. R. Kripalaini, Rector, Patha-Bhavana, Visva-Bharati.
16. Tan Yun-Shan, Director, Cheena-Bhavana, Visva-Bharati, (Director, China Centre).

Pages

WRITINGS OF TAGORE, NEHRU AND TAN YUN-SHAN

SELECTED CORRESPONDENCE BETWEEN TAN YUN-SHAN AND INDIAN LEADERS

SINO-INDIAN CULTURAL SOCIETY

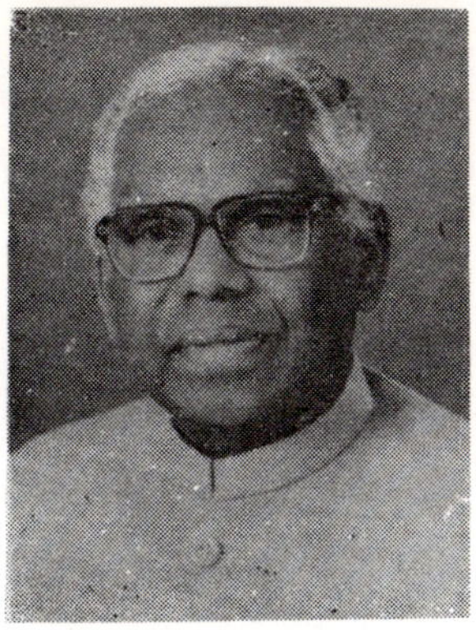

